WAYMARKS
FOR THE
JOURNEY

WAYMARKS FOR THE JOURNEY

Daily prayer to change your world

RAY SIMPSON

Augsburg Books
MINNEAPOLIS

WAYMARKS FOR THE JOURNEY
Daily prayer to change your world

© Copyright 2009 Ray Simpson.
Original edition published in English under the title WAYMARKS
FOR THE JOURNEY by Kevin Mayhew Ltd, Buxhall, England.

This edition published in 2020 by Fortress Press. All rights reserved.
Except for brief quotations in critical articles or reviews, no part of
this book may be reproduced in any manner without prior written
permission from the publisher. Email copyright@fortresspress.com
or write to Permissions, Fortress Press, PO Box 1209, Minneapolis,
MN 55440-1209.

Cover image: © iStock 2020: Silhouette of a signpost in a colorful
sunset stock photo by Angel Mato
Cover design: Emily Drake

Print ISBN: 978-1-5064-6040-6

Contents

About the author	6
Introduction	7
January Three life-giving principles	10
February Learning	72
March Guidance for the journey	130
April Rhythm of life	192
May Lifestyle	252
June Creation	314
July Healing	372
August Growing	436
September Transforming	498
October Community	558
November Outreach	620
December Flame and struggle	680
Footnotes	743

About the author

Ray Simpson is the founding guardian of the international Community of Aidan and Hilda and the principal tutor of its Celtic Christian Studies programme. He lives on the Holy Island of Lindisfarne where many pilgrims come to the Community's Retreat House, library and Spirituality Centre, the Open Gate. An Anglican priest, he was previously also a Free Church minister in a fresh expression of Church sponsored by six church streams at Bowthorpe, Norwich. Ray is the author of numerous bestselling books on Celtic Spirituality. He writes a weekly blog on www.aidanandhilda.org.

Introduction

Jesus did not call people to join an organisation, but to follow a way of life: 'I am the way, the truth and the life,' he said (John14:6), and, 'the way is wide and easy that leads to destruction: the way is narrow and hard that leads to life,' (Matthew 7:13, 14).

Many Christians seek to discern the way God calls them to walk. Although the final destination is not on this earth, they can see certain waymarks. The Way of Life of the Community of Aidan and Hilda, for example, has ten waymarks. These form the framework for this year's worth of readings. They may lead us away from our comfort zones on to a road less travelled. If we get lost, we look out for the guideposts, or waymarks. If we keep these in sight we will not go far wrong.

Each daily reflection has a

Reading – a paraphrase of a Bible passage. I suggest that you read this slowly, more than once.

Reflection – building on the reading and the theme of the month.

Pause for thought – a focus for thought or action.

Prayer – pulling the reading, reflection and pause for thought together into an address to God.

Today's step – to enable a move away from what is destructive towards what is life-giving.

Spiritual breathing exercise – All the time our bodies breathe in a three-fold rhythm: in – out – rest. Become aware of this rhythm. With practice we can combine this three-fold rhythm with three words or phrases that 'breathe' through our souls. We do this for some minutes at the start of the day, and whenever we have spare moments throughout the day – even when we are travelling or working. In this way the prayer book becomes a living companion wherever we are.

I use the pronouns 'he' and 'him' for God only because the English language has no gender-inclusive pronouns. According to the universal Christian Church God embraces and transcends both female and male; it is heresy to teach otherwise.

I completed this book on Saint Aidan's Day, looking out to Bamburgh where Aidan died, and to the sky above in which a young man, Cuthbert, who became the greatest of English Christian leaders, discerned Aidan's exit to heaven in a trail of light.

A good book is a person's precious life-blood outpoured. May it be so.

JANUARY 1

A way of life

Bible reading

God says 'I gave Levi a covenant of life and well-being. This called for deep, respectful awareness, which he gave me. People gained true instruction from him; nothing false came from his lips. He walked with me in integrity and turned many from futile ways. I want such people today, people who guard knowledge and carry out my message.'

Malachi 2:5–7

Reflection

We begin the journey into a new year with God's call to follow a way of life. This contrasts with the many sterile ways that dominate present society. God issues fresh calls in different generations. Long ago he asked a little-known tribe, named after Levi, a son of Jacob, the founder of ancient Israel, to make an unconditional commitment (a covenant) to such a way of life. God pledged to give well-being: the people promised to give themselves to God.

Often people delude themselves that to feed their bodies on artificial foods – manufactured so that they desire to eat too much – will fill them with life. In fact they become weighed down, obese, they sink into a half-life. It is like that with what we feed our minds on. Fast and false images infect us like a virus through the proliferating media. If we bow down to them they cause us to become unreal, disconnected from ourselves, from others, from God, the source of good.

God is revealing to people today something like the covenant he gave to Levi in biblical times; it is a way of life and well-being. God calls us, not just the people who lived in biblical times, to respond with respectful awareness, and attentiveness. How may we begin? Picture ourselves at a crossroads. One road is that of endless, empty chasing after things such as foods, fashions, fame, fancies, feelings. The alternative road is that of being true to oneself, pausing to reflect, tuning in to the source of good.

This we may indeed call a way of life.

Pause for thought

What am I attached to that is false or that will fade?
Where do I sense God's presence in myself;
in the people around me; in the place where I am?

Prayer

Great God of mercy, your world is becoming a wasteland;
calm us to prepare a way for you.
May we discover and live ways that are life-giving:
ways of integrity, respect, and awareness of your presence in all.

Today's step

I step
away from what is sterile
towards what is life-giving.

Spiritual breathing exercise

Your way in.
My way out.
Life.

JANUARY 2

Three life-giving principles

Bible reading

Blessed are the poor in spirit,
for theirs is the kingdom of heaven.
Blessed are the pure in heart, for they will see God.
Blessed are the meek, for they will inherit the earth.

Matthew 5:1, 8, 5

Reflection

These timeless, universal and life-giving words of Jesus are the best place to start our journey through the year. They are called The Beatitudes. I think of them as The Beautiful Attitudes. If these had been as central to Christianity as its creeds, how different would things be? Please notice that little word 'for'. There's no point in being poor, pure or meek for their own sake; the point is they are the only way into the infinite treasures of gaining heaven, seeing God and inheriting the earth. Some people call these three Beatitudes 'the three life-giving principles of simplicity, purity and obedience'. Simplicity leads us into God's generosity. Purity leads us into God's love. Obedience leads us into God's freeing community.

These life-giving principles are like roots which sustain everything we do. They are the source of blessings. Their opposite, the primal drives that make gods of money, sex and power, turn these blessings into curses. Everywhere people seem on a frantic drive to acquire things, misuse others for selfish pleasure, and selfishly control life. Simplicity frees us from the clutter that weighs us down. Purity frees us from the divided allegiances which fragment us. Obedience frees us from enslavement to our own or another's ego-driven agenda.

Simplicity acquires only what is life-giving. Purity gives and receives only what brings well-being. Obedience shares, listens and gives everyone their worth. Simplicity means we are stripped of everything that is superfluous to our calling. Purity means that we are purged of every passion that is divorced from God's love. Obedience means that we are aligned to what is good, not to our self-will.

Simplicity removes the fuss which drags us down. Purity removes the lust which ties us up. Obedience removes the rust which corrodes our ego when it is left to itself. These are three great gifts that can transform us.

Pause for thought

What three things can I throw away:
something I fuss about;
something I lust over;
something I try to control?

Prayer

Remove the clutter from my life, Lord,
and give me the grace of blessed simplicity.
Remove the divided affections from my life, Lord,
and give me the grace of undivided love for all.
Remove the dominating spirit from my life, Lord,
and give me the grace of seeking the good in the other.

Today's step

I step
away from what binds
towards what frees.

Spiritual breathing exercise

Simply your way.
Purely your love.
Only your will.

JANUARY 3

There's a monk in everyone

Bible reading

People who weep now are blest, for they will laugh. Those who laugh at everything now will one day be crying their heart out. People who are hungry now – whether for food or for what's right – will one day be satisfied. But you who are self-satisfied and over-fed now will one day realise how empty you are.

Luke 6:21, 24, 25

Reflection

Monks and nuns apply those three life-giving principles in one particular form – through the vows of poverty, chastity and obedience. Although we may hold these brothers and sisters in high regard, most of us have to earn a living, parent children or make our own way in life. We may even doubt whether the monastic vows have always been life-giving even for monks and nuns. Those vowed to poverty have everything provided by their monastery: can that be an evasion of responsibility? Some people who have embraced celibacy at a young age may repress sexual attractions that could be from God. Certain monks have obeyed directives of a superior that have been wrong and which have diminished them as human beings.

We need to remember that the traditional monastic vows – poverty, celibacy, obedience to a superior – are only one expression of the life-giving principles; these principles can be applied in different ways that are right for each person. God may entrust someone who simply wants to do his will with responsibility to handle money. This helps them grow. God may entrust someone who is pure in heart to parent a large family. This helps them love. Obedience, lived as a life-giving, universal principle, might mean doing what the doctor, the plumber or the soul friend advises.

Raimundo Panikar[1] views the monk as an element that is in every person. He sees his monastery as the entire planet. For Panikar the fundamental monastic principle is blessed simplicity. The monk is the one who learns to say 'no' to all that fragments or creates barriers. But the modern monk does not say 'no' to anything that is real; he achieves simplicity through integration, not denial.

Pause for thought

If you wish to enjoy all, wish to possess nothing.
If you wish to be all, wish to be nothing.[2]

Prayer

Nothing in my hands I bring,
simply to your Cross I cling,
naked, come to you for dress,
helpless, look to you for grace.
Dirtied, to the fountain fly;
wash me, Saviour, or I die.[3]

Today's step

I step
away from what separates
towards what unites.

Spiritual breathing exercise

Possess nothing.
Enjoy all.
Be at peace.

JANUARY 4

Through simplicity to generosity

Bible reading

Jesus said, 'How hard it is for rich people to enter God's economy.' 'Look here,' said Peter, 'we've left everything to follow you.' 'No one who has left their homes, loved ones or jobs to follow me will miss out,' Jesus assured him; 'they will receive a hundred times as much in this age, and something infinitely more precious in the next – eternal life.'

Mark 10:23, 28–30

Reflection

Simplicity leads us to become aware of God's generosity and to live out of providence. No longer distracted by many things – inessential things that we want to acquire, possess or just dream about – we are free to become conscious of the leaf greening, the bird chirping, and our heart singing. We rejoice in the taste of the simplest food, in the vitality of water poured into a glass, and in the wonder of our own bodies. Above all, we marvel at the divine presence everywhere present, understanding, warming, giving. Then, because we realise that the best things in life are freely given – like the earth and the air – we become grateful and generous. We cease to manipulate people in order to make them like us, do what we want or make us successful. Good people will like us the better for that, and we will experience the glow of deep-down trust.

Surely, there are hardships? Yes, plenty – Jesus warned of these. But no hardship, however extreme, can take away the generosity of God from our lives. We should not make a fetish of poverty. If we have really dedicated everything to God he may trust us to handle wealth, but he may also ask us to give it all away!

Simplicity means the willingness to be poor or rich for God according to God's direction. We resist the temptations to be greedy or possessive, and we will not manipulate people or creation for our own ends. We are bold to use all we have for God without fear of possible poverty.[4]

Pause for thought

What do I need to leave behind
because it gets in the way of God's generosity?

Prayer

Generosity of God, spilling over into creation,
we bless you for flowers and their wealth of beauty,
for creatures and their glorious variety,
for seas and seasons and scents;
may we, too, reflect your boundless generosity.

Today's step

I step
away from what I want to grab
towards what I can give.

Spiritual breathing exercise

Generosity in.
Meanness out.
Ooh!

JANUARY 5

Clearing the clutter from our lives

Bible reading

Bearing in mind the inspiring example of so many others, let us throw off everything that weighs us down and the sin that so easily entangles us, and with perseverance keep running the race marked out for us, keeping our eyes fixed on Jesus who himself has set out our course, and is both the starter, the coach who helps us perfect our running, and the finishing post.

Hebrews 12:1, 2

Reflection

There is no merit in seeking simplicity for its own sake; we seek to live simply for God. If we are weighed down by excess baggage we cannot walk, let alone run, the course God has set out for our lives. We cannot be what we are meant to be. The writer of this letter to Hebrew Christians does not liken our lives to a competition – there is a course specially designed by God and uniquely suited to each person. If we are to find our right way in life, be true to ourselves, and give our utmost for the Highest until we pass the finishing post with our final breath, we have to free ourselves from the attachments which drag us down, entangle our relationships or come between us and God. These prevent us from being the person we were born to be, and from living out our calling on earth.

In a world of increasing complexity we yearn for simplicity, but institutions sink under mountains of paper, and we succumb to the tyranny of a myriad competing demands both within and without us. Choice fatigue afflicts most people in the industrialised world. Because God has made each of us differently, the things that weigh us down will vary. The 'weights' are different for each person.

The point is to clear out of our lives, as far as we can, whatever clutters our spirits.

When we clear out junk, we do not sit back feeling self-satisfied, we turn our eyes upon Jesus. He is the true athlete of the Spirit.

Pause for thought

What activities,
relationships,
possessions,
clutter my spirit?

Prayer

Divine Saviour, your birth in the stable at Bethlehem
reveals the simplicity of the Father's love;
help us, like you, to fling away burdensome accessories,
and live in simplicity and joy.

Today's step

I step
away from disorder
towards order.

Spiritual breathing exercise

Ring in joy.
Ring out clutter.
Stay in joy.

JANUARY 6

Living simply in God's generosity

Bible reading

Seek God in simplicity of heart. God is not to be found by people who deceive and dissemble. God reveals himself to those who show childlike trust. Divided and devious thoughts put up walls . . . To exist: for this God created all things . . . God created human beings to be immortal, to reflect his own generous nature.

Wisdom 1:1–3, 14; 2:23

Reflection

We do not embrace simplicity for its own sake, but because it is the indispensable means by which we may live out of God's generosity: God's providence.

Recognise to whom you owe the fact that you exist, breathe, understand and are wise; and, above all, that you know God and hope for the kingdom of heaven and the vision of glory.

What benefactor has enabled you to look out upon the beauty of the sky, the sun in its course, the circle of the moon, the countless number of stars, with the harmony and order that are theirs, like the music of a harp? Who has blessed you with rain, the art of husbandry, different kinds of food, the arts, houses, laws, states, with a life of humanity and culture, with friendship and the easy familiarity of kinship?

> Is it not God who asks you now in your turn to show yourself generous above all other creatures and for the sake of all other creatures? Because we have received from him so many wonderful gifts, will we not be ashamed to refuse him this one thing only, our generosity? Though he is God and Lord he

is not afraid to be known as our Father. Shall we for our part repudiate those who are our kith and kin?[5]

In simple trust we abandon ourselves to the divine providence, which orders all things, sustains all creatures, and loves all souls. Yes, we take initiatives and exercise responsibility, and sometimes these can be complex, but always we ask, 'What is the simplest way to achieve the divine ends?'

Pause for thought

What do I depend upon most – a possession, product, point of view, person or God?

Prayer

Break in me the drive to manipulate others.
Embolden me to clear out the clutter.
Inspire me to give all in trust that you will provide.

Today's step

I step
away from dissipating
towards trust.

Spiritual breathing exercise

Generosity in.
Grasping out.
Overflowing.

JANUARY 7

Simply divine self-giving

Bible reading

When we love God we can't fail to recognise that everything he does is for the good of us all. If anyone wants to dispute this, what will they say in the light of this fact: God spared nothing, not even his own Son? If God gave so unstintingly in this way, won't he also give unstintingly to us now, through Christ?

Romans 8:28, 31, 32

Reflection

If we do not make simplicity our daily intention, clutter accumulates in our stomachs, brains, activities and possessions; we feed off false sources and we do not live out of the generosity of God. This is not an easy generosity, but it is sublime.

W. H. Vanstone[6] writes, 'The image of creation suggested by popular devotion . . . (conveys) an impression of easy control and limited endeavour, of resources held in reserve and power unused. There is nothing of the giving of self, and therefore nothing of the authenticity of love, in activity so light and easy.'

He tells a story which reflects in a human life the self-giving of God. A student doctor observed a brain operation in a London hospital. 'It was the first time this particular brain operation had been carried out in this country. It was performed by one of our leading surgeons upon a young man of great promise for whom, after an accident, there seemed to be no other remedy. It was an operation of the greatest delicacy, in which a small error could have had fatal consequences. In the outcome the operation was a triumph: but it involved seven hours of intense and uninterrupted concentration on the part of the surgeon.

When it was over, a nurse had to take him by the hand, and lead him from the operating theatre like a blind man or a little child.' This, one might say, is what self-giving is like: such is the likeness of God, wholly given, spent and drained in that sublime self-giving which is the ground and source and origin of the universe.

Pause for thought

What action of mine can I recall that best illustrates the 'no expense spared' spirit?

Prayer

Generosity of God, spilling over into creation,
we bless you for flowers and their wealth of beauty,
for creatures and their glorious variety,
for seas and seasons and scents.
May we, too, reflect something of your glorious generosity.

Today's step

I step
away from half-hearted giving of myself
towards doing something with all my heart.

Spiritual breathing exercise

Give all.
Withhold nothing.
Fullness.

JANUARY 8

Simplicity – stripped to the core

Bible reading

Jesus warned his friends: 'You know the tradition that if you are in a court, in order to convince people that you do not make a false statement you call God, or heaven, or the earth, or your city or some other body or your own head as your witness. Don't do this, for you have no power even to change what nature has put on your head. Simply say "yes" or "no"; anything else you contrive to add to these plain words comes from an evil source.'

Matthew 5:33–37

Reflection

In a desert there is no room for the comforts and conveniences of contemporary life, and there is a simplifying of expectations and lifestyles. There is a simple choice between yes and no. In the Bible and in Christian history believers have created temporary or inner deserts, where they are stripped down, to get to the core of reality. In the desert we realise that the life of simplicity is a life that is not embellished, elaborate, affected, deceitful, artificial, vain, pretentious, or ostentatious.

In the desert we also become aware of sand and stars. These were the simple signs of God's covenant with Abraham. At the time of the Exodus, the Israelites were told to make the simplest provisions for their desert journey into freedom (Exodus 13). When they were hungry in the desert they were sent provisions but were told only to collect what they needed (Exodus 16). The prophets found the simplest things to be of great significance. Samuel hears a quiet voice in the night (1 Samuel 3). Elijah encounters God in a sound of sheer silence (1 Kings 19:11, 12). Naaman the Syrian at first rejects as folly so simple a remedy as washing in the river (2 Kings 5).

Jesus 'emptied himself' (Philippians 2); he eschewed showmanship, prayed and spoke simply from the heart, possessed little, and focused on simple things such as bread and wine. In parables such as that of the rich man who stored up goods he had no need of, Jesus warns against hoarding material treasures, which moth and rust erode, and urges his ambitious disciples to be as a little child (Matthew 18:3).

Pause for thought

What words have I spoken in the last day or two that were convoluted?
What does that tell me?

Prayer

Dear God,
you are the true and real one.
Help me to be true, help me to be real,
help me to know my own mind.
Help me to know to what I must say 'yes'
and to what I must say 'no'.

Today's step

I step
away from doublespeak
towards plain speech.

Spiritual breathing exercise

Yes.
No.
Real good.

JANUARY 9

Simplicity – willing to be poor or rich

Bible reading

I prove myself to be a true servant of God by my willingness to endure whatever comes. With the Spirit's gifts of integrity and insight I face honour or dishonour, fame or rejection. I may be dying, but even in that I experience life. I may be poor but I am a means of wealth to many. Even though I may have nothing, in reality I possess everything.

Paul's Second Letter to the Corinthians 6:3–10

Reflection

Saint Aidan, who restored Christianity to the English in the seventh century, was poor for God. He chose, as a monk, to have no possessions of his own and, as a bishop, to give to the poor whatever money rich people gave him. Oswald, the king who invited Aidan, was rich for God. He chose to use his wealth and power to fund a Christian mission to his people, and to serve the needs of the poor. He was probably the first Anglo-Saxon king to appoint an officer for the welfare of the poor. The story of how Oswald instructed his officer to break up the silver used at his Easter banquet and distribute the pieces, as well as food, to hungry people outside, reveals the spirit in which he handled wealth.

Jesus observed that it is easier for a camel to go through a small opening, known as the eye of the needle, than for a rich person to enter the kingdom of heaven, yet he affirmed that a rich person such as Abraham would be at the top table in the kingdom of heaven.

It is doubtful that the world can develop the infrastructures and trades that enable its populations to live in dignity without the contribution of rich people. Certain business people have given away ninety per cent of their profit to good causes. But how many of us can be relied on to use money as a trust, rather than to let it take over our lives?

Pause for thought

What do I need?
Am I willing to give away everything I don't need?

Prayer

You who became poor to make many rich,
in your last days on earth
you promised to leave us the Holy Spirit.
As we meet and eat
may your Spirit come like blood into our veins
so that we will be driven entirely by your will.
Blow over the wealthy people so that they will be humble,
blow over the poor people
so that they will receive their true worth.[7]

Today's step

I step
away from something I clutch at
towards an act of selfless giving.

Spiritual breathing exercise

Possessive – no.
Enough – please.
Shalom.

JANUARY 10

Living simply from the deep centre

Bible reading

You who live in the secret place of the Most High,
spend your nights in the shelter
of the One who overshadows.
Say to the Eternal, 'My refuge, my place of safety,
my God in whom I trust.'

Psalm 91:1

Reflection

Twenty-first century life is overcrowded and ever more complex. Networks, means of communication, the number of acquaintances, stepchildren and relatives multiply as do 'necessary duties' associated with them. Before we know it we are weighed down with jobs, committees, appointments. We are crushed by the demands and expectations laid upon us. We are too busy to be good partners, good homemakers, good companions to our children, good friends to our neighbours, and we have no time at all to be friends with the friendless.

Yet if we withdraw in order to snatch quiet hours with ourselves or our families, guilt mounts, and the whispered complaints of others, real or imagined, crowd our being. So we limp from one thing to another, only half attentive, never savouring a moment or a meeting to the full. The time when we enter into deep composure in the divine presence is put off, as Shakespeare might have said, until tomorrow and tomorrow and tomorrow. Today is much too full to enter into our true home in God.

Thomas Kelly[8] said we are wrong to blame our plight upon external circumstances. The root of our problems lies in our lack of skill in the inner life. The outer distractions reflect a lack of inner integration. We are trying to be several selves at once, without all our selves (for example the parental self, the business self, the religious self, the social self) being organised by a single, integrating life within us. These selves shout their conflicting claims and we get a quick decision by heeding the loudest. This leaves disgruntled minorities. We are called to slip out of these into the divine centre.

Pause for thought

What is the loudest and most fretful voice shouting at me?
What is the deepest voice of the divine centre saying?

Prayer

Holy God,
help me to live in the still centre
of the world's whirring wheels,
where everything is led by you,
where all is one, and we are at peace.

Today's step

I step
away from fretful, short-term demands
towards the silent centre
where these demands are integrated.

Spiritual breathing exercise

Being in.
Fretting out.
Deep peace.

JANUARY 11

Living simply that others may simply live

Bible reading

For the first time a great number of Greek-speaking people became Christians, not just Jews. In places like Phoenicia, Cyprus and Antioch a great many people were brought to the Lord. At that time some prophets came from Jerusalem to Antioch and predicted there would be a severe famine. This took place during the reign of the Roman Emperor Claudius. The disciples in these Greek-speaking areas determined that, according to their ability, each would send relief to the believers in Judea. This they did.

Acts 11:19–30

Reflection

In theory, a person could pursue simplicity in the cause of an evil. In practice, the pursuit of evil requires manipulation and subterfuge, which breeds confusion and complication. Lies multiply. Truth simplifies.

Our dedication to simplicity is not an end in itself. It is so that we may simply love God, and others. The headline, 'We live simply that others may simply live' was first used by Christian Aid. By reducing our excessive consumption of foods, or by abstaining from eating foods that are more needed in the land where they are grown or reared, for example, we reduce costs, pollution, and unfair reward for poor food-growers.

The Quaker William Penn observed that we can either keep the ten commandments of God or we condemn ourselves to be ruled by the ten thousand commandments of people. Our society is saddled with the bureaucracy bred of dishonesty. Imagine how our bureaucracies would change if those who administer them lived in the Quaker simplicity of a William Penn?

Some Christians forego a meal, and send the money they have saved to people in a famine area, as those early Christians sent money when their brothers and sisters suffered famine in Judea. Organisations such as CAFOD and Christian Aid exist to help us do this. In Christian tradition Friday is the best day to do this habitually, for by missing lunch on Friday we are in solidarity with Jesus, who was without food, on the Cross, during Friday lunchtime.

Pause for thought

Become aware of each thing I eat today.
How simple is its journey to my table through the food chain? What is my response?

Prayer

Lord of earth and heaven,
the food I eat is earth, water and air
coming to me through pleasing plants or creatures.
When I eat, help me to keep these in mind
and to keep it simple.

Today's step

I step
away from quick gratification
towards thoughtful eating.

Spiritual breathing exercise

Savouring in.
Gobbling out.
Enough!

JANUARY 12

Living simply in trust

Bible reading

There is great gain in being close to God and being content in this. We brought nothing into this world, so it follows we can take nothing out. If we have food and drink, we will be content with these. In contrast, those who want to be rich fall into temptation, and become trapped in many senseless desires that drag them down into ruin. For the love of money is a root of all kinds of evil, and in their drive to be rich some believers have strayed from a relationship of trust. But you, God-lover, shun all these, and pursue right living, godliness, faith, endurance, love and gentleness.

1 Timothy 6:6–11

Reflection

The generosity of God, not the lust for money, is the deepest reality in which we should move.

We recognise that the love of money is the root of all kinds of evil and that no human being can serve both God and money. This false love of money is rooted in the desire to control. It is in fact also possible to choose poverty for a false reason, for example because it makes it easier for us to control everything in our life, though it is little. God's ultimate purpose for our lives is that we live for God's glory. God will give us everything there is if we can handle it for his glory. God says to us, 'If it is my will, you can afford it. If it is not my will, you shouldn't want to afford it.'

So we see that there are different layers of character formation in relation to money. The bottom layer of character formation is to practise abstinence, to learn to do without. Some of us are so eaten up with the craving for money that we need to stay in that bottom layer. But there is a higher stage in character formation. This is when our spirits are free to trust God for everything. When we are poor and in need, we discover streams of resource in the great God of all creation. These can be streams of enterprise and faith projects to serve the world.

Pause for thought

What is God saying?
Am I willing to use all as God directs?
Am I willing to give away all as God directs?

Prayer

All that I am,
all that I have,
all that I do,
all that I'll ever be,
I offer now to you.

Today's step

I step
away from money-grabbing
towards God's wealthy ways.

Spiritual breathing exercise

Let go.
Let God.
Blessing.

JANUARY 13

For richer or poorer

Bible reading

Joseph's brothers came from their famine-stricken land to Egypt, where, unknown to them, Joseph, whom they had left as dead, had risen from the penury of prison to become the Emperor's chief of staff. When they realised the chief of staff was their brother, Joseph said to them, 'Do not condemn yourselves because you sold me to be brought here as a slave, for it was God who sent me before you to preserve the life of many. The famine has been here for two years, and will continue for another five, but through divine guidance I have stored enough food to last for this period. God has made me a father to the Emperor. I am in charge of his whole household and rule over the entire land of Egypt. Tell my father to come and settle here. I will provide for you all. You shall not sink into poverty.'

Genesis 45:5–11

Reflection

Joseph had to be brought into the poverty of a prison, and tested to see whether he would trust in God alone. When he passed that test he was trusted with the wealth of superpower Egypt. Nehemiah and Daniel were also men of means who used their position, resources and contacts for God.

Traditional religious orders within Christianity usually require those who are to become monks or nuns to make a vow of poverty. Poverty usually means having no property, capital or other possessions. These may be sold or given to the monastery. Some monasteries return an amount of capital if a member withdraws and goes back to a secular life. John Chrysostom, a fourth-century leader of the Eastern

Church wrote: 'What are we to fear? The confiscation of our goods? "We brought nothing into this world and we shall surely take nothing from it." . . . I have no fear of poverty, no desire for wealth.'

This monastic life of poverty is one calling among many. The suggestion that certain people may be called to be rich has raised eyebrows. 'I do not think this is possible,' I have been told, 'for did not Jesus say it is more difficult for a rich person to enter the kingdom of God than for a camel to go through the eye of a needle?' Jesus said that, but he also added, 'With God all things are possible.'

Pause for thought

Joseph did something about the dreams God gave him.
What dreams does God give me?
What am I doing about them?

Prayer

God of destiny,
who through dreams brought Joseph from poverty to plenty,
weave your dreams into our lives,
and make us content with your will,
in bad times and in good.

Today's step

I step
away from burying my dreams
towards realising my dreams.

Spiritual breathing exercise

Dream in.
Despair out.
God provides.

JANUARY 14

Living simply to give

Bible reading

The person who sows little will reap little. The person who sows generously will reap generously. Each of you must give of your own free choice, not grudgingly, because of the demands of others, for God loves a cheerful giver. God is able to provide for you every kind of blessing in abundance, so that you, in turn, may give abundantly to others.

2 Corinthians 9:6–8

Reflection

The 'prosperity gospel' tells people that if they follow God's laws they will increase their prosperity. This contradicts Jesus' teaching and common experience. 'The sun and rain fall on good and bad alike,' said Jesus. Neither prosperity nor poverty necessarily reflect a person's standing with God. Moreover, if our aim is to be rich, or if we are driven by the desire for riches then we cannot enter the kingdom of God. But if, like Abraham, we are called and are willing to leave all, and then are also promised a good material as well as spiritual inheritance, we are blessed indeed.

There are billionaires who tithe ninety percent of their income. Often those who tithe so generously wish to remain anonymous. This can be a sign that they have no wish to control or glory in riches; they have truly put them at the Lord's disposal. The reward is the satisfaction of being used to bring well-being of body and soul to others.

There is more happiness in giving than in receiving.

Jesus, Acts 20:35

He is no fool who gives what he cannot keep to gain what he cannot lose.

Jim Elliot, missionary and martyr

JANUARY 14

God has given us two hands – one for receiving and the other for giving.
Billy Graham, American evangelist

We make a living by what we get, but we make a life by what we give.
Winston Churchill

Pause for thought
Have I prayed over my assets, whether they be large or small?

Prayer
God bless this money for what it can make possible –
the nurturing of my body or mind,
a pat on the back for work well done
the enlarging of my horizons,
expressing love to others through gifts,
for it is in giving that I shall receive more than I can ask.

Today's step
I step
away from hoarding my assets
towards multiplying or distributing my assets.

Spiritual breathing exercise
Your wealth in.
My wealth out.
Giving.

JANUARY 15

Purity – giving our whole being to God

Bible reading

God is love, and whoever lives in love, remains in God and God in them. This is how love is made complete in us; this is how, on judgement day, we will be able to look God in the face, because we express divine love in our lives in this world, in relationships.

1 John 4:16–18

Reflection

> Purity means we are wholehearted, not divided, in relationships. It means accepting and giving God our whole being, including our sexuality. We love all people as Christ commands, and accept Christ's teaching about marriage and celibacy. We respect every person as belonging to God, and we are available to them with generosity and openness.[9]

We do not embrace purity for its own sake, but as an indispensable means of living in the love of God. If we allow our affections to be pulled in contrary directions, we fail in both human and divine love. If, however, we fling our affections out of the down-drag of partiality into the ever-replenishing source of love, we can live the fullness of both human and divine love.

In merely human love, we try to possess the many without caring for the One. But if we do not possess the Source, then the many human loves fail us and we fail them. With divine love, we go first to the Source, and from there we go to the many. In human love there is demand or, at least, expectation. But in divine love there is no such thing as demand or expectation. In divine love we just give what we have and what we are . . . We give, and even if our love is not accepted, we do not mind. We shall go on giving, for we are all love.

In human love, when our expectation is not fulfilled, we sometimes try to withdraw from the person to whom we have offered our love. In divine love, it is never like that. With divine love we try to become one with the weakness, imperfection and bondage of others. Although we have inner freedom, we use this inner freedom not to lord it over others, but to become one with their imperfections. In this way we can understand and serve them at their own level, with a view to transforming their imperfections.

Pause for thought

The capacity of human love is so limited that we cannot expand ourselves and totally embrace one another. There is bound to be a feeling of supremacy. But in divine love there is no such thing as superiority and inferiority.

Prayer

O God you have prepared for those who love you such good things as pass our understanding. Pour into our hearts such love towards you that we love every person and every thing with your heart of compassion.

Today's step

I step
away from demand
towards compassion.

Spiritual breathing exercise

Acceptance in.
Snatching out.
Love.

JANUARY 16

Pure gold

Bible reading

God has saved up for you a heritage in heaven that never fades. This is a great joy to you, so that even though you go through all kinds of trials in the short term, your faith will emerge as something purer, more valuable than gold. Gold has to be purified by fire, yet even that eventually perishes. Your life of faith also has to be purified like that – but in contrast to gold will never dissolve.

1 Peter 1:4–7

Reflection

Most of us would like to be described as 'pure gold', but few of us want to go through the process that makes us pure. We become pure only when the false ingredients are removed in molten fire.

This life-giving principle of purity is universal, and can be applied to every aspect of our lives, including each of the ten waymarks featured in this book.

To be pure in our learning is to develop the talents we have, not to cover over the reality with mere paper qualifications.

To be pure in the way we relate to a soul friend is to be transparent; to entrust our deepest thoughts, feelings, failings, doubts to them without regard to their opinion of us.

To be pure in our prayer, we refrain from bending God to our will.

To be pure in our work we do (as far as circumstances permit) what God puts into our hearts, and we do it with undivided attention.

Purity in recreation means we refrain from doing things to escape from ourselves.

Purity in interceding to overcome evil with good comes from a desire to see God's righteousness prevail, not from a lust to empire build or be self-righteous.

Purity in our lifestyle means holding on to nothing that we do not need, speaking no evil, and treating all people with respect.

Purity in relation to creation means we respect its integrity, and resist those who market products that violate creation by deceiving customers.

Purity in healing means we only want what Jesus wants for the other person and place.

Purity in relation to unity means that our agenda is never 'we'll walk with you if you will arrange yourselves around us'.

Purity in relation to mission means that we trust what is good in each person, whatever their religion, class or ethnic background and give them equality of regard.

Pause for thought

Are there double standards in the way I treat people?

Prayer

May the fire of the Spirit
kindle in me a great blaze,
consuming all that is of my ego,
leaving only that which is from you.

Today's step

I step
away from double-minded ways
towards acts and attitudes that are like pure gold.

Spiritual breathing exercise

Gold in.
Dross out.
True.

JANUARY 17

The eye of the eagle

Bible reading

The light of the body is the eye. So if your eye is clear, your whole body will be filled with light. But if your eye is diseased, then your whole body will be filled with darkness. There can be nothing worse than for your whole being to be in the dark.

Matthew 6:22, 23

Reflection

The point of Jesus' words is that we keep our eye on the ball. The eye of the body is a parable of the eye of the soul. If our physical eyes deteriorate, we become unfit to drive a car, because we are likely to crash. If our inner eye is clouded, we become unfit to drive on the road of life. We miss the essential points. We either crash or we go round in circles.

Celtic Christians believed that the eagle was the only bird that could gaze directly into the sun without being blinded. The eagle is the symbol of John the contemplative Gospel-writer, who gazed into the face of Jesus, and who looked at the world with eyes of love. The phrase 'the single eye' refers to this pure way of looking at the world, to a seeing that is not distracted by fanciful or false sights, to an orientation towards God that prays, 'You be my vision.'

This teaching of Jesus is about purity. Purity in our motives enables us to focus on what is important from eternity's point of view. Huge consequences flow both from purity and from impurity. If we are pure we become free in spirit, wise in mind, beautiful in attitude, alert in body, noble in service. If we are impure we become closed to other people, inconsistent in our behaviour, divided in our emotions, confused in our calling, stiff in our bearing.

Pause for thought

What things distract my attention?

Prayer

Open my eyes that I may see
each thing that you bless:
the beauty of a flower,
the grace of a creature,
the goodness of a person,
eternity in a grain of dirt.

Give me the eye of the eagle that
gazes into your face,
traces the movement of your hand,
sees into the depths of your heart,
follows the reaches of your mind,
glimpses the horizons of your spirit.

Today's step

I step
away from emotions that divide
towards emotions that accept all.

Spiritual breathing exercise

See God in all.
See nothing self-serving.
Your gaze.

JANUARY 18

Good and bad fruit

Reading

A good fruit tree will not produce bad fruit; nor will a diseased fruit tree produce good fruit. You can tell the quality of a tree by its fruit. You know perfectly well that no one can pick figs for the meal table from a tree full of thorns, or grapes from briars. Good persons produce good things from the goods they have stored in their hearts. Bad persons sooner or later come out with the bad things they have stored in their hearts. Whatever comes out of the mouth has flowed from what is stored in the heart.

Luke 6:43–45

Reflection

Purity is consistent. Purity does not put on faces, or treat one person differently from another. There is no gap between the inner and the outer life in a pure person.

A monk saw someone who looked like a Christ figure come to offer advice. The monk was beguiled and confused, until he exclaimed, 'Where are the scars?' Once he realised that this figure had no scars, as Christ had, he knew it could not be Christ, so he commanded the visitor to depart.

The scars on Christ are a reminder of the 'integrity test' he passed with such flying colours. Christ's trials, which he underwent voluntarily, were like the fire which purifies gold. We do not seek trials, or stretching circumstances that threaten to pull us in different directions, but we will have to face them. If we remain true to ourselves and God, we will come out with our purity increased. Then we shall be able to say the words Tennyson puts into the mouth of Sir Galahad: 'My strength is as the strength of ten, because my heart is pure.'

'Live pure, speak true, right wrong, follow the King –
Else, wherefore born?'[10]

Pause for thought

What threatens to pull me in contrary directions?
What is purity's response?

Prayer

Give me your firelight, Holy Spirit,
as I go down
into the things stored
in my memories, dreams and hurts.
Journey with me beyond these
to the seed of my nature you planted in me at my beginning.
May I become that seed, which is my true self,
and may it grow and produce much fruit.

Today's step

I step
away from deceitful ways
towards the pure seed of my true nature.

Spiritual breathing exercise

Good roots in.
Bad roots out.
Life.

JANUARY 19

Single-minded

Bible reading

I treat every thing in life as trash to be thrown away, in contrast to the infinitely better experience of knowing The Greatest, Jesus Christ. All I want is to know Christ, and the fellowship of his sufferings, and the power of his resurrection. This desire is not yet a complete experience. But one thing I do: forgetting what is behind I press on towards the goal that lies ahead with every fibre of my being. All of us who are mature should think like this.

Philippians 3:7–16

Reflection

Jesus' words 'Blessed are the pure' have sometimes been translated as 'Blessed are the single in heart'. Celtic Christians are renowned for their single-mindedness. This is what the term 'Celtic fire' expresses. Anything that is artificial or false is burned; then only the eternal uncreated fire of love remains. Someone else referred to them as 'God-intoxicated Christians'.

This is not the same thing as being stubborn people, intent only on our own blinkered way. The world has too many of these. Purity is not about repressing anything. We hold before God everything – our emotions, cravings, aspirations. We work to integrate emotions that fly in all directions. We discard what does not truly belong to our deepest being. This is what the apostle Paul here writes about – the willingness for everything to be exposed and scrutinised in the light of Christ, of his values and of his qualities of suffering love.

A delightful folk story that someone wrote down about the Life of Brigid in the ninth century[11] shows the competitive streak in those two great saints, Brendan and Brigid, being used, not for gold or worldly glory, but for God. Brendan asked Brigid to bear witness to what degree she 'had the love of God more than others'. Brigid urged Brendan to give his answer first. 'From the day I took vows I never travelled more than seven furrows without focussing my mind on God' Brendan declared. 'That is good,' said Brigid, but she went on: 'from the hour I set my mind on God I never took it from him for a moment!'

Pause for thought

What wayward impulse do I need to hold before God – either to integrate into my life or send on its way?

Prayer

Lord, I leave behind with you affections, habits and attitudes which are no part of a whole life.
This one thing I do,
I look to you and to the fellowship of your sufferings
and to the power of your resurrection
and to the goal
of the whole created universe
becoming one with you.
So help me God.

Today's step

I step
away from thoughts which lead astray
towards the single goal.

Spiritual breathing exercise

Single heart in.
Straying thoughts out.
Goal.

JANUARY 20

Purity preserves the world's goodness and gives taste to life

Bible reading

Jesus said, 'You who follow my way are like a preservative – its ingredients preserve a food's goodness and give it taste. You are the preservative of the world. You give taste to life. If you lose the essential ingredient, what use are you? You are good for nothing. You are fit only to be thrown out with the rubbish.'

Matthew 5:13

Reflection

This passage highlights the benefits of purity. In Jesus' day salt was the main preservative for fresh foods, which soon went bad without it. The phrase 'you are the salt of the earth' makes the point that without purity, everything in human affairs goes bad, or turns sour. In the case of salt, it does something more, it makes food tasty. A pure person can give taste to a conversation, a gathering or an institution.

How do we lose our saltiness, our preservative quality? Relationships decompose when we are one thing to this person and another to that person. Businesses decompose when a person's word cannot be relied upon. Organisations and neighbourhoods decompose when colleagues and neighbours cannot be trusted. No one's motives can be relied upon. Everything becomes a means to an end, the end being someone's vain glory.

How do we become like salt, that is, how do we become true? Think on this vision given to Mother Julian: 'I beheld a little thing no bigger than a hazelnut (as it seemed to me), lying in the palm of my hand, and it was as round as a ball. I looked at it with the eye of my understanding and thought: "What can this be?" And I was answered generally "It is all that is made!" I gazed with astonishment, wondering how it could survive because of its littleness. It seemed to me that it should presently fall into nothingness. And I was answered in my mind: "It lasts and always will last because God loves it." And so everything receives its being from the love of God.'[12]

Pause for thought

What in me is not true, tried and tested?

Prayer

Lord,
make me true, like an arrow;
make me dependable, like rock;
make me deep, like an anchor;
make me incorruptible, like salt.

Today's step

I step
away from that which corrupts
towards that which preserves good.

Spiritual breathing exercise

Goodness in.
Corruption out.
Your preserve.

JANUARY 21

Purity – the route to thriving friendship

Bible reading

God says, 'Ask me to forgive all your sins. No longer put your trust in false gods. Acknowledge that an orphaned people find compassion only in me. Then I will heal your fragmented life and love you freely, and you will become like a great cedar tree under whose branches people gather and find shelter.'

Hosea 14:2–9

Reflection

Purity is the soil in which friendship thrives; it frees us to be available to everyone as they are, without making them a sex object.

> The media continually takes the line that romance is indispensable and sex vital to personal fulfilment. Sex is seen as a safe, low-consequence activity engaged in by just about everyone – except, oddly, within the context of lasting marriage, where it can often represent stagnation and freedom-curtailing responsibility.
>
> In the real world, friendship runs the risk of being demoted . . . Rootlessness and mobility have encouraged the expectation that our partners should fulfil the role of every other kind of relationship, and the same is true in reverse, as friendships become increasingly sexualised . . . Sexual relationship is one part – an important part, but only a part – of God's relational plan for us. It is not his only solution to loneliness, or even his first.

Humans were never meant to live in isolation. Even those biblical characters who apparently led solitary lives had strong friendships.

The Bible does not see Jesus or Paul as relationally deprived because it never equates love or relationship with sex . . . We need to recover in our churches and for our culture the possibility of intimacy without eros.[13]

Pause for thought

Can I allow my friends to be who they are?

Prayer

Father,
free us to enjoy and not possess another;
and to be who we are.
Grant us the purity within which friendship thrives;
restore to us the joy of communion.

Today's step

I step
away from sexual projection
towards freeing friendship.

Spiritual breathing exercise

Friendship in.
Lust out.
Communion.

JANUARY 22

Obedience – joyful abandonment to God

Bible reading

If you obey my commands you will remain within my love, just as I have obeyed my Father's commands and remain within his love. I have told you this so that my joy may be in you, and that your joy may be complete. My command is this: love each other as I have loved you. No one can have a greater love than to lay down their life for their friends. You are my friends if you do what I command you.

John 15:9–14

Reflection

> Obedience is the joyful abandonment of ourselves to God.[14]

According to one of the early Church fathers, joy is the echo of God in us, and joy and obedience are two sides of the same coin. You cannot have one without the other. In Christian tradition the disobedience of the human being, which is spelt out in the story of Adam and Eve (Genesis 2), is understood to be the root of all other evils. Obedience is the source of all blessings. That is why we are called to obedience.

This passage assures us that the obedience we are called to is nothing to do with subservience to authority that is wrongly used. Rather, it is about developing such a relationship of love that we gladly yield our selfish desires out of love for the other – God above all, and then, also, those with whom we are called to relate.

The true nature of obedience is modelled for us by the Trinity – the three loves in the heart of God. Within the

Trinity obedience is always voluntary, it is always an act of unconditional love which is at once both humility and majesty. The three divine loves did not snatch at what, in our human terms, we might regard as their 'rights'. Christ, on earth, accepted limits and obeyed even to the point of death. When Christ says he obeyed his Father's commands he was also, so to speak, obeying himself; Christ and the Father each chose an identity of purpose. Through his obedience, Christ fulfilled his destiny. It is like that with us.

Pause for thought
What do I do that I don't sense the Father doing?

Prayer
Make me eager to align my will with yours.
Give me joy in my heart, keep me serving.
May I grow in intimacy with you,
until my every act is a glad response to your promptings.

Today's step
I step
away from self-will
towards joyful abandon to your will.

Spiritual breathing exercise
Your will in.
Self-will out.
Joy.

JANUARY 23

Obedience – attentive listening

Bible reading

My teaching is not my own, but the one who sent me . . . The Son can do nothing of his own accord, he does only what he sees the Father doing; whatever he does, the Son does also. The Father loves the Son and reveals to him all that he himself is doing . . . I can do nothing of my own accord: I exercise judgement in human affairs as I am taught by God, because my aim is not my will but the will of the One who sent me . . . In the prophets it is written 'they will all be instructed by God'. Everyone who has listened to the Father and learned from him comes to me . . . What I have heard from the Father I tell the world.

John 5:17, 19, 20, 30; 6:45; 8:28

Reflection

> The root of obedience is attentive listening to God, because the longing of our hearts is to obey him.[15]

The word 'obedience' comes from the Latin word 'audire', meaning 'to hear'.

As the deer in a parched land longs for the watering places, so every human heart longs, deep down, for God's will. Jesus was so attentive to his Father's will that he said 'I can do nothing on my own, I speak as the Father instructed me' (John 8:28). That, too, is our ideal. For those who commit to this attentive listening, nothing counts so much as God's slightest wish. Holy obedience sets in, sensitive and selfless as a shadow, and when this happens renewing divine forces are released, and history changes.

Thomas Kelly[16] observes that this holy obedience leads us to embrace the suffering of others. In doing this our hearts are stretched. Christ enacts in our hearts the willingness to welcome suffering and to know it as the final seal of God's gracious love. He speaks within us, to our truest selves and disquiets us with the world's needs. By inner persuasions he draws us to a few tasks, our tasks, and gives us the seeing eye of the sensitised soul and the grace of unflinching obedience.

Pause for thought

How is God disquieting me?

Prayer

Make me attentive to your clear commands.
Make me attentive to the sighing of your world.
Make me attentive to your whispering tones.
Make me attentive to your slightest wish.

Today's step

I step
away from blaring
towards listening.

Spiritual breathing exercise

Your voice in.
My voice out.
Speak.

JANUARY 24

Obedience means respect

Bible reading

Respect those who work so hard among you, who oversee you and keep you on the right path. Theirs is a high calling. Give them the highest honour. Live together in peace. Challenge the person who does not play their part; encourage the shy, help the weak, and be patient with every one. Make sure that no one pays another back for some wrong. Always try to be kind to one another, and to everyone else.

1 Thessalonians 5:12–15

Reflection

> We honour those whom God has placed in authority over us, and we seek to recognise and respect the gifts, roles and authority of those who work alongside us in the community of the church.[17]

Those who welcome God's grace will submit joyously to all rightful authority. They know that God rules over everything in heaven and earth. The principle of obedience means that we give each person the respect due to them. The transforming dynamic of the early Christian Church enabled Christians to leap across their previous religious frameworks, cultural ghettos and conditioned reflexes, and meet face to face. They inevitably faced profound disagreements. It would have been easy for them to have belittled or written off as 'an axis of evil' those who differed from them. Yet both the apostle Paul in this letter to the church in Thessalonica, and Peter in his first letter, frequently implore Christians not only to respect parents, as was generally taught, but to show respect even to unpopular people. And Christians are called to model this respect within the Church by honouring those who have oversight.

Citizens, wrote Peter, should respect their national leaders, employees should respect their employers, married people should respect their spouses: in fact people should respect everyone (1 Peter 2:17,18; 3:7).

Each person is made in God's likeness. For the Body of Christ to function well, and for society to function well, many roles are required. Each should be respected. Respect does not mean we acquiesce in what is wrong. If someone abuses their trust, we show respect by confronting this and holding them to the highest.

Pause for thought

As I look back over the past day or two, is there someone to whom I have not given due respect?

Prayer

Holy God, author of life,
by sharing our life on earth
you declare every life to be sacred.
Imbue us with deep respect for each person
and for each of the many roles that are needed
to sustain a cohesive world.

Today's step

I step
away from despising someone in my heart
towards honouring them.

Spiritual breathing exercise

Honouring in.
Despising out.
Respect.

JANUARY 25

Obedience includes accountability

Bible reading

A human being has one body, but this has many parts. The wider, multi-racial community is like a body which has Christ as its head. One part of this body does not make the whole. If the foot should say, 'Because I am not the hand I can go my own way' is it not still in fact part of the body? If the ear should say, 'Because I am not the eye I need take no notice of it', it is still actually part of the body. If the whole body were an eye where would it get its hearing? If the whole body were an ear, where would it get its sense of smell? There are many limbs but one body, so no part of the body is able to say to another, 'I have no need of you'. Indeed, it is essential to the body's good functioning that its stronger parts honour the weaker parts. Thus if one member suffers, all suffer; if one member is honoured, all are honoured.

1 Corinthians 12:12–26

Reflection

Obedience to God (the vertical) can become a pious delusion if we do not test this against obedience to others (the horizontal). The human heart is deceitful, and God has designed us to develop obedience in the context of both the human family and the spiritual family of the Church.

How was obedience expressed within the Body of Christ after its Head left this earth? Jesus appointed seventy missionaries and told them 'Whoever listens to you listens to me' (Luke 10:16). Early Christians recognised that heeding the teaching of the apostles was fundamental to following Christ. Early Church members were also urged to esteem their elders (1 Thessalonians 5:12). Yet this was never taken as subservience. Paul, following the light of conscience, lovingly confronted Peter, the leading apostle, because he was man-pleasing fellow Jews when he refused to eat a meal with uncircumcised non-Jews. We may assume, however, that whenever Peter was fulfilling his God-given role, Paul honoured it.

The functioning of the parts of the human body is a brilliant parable of the nature and purpose of obedience. Obedience lies in humbly playing my part and working with, not in place of, each other member of the body. Each person has a calling, a role, a gift, however small. When they exercise that, we should accept their authority. If a doctor tells me what to do about an injury, I do not dismiss the suggestion without good reason. If, however, someone tries to usurp another's role, or abuses their own role, I do not collude. Obedience requires accountability, but it also requires discernment.

Pause for thought

Is there anyone whose part in 'the body' I do not honour?

Prayer

Christ,
Help me to see each member of your body as you see them.
May I support each person in their calling,
may I honour the weak,
may I relate well to other members of the body
as I make my contribution.

Today's step

I step
away from wilful independence
towards a partner in the body.

Spiritual breathing exercise

Partnership in.
Self-sufficiency out.
Obedience.

JANUARY 26

Obedience is rooted in humility

Bible reading

Do not look out just for your own interests, but also for the concerns of others. Have the same attitude as Jesus the Christ. Although he was essentially divine, he gave up his divine 'rights', and became as we humans are. He humbled himself, became a servant, and carried his obedience even to the point of death. Because he was willing to stoop so low, God has lifted him up so high, that whenever his name is mentioned every knee in heaven and earth shall bow . . . Therefore as you have always obeyed in my presence, complete the working out of your calling, for it is God who wills you to work for his pleasure, not yours . . . that you may be like stars that shine in the dark.

Philippians 2:4–10, 13, 15

Reflection

This passage reveals the divine secret of obedience. The obedient person follows in the footsteps of Christ, who gave us the pattern of obedience that leads to greatness. The obedient person puts their whole trust in God. The proud and those who are a law to themselves prevent the indwelling of God's grace and peace, whereas the Holy Spirit enters into the soul of the obedient, bringing deep contentment.

Humility is closely linked to obedience. Humility is not about self-disgust. It is knowing that anything we do or think that pulls away from God is worthless. Humility is acceptance that God is the source of every inspiration, action and outcome that has worth. This humility does not hold us back, it can make us bold. Out of humility came the thunder of the prophets.

Why did the holy fathers of the early Church set obedience above fasting and prayer? Because feats of spiritual endeavour without obedience foster glory. Obedient people heed their spiritual guide, are therefore free from care and can pray with an undistracted mind.

> Had the fallen angels observed obedience they would have continued in heaven, singing the praises of God. And had Adam not disobeyed he and his seed would have remained in paradise.[18]

Pause for thought
What am I holding back?

Prayer
I give myself to you, Lord,
my will I hand to you.
I yield to those who heed you, Lord,
now free my heart to sing.

Today's step
I step
away from insisting on my views
towards accepting yours.

Spiritual breathing exercise
Your will in.
My will out.
Freedom.

JANUARY 27

The fruit of obedience

Bible reading

Then you will once again obey God and carry out the commands he has given you. The Lord will prosper you in the fruit of your body, in the fruit of your livestock, in the fruit of your soil. The Lord will again take delight in prospering you as he did your ancestors when they obeyed what is written in the Book of the Law.

Deuteronomy 30:8–10

Reflection

Obedience to God is the most fundamental thing required of us. Yet the heart is deceitful; many of us do not know the difference between our own ego and God's will, and we claim we are obeying God when in fact we are going our own way. We may even quote Scripture texts, circumstances and words of others to claim divine support for what we selfishly do.

A test of whether we obey God is whether we are transparent with someone in oversight to whom we give account of our time and money. The fourth-century desert Christians shared all their thoughts with an elder and carried out their advice with alacrity as an act of obedience – through accountability to community.

A story did the rounds of the fourth-century desert Christians which serves as a parable to us. A spiritual father named John the Dwarf lived in the Egyptian desert at Skete. He accepted an old man as his helper. John placed a bit of dry wood in the earth and asked the old man to water it each day with a bottle of water until it bore fruit. The old man had to leave each evening and walk a long distance to fill up the bottle from a spring. He did this uncomplainingly for three years, until the wood sprouted into a tree. John took a twig from the tree to the Sunday gathering of the brothers and held it up. 'Look at the fruit of obedience' he said.

Pause for thought

Is there some mundane duty
I need to carry out as an act of obedience?

Prayer

Bend my will to the holy yoke of obedience, O Lord.
Make me faithful in the little things.
May every necessary chore become an act of worship.
And grant that some fruit may fall upon us.

Today's step

I step
away from vain argument
towards obedience in the little things.

Spiritual breathing exercise

Faithful duty in.
Fickleness out.
Fruit.

JANUARY 28

Obedience means getting real

Bible reading

When Christ entered this world he said, 'I come to do your will. I know that you do not want external rites and sacrifices. You have prepared a human body for me to assume so that I may accomplish your will, not in symbol but in reality, as the Psalmist pre-figured.'

Hebrews 10:5, 7

Reflection

We find in the life of Jesus the fundamental example of obedience to God. As the writer of the Letter to the Hebrews points out so well, every aspect of the life and ministry of Jesus was shaped by his intense desire to follow the will of the Father. Even when he faced a painful and humiliating death his obedience, his attentive listening, to the divine will gave him resolve and courage: 'Abba, Father, all things are possible to you. Take this cup away from me, but not what I will but what you will' (Mark 14:36).

The uncreated Christ knew his identity and calling lay in doing the Father's will, which was to lay down his life on earth. We created mortals find our identity and our calling in doing the Father's will. Obedience to this is the joyful discovery of our true selves. We freely, and with delight, carry out God's laws because we know that in them lies our good. The root of obedience is to accept who I actually am – to accept the bits I tend to deny or run away from or rebel against. When I accept myself I then accept my relation to others. Of course, we all have bits yet to be discovered and connected with the whole. Obedience lies in the integrity of the search.

What if part of me is a runaway, or is out of kilter with the other parts? What if another organ of the body is abusing its role and trying to usurp me? It can't, because I am obedient to myself – to my call, to my maker's original intention. So I say 'no' to a usurper, in love, while still respecting their rightful role, in obedience to the Body of Christ.

In this understanding of obedience we do not hand over our moral choices to a 'superior'. However, my ego also tries to usurp others. In order to be obedient I practice dethroning my ego. So we do accept to do some things that we would not choose to do, in order to learn the humility of service. But we 'give' those acts of humble service through our own free will – we are not therefore demeaned. Each day we laugh at little inconveniences suffered in the greater cause.

Pause for thought

Experiment. Find out if it's true that doing God's will brings freedom.

Prayer

O Christ, you laid your life down for us.
May each thing I do this day be a laying down of my life.

Today's step

I step
away from doing things my way
towards doing things Christ's way.

Spiritual breathing exercise

Your way in.
My way out.
I come.

JANUARY 29

Holy disobedience

Bible reading

Xerxes, king of a vast empire of many religions and races, commanded that the beautiful Esther, who was brought up by a god-fearing Jew named Mordecai, become his concubine. The king promoted a man named Haman as his senior officer. He hated God-honourers, and persuaded the king to issue a decree banning any subject from worshipping anyone but the king. Mordecai continued to pray to God as before. This infuriated Haman, who decided to have him and other Jews killed. Mordecai, realising what was planned, advised Esther to make herself especially alluring. Sooner or later the king would invite her into his presence and allow her to ask him a favour. This happened. Esther asked that the king spare the God-honourers in his kingdom. And so he did.

The Book of Esther

Reflection

A tradition has developed within Christianity of 'holy disobedience'. This means that in order to be obedient to God and do what is right, we sometimes have to be disobedient to an authority which is undermining what is right.

Mordecai remained obedient to the law of God and Esther remained obedient to her adopted parent even though this meant they disobeyed a pernicious new law of an empire whose laws they had hitherto obeyed. The midwives Shiphrah and Puah were obedient women; so they had to set aside the Egyptian emperor's orders to kill every Jewish baby at the time Moses was born in order to obey God. Jesus allowed his disciples to pick wheat grains on the Sabbath even though it broke the letter of the law that their religious leaders had drawn up. Churches throughout the world honour martyrs who have suffered death by burning rather than disown Christ and worship an emperor. In the last century methods of non-violent civil disobedience were effective in overturning wrong treatment of slaves' descendants in the USA, and occupied peoples in India and Africa.

Disobedience is not holy unless those who practise it have first learned the habit of obedience to another. It is not holy if the desire is to stir up trouble, draw attention to oneself or get one's satisfaction from protest rather than living God's way of life. Disobedience should be done in sorrow, as a last resort, and with a desire to turn bad law promoters into friends.

Pause for thought

Am I transgressing a higher obedience by subservience to a regulation that harms others?

Prayer

Christ,
who succumbed to a death sentence
rather than deny your call,
scatter upon me a little of your courage,
a little of your fidelity.
May I not, through fear,
disobey your call.

Today's step

I step
away from collusion
towards fidelity.

Spiritual breathing exercise

God-pleasing in.
Man-pleasing out.
Mmm.

JANUARY 30

Obedience is the gateway to freedom

Bible reading

I run in the path of your commands, for you have set my heart free.
Psalm 119:32

I will walk about in freedom, for I have sought out your precepts.
Psalm 119:45

If you love me, you will obey what I command.
John 14:15

They promise them freedom, while they themselves are slaves of depravity – for a person is a slave to whatever has mastered them.
2 Peter 2:19

Reflection

Freedom is not the aimless licence to do whatever we like regardless of the consequences, it is the joyful discovery of our true selves which we find in a relationship of love with God. We freely, and with delight, carry out God's laws because we know that in them lies our good. True freedom is not freedom to sin. It is freedom from the power of sin.

The story of a Tibetan monk is a parable for us. During a savage Chinese occupation of a village the monks fled to the mountains, all, that is, except one. The deputy informed the commander of this. The angry commander kicked in the monastery gate and glowered at the monk: 'Do you know who I am? I can run you through with the sword without batting an eyelash.' The monk replied: 'And do you know who I am? I am he who can let you run me through with a sword without batting an eyelash.' Such fearless obedience demands from each one of us the conversion, to be free, detached and centred in God. It speaks of the power that is based neither on domination nor position, but on a freedom in one's being that no one can take from us.

People who have given themselves over to the will of God have no fear of death; they have excised their own will. They are free to do anything on earth and to see God in heaven.

The fathers call psalmody a weapon; prayer – a wall; pure tears – a bath; and the blessed obedience – the profession without which none of the passionate will see the Lord.[19]

Pause for thought

If I had no fear of death or anything this world can do to me, what would I do now?

Prayer

Set our spirits free to soar wherever you climb.
Set our feet free to trek wherever you go.
Set our mouths free to say whatever you command.

Today's step

I step
away from fear
towards an act of faith.

Spiritual breathing exercise

Faith in.
Fear out.
Freedom.

JANUARY 31

Obedience is the gateway to community

Bible reading

Jesus came from his home town of Nazareth to be baptised in the river Jordan by John the Baptiser. John, who thought he was not worthy even to tie up Jesus' sandals, demurred, but Jesus explained that this was a way for him to perform obediently whatever was right. As Jesus came up from the water John saw the Spirit alight upon him like a dove. A voice from heaven said, 'This is my beloved Son in whom I delight.'

Matthew 3:13–17

Reflection

There are different expressions of obedience. In the first place we may obey a general command of God such as you shall not kill, steal, covet or commit adultery (Exodus 20) – but our minds may be closed to inspiration. We may obey a particular inspiration that comes to us, such as to do or say something – but certain of our feelings may still be dammed up and therefore closed. We may, in time, become willing to journey into pain, love or healing – but the framework in which we live our lives may still revolve around ourselves rather than the needs of the world. A fourth expression of obedience is to obey a call to seek justice without limits of time and place.

This kind of obedience liberates us from the tyranny of our own ego-driven agenda, and enables us to experience community, for the root of obedience is not subservience, it is trust.

This is expressed most clearly in Jesus' baptism by John. Jesus and John trusted that the other would obey God. Jesus submitted to entering into that muddy stream, in order to model for us, as the representative of the human race, the obedience of solidarity. The Spirit delighted to be present in a visual way. The Father delighted to be present in an audible way. The Three were One. They were community.

Pause for thought

Meditate on Rublev's icon of the Trinity: each is eagerly, humbly, attentively looking and listening to the other, seeking not their own interests but that of the other. Practise reflecting this attitude, first towards God, and then towards a different person each day.

Prayer

The Immortal who bowed the heavens
bowed his head before a mortal.
The Uncreated entered the stream of created life.
God becomes one with us, and we are made one with God.
Father-love cascades over the Son; the Spirit pours upon him
God in Trinity is revealed.
Dear God, give me an obedience that leads to such glory.

Today's step

I step
away from disdain of the other
towards mindfulness of the other.

Spiritual breathing exercise

Obedience in.
Wilfulness out.
Oneness.

FEBRUARY 1

Waymarks on the journey

Bible reading

This is what God says: Imagine you are at a crossroads. Look around with care. Ask where the ancient paths are. Ask where the good way is. Then walk along that way. Your bodies may get sore but your souls will be refreshed.

Jeremiah 6:16

Jesus said to his apostles, 'You know the way I am going to take.' Thomas said to him, 'No we don't. How can we know the way?' Jesus replied, 'I am the way, the truth and the life.'

John 14:4–6

Reflection

The ancient paths that the prophet Jeremiah refers to are paths of listening to God and obeying, such paths as Abraham, Jacob, and Moses followed – they are moral and spiritual paths. The way that Jesus refers to is a continuation, but at a higher level. It is the way of close relationship with God. We follow wherever our closest friend leads.

Christianity began as a way of life. The first Christians were known as 'followers of the Way', (Acts 9:2). The Christian Way is not pre-determined like a motorway that goes from A to Z, it is a journey into the unknown. It is only as we abandon ourselves to divine leading that the next steps are revealed to us.

In his book *The Road Less Travelled* Scott Peck refers to a poem by Robert Frost of a traveller who reached a fork in the road. Both roads ahead of him looked similar. He wanted to explore them both, but knew that he could not. So he chose the road that looked less travelled, sensing that this would enable him to make a more authentic journey.

Pause for thought

Visualise yourself as being at a crossroads. What choices are before you? Which way should you take?

Prayer

Eternal Guide,
you led our forebears by cloud and fire:
lead us through the days and years.
You led your saints by sign and sail:
lead us now through whisper and wind.

Today's step

I step
away from self-centred paths
towards the path of life.

Spiritual breathing exercise

Good way in.
False way out.
Destiny.

FEBRUARY 2

Learners for life

Bible reading

You shall love the Lord your God with all your heart, and with all your soul and with all your mind.
Matthew 22:37

Study to present yourself to God as a tried and tested 'work in progress', as someone who has no cause to be ashamed for wasting time, talent and thought, but as someone who correctly understands the word of Truth. Avoid idle talk and futile controversies.
2 Timothy 2:15, 16

Reflection

> Anyone who stops learning is old, whether at twenty or eighty. Anyone who keeps learning stays young. The greatest thing in life is to keep your mind young.[1]

Every human being is born to study, for God has given each of us a mind. When Jesus was asked which of God's commands to the Jews was the greatest, he included in his reply the command to love God with all our mind. What does this mean? It means that we reflect on Scripture, nature, wise people, and on the learning experiences of life. Sensible persons try to learn something good every day. They are always learners; that is what it means to be a disciple.

Western people are obsessed with the craze to accumulate more information as a tool of the ego, or to acquire academic certificates that give them status. Study that is divorced from the living of a whole life becomes a curse, not a blessing. It mistakes cleverness for wisdom. It can become the tool of pride, power and prejudice until the very term 'study' is given a bad name. It is essential that study is not understood merely as an academic exercise. All that we learn is not for the sake of study itself, but in order that what we learn should be lived. The most brilliant academics, if they lack humility and limit study merely to the head, may miss out on wisdom. In this way of life study is holistic – the head through the heart.

Aidan taught the clergy many lessons about the conduct of their lives but above all he left them a most salutary example . . . All who accompanied him had to engage in some form of study . . . This was the daily task of Aidan and all who were with him.[2]

Pause for thought

If purity is the benchmark for my studies, how will they change?

Prayer

God of Wisdom, teach me to
use my mind well,
study with a humble heart,
relate the parts to the whole,
explore things with wonder,
listen to those who know more than I
and learn from my mistakes.

Today's step

I step
away from chasing futile fancies
towards learning wisdom.

Spiritual breathing exercise

Good learning in.
Futile learning out.
Wisdom.

FEBRUARY 3

Head through the heart

Bible reading

Some words of advice from the wise King Solomon: Listen, my children, to a father's instruction. Pay careful attention and learn understanding. I give you good counsel: do not turn away from it . . . Acquire wisdom; whatever the cost, gain understanding. Never forget her. Never stray from her, and she will do well for you. Embrace her, and she will make you great.

Proverbs 4:1–12

Reflection

> It is essential that study is not understood merely as an academic exercise.[3]

> I had learned many English words and could recite part of the Ten Commandments. I knew how to sleep on a bed, pray to Jesus, comb my hair, eat with a knife and fork, and use a toilet . . . I had also learned that a person thinks with his head instead of his heart.[4]

This way of life offers an alternative approach to study – we learn with our head through the heart. Following the great teachers of the early Church we believe that reality is grounded in God, and that in God knowledge and commitment are not divorced, for God is love. To be made in God's likeness means that we can see no one and nothing as it truly is without seeing as God sees.

Ultimately we only know the truth by living it. Our goal is that the mind is always linked to the heart. Some people find that quantum physics throws light on this truth. The objects of study, we now learn, cannot be wholly divorced from the subject who studies them; they are affected by them. Everything is interlinked. Much scientific advance has come from experimenting on the basis of an informed intuition.

This holistic approach to learning does not lessen the importance of integrity in academic study, the need to compare like with like and not to make unsubstantiated claims, it is rather a cry for all-round excellence.

Pause for thought

Connect up some new thought in your head with a feeling in your heart or with an action.

Prayer

All-knowing God, make fruitful my learning.
May I acquire information that forms me for a good purpose and does not distract me from it.
May I link up what I learn today with what I already know, and so become more whole.
May I offer to you in love what I learn,
so that it shows in my words, my silences, and my actions.

Today's step

I step
away from the acquiring of arrogant head-only knowledge towards humble head-through-the-heart learning.

Spiritual breathing exercise

Humble learning in.
Prideful study out.
Whole.

FEBRUARY 4

Think things through

Bible reading

In the last week of Jesus' life he made his entrance into the capital city on a donkey. When his mission team had reached the Mount of Olives he directed two of them to a specific place where they would find two donkeys tethered and, upon hearing them repeat their password, would release these to them. Jesus rode on one of these. After a triumphal entry into Jerusalem, Jesus did a careful reconnaissance of everything in the temple area before returning to Bethany in the evening.

Mark 11:1–11

Reflection

Jesus thought things through. He did not bump into one thing after another as we are all too prone to do. He was not the plaything of circumstances. Yes, he was heading for trouble, and some key actions would be dictated by others, but always he knew how he would respond and where he would go. He must have planned the provision of the donkey and the procession which was symbolically significant and a fulfilment of the prophecy that 'Your king will come to you upon an ass.' He 'looked around at everything' says one Bible version[5]. Why? Perhaps so that he could plan the timing and the place of his final teachings in the temple compound, where he would upturn the stalls of bent traders, and where he would walk out and back to the temporary sanctuary of friends. It was important that he did the symbolically right thing on the right day – the Passover Meal and his death took place as the ceremonial lambs were being slain.

Let us order our priorities so that we do not waste time on unnecessary tasks. By delegating, as Jesus delegated the travel and meal arrangements, we leave ourselves free to do the work that only we can do. Clearly define any duties we delegate, and make sure the person who carries them out knows exactly what is expected of them. Don't delegate exceptional tasks which require knowledge, sensitivity or authority that belong to you. Even if we are the willing pair of hands rather than the person who delegates, we can still think things through.

Pause for thought
How may I relate what I do to the wider pattern of God at work?

Prayer
Lord,
help me to think things through,
to sense the season,
and to relate what I do to the signs of the times.
Help me to act and speak appropriately.

Today's step
I step
away from 'the bull in the china shop'
towards thought-through action.

Spiritual breathing exercise
Thoughtlessness out.
Thoughtfulness in.
Bullseye.

FEBRUARY 5

Learn from the Bible

Bible reading

Every God-inspired Scripture has value – for sound instruction, to point out and convict us of sins, to correct errors, and to train us in a godly way of life. Its purpose is that every God-honourer may be complete, skilled and thoroughly equipped to do every kind of good work.

2 Timothy 3:16 ,17

Reflection

> We present you with this Book, the most valuable thing that this world affords. Here is wisdom; this is the royal Law; these are the lively Oracles of God.[6]
>
> Daily Bible reading is at the heart of this Way of Life.[7]

For some readers, this is obvious, but to others it needs explaining. God has spoken to many people, at many times, in many ways – through visions, flashes of inspiration, a turn of events, poetry, prayer or planning processes. Sooner or later these were recorded by a trained scribe on a scroll. Scrolls – of law and history, poetry and biography, stories and sayings – were collected and edited. Certain of these grew in moral authority over time. There was evidence of God's Spirit at work in the whole process – the original revelation, the good and bad response to this, the recording and editing and reflecting. In the second century leading Jewish scholars drew up a list of those books that had commonly agreed divine authority. Jews call this the Torah and Christians call it the Old Testament. In 382 the bishops of the Christian Church added to this list twenty-seven of the many writings about Christ and his apostles that were circulating. This list included four Gospels (accounts of

Christ's life based on first-hand memories), letters written by apostles, the Acts of the Apostles, and the Book of Revelation.

Neither the Jewish nor the Christian scholars claim that each book is equally inspired. They do, however, believe that God's Holy Spirit is sufficiently evident in the original revelations, the recording of these and the responses to them, for these to be in our Bible, and to be valued and studied as sacred Scriptures that God has given for our present and our eternal benefit.

Pause for thought
What does God want to correct or point out to me today from Holy Scripture?

Prayer
All-seeing God, who has given to us the Holy Scriptures,
help us so to value them,
to read, mark, learn and inwardly digest them,
that we may grow in wisdom
and in understanding of your ways
now and for eternity.

Today's step
I step
away from my thought
towards God's word.

Spiritual breathing exercise
Your word in.
My words out.
Eternity.

FEBRUARY 6

Be inspired through Scripture

Bible reading

Before you explore other matters it is vital that you understand that no prophecy that has been recorded in our Scriptures should be used to bolster your personal point of view. No such prophecy was worked up by human enthusiasm. These prophecies came as people spoke from God, moved and impelled by the Holy Spirit. There were – and there still are – false prophets, who belittle the True Way. You can tell them because they draw people to themselves rather than to God.

2 Peter 1:20, 21; 2:1

Reflection

> The Bible is alive, it speaks to me;
> it has feet, it runs after me;
> it has hands, it lays hold on me.[8]

Some readers will never question anything in the Bible; others will ask, 'How can we know which parts of the Bible are good for us today, and which parts are not?' A seeker read the psalms and said, 'I don't want to believe in a God who tells people to kill'. In order to understand each bit of Scripture, we place it in the context of the overarching purpose of all Scripture – which is to build up our love of God and neighbour. Put yourselves, so to speak, in God's shoes. The human race was a cesspit of savagery. God called out a people, the Jews, taught them lessons, and gave them guidelines for civilisation. These required the punishment to be proportionate to the crime. The first five books of our Bible contain these guidelines. Then God sent prophets to give them visions of further advance. These are contained within the Books of the Prophets. Eventually God sent Jesus, who brought in a way of life based on forgiveness, and personal communion with God. The New Testament describes this. Jesus makes clear, when questioned about how to understand the Jewish Scriptures (our Old Testament) that he came to fulfil them. That is, their underlying purpose was fulfilled in Jesus.

Saint Augustine of Hippo went so far as to say that a person who sees in some Scripture a lesson that helps them build up love has not been deceived, even though they have not understood the exact meaning the author intended in that particular passage. The test of whether words come from God is their purity: is the motive to draw us to God or to the speaker?

Pause for thought

Which words draw me towards God, and which to a human?

Prayer

Eternal Word of God,
whose Spirit moves prophets, recordists and readers,
give me discernment of spirits
and help me understand every part of Scripture
in the light of the True Way.

Today's step

I step
away from self-opinionated words
towards words from the heart of God.

Spiritual breathing exercise

God is truth in.
Self-advertisement out.
Your Word.

FEBRUARY 7

Memorise Scripture

Bible reading

Moses told the people: I have given you God's commands, guidelines and discernments which you are to follow when you settle in your own land. Listen and carry these out that you may do well. Store these words in your hearts. Teach them with care to your children. Talk of them when you sit at home and when you travel, before you sleep and when you rise up. Write them down and tie them round your heads. Inscribe them on your door and gateposts.

Deuteronomy 6:1–9

Reflection

> We encourage the Celtic practice of memorising Scriptures.[9]

Aidan's effective evangelisation of English-speaking people in the seventh century began with a few Christians who walked from their Lindisfarne base to mainland villages memorising Scripture as they went. But why bother to do this in an age of mass-produced Bibles? Because if inspired words are to do any good they need to leap from a page into a heart, from the moment into the memory, from the external into the inside of a person. Because, as our Bible reading points out, a nation's well-being depends upon taking to heart God's guidance on a daily basis.

Aidan's disciples learned psalms first, and then a Gospel. I find that I am good at learning a few verses and am equally good at forgetting them! However, the act of repeating them slowly has a beneficial effect. I meditate as I memorise and the words become food for my mind throughout that day. Even if, weeks later, I cannot recall the exact reference or the exact words, they are nevertheless stored in my unconscious memory cells and they do their cleansing work.

The Celts believed that the recitation of Scripture, whether during corporate worship or when they walked, held a godly power. As we might say today, 'A verse a day keeps the doctor away.'

Why not use odd moments, such as when you are travelling, queuing, resting or in the washroom to run through in your mind how many verses of a book of the Bible you can recall – and then add one more verse?

Pause for thought

What verse of Scripture can I remember from yesterday's reading?

Prayer

Lord, you remember me and know my every thought.
Help me to remember you, and know your words to me.

Today's step

I step
away from futile words
towards Scripture memory.

Spiritual breathing exercise

. . . (a word from today's memory verse) in.
. . . (a word from yesterday's memory verse) out.
. . . (repeat today's word).

FEBRUARY 8

Reflect on Scripture

Bible reading

How I love your Law! I ponder it all day long. I never let go of your commands: they make me wiser than my opponents. I have more insight than my teachers because I constantly reflect upon your instructions and then carry them out. I turn away from evil ways in order to keep your word. The reason I resist the course of evil is that I let you be my teacher. I refuse to swerve from the directions you give. Your sayings are sweeter than honey to me, I learn to savour them.

Psalm 119:97–103

Reflection

Lectio Divina (Divine Reading) is an ancient practice that is fast reviving. This Latin expression comes from the theologian Origen of Alexandria (d.254) and refers to a prayerful reading of Scripture with attentiveness and openness to God speaking through the Word.

In the twelfth century a Carthusian monk suggested these four explicit steps: The faith-filled reading of Scripture (lectio) leads to thoughtful reflection upon what has been read (meditatio), which results in fervent prayer to God (oratio), and this prayer leads into silent communing with and enjoyment of God (contemplatio).

1. Reading (lectio). Choose a passage with thought. You may choose any passage that speaks to your present condition; you may go through a book in the Bible section by section; or you may follow a lectionary or Bible reading plan.

2. Reflection (meditatio). Read it slowly several times. Stop at words or phrases that speak to you. Mull them over. Let them sink in. Ask yourself both 'What do I

think about this?' and 'What do I feel about this?' Share your thoughts, feelings, questions, hopes with God as you would with a friend.
3. Response (oratio – prayer). Prayer is a response to the passage. It may be an arrow prayer, thanksgiving, repentance, praise, or asking for help.
4. Relaxing (contemplatio – abiding). Relax and enjoy God's presence for a while. Write down or remember any key thoughts or feelings the passage has sparked in you, or any action you have been prompted to take. If possible, share these with a soul friend or someone else you trust.

You can return to reading and move on further through the passage, starting the process again.

Pause for thought
What does Jesus say to you through today's passage? What action will you take?

Prayer
Risen Christ, as I read this passage,
may I be aware that you are here with me.
Eternal truth flows through the words I read.
But you know the particular word that I most need now.
I open myself to you.
Please speak to me.

Today's step
I step
away from rush
into reflection on your words.

Spiritual breathing exercise
Your word in.
Vain thoughts out.
Sweet.

FEBRUARY 9

Visualise Scripture

Bible reading

The heartfelt prayer of a person with integrity works wonders. Reflect back on the scriptures that tell the story of the prophet Elijah. He was a frail human being just like ourselves, but he prayed persistently for rain to be withheld, and it was dry for three and a half years. Then he prayed again, the rain fell and crops grew.

James 5:16–18

Reflection

> If you wish to draw profit from these meditations (on the scriptures), set aside all cares and anxieties. Lovingly and contemplatively, with all the feelings of your heart, make everything that the Lord Jesus said and did present to yourself, just as though you were hearing it with your ears and seeing it with your eyes. And then all that will become sweet to you, because you are reflecting upon it with longing and savouring it yet more.
>
> And even when it is related in the past tense you should contemplate it all as though present today. Go into the Holy Land, kiss with fervent spirit the earth on which the good Jesus stood. Make present to yourself how he spoke and went about with his disciples, with sinners; how he speaks and preaches, how he walks and rests, sleeps and wakes, eats and performs miracles. Write down in your heart his demeanour and his actions.[10]

This way of reading the Gospels has been criticised as vain imaginings, but in this passage from the Letter of James, he uses the Bible in just this way: the prayer dynamic of Elijah can inspire a stronger prayer in us. Of course, these humble prayer visualisations are not historically true, but they can bring us into touch with reality – the reality of the living Christ in the depths of our own being. Another objection is that we may hear our own thoughts, not those of God. Jesus said, 'by their fruits you shall know them'. When these thoughts bring peace, light, strength, joy, love then we may receive them as from God.

This way of reading the Gospels does not help all types of personality, but for some it is a way of becoming a child, as Jesus asked of us. When we do this he will give us the hidden wisdom he has reserved for little children.

Pause for thought

What strikes me most in today's passage?

Prayer

Make me sensitive, Lord,
to your tones, your style, your feelings
as I recall your work in Bible times.
Re-envision me.
Recharge me.
May I touch the earth that you touched.
May you touch the earth upon which I stand today.

Today's step

I step away
from the dead letter
to an inspiration for me, today.

Spiritual breathing exercise

Relocation in.
Dislocation out.
See.

FEBRUARY 10

Apply Scripture

Bible reading

Abraham continued to place his hope in God's promise that he would be the father of many peoples, even when his wife was past the age for child-bearing. Because his faith did not weaken, he let neither his own old age nor his wife's infertility undermine his trust in God. He continued to give glory to God and to proclaim his faith that God was able to perform what he had promised. This was not recorded just to honour Abraham, it was written down for us, too, in order that God may include us in Abraham's company if we really believe he raised Jesus from death.

Romans 4:18–24

Reflection

The apostle Paul here urges his Jewish readers to apply their Scriptures to their own situation.

We all need regularly to apply Scripture to our own situation. When we read the Gospels, for example, we may ask ourselves questions such as these: What words stand out? What do I feel? What might God be saying? What do I say to God? How do I act on what God is saying? What do I most want God to do in me today?

> When Love itself walked this earth where would I have been?
> Would I have been Judas with the silver weighing down his heavy soul?
> Would I have been like Pilate, washing clean his dirty hands inside a bowl?
> Would I have been Peter in denial even before the cock had crowed?

Would I have been shouting 'Guilty – now be free',
joining voices with the crowd?
Would I have been the soldier who saw what others
round him couldn't see?
Would I have been Thomas in his doubting what
his eyes could clearly see?
Would I have been the mother at the Cross, the cost
of loving?
Magdalene in the garden, tears of grief all the
desire?[11]

Pause for thought

What does God say to me through today's Bible reading?

Prayer

Holy God, holy and mighty
who brought to birth an heir in Sarah's barren womb;
bring a new thing to birth in my barren places.
Holy God, holy and mighty,
I would have faith to move mountains
but my faith is weak, like a little seed.
Encouraged by Abraham's example,
I give this seed to you, Lord.
Take it, water it and multiply it.
That there may be much fruit.

Today's step

I step
away from the down-drag of my unbelief
toward's Scripture's uplift of my fragile faith.

Spiritual breathing exercise

Faith in.
Doubt out.
Birth.

FEBRUARY 11

Learn from the Torah

Bible reading

You shall have no other gods but me.
You shall not carve gods that are not God at all.
You shall not dishonour God's name as a swear word.
You shall rest and savour God's presence on the seventh day.
Honour your father and mother.
Do not murder.
Do not steal someone else's spouse.
Do not steal anything. Do not lie to a court.
Do not covet anything that belongs to another.

Exodus 20:1–7

Reflection

The first five Bible books are known as the Torah, the Pentateuch or the Books of Moses' Laws. Genesis means beginnings. It gives insight into the beginnings of creation, the human race, and the people, starting with Abraham, who became a God-guided nation. The gripping theme of Exodus is the Israelites' freedom struggle, under Moses' rallying cry 'Let my people go', and the enshrining of basic laws for a civilised society such as today's reading, 'The Ten Commandments'. In Leviticus the Jews stand still during their forty years' on-off journey to their new land, God gives them detailed regulations about the soul of the new society – the honouring of God in ceremony and prayer under the oversight of the priests of Levi's clan. The Book of Numbers jumps a generation. It is a time of consolidation as they journey to the border of Canaan, during which they add up their numbers, and clarify important matters such as women's rights, rights of asylum, and how to deal with civil strife. The last book, Deuteronomy, meaning a renewed presentation of the law, connects the laws with a new generation as it increases in understanding. These come in the form of five addresses from Moses. They include the injunctions to love God and one's neighbour. Jesus referred to these as the two greatest commandments; in the light of these all lesser commands should be interpreted. In Christian tradition the ceremonial laws are superseded, but can inspire us to live what they symbolise; the social regulations are not necessarily applicable to our much-different conditions, but we should build upon them, not go back to the barbarism that preceded them; the moral guidelines, such as the Ten Commandments, remain in force as a lowest common denominator in our law courts, but love must reign supreme.

Pause for thought

Give yourself marks out of ten for how you fulfil each of the Ten Commandments.

Prayer

I will sing to you, Almighty God,
for you are my strong defender,
you are my forebears' God and I will praise your greatness.
Holy and Mighty One, who among the gods is like you?
Who is like you in holiness?
Who is like you in glory?
You rule in glory for ever.[12]

Today's step

I step
away from complaining and blocking God's path
towards whatever God is opening up.

Spiritual breathing exercise

Yahweh in.
Idols out.
Be.

FEBRUARY 12

Learn from Wisdom Writings

Bible reading

Maxims of King Solomon, the son of David, for gaining shrewdness, understanding and a grasp of wise sayings, for training in right conduct, duty, goodness and integrity, for imparting insight to the ignorant, knowledge and good sense to the young, understanding of proverbs, parables and riddles of prescient minds . . . Reverence for the Eternal God is the beginning of wisdom . . .

Proverbs 1:1–7

Reflection

'He's a canny man,' I was told. 'He knows the locals inside out, he knows about fishing and the weather, and he knows his God. His spirituality – unlike that of most people I know – is grounded and down-to-earth.' The Wisdom books feature people like that. The pithy sayings of shrewd counsellors and agony aunts were collected and published, for example, in our Book of Proverbs. They include practical, common-sense insights into what to look for in a spouse, a workmate or a student.

Maybe you find yourself in a crisis where people you care about are threatened, and you ask, 'What can I do?' Read the Book of Esther. Perhaps your heart begins to bleed for a country that lies in ruins and you wonder if someone you know could be a link in a rescue operation? Read the Book of Nehemiah. Maybe you are in a situation where a bad chapter has ended; a page has been turned but the page is blank. How can something good be written on that page? Read the Book of Ezra. And so on.

The third sub-division of the Old Testament is known as The Writings, by Jews, and as The Wisdom Literature by Christians. It includes all the books that are not in the

Law or the Prophets, and each one of them can reveal to you how a big door can swing on a little hinge. The Spirit who breathed through those Writings can show you how you can be such a hinge today.

Pause for thought

What is the most shrewd saying you can find in the Book of Proverbs?

Prayer

Almighty God, nothing on earth can compare with you,
nothing on earth can contain you.
If we, your people, experience failure but turn again to you,
forgive us and restore us.
If there is drought or famine and we cry to you,
send us rain and revive the crops.
If those who have warred and wasted the land
confess and say sorry to you,
hear from heaven, forgive us, and heal our land.[13]

Today's step

I step
away from sloth
towards the way of the ants.[14]

Spiritual breathing exercise

Good sense in.
Silliness out.
I know.

FEBRUARY 13

Learn from the prophets

Bible reading

The word of God came to Jeremiah: 'Before you were born I set you apart to serve me.

I have appointed you a prophet to the nations. Go to whomever I send you and say whatever I tell you. Do not fear them, for I am with you to look after you. I put words into your mouth. I set you over nations, to uproot and overthrow, to build and to plant.

Jeremiah 1:4–10

Reflection

To begin with, Israel's prophets were known as seers, because they saw into the state of their people with penetrating eyes. Then schools of prophets emerged, led by the likes of Elijah and Elisha, who learned to listen to God in wilderness places. Prophets became a recognised stratum of society – but some of these, like prosperity Gospel preachers today, told rulers what they wanted to hear, no doubt in return for favours. Certain people who were not professional prophets bucked this trend, including a village shepherd named Amos, who had the courage to tell wealthy women who oppressed their servants that they behaved like cows, and that they should let justice flow like a river. Then there was poor Hosea, whom God told to liken his people to his own faithless wife, and to liken God's love for them to Hosea's continuing love for her. The Bible contains twelve books about these more provincial figures, whose prophetic speeches were nonetheless seminal and searing. Finally, it contains four major books about prophets who strode across the stage of their times. These prophets, especially Jeremiah and Ezekiel, acted out prophetic actions. Ezekiel tied two sticks together, to call for the divided nations of Israel and Judah to unite again. Jeremiah went to a potter's kiln, and likened the nation to the marred pot which the potter had to reshape. Isaiah had a big vision that reached far into the future: many of his messages were taken by the first Christians to have found fulfilment in the life and death of Christ. Much of G. F. Handel's marvellous oratorio *The Messiah* consists of such passages. It repays study.

Pause for thought

If our people are like a faulty jar in the Divine Potter's hand, how does he need to rework the clay?

Prayer

Give to us your prophet's touch, True and Faithful One:
the fire that never dies away,
the eyes that see beyond today,
the words that cut more sharp than blades,
the truth that wakes the sleeping shades.

Today's step

I step
away from what is faulty
towards what is rightly shaped.

Spiritual breathing exercise

Faulty clay out.
Malleable clay in.
Yours.

FEBRUARY 14

Learn from the Psalms

Bible reading

I will extol the Lord at all times, his praise will always be on my lips . . . Glorify the Lord with me; let us lift up his name together . . . Taste and see that the Lord is good. Happy the person who takes refuge in God.

Psalm 34:1–3

Reflection

> It is better for the sun to stop its journey than for the Psalter to remain unread in the homes of Christians.[15]

In the psalms we see a nation vividly alive, with all its human needs spread before God. The psalms provide a framework through which God led a people to build up an authentic and suitable pattern of worship. The Psalter reflects fundamental human needs, flaws and aspirations and therefore has become a priceless treasure house for many peoples. Christians read into them knowledge about God and life that was known only by later experiences. Calvin observed that the psalms are a mirror of the human soul: they reflect every season and stage of life.

Their variety is wonderful. There are services for daily morning (3, 43) evening (4, 141) and night (134) prayer. There are liturgies for great festivals such as Passover and Harvest. There was a collection of psalms used by pilgrims coming up from Babylon, drawing lessons from the dangers and emotions of the desert route (120–134). There were orders of service for the sick (6, 13, 16) and for marriage (45). The national army was constantly going into battle, and there were orders of service to be used on the field before battle (20, 56), in defeat (10, 52, 54, 59, 60, 79) and after victory (9, 17, 21, 30, 68, 76). There were devotions for days of fasting and humbling (31, 35, 37, 40, 69, 74, 77, 80, 102). There are services of pure praise and worship of God as seen in history (105, 114), and in creation (19, 29, 92, 104, 148). There are psalms intended for instruction, such as the prefixes to various collections (1 to the whole psalter, 2 to Book 1 and so on). And there were deeply personal psalms for use in private devotion. Perhaps the most loved of these is the Shepherd Psalm – 23.

Pause for thought

You could write your own psalm or, if you read this book year after year, you could devote a season to looking up each of the psalms mentioned above.

Prayer

I love you, Lord, and I lift my voice
to honour you and to rejoice.
As thirsty deer go down to the pool,
so my thirsty soul is refreshed in you.
By day you guide me along the way,
at night you guard and with me stay.

Today's step

I step
away from surface babble
towards deep songs of the heart.

Spiritual breathing exercise

Heart-songs in.
Forth out.
Tryst.

FEBRUARY 15

Learn from the Letters

Bible reading

From Paul, Silvanus and Timothy to the church in Thessalonika . . . We continually thank God for you because your faith is growing so wonderfully and your love for one another never stops increasing. Of all the churches we take special pride in you for your constancy and faith under the many persecutions and troubles you have to bear . . . We wanted to make a return visit to you. Our delay was not for want of trying. It was Satan who blocked our path . . .

1 Thessalonians 1:1–3; 2:17, 18; 5:12–14

Reflection

Twenty-one of the New Testament's twenty-seven writings are letters, usually from travelling apostles such as Paul, to the Christians who make up the Church in a place they have visited. A typical letter achieves at least three things. It thanks the believers for some valued quality; it shares some news that helps them keep in touch; it teaches or challenges where there is a weakness. Think about a church known to you. What in it can you thank God for? What news might it be helpful to share? What weakness might you help them to overcome at the appropriate time, through challenge or encouragement?

The last book in the Bible, Revelation, contains seven letters of a different kind (Revelation, chapters 1–3). These were given by the risen Christ in a vision to John, who was under house arrest on Patmos Island. Each letter discerns something good and something bad about the character of each of seven cities. It then speaks to the seven churches in them. The aim of each letter is to build up the 'yeast' (for example, faith, hope and love) in the church that transforms the 'dough' of their cities, and to root out negative qualities that they imbibe from their city. One church, Laodicea, is neither burning with faith nor frozen with unbelief. Because it is luke-warm, Christ says he will spew it out of his mouth. The church I once served invited the risen Christ to reveal something similar to them. Church members prayed, reflected and wrote down the letter they thought Christ might have them write. It was a salutary and transforming exercise.

Pause for thought

What might Christ want to write to your church?

Prayer

Risen Christ,
you come with searing white purity of understanding,
you come with flaming, all-seeing eyes;
you come perfectly formed,
like a burnished bronze sculpture
and your voice is like the sound of many waters.
Come to our church:
teach her, cleanse her, forge her.
Speak to her in many-voiced splendour
until the surrounding population
sees something of you reflected through her.

Today's step

I step
away from luke-warmness
towards my first love.

Spiritual breathing exercise

Unbelief out.
Trust in.
Christ.

FEBRUARY 16

Learn by asking questions

Bible reading

When Jesus was twelve years old his parents went with him and a large local contingent to the big city for their great annual festival. They had travelled a whole day on their return journey when they realised Jesus was not with them. He had stayed behind, and made his way to the leading religious teachers. His parents found him in the temple courts, sitting among the teachers, listening to them and asking them questions. Everyone who heard Jesus was amazed at his understanding and at his answers to questions the teachers put to him in discussion.

Luke 2:41–47

Reflection

Jesus was hungry to get the best learning available, and did something about it. He listened before he rushed in with ill-thought questions. Then he asked good questions, that sought to relate his people's faith story to his own unfolding discernment of God's will. These three things we, too, can do, directly, or through the internet and books.

For some readers, organised study can be a way of learning. We study in order to think, build up a memory and put this in a logical order, apply general information to particular circumstances, express ourselves clearly. We seek an ability to understand an issue and different points of view, to relate one piece of material to another, to draw lessons from the material. We do not gloss over key points. To avoid getting bogged down in irrelevant data, skim an article or book in order to find out whether it is relevant to your study aim, whether you should consult just a chapter or a theme word included in the index. Pick out its key ideas. To do this, look for summaries near the start or end of chapters, or at section headings, and note the main points down in a notebook. Find out who are the sources with authority. Do not make dogmatic statements without good reason.

In short, like Jesus, we seek understanding.

Pause for thought

What is the most important unresolved question bubbling up within you?

Prayer

Eternal Truth,
grant me humility to realise how little I know.
Give me clarity to know what is best for me to learn.
Show me a good way to do this.
Form me in the art of asking useful questions.
Help me grow, like Jesus, in understanding.

Today's step

I step
away from selfish accumulation of knowledge for its own sake or for vain glory
towards true learning.

Spiritual breathing exercise

Let go.
Listen.
Learn.

FEBRUARY 17

Learn from history

Bible reading

These are some maxims of King Solomon, copied out by scholars under Hezekiah, King of Judah: Mystery is God's glory . . . Remove the dross from silver and it shines out pure . . . Never be in a hurry to talk about something you have seen; it is better to first talk it over with the person concerned . . . An apt word is like a priceless necklace . . . A messenger you can trust is like ice in a drink . . . If your enemy is hungry, give him food . . . Lazy people imagine they are wiser than twelve people who talk things through.

Reflection

History can be dismissed as 'one damn thing after another' or treated as the story of how great people have shaped changing circumstances for better or worse, and ultimately it can be seen as his story.

> King Alfred, amid wars, numerous interruptions and ailments gave instructions to his craftspeople and animal trainers, making to his own design many wonderful new treasures, reading aloud from books and learning poems by heart. All these things he did with great application and to the best of his abilities. He invariably listened daily to the divine church services, participating in certain psalms and prayers. His habit was to listen eagerly and attentively to Holy Scripture being read. He did not cease, by day and night, from giving instruction in virtuous behaviour and literacy to the children of his staff.
>
> He resembled the highly esteemed King Solomon, who sought wisdom from God. God stimulated King Alfred's intelligence from within, not from without,

as it is written 'I will hear what the Lord God speaks in me' (Psalm 84:9).

Like the clever bee, who in summer departs from its honeycomb in order to gather flowers of many grasses and shrubs, and brings them home, the king sent for luminaries from other countries. By day or night, even while he was in the toilet, he asked them to read to him aloud. Through their teaching the king's outlook was considerably broadened, and he had many books translated into English and educated the clergy.[16]

Pause for thought

Think of history. What bit of history comes to mind? What lesson can you learn from this?

Prayer

Shaper of nations, who through leaders and prophets
gave guidance that would make a people great,
teach us the ways of true greatness.
Key to Destiny, unlock our capacity to learn.
Wisdom, informing all peoples, bring us the mind of God.

Today's step

I step
away from not bothering
about how we have come to be what we are
towards learning the lessons of history.

Spiritual breathing exercise

Recollection in.
Blindness out.
His story.

FEBRUARY 18

Learn through good reading

Bible reading

Whatever is true, whatever is noble and worthy of honour, whatever is just, whatever is pure, whatever is loving, whatever is kind, if there is any virtue, anything praiseworthy, reflect on these things and keep them in your minds.

Philippians 4:8

Reflection

> It requires discipline to let God and not the world be the Lord of our mind. It requires us not just to be gentle as doves, but also cunning as serpents! That is why spiritual reading is such a helpful discipline. Our thoughts and feelings would be deeply affected if we were always to carry with us a book that puts our minds again and again in the direction we want to go. There are so many good books about the lives of holy men and women, about remarkable examples of peace-making, about communities that bring life to the poor and the oppressed, and about the spiritual life itself.[17]

An important discipline in the life of the Spirit is spiritual reading. Through spiritual reading we have some say over what enters our minds. Each day our society bombards us with myriads of images and sounds . . . The words yell and scream at us: 'Eat me, drink me, buy me, hire me, look at me, talk with me, sleep with me!' Whether we ask for it or not is not the point; we simply cannot go far without being engulfed by words and images forcibly intruding themselves into our minds. Even if we were to read for only fifteen minutes a day in such a book, we would soon find our mind becoming less of a garbage can and more of a vase filled with good thoughts.

It is good to find out, to explore, in order to discern aright, but do we really want our mind to become a refuse bin? Do we want our mind to be filled with things that confuse us, depress us, arouse us, repulse us or attract us whether we think it is good for us or not?

Pause for thought

What will I fill my mind with today?

Prayer

Divine Source of truth, beauty and goodness,
our minds are like a field.
In this field, please grow many good things,
many beautiful things, and many true things with deep roots.
Teach us also how to weed and sift and sort,
how to water and prune wisely.

Today's step

I step
away from mindless trivia
towards the good, beautiful and true.

Spiritual breathing exercise

Thought in.
Trivia out.
Mature.

FEBRUARY 19

Learn through eyes and ears

Bible reading

Jesus' disciples asked him why he spoke to the crowds by giving messages hidden within a story. 'The reason,' Jesus explained, 'is that they look without seeing and listen without hearing or understanding. When this happens to people they fulfil a prophecy of Isaiah: "You will keep on listening but not understand; for your ears have grown hard of hearing, and you have shut your eyes for fear of what you would see if you kept them open, understood with your heart, and were to be converted and healed."'

Matthew 13:10–15

Reflection

> All sorts of bodily diseases are produced by half-used minds.[18]

God has given us the five senses that we may see, hear, think, touch, and scent external things in his vast and wonderful creation. In this passage, however, Jesus refers to the inner eyes and ears with which each person is also equipped. These are the roots into our souls.

Some of the folk in the crowds to whom Jesus referred no doubt thought of themselves, so to speak, as 'good church people', yet they were not learning from Jesus. A person can sit in a church pew all their lives and exit this world in a coffin, still none the wiser.

Why is this? We all have a propensity to focus on what makes us feel good, secure, superior, and we instinctively shut out what unsettles these feelings, even in the name of God or the Bible. How may we cease to be spiritually deaf and blind? First, we invite Christ into any area of our lives which we unconsciously keep closed and out of view. Second, we practise asking God to speak into our fears, anger, laziness, prejudices – through Scripture, through critics, through conscience.

We have the same eyes and ears as before, but what we look out for and listen for begins to change.

Jesus links healing with openness. A person who closes off some part of reality develops defences – hardness, tension, blind spots – and these make us dysfunctional. Let us listen and learn.

Pause for thought

What blind spot might I need to address?

Prayer

We pray for the cleansing of our perceptions
that we may hear,
that we may see,
that we may understand with our hearts
and that we may be healed.

Today's step

I step
away from closed eyes
towards open eyes
I step.

Spiritual breathing exercise

Hearing in.
Hardness out.
Healed.

FEBRUARY 20

Learn from daily life

Bible reading

People learn from one another as iron sharpens iron.
Proverbs 27:17

Evaluate yourselves to see whether you are showing the fruits of faith in your lives. Test yourselves. Don't you realise that Jesus Christ is in you?
2 Corinthians 13:5

If you are exasperated, do not let the sun go down upon your anger. Leave no foothold for the devil to get in while you sleep.
Ephesians 4:26, 27

Reflection

The unexamined life is not worth living.[19]

A person who is completely insulated learns little. Even the desert fathers were taught that they found God through their neighbour. However, as we brush up against one another in daily life, we may just become exasperated, and go to sleep exasperated, having learned nothing. The ancient Christian practice known in Latin as the *Examen* enables us to learn from life.

Before you sleep, become present to God and invite the Holy Spirit to guide your thoughts. Then carefully recall and process the events of the day. Who did you meet? What did you do? What were the interactions? Review your hopes and hesitations, and search for the internal movements of your heart. Some blessing may come to mind: thank God for it. Some failure is recalled. Say sorry for any wrong, presumptive acts or reactions, but also ask the Holy Spirit for insight. Could certain things have been avoided or done better? A person or situation is like a red rag to a bull? How would Jesus, if he were in my shoes, handle the red rag?

Some situations will show that your heart was divided—wavering between helping and disregarding, scoffing and encouraging, listening and ignoring, rebuking and forgiving, speaking and silence, neglecting and thanking. What reactions helped or hindered you? See where Christ entered your decisions and where you might have paused to receive his influence. Before you sleep, place all this into Christ's hands and ask the Holy Spirit to work in you – and in those you have recalled – during the night.

Pause for thought

What lesson can I learn from the ups and downs of this day?

Prayer

Examine me, O God, and know my thoughts.
Reveal to me the cause of any divided or angry thoughts.
I place failures and frustrations into your hands.
I give thanks to you for these blessings . . .
Take what I have learned, and work in me as I sleep,
that tomorrow I may be more effective as a human being.

Today's step

I step
away from unexamined anger
towards reflective integration.

Spiritual breathing exercise

Sifting in.
Exasperation out.
Sunset.

FEBRUARY 21

Learn through creative arts

Bible reading

God told Moses: I have called out Bezalel and have filled him through my Spirit with wisdom, knowledge and skill in every kind of craft, in design, in gold, silver and bronze work, in stone cutting and wood carving and in enabling others to carry out all kinds of work. To help him I have given Oholiab, and all sorts of other people whose hearts I have endowed with the ability to make everything that I have in mind . . . including furniture, clothing and fragrancies. Do everything as I have asked of you.

Exodus 31:1–11

Reflection

> We encourage learning through the use of creative arts.[20]

We learn by thinking, memorising, and also by doing. As we create we 'see' new ways, we bring something buried to light, and we reflect. Some types of personality cringe at the thought of doing a creative art. Maybe they fear making a fool of themselves, so they dismiss it as a waste of time. Yet the Creator has made every one in his likeness. We are co-creators. Some seed of creative potential is planted in each of us.

Andy Freeman[21] writes:

> The arts and creativity are a great gift that God has given to humankind. We live in a world where music can lift the soul, where stories can ignite the imagination. Medical studies have shown the benefits of laughter. Painting and photography can deepen our appreciation of light, colour and detail. God has inspired artists to give us representations of historical

events. He has gifted scientists to discover incredible media that allow us to see our world like never before. We even live in an age where the arts can help those who struggle with learning difficulties, through art and music therapy.

There are some things that we can only discover about ourselves or the world through creative experiments.

Pause for thought

What creative potential in me cries out to be developed?

Prayer

Great Creator, I am made in your likeness
and you call me to be a co-creator with you:
water the seeds of creativity you have planted in me,
let not fear, over-busyness or low self-image
hold me back from letting these come to flower.
May I, in a second-hand and sterile society,
be a sign of your creative life.

Today's step

I step
away from the sterile treadmill
towards some creative action.

Spiritual breathing exercise

Creative life in.
Sterile life out.
Life.

FEBRUARY 22

Learn from stories

Bible reading

After King David had engineered the death in war of the man whose wife he desired, God told the prophet Nathan to call on the king and tell him the following story: A rich man with much livestock and a poor man with only one lamb lived in the same town. The poor man's family cared for their lamb and treated it as a pet. A traveller called on the rich man and asked for hospitality. The rich man gave him nothing of his own; instead he slew and cooked the poor man's only lamb. David was angry and said the rich man should be punished. 'You are that man' said Nathan.

2 Samuel 12:1–7

Reflection

> There is a point to a good story. Stories are not an indulgence of the few, they are the life-blood of the many. Stories are the secret reservoir of values: change the stories individuals and nations live by and tell themselves and you change the individuals and nations. Individuals and nations are largely the stories they feed themselves. If they tell themselves stories that are lies, they will suffer the future consequences of those lies. If they tell themselves stories that face their own truths, they will free their histories for future flowerings.[22]

Jesus was the hero of the greatest story ever told, and was also one of the world's greatest storytellers. It repays us to study that greatest story above all, and secondly to study the stories Jesus told. Thirdly, it repays us to study other great stories that have passed the test of time or which carry eternal truth, or which bring insight into the human condition. Some of these great stories have been made into films: *The Lord of the Rings*, *The Chronicles of Narnia*, *Les Misérables*, *The Brothers Karamazov*, *The Little Prince*, to name but a few. TV soaps are stories. Some stories have entertainment value: they relax our minds but do not improve them. They have their place. Many stories are much ado about nothing. They waste our time. Why not make and add to a list of stories that are worth telling?

Pause for thought
Recollect a story of worth. What do you learn from this?

Prayer
Kindle our imaginations,
rivet our attention with graphic truth,
restock our memories with noble themes.

Today's step
I step
away from a closed imagination
towards the good story.

Spiritual breathing exercise
Visualisation in.
Rigidity out.
Good story.

FEBRUARY 23

Learn from truth

Bible reading

Jesus said to those who put their trust in him, 'You really are my disciples when you live by my teachings. When you do this you will know the truth and the truth shall set you free.' They replied: 'We have never been in prison, so what do you mean?' Jesus explained, 'Any person who lives selfishly becomes enslaved. A slave is usually only employed for a period. If you are a son or daughter (a free citizen) you remain so for ever. So if I liberate you, you are free in that way.'

John 8:31–36

Reflection

We will be told: What can literature do against the pitiless onslaught of naked violence? Let us not forget that violence does not and cannot flourish by itself; it is inevitably intertwined with lying. Between them there is the closest, the most profound and natural bond: nothing screens violence except lies, and the only way lies can hold out is by violence. Whoever has once announced violence as his method must inexorably choose lying as his principle. At birth, violence behaves openly and even proudly. But as soon as it becomes stronger and firmly established, it senses the thinning of the air around it and cannot go on without befogging itself in lies, coating itself with lying's sugary oratory. It does not always or necessarily go straight for the gullet; usually it demands of its victims only allegiance to the lie, only complicity in the lie.

The simple act of an ordinary courageous man is not to take part, not to support lies! Let that come into the world and even reign over it, but not through me. Writers and artists can do more: they can vanquish lies! In the struggle against lies, art has always won and always will. Conspicuously, incontestably for everyone. Lies can stand up against much in the world, but not against art. Once lies have been dispelled, the repulsive nakedness of violence will be exposed – and hollow violence will collapse.

Proverbs about truth are well-loved in Russia. They give steady and sometimes striking expression to the not-inconsiderable harsh national experience: 'One word of truth shall outweigh the whole world.'[23]

Pause for thought

What prevalent lie do I need to expose?

Prayer

God, eternally True,
save us from
complicity in the lie,
the refusal to speak out,
the acquiescence in misrepresentation.
Steel us to speak out,
to expose what is wrong,
to vanquish lies
in the strength of the One who was put to death by a lie
but remained undefeated.

Today's step

I step
away from acquiescence in the Lie
towards salute to the Truth.

Spiritual breathing exercise

Truth in.
Lies out.
Freedom.

FEBRUARY 24

Learn from goodness

Bible reading

The king said to them, 'I was hungry and you gave me food, I was thirsty and you gave me drink, I was a stranger and you took me in, I was lacking clothes and you gave me things to wear, I was sick and you visited me, I was in prison and you visited me.' 'When did we do these things?' they asked. 'Whenever you did these things to the least of my subjects, you in fact did them to me' the king replied.

Matthew 25:34-40

Reflection

There is that of God in every person.[24]

We may learn from the Quakers to look for that which is good and of God in each person. In preparing to write today's reflection I became attentive to each person who crossed my path. From one person I learned to listen, and from another to speak with grace. From one person I learned to put myself out for someone, and from another to have a light touch and be able to laugh at myself. I learned good bodily posture from this person, and the stature of self-acceptance from that person.

A pagan farmer intended to stab Saint Patrick, who had arrived on his mission to Ireland seeking overnight hospitality. When the farmer, whose name was Dicu, looked into Patrick's face, he saw nothing but goodness, and became his friend. Patrick learned from this good man to change his missionary schedule. He stayed with him, let friendship ripen, baptised him, blessed the entire area, and established little communities of faith there.

Ole Gunnar Solskjaer was famous for scoring the last-minute goal that won the European Football Cup for

Manchester United in 1999. Upon his retirement in 2008 he used the proceeds of his multi-million pound benefit match to build ten schools in southern Africa run by UNICEF, the worldwide children's charity. He gave his entire earnings from a £70,000 per year kit deal with Nike to UNICEF, as well as £30,000 he was due to be paid for advertising a Norwegian cheese.

Pause for thought

What good thing can I learn from the person I last met?

Prayer

Christ of the people
who learned lessons in your home, in the temple
and at the carpenter's bench:
make me humble to learn facts from others,
make me observant to learn goodness from others,
make me reflective to learn from others' mistakes.

Today's step

I step
away from a couldn't-care-less attitude
towards the good in another.

Spiritual breathing exercise

Look-for-good in.
Don't-care out.
Goodness!

FEBRUARY 25

Learn from beauty

Bible reading

The male lover: How beautiful you are, my beloved, how beautiful! Your eyes are like pools, your neck is like a fine tower. Your head is held high like a mountain, your lips could distil wild honey! How fragrant your perfumes and the scent of your garments. You are like an enclosed garden, a fountain, a flowing stream. You are as beautiful as the world's most beautiful city.

The bride: Your appearance is like the cedar among trees. Your hands are golden, rounded, set with jewels. Your belly is like a block of ivory covered with sapphires. Your hair is black as the raven. Your conversation is sweetness itself.

The Song of Songs

Reflection

Beauty is the radiance of truth; the fragrance of goodness.[25]

Perhaps then the old trinity of truth, goodness, and beauty is not simply the dressed-up, worn-out formula we thought it in our presumptuous, materialistic youth?

If the crowns of these three trees meet, as scholars have asserted, and if the too obvious, too straight sprouts of truth and goodness have been knocked down, cut off, not let grow, perhaps the whimsical, unpredictable, unexpected branches of beauty will work their way through, rise up to that very place, and thus complete the work of all three?

Then what Dostoevsky wrote – 'Beauty will save the world' – is not a slip of the tongue but a prophecy. After all, he had the gift of seeing much, a man wondrously filled with light.

And in that case could not art and literature, in fact, help the modern world?[26]

We can learn through beauty because God is the source of beauty, and each glimpse of beauty can become a teacher of our soul, revealing to us some quality of God, wooing us, beckoning us, leading us one more small step into the mystery of God. Beauty teaches us that production figures and league tables, the mere amassing of data, are not the whole truth about this world or the next. Beauty leads us beyond itself.

Pause for thought

What expression of beauty has most moved you in the last day? What may you learn from it?

Prayer

Uncreated beauty,
who graces everything that has been created,
as the hand is made for holding and the eyes for seeing.
Grant that I may behold your beauty
in the sunlit faces of our world,
in the wild flower's beauty, and in the lovers' embrace,
in a mother's love, in the face of a steadfast man,
and in the twilight of the gloaming
until the beauty that is within me
comes forth and sings to you.

Today's step

I step
away from my ugly intentions
towards the beauty reflected in another.

Spiritual breathing exercise

Beauty in.
Ugliness out.
Glory.

FEBRUARY 26

Learn from nature

Bible reading

Observe the birds. They don't spend their time sowing seeds, collecting up crops or stacking things in storehouses, yet your heavenly Father feeds them. Are you not worth more than they? . . . Learn from the wild flowers. They do not get stressed making themselves clothes, yet not even the world's biggest royal star is clothed like one of these.

Matthew 6:26–29

Reflection

> What is God's will?
> That we should live
> according to the laws of his creation.
> What is best in this world?
> To do the will of our Maker.
> How do we know those laws?
> By studying the Scriptures with devotion.
> What tool has our Maker provided for this study?
> The intellect which can probe everything.
> And what is the fruit of study?
> To perceive the eternal Word of God
> reflected in every plant and insect,
> every bird and animal,
> and every man and woman.[27]

Jesus encourages us to be bird watchers and to learn from nature. Celtic Christians encourage us to learn something each day from two books: the Book of Scripture and the Book of Nature. This is not just something for people who live in the countryside. Creation is the backdrop against which all of us live our lives. It is above us and beneath us and, even in inner-city 'concrete jungles', it is all around us.

And hark, how blithe the Throstle sings!
He, too, is no mean preacher:
Come forth into the light of things,
Let Nature be your teacher.[28]

Pause for thought

Think of something in nature. What does it teach you?

Prayer

Earth teach me stillness as the grasses are stilled with light.
Earth teach me humility
as blossoms are humble with beginning.
Earth teach me courage as the tree which stands all alone.
Earth teach me limitation
as the ant which crawls on the ground.
Earth teach me freedom as the eagle which soars in the sky.
Earth teach me resignation as the leaves which die in the fall.
Earth teach me regeneration
as the seed which rises in the spring.
Earth teach me to forget myself
as melted snow forgets its life.
Earth teach me to remember kindness
as dry fields weep for rain.[29]

Today's step

I step
away from a know-all attitude
towards the Book of Nature.

Spiritual breathing exercise

Nature in.
Know-all out.
Imbibe.

FEBRUARY 27

Learn from God's hand in history

Bible reading

Faith means that we are confident of what we hope for, convinced of what we do not yet see. The biblical record of people of faith illustrates this. It was by faith that Abel gave God a more fruitful offering than his brother Cain. He died, but by his faith he is speaking to us still. It was by faith that Enoch was not overtaken by death, but taken by God direct to heaven. It was by faith that Noah, after God told him of the flood that was as yet not on the horizon, constructed an ark that saved his whole household. It was by faith that Abraham obeyed the call to leave his familiar homeland and journey out into an unknown land that God promised him.

Hebrews 11:1–9

Reflection

> What is important is to remember that it is not the way in which we record our existence, but that we do record it. In the air, and everywhere around, we must remember how the streets ring out for every soul that thought and felt and passed through them in weakness and in strength.[30]

To remember God's hand in history is a biblical requirement. Look up any Bible concordance and you will find that the word 'Remember' comes over and over again. We learn from the history of God's people about ways in which God guides and shapes his people. We also learn from their failings, by observing the consequences of their disobedience – the law of reaping and sowing. Perhaps the most terrible consequence of the Jews becoming greedy and self-centred was their exile to a foreign land.

This biblical mandate to learn from God's hand in history does not cease with the Old Testament, nor, indeed, with the New Testament. I like to think of the Acts of the Apostles, in our New Testament, as chapter one of a book that is still being written. Chapter two may be thought of in these words: We study the history of the Celtic Church, becoming familiar with such saints as Aidan, Brigid, Caedmon, Columba, Cuthbert, David, Hilda, Illtyd, Ninian, Oswald and Patrick. In the coming days we shall learn from them.[31]

Pause for thought
What is the most important lesson you can learn from one of the characters mentioned in the Bible reading?

Prayer
We thank you for great people of faith
who light up our night
and urge us on to heavenly virtues.
May we learn from those who:
overcome heroic odds with nobility of spirit,
are gracious in defeat and magnanimous in triumph,
show us how to truly love,
are content with little things.

Today's step
I step
away from a spirit of defeat
towards the faith of inspired believers.

Spiritual breathing exercise
Faith in.
Defeatism out.
Heaven.

FEBRUARY 28

How to study

Bible reading

Wisdom will not enter a deceitful soul
nor stay in a body that is hostage to sin.
A holy spirit of learning shuns what is false,
flees reckless thoughts
and is affronted at the approach of wrong.
Wisdom is a kindly friend to mortals.

The Wisdom of Solomon

Reflection

> All that we learn is not for the sake of study itself,
> but in order that what we learn should be lived.[32]

When the Community of Aidan and Hilda realised there was a need to offer study programmes, we sought guidance from our advisers. 'When the universities were removed from the monasteries they lost something,' Dr. Ian Bradley, of St. Andrews University pointed out.

The head was divorced from the heart, and study became less holistic. Now, colleges are run as businesses, and it is in their interest to tell everyone that they have done well enough in one course to pay to enrol on the next course. Colleges feed the frenzy for honours. We were advised to restore the love of learning for itself, and to aspire to honour, more than honours.

There is no one right way to study; the important thing is to find what is right for you. The spectrum of study may move from the non-reader who listens to CDs, or learns some key Scriptures and prayers, to the scholar, who goes to the original language of the sources. Most of us are somewhere in between. The most important thing is to develop a Christian mind.

Don't waste time. Always have something edifying to read with you, whether you are travelling or in a queue. It can be good to become expert in one subject whether it be flower arranging, the night sky, or an aspect of computer technology. To learn how such things work is to have learned much more than these things in themselves. It helps us to become observant people, to distinguish between the shoddy and the good. To follow the Lord of sincerity and truth means that in our searching we are true to what we already know, but we make room for every new fact. We proceed from the known to the unknown.

Pause for thought

'I don't think much of a man who is not wiser today than he was yesterday,' said Abraham Lincoln. In what way am I wiser?

Prayer

Bend our minds to holy learning.
Give us
wisdom to know the nub of things,
memory to recall the important things,
and clarity to express what we learn.
May your truth reshape us
and may we always walk humbly in the light.

Today's step

I step
away from time-wasting
towards attentiveness.

Spiritual breathing exercise

The holistic in.
The foolhardy out.
Learning.

FEBRUARY 29

Don't leap over the saints

Bible reading

Never forget how the people provoked God when they were hungry and thirsty during their march to freedom through the desert. Do not forget how I, Moses, went up the mountain to receive God's laws which I wrote down on stone tablets; how I remained forty days there, fasting, and how you turned away from God and made a false god for yourselves. Never forget how I lay prostrate before God for forty days, imploring him to have mercy on you, and how God listened to me.

Deuteronomy 9

Reflection

> In addition, we study the history of the Celtic Church, becoming familiar with such saints as Aidan, Brigid, Caedmon, Columba, Cuthbert, David, Hilda, Illtyd, Kevin, Ninian, Oswald and Patrick. We remember their feast days and consider them as companions on our journeys of faith. We also bear in mind their strong link with the Desert Fathers and Mothers and the Eastern Church, and wish to draw them too into our field of studies.[33]

Since you may only read today's reflection once every four years, you may assume that the least important aspect of life-long learning has been saved for this leap-year day. Not so. Learning from inspired men, women and children – including those who some parts of the church put on the roll call of saints – is so important that we will devote the whole of December to it.

But before we leave this month's readings on life-long learning, ponder these perhaps stereotypical, but challenging words:

Love without courage and wisdom is sentimentality,
as with the ordinary churchgoer.
Courage without love and wisdom is foolhardiness
as with the ordinary soldier.
Wisdom without love and courage is cowardice,
as with the ordinary intellectual.
But the one who has love, courage, and wisdom
moves the world.[34]

Pause for thought

Think of one way you can grow in love, in courage and in wisdom.

Prayer

O God, eternal love, courage and wisdom,
may the love in our hearts be growing,
may the courage in our guts be galvanised,
may the wisdom of our days be garnered.

Today's step

I step
away from overlooking things
towards garnering them.

Spiritual breathing exercise

Mindfulness in.
Forgetfulness out.
Wisdom.

MARCH 1

Life is meant to be a journey

Bible reading

When you have settled in the land that God promises to give you, dedicate to God the first of your crops and say before the altar: 'My forebear was a wandering Aramean, who went down to Egypt and became a great people. But the Egyptians oppressed us, so God brought us out with signs and wonders, and led us to this place.' Now you are in this land I want you to give one tenth of your produce to those who lead your worship and to the poor and orphaned . . . and then to declare that you will walk in God's ways.

Deuteronomy 26:1–12, 17

Reflection

The Scriptures constantly teach that we are to view our life as a journey. In Moses' time it took God forty years to teach the people, speaking through the movements of cloud, to move on whenever they received the divine prompt, and to stay still whenever they did not receive it. When they reached their promised land they would often repeat in their worship those words that their ancestor was a wandering Aramean whom the Lord delivered from captivity. They linked this awareness of how God had led them in the past, with the need to share their goods with the needy in the present. In this way they entered into an abiding covenant with God, and were committed to 'walk in his ways'.

The first Christians were known as 'The Way' (Acts 9:2). Like the prophet they could say, 'My soul is hungry for you, O Lord, as I travel' (Psalm 84:5–7). They knew that 'There is no permanent city for us here on earth' (Hebrews 13:14).

Pause for thought

Look back on your life as a journey; what significant turnings has God led you to take?

Prayer

In our journeying this day
keep us, Father, in your way.
Guide us, Saviour, by your word,
you alone be overheard.
May we, Spirit, with you walk
in our thoughts and in our talk.
In our friendships let us be
in the Blessed Trinity.

Today's step

I step
away from my ways
towards God's ways.

Spiritual breathing exercise

Dedication in.
Stubbornness out.
Journey.

MARCH 2

To journey we have first to leave!

Bible reading

When Jesus learned that John the Baptiser had been imprisoned he journeyed to Galilee. While he was walking beside the Sea of Galilee he saw two brothers he had befriended on a previous visit, Simon (who would be called Peter) and his brother Andrew, casting their fishing net into the water. 'Come and follow me,' said Jesus, 'and I will teach you how to fish for people.' At once they left their nets and followed him. As he walked further on he saw two other brothers, James and John, in a boat with their father Zebedee. They were preparing their nets. Jesus called them, and they, too, immediately left both their nets and their father and followed him.

Matthew 4:12, 18–22

Reflection

Surely one reason Jesus chose those two pairs of brothers to be his apostles was that they were willing, without any ifs and buts, to leave things of secondary importance in order to follow what was all-important. Can we hear Jesus speaking to us, too, in words such as these?

> In order to journey in this way you must first of all lay the past down at my feet. Leave behind your opinions, plans, prejudices, feelings, idle thoughts. Unhelpful relationships and pursuits: all have to go. When you lay all at my feet something happens; the present becomes my presence; my divine presence is the feast and you are held captive by my heart of love. Then your vain hopes, dreams and diversions will soon be left behind. False ambitions and comfort in the present will fade from view as the vision of things of eternal worth grows stronger.

Pause for thought

What do I need to leave behind?

Prayer

Jesus, I will follow you.
I am willing to leave behind whatever gets in the way.
I leave behind 'the nets' that, though good,
are the enemy of the best.
I leave behind the tangles that are not for me to unravel.
I leave in your hands those who are dear to me,
but who can thrive without me.
Jesus, you may lead me up or down hill,
you may lead me to the unknown or to the familiar,
wherever you lead, I will follow.

Today's step

I step
away from second-best routines
towards you.

Spiritual breathing exercise

Your best in.
Second-best out.
Will travel.

MARCH 3

To live is to journey

Bible reading

As Jesus and his followers walked along the road a man shouted out, 'I will follow you wherever you go.' Jesus replied that although even foxes have holes and birds have nests for refuge, the Peoples' Son had no such place. He said to someone else, 'Follow me.' But this man asked if he could first see to his father's funeral arrangements. 'Let people who are dead to my call take on things like funeral arrangements,' Jesus said, 'but you go out and proclaim that God's kingdom is here.' Yet another person promised to follow Jesus, but wanted first of all to go back home and say goodbye. 'No one,' Jesus said, 'who puts their hand to the plough and then looks back is suited for service in God's kingdom.'

Luke 9:57–62

Reflection

> My children, I have called you to journey every day of your life, from your womb, to your tomb, in fair weather and foul. To cease to move is to die. Do not delude yourselves that your destiny is to possess, to hold on to what you have. The purpose of your life is to travel towards your destiny, into the heart of human good, into my heart.[1]

> Some people travel in straight lines:
> sat in metal boxes, eyes ahead,
> always mindful of their target,
> moving in obedience to coloured lights
> and white lines,
> mission accomplished at journey's end.

Some people travel around in circles:
trudging in drudgery, eyes looking down,
knowing only too well their daily,
unchanging round,
moving in response to clock and to habit,
journey never finished yet never begun.

I want to travel in patterns of God's making:
walking in wonder, gazing all around,
knowing my destiny, though not my destination,
moving to the rhythm of the surging of his spirit,
a journey which when life ends,
in Christ has just begun.[2]

Pause for thought

Going round in circles,
climbing a ladder
or journeying into the heart of God.
Which most resembles my life?

Prayer

Jesus, may we journey with you,
firm in the faith,
loyal to your teaching,
obedient to your Father's will,
encompassed by the Spirit
along the way that leads to life.

Today's step

I step
away from fleeing or pushing
towards the One who beckons.

Spiritual breathing exercise

Following in.
Spectating out.
Life.

MARCH 4

To grow is to move

Bible reading

Jesus once told this story-with-a-truth-for-humans: A land-holder planted a fig tree and came back each year to inspect it. On his third visit he found it had still not borne fruit. He advised his chief gardener to cut it down, since it was taking up space that could be used for fruit-bearing plants. 'Give it one more chance,' the gardener said. 'I will loosen the earth all around it and dig in some good manure, then hopefully it will bear fruit next year. If it still fails to bear fruit, I promise I will then cut it down.'

Luke 13:6–9

Reflection

Jesus used many images of growth in plants to illustrate the need for people to grow in body, mind and spirit. Growth infers movement, responsiveness to one's environment, to God's Spirit within. Refusal to change is alien to growth. To grow is to journey.

> My children, the genius of this Way of Life is that your obedient journeying in common with fellow travellers frees you to be your true, unique self. Certain of God's children have been called to live in community under one roof, where each keeps the same rules of the house. Some of these have, through obedience to these rules, found their true selves, but others have become prisoners: the letter kills, the spirit gives life. God may, indeed, call a few of you to live under one roof, but most of you are to be pilgrims for love of God who travel wherever God takes you.[3]

Pause for thought

To make this journey takes its toll, but thankfully the sufferings that help us grow come in stages, not all at once.

Prayer

Lead me from that which binds to that which frees;
lead me from that which cramps to that which creates,
lead me from that which lies to that which speaks truth,
lead me from that which blights to that which ennobles.
Lead me from that which hides to that which celebrates;
lead me from that which fades to that which endures.

Today's step

I step
away from hardness
towards receptivity.

Spiritual breathing exercise

Nutrients in.
Shutters out.
Growth.

MARCH 5

Don't fossilise nice moments

Bible reading

Jesus began to brief his apostles that he had to journey into Jerusalem and into betrayal and death . . . Six days later he took Peter, James and John up a mountain. There he was transfigured. His clothes became dazzling white. The epochal national heroes Elijah and Moses appeared out of nowhere to support and converse with him. Peter, however, said, 'Rabbi, let's build huts for each of us so we can stay put. It's good here.' He did not know what he was saying. Suddenly a cloud enveloped them and a voice said, 'This is my Son, whom I love. Listen to him!' Before they knew it the only person they could see was Jesus; they went down the mountain with him.

Matthew 17

Reflection

> In a world of travel and global communication, faiths that seem to be fighting ancient turf wars rather than to recognise that we are all on a journey are rejected by the open hearted and taken over by the fearful.[4]

Peter did not want either Jesus or himself to journey on into a future that looked bleak. So he tried to stop the journey and stay on the mountain top. We, too, try to capture a snapshot of a happy moment and make an idol of the snapshot, for we shrink from 'losing' the feeling of that moment, from moving on, moving down into a valley.

In reality we do not cease to change, to move any day of our lives. Every second a human life is creating a new body. It is said that we make a new liver every six weeks, a new skeleton every three months, a new stomach every five days, a new skin every month. 99.99 per cent of our bodies is empty space – a bunch of atoms whirling around.

Is Jesus saying something like this to us? 'You have to keep walking. Never let a home or even a hermitage enmesh you in the comforts of cherished habits or even in self-centred tranquillity. Always alert, your path is to "the bourne from which no traveller returns". This bourne is my love. Love must goad you on until you are incapable of finding your satisfaction in any mere human shelter.'

Pause for thought

What snapshot experience do I try and ossify rather than move on?

Prayer

Father, you call us to listen to your Son and follow him.
Forgive us for fossilising good experiences.
Help us, rather, to use them as launching pads,
strengthened to go into the valleys of discontent,
willing to give even our lives for you,
reassured that, whatever trials we pass through,
we shall rise with you in glory.

Today's step

I step
away from nostalgia
towards destiny.

Spiritual breathing exercise

Journey in.
Standstill out.
Victory.

MARCH 6

Even the house-bound may journey

Bible reading

O God, our help in ages past,
our hope for years to come,
our shelter from the stormy blast,
and our eternal home.
Beneath the shadow of your throne,
your saints have dwelt secure;
sufficient is your arm alone,
and our defence is sure.
Time, like an ever-rolling stream,
will bear us all away;
we fade and vanish, as a dream
dies at the opening day.[5]

Reflection

> What then are you, human life?
> You are the road to life, not life itself,
> you are a real road but not a level one,
> long for some, short for others,
> broad for some, narrow for others,
> joyful for some, sad for others,
> for all alike, fleeting and irrevocable.
> A road is what you are, a road,
> but you are not clear to all.
> Many see you
> and few understand you to be a road.
> For you are so wily and enticing,
> that few know you are a road.
> Therefore you are to be questioned,
> but not believed and given bail.
> You are to be traversed but not inhabited.

> For no one dwells on a road, but travels it,
> so that those who walk upon the road
> may dwell in their homeland.[6]

'It is all very well for hermits to be constantly journeying,' someone points out, 'but I have family and work responsibilities; these are fixed points in my life.' Every relationship lives and moves. We can always choose how we respond to those we work and live with. 'You cannot step into the same river twice because new water is flowing in', wrote Heraclitus. In everything God can speak to us. So, although, for the time being, certain things may seem fixed in our situation, the way we relate to these constitutes our journey.

Pause for thought

How should I respond to what today brings?

Prayer

Leaving what is past,
we journey in your light.
Seeking what is just,
we journey in your truth.
Forgiving those who harmed us,
we journey in your love.
The eternal Creator keep us,
the beloved Companion beside us,
the Spirit's smile upon us.

Today's step

I step
off the pedestal
to go out in faith.

Spiritual breathing exercise

Open heart in.
Closed heart out.
Eternal home.

MARCH 7

Keep right on to the end of the road

Bible reading

Have you still not realised that the everlasting God, who creates one end of the earth to the other, never faints, grows weary or runs out of knowledge? God energises the faint and empowers the weak. Even youths flag, and young men run out of steam, but those who wait upon God shall renew their strength. They shall soar like eagles, run and not grow weary, walk long distances without becoming faint.

Isaiah 40:28–31

Reflection

Many spend their lives running away from this call to journey, in the fear that if they are stripped of worldly securities there would be nothing left, or that they would not know contentment. The truth is that, if we are truly open to whatever is God's best for us, we will find deep contentment and be renewed each day of our journey.

In order to be continually renewed in an endless adventure we must hold lightly to the things that become addictive; this enables this world and the next to come into perspective. Secondly, we must hold before us awe of God, and awe of our death; for as the Son of Sirach says: 'Remember your end and you will not sin' (Ecclesiasticus 7:36).

Imagine angels escorting you on your right and your left as your soul leaves your body, carrying you through purifying fire into ever greater light, always journeying nearer to the heart of God.

Pause for thought

Hold before you God and your final day on earth throughout today. Never give up. Keep right on to the end of the road.

Prayer

As fish live in water may I live in you.
As birds soar high and carefree may I soar with you.
As deer run straight and graceful may I run with you.
As water flows so freely may I flow with you.

Today's step

I step
away from something that threatens to become addictive
towards the flow of God's movement in my soul.

Spiritual breathing exercise

Flow in.
Fixation out.
Go.

MARCH 8

The last passage

Bible reading

Our human body is like a tent. We only live in it temporarily. If our 'tent' is destroyed, be assured that we have another dwelling place. This is not made by human hands. It lasts for ever. So if, at times, our aches and pains make us groan, remember that God has prepared for us this spiritual body. You're not convinced? The Spirit of God in your heart is a witness to the reality of the eternal spiritual home God has prepared for us.

2 Corinthians 5:1–5

Reflection

With the advance of medical technology, the average life span is getting longer. Some people find themselves in an institutional home, unable to do, see, hear, remember or talk much. They can feel lonely, since so many of their friends have already passed on. They can be tempted to despair, to suicide or to give in to constant complaint. To a pilgrim for the love of God each day that God grants us, however, is an opportunity to give our best for God's highest. Each day is to be lived. Each person we come into contact with is to be loved.

Although many of our faculties may be lost, those faculties that remain may be used to the full. The face may be used to smile. The lips may be used to thank. A hand may be used to salute or show friendship. Each day God keeps us on this earth is an opportunity to reach out to another, to take an interest, to show that every life is worthwhile. Trials are a means to develop fortitude and humility.

At the very end, the things of this world fade. We need to be set free from the ties that would bind us to this earth, for now we see it has been but our temporary home. Light beckons. What Orthodox Christians name *The Great Passage* begins.

Pause for thought

Look back with gratitude.
Look up for help.
Look out for an opportunity
to make someone else feel worthwhile.

Prayer

Guide me, good and great Redeemer,
pilgrim through this barren land.
I am weak, but you are mighty,
hold me with your powerful hand.

When I reach the river's crossing,
lead me to the other side.
Hold me in your heart for ever,
always I'll with you abide.[7]

Today's step

I step
away from grumbling
towards gratitude.

Spiritual breathing exercise

Care in.
Complaint out.
Reflection.

MARCH 9

Journey with a soul friend

Bible reading

Each person is like an organ in a human body; each has a distinctive part to play. We all know that God has appointed people like apostles, prophets, teachers, and those who work miracles. God also calls people to less public roles, such as those who have the ability to give to and receive from another person.

1 Corinthians 12:28

Reflection

> A soul friend seeks to discern with us where we are on our spiritual journey.[8]

The early Irish Christians used to say that a person without a soul friend is like a human body without a head. The Irish word for soul friend – anam cara – is increasingly being used again. Another term for this person is the spiritual companion. This comes from the French, meaning one who shares bread with you. The Norwegians who follow this way of life felt that they had no suitable translation for this person. So they use the word 'medvandrer'. This means someone who walks beside you at your own pace.

Imagine you are backpacking and someone comes with you. Before long you are too tired to walk and you sit down. 'What's in your backpack?' the other asks, 'Open it up and let me see.' As the accompanier sees all the things that have been laid out he or she asks, 'Do you need this, or that? Why don't you leave this here?' If the backpacker heeds this advice, he can go on exploring. If he does not heed it, he remains stuck or he has to go back to where he started.

On a physical journey we may have a map and a compass. On the spiritual journey we have an inner compass. We need to learn how to use this. To talk through with a travelling companion how we have been led so far, how we know when we are lost, and how to tell what the inner compass is saying can be invaluable, even life-saving.

Pause for thought

What do I most want to share with a companion on my journey?

Prayer

Christ of the journey,
you allowed yourself to journey alone when necessary,
but you invited treasured friends
to share much of the journey with you:
sacred moments and frightening ordeals,
humdrum tasks, tiring days, draining duties.
Share my journey.
Lead me to a companion on my journey,
to a true friend of my soul.

Today's step

I step
away from isolation
towards a soul companion.

Spiritual breathing exercise

Companionship in.
Self-sufficiency out.
Friendship.

MARCH 10

Two together in God's presence

Bible reading

During their long march to the promised land the people complained about their hardships. Moses, aggrieved, asked God, 'Why did you tell me to carry this people in my arms as a nurse carries an infant? I can't carry them on my own, the burden is too great.' God told Moses to bring seventy leaders who would stand with him in the Tent of Meeting. The Spirit came upon them and they prophesied. However, this also happened to two of the seventy who had stayed outside. Someone reported this to Moses. Joshua, son of Nun, who had been Moses' assistant since youth was horrified. 'Stop them,' he said to Moses. Moses said, 'Do not be jealous on my behalf. I wish all God's people were prophets and that God would put his Spirit upon them.'

Numbers 11:10-29

Reflection

This reading tells us something about the character of Moses and something about how he mentored Joshua. Power usually corrupts but in Moses' case it did not. He was humble and true. His greatness as a leader was that he was not threatened when those around him developed gifts that attracted attention – he loved to encourage others to grow in God-inspired leadership, and he wanted his protégé to understand this.

Moses first noticed Hoshea, son of Nun, as a young man of potential in the tribe of Ephraim. He gave him a new name – Joshua. Perhaps this was a way of re-envisioning him. When a hostile tribe attacked, Moses asked Joshua to choose warriors and confront the enemy, while he himself stood on an overlooking hill, arms raised in prayer.

Following victory, God told Moses to write a divine assurance on a scroll and to make sure Joshua heard this being read out (Exodus 17). Later, Moses took seventy leaders halfway up a mountain, but he himself went to the top with Joshua, who was privy to the most intimate communings with God. I wonder what they shared together during that extended time on the mountain? Later, when the people complained and fell prey to the twin gods of greed and power, Moses heard their demonstrations below and wrestled with God. Joshua shared these wrestlings, too (Exodus 24, 32, 33).

What a mentoring! What a combination of 'the warrior' and the 'spiritual person' developed in one younger person. *That* was a soul friendship.

Pause for thought

Is there something I try to do on my own which I should share with another?

Prayer

Father, you give us many gifts that we may share them in the work of building up your people. Help us to receive deeply, and to give ourselves generously, that in the work to which you call us we may know the wonder of your presence in another human life.

Today's step

I step
away from tittle-tattle
into the presence.

Spiritual breathing exercise

Presence in.
Pride out.
Aah.

MARCH 11

Share things of the Spirit

Bible reading

Mary, realising that she was pregnant, hurried to her cousin Elizabeth in the highlands of Judah.

As soon as Elizabeth heard her cousin's greeting the child in her own womb leapt and she was filled with the Holy Spirit. 'You are the most blest of women,' she told Mary, 'and the child in your womb is blest. Why should I be honoured with a visit from such a mother of God? For the moment I heard your voice my baby leapt in my womb for joy. You are blest because you have shown such complete faith. The things that God has told you that you have shared with me will, I know, really happen.' Mary said, in Elizabeth's hearing, 'I give glory to God.'

Luke 1:39–46

Reflection

Elizabeth and Mary were soul friends. They had such a rapport that Mary felt she could share with Elizabeth intimate matters that no one else would take seriously. They were both humble servants of God, dedicated to being led by God's Spirit. Elizabeth could shout aloud prophetic words, and Mary could burst into inspired song. They were at home in each other's presence. Such rapport is rare, but it can grow over time.

> A soul friend is like
>
> water for a picked flower, or
> gentle rain on seedlings;
>
> the warmth of eiderdown, or
> a fire to a cold hearth;
>
> a lighthouse in the dark, or
> an anchor to a blown ship;

play after hours of toil,
and the lightness of thistledown;

a window on a new world, or
secateurs to an overgrown rose;

clear air in a smoky room,
or a guiding star for a journey.

such friends are freeing as love,
with the healing touch of Jesus.

so is Christ to you –
so may you be for many more.[9]

Pause for thought

What most intimate concern of the Spirit do I need to share?

Prayer

May the One who fathers, the Christ who succours,
and the Spirit who counsels
bring divine blessings to birth in us;
may they grant us gifts of friendship and discretion,
integrity and understanding,
faithfulness and spiritual strength;
and the ability to be ourselves in the presence of the other.

Today's step

I step
away from isolation
towards sharing in the Spirit.

Spiritual breathing exercise

Sharing in.
Burden out.
Bliss.

MARCH 12

Questions on the journey

Bible reading

If I have washed your feet, then you are to wash one another's feet . . . As the Father has loved me, so I have loved you . . . I have shared these things with you that you may have peace . . . Father, I have shown your character to those you have given me . . . I have given them the words you have given me . . .

As he was dying Jesus saw his mother Mary and the disciple who had felt especially loved by him standing nearby. 'Take him as your son' Jesus said to Mary. 'Take her as your mother' he said to the disciple, John.

John 13:14; 15:9; 16:33; 17:6, 8; 19:26, 27

Reflection

Mary and John became soul friends. It was a spiritual mother-son relationship. Before his death, even Jesus, although he was way ahead of his closest friends in discerning the Father's will, nevertheless needed close companions who would share his journey. That is no doubt why, on several occasions, he chose three disciples, Peter, James and John, to share special moments of testing or illumination. Of these three, John seems to have emerged as the most intuitively close to what was in Jesus' heart. At the last supper it was he who leant against Jesus and whispered in his ear.

John and the twelve asked Jesus lots of questions. Chapters 13–17 of John's Gospel are Jesus' answers to these questions, and his preparing them for what lay ahead. These chapters are a supreme example of spiritual formation. By praying to the Father from the depths of his heart, in the presence of his disciples, Jesus not only continued his authentic journey, he modelled a way of praying that spiritually formed them. The fact that John years later wrote down his reflective recollection of this prayer bears eloquent witness to this.

We will have many questions, many needs on our journey:

> A fear to overcome? A challenge to tackle? A need to meet? A person to love? An injustice to right? Ways of prayer to explore? A talent to develop? A skill to learn? A discipline to master? A relationship to tend? A habit to break? Physical fitness to achieve? Knowledge to acquire? A place to visit? A virtue to grow?

Pause for thought

Which of these things is a priority to talk through when I next meet with a soul friend?

Prayer

Christ of fearless love.
Take me to my point of greatest weakness
and let me find you there.
May your strength be made complete in my frailty.

Today's step

I step
away from misery
towards companionship of love.

Spiritual breathing exercise

Trust.
Share.
Joy.

MARCH 13

The spiritual fitness coach

Bible reading

Dear Timothy, my treasured child in the Faith, don't give credence to the fanciful talk that goes the rounds; focus on the things that build people up in God. Do not be put off by people who despise your youth. Keep up your reading. Stir up the gift that was given you when you were ordained. Meditate on these things with full concentration. I constantly remember you in my prayers. Be strong. Commit to memory my teachings. Endure hardship. Study in a way that pleases God. Flee youthful lusts. Avoid stupid disputes. Do not be put off course – times are coming when nearly everyone will promote godless living in the name of God. Keep on giving out the message, in season and out of season. Challenge and encourage others with longsuffering.

1 Timothy 1:2 ,4; 4:12–15; 2 Timothy 2:3–5

Reflection

The apostle Paul's two letters to his young apprentice Timothy are in part letters of spiritual direction, as these extracts reveal. A soul friend such as Paul helps a seeker to grow in their relationship with God and others, explore different ways of praying, reflect on the promptings of the Holy Spirit, feed on Scripture, gain awareness, confront things that are wrong, find strength in times of adversity, apply the gospel to each area of life, and maintain a good balance of prayer, work and recreation.

Paul and Timothy were known as followers of The Way. In the context of the faith journey, the seeker shares with a soul friend how God has led them since they last met, where they have gone astray, anything that has brought them to a halt or to a crossroads. They seek to address these, and to discern the next steps of the journey.

Paul was a coach whose aim was to build Timothy's fibre. Elsewhere in his letters he encouraged Timothy to learn fitness from the athlete, toughness from the soldier and productivity from the farmer.

Pause for thought

In the light of Paul's advice to Timothy, what do you need to learn?

Prayer

God be with us at every leap,
Christ be with us on every steep,
Spirit be with us in every deep,
each step of the journey we go.

Today's step

I step
away from diversions
towards Christ's training.

Spiritual breathing exercise

Gospel in.
Flab out.
Fitness.

MARCH 14

Seek out a wise elder

Bible reading

Do not bare your soul to anyone: you may invade their personal space and dispel their happiness. Do not consult with people who lack mental discipline, for they cannot keep a confidence. If you really want to, you can gain spiritual fitness. If you love to listen, you will gain wisdom. Seek out an elder who is wise and attach yourself to that person. If you find a discerning person, rise early to visit them.

Ecclesiasticus 8:19, 17; 6:32–36

Reflection

The desire to be built up in the Faith through close fellowship with another Christian, which characterised the New Testament Church, began to fade over time. That changed in the fourth and fifth centuries when Christians who were all-out for Jesus went into the deserts of Egypt, Syria and Palestine. The desert became a training ground of the Spirit. Those who overcame the hurdles became known as athletes of the Spirit. The older, wiser ones were called Abbas or Ammas (we might say Poppa or Mama) and were sought out as soul friends.

News of these spiritual fathers and mothers stirred the imagination of sincere Christians in the towns, and they began to seek out desert fathers and mothers as guides. Young people would test out whether they, too, could live this way, by choosing an Amma or Abba to be their soul friend. They would share the work, the prayers, the silence and the cell, and learn from the life as much as from the words of the older Christian. So these soul friends were cell mates.

Busy town Christians would make journeys to some wise old desert elder and ask him or her to be their soul friend for a weekend. Desert hermits would pay visits to one another, and those with the clearest spiritual discernment would bring to light hindrances to spiritual growth that needed attention. When Abba Helle[10] was staying with some brothers, they so trusted him that when he revealed the secret counsels of each of them, saying that one was troubled by fornication, another by vanity, another by self-indulgence, and another by anger, they could only respond, 'Yes, what you say is true'.

Gradually collections were made of the sayings of the Ammas and Abbas. This was one of their sayings: 'Let us each give his heart to the other, carrying the Cross of Christ'.

Pause for thought
To whom can I give my heart to, carrying the Cross of Christ?

Prayer
Gentle God, reveal to us the beauty of sensitive friendship.
Help us to create such stillness in our inner being
that we become aware of your gracious movements
in the souls of others.

Today's step
I step
away from the wayward impulse
towards the wise friend.

Spiritual breathing exercise
Trust in.
Treachery out,
Tryst.

MARCH 15

The annual retreat

Bible reading

On the fifteenth day of the month when you have gathered in the harvest, set apart eight days. Dedicate this period to God. Begin and end with a day of rest. On the first day get some leafy branches and strong boughs of wood and build a shelter. Use this as a time of praise and appreciation of God. It should be your first priority, and that of every citizen, to do this every year. This practice will keep alive the memory of my guiding hand in the life of the people.
Leviticus 23:39–43

Reflection

> Regular retreats: The outworking of this depends on the individual's own lifestyle, but we encourage regular days of quiet and reflection, and also an annual retreat.[11]

A human being is not a machine that can output without input. From time to time we need to retreat in order to advance. The great religions recommend retreats. In Moses' time God advised the people of Israel to spend one week a year living in shelters. Sometimes these were on the roof of their houses. This practice took them out of their comfort zones, and out of their habit of taking things for granted. In the hot, dry climate of Moses' people, they often had no roof in their temporary shelters; they looked out on to God's open skies and appreciated Providence. Jews in wetter climates still mark this 'Festival of Tabernacles' in some way, such as erecting tents in the garden.

This idea, which modern retreats also help to fulfil, is to get us 'away from it all', to unclutter us, to free us from depending too much upon *things*.

People today go on retreats to get rid of stress, to find a breathing space; to read, reflect or journal; to talk with someone; to listen to creation; to sort out priorities; to find divine perspectives.

Pause for thought

Which of these reasons for making a retreat is most important for you?

Prayer

God of our forebears,
help me to get out of the box
and find the place where I may re-orient my life with you.
Teach me to go wherever and do whatever it takes
to stop running life my way.

Today's step

I step
away from the daily round
and retreat into God space.

Spiritual breathing exercise

God-space in.
Ego-space out.
There!

MARCH 16

Come apart

Bible reading

The twelve apostles, whom Jesus had sent out in twos on the campaign trail, came back together and reported to Jesus the many things they had done and taught. Jesus said, 'Now you, too, need to come apart into a deserted place and rest awhile.' For many people were coming and going and they often had no time even to eat. So they departed on a boat in private.

Mark 6:7, 30–32

Reflection

Jesus called his disciples apart for various purposes. On this occasion the purpose was to get some rest. Although it is good to make a retreat, it is not as easy as you may think! You may find it difficult to get away; and when you arrive, you may find it hard to get into focus.

If you arrive exhausted, take time to sleep, walk, eat, and relax. If you come with deep hurts, perhaps buried under 'overload', be gentle with yourself. Remember, rest is still God's best and normal way of healing. This is also true if you have been suffering deep depression. In that case good food and fellowship should come before intense prayer or solitude.

The pressures of modern life, and even a change in our normal routine, can make us tense. If you arrive tense, take time to unload and unwind. One way to do this is to make a list of the things that you must attend to on your return and hang them up on an imaginary clothes line to return to later. Another way to unload is to go to a deserted waterside, take hold of a stone which represents something you need to offload, fling it into the water, and repeat. Some people build a cairn of stones during their retreat. Each stone can represent some stress or difficulty you wish to leave behind.

Before we can have the energy to resolve conflicts or engage in spiritual exercises, we need to learn how to receive new energies into ourselves.

Pause for thought

Try the sunbathing exercise. Imagine first the sun in the sky shining upon you, warming, relaxing and nurturing you. Now repeat the exercise, thinking of Jesus as the uncreated sun and let him warm, relax and nurture you. Breathe it in deeply and rhythmically, saying words such as 'I breathe in love' or 'warmth' or 'peace'.

Prayer

May the sun of suns shine upon me,
bringing peace and poise.
May the healing rays come through me
until I frolic like the lambs.

Today's step

I step
away from the fret
towards the rest.

Spiritual breathing exercise

Sun in.
Stress out.
Aah!

MARCH 17

Retreat to advance

Bible reading

God is my shepherd,
who refreshes me in green pastures,
restores me by quiet waters,
and leads me into the right ways.
Even though I walk through the valley
of the shadow of death,
I will fear no evil, for you are with me,
your protecting staff comforts me.
You prepare a feast for me
even when hostile people surround me.
You anoint me with oil and my life overflows.
Surely goodness and mercy shall follow me
all the days of my life,
and I will dwell in your presence for ever.

Psalm 23

Reflection

Jesus likened himself to the Good Shepherd. If at one time he took his apostolic flock away for a rest, on other occasions he took them into retreat in order to share his thoughts with them, to pray in their presence, to prepare them for an advance.

Before Jesus began his public campaign he spent forty days in a desert; before he chose his team of twelve he spent a night on a mountain. He taught his disciples to follow a similar pattern of retreat before advance. God's advice to three of Jesus' friends who were on retreat on the Mount of Transfiguration was to listen to his Son (Mark 9:2–8). That is always central to a retreat.

In some countries, such as the UK and Ireland, there are retreat associations. These give advice on different kinds of retreats, and list retreat houses. Not everyone can afford or have access to these. If you live in a hot country, desert places may be easy to find. If you do not, there is another way. In Britain, for example, the garden shed is becoming a place of sanctuary for millions. The garden shed was voted into the Millennium Dome's display on national identity as one of the top 100 symbols of Britishness. By the time the Dome closed the number of British homes with a garden hideaway had risen to an estimated 9.6 million[12]. Readers in most countries can make or find a shed. Certain people who live in a noisy city centre play calming music, and that becomes their retreat setting.

Pause for thought

What do you most need to do on a retreat?

Prayer

I will come apart with you, Lord,
that you may still my heart.
I will come apart with you, Lord,
that you may stock my mind.
I will come apart with you, Lord,
that you may steel my will.
I will retreat with you, Lord,
that together we may advance.

Today's step

I step
away from a routine that debilitates
towards a break that renews.

Spiritual breathing exercise

Space in.
Fuss out.
Advance!

MARCH 18

Journalling

Bible reading

O Lord, you have searched me. You know everything about me, even when I sit down and rise up. You understand my thoughts even from a distance. You encompass me as I journey and as I sleep. You know my funny ways. Not one word comes out of my lips that you do not hear. You guard me in front and behind; you lay your hand upon me. Such knowledge is so wonderful I can hardly take it in. Where in the world could I be out of the range of your Spirit? Even in outer space you are there! Even in the depths of hell, there, too, you are. I will praise you also for the amazing way my body is formed. My thoughts are precious to me.

Psalm 139:1–8; 14, 17

Reflection

The Christian Reformer John Calvin described the psalms as 'the mirror of the soul'. In the psalms many types of people wrote down thoughts about their hopes and fears. Often they addressed these to God in the form of reflections. Sometimes they wrote prayers. At times their anger got the better of them, and they expressed raw, vengeful emotions. They examined themselves and journeyed into the depths of the soul. They identified themselves with the fate of their society, and invited God to challenge, shape and heal their nation, and much more. They wrote all this down on scrolls which have become the world's greatest collection of psalms.

People who make retreats often jot down words and thoughts that seem important to them. Many find it useful to keep a journal. Here are some things you might find helpful to write down: your deepest desires; memories that have shaped you; dreams; striking words you have heard or read; things that make you angry or that you run away from; people you need to forgive; things you need to give up; steps you need to take; people to pray for; attitudes that need to change; hurts that need healing; how to arrange your time; ingredients of a healthy diet for body, mind or spirit.

Pause for thought

Write down what most strikes you now.

Prayer

Search me, O God and know my heart.
Sift me, and know my thoughts.
See if there is anything out of place in my life.
Lead me in the way everlasting.[13]

Today's step

I step
away from reflex actions
towards reflection.

Spiritual breathing exercise

Thoughtfulness in.
Thoughtlessness out.
God.

MARCH 19

Poustinia

Bible reading

When you pray, do not put on airs, or make a public show of it as some religious figures do. Do not gear your prayers to what others notice. It is much better to go to your room and shut the door. When you have shut the door, pray to your Father in solitude. God, who sees what you do in secret, will reward you if you do this.

Matthew 6:1–6

Reflection

As a child in Russia, Catherine Doherty and her mother would visit a poustinia. This is the Russian word for a desert-like hermitage for one person. The poustinik, however, was not just a hermit, there was a gracious hospitality about him. He was a listening person. He was available. When Catherine first moved to the West she thought it would be impossible for such a place to exist or for such a life to be lived. She was led, however, to create just such a place. She gathered a spiritual family, gave her possessions to the poor, and established Madonna House. She wrote the following in order to help her friends grasp the ethos of the poustinia:

> The poustinia must be stark in its simplicity and poverty. It must contain a table and a chair. On the table there must be a Bible. There should also be a pencil and some paper. In one corner are a basin and a pitcher for washing up. The bed, if bed there be . . . Drinking water, a loaf of bread . . . For those who are not accustomed to eating their bread with water, there are the makings for tea or coffee. Prominent in the poustinia is a cross without a corpus, about

six feet by three feet, which is nailed to the wall, and an icon of Our Lady in the eastern corner, with a vigil light in front of it. The cross without a corpus is a symbol of one's own crucifixion on it, for those of us who love Christ passionately want to be crucified with him so as to know the joy of his resurrection. But of course there is so much more than the physical aspect of a place like that . . . It is God who leads a soul to the desert, and the soul cannot remain in the desert long unless it is nourished by God.[14]

Pause for thought

How might you create and arrange a poustinia?

Prayer

Lead, me, Lord into a place of prayer,
to live simply, silently, and alone with you
so that I may die to myself quicker
and Christ may grow in me faster,
so that you may give more of him
to the world that hungers for him.[15]

Today's step

I step
away from paraphernalia
towards poustinia.

Spiritual Breathing Exercise

Silence in.
Superfluities out.
Poustinia.

MARCH 20

Desert places

Bible reading

Moses was looking after the flocks of his father-in-law, Jethro. He led the flock to the far side of the desert and came to Horeb, which was to be named God's Mountain. A bush caught his eye. It was burning, and the flames refused to die down. Moses turned aside and went towards it. There God called to him, 'Moses, Moses.' 'I am here,' Moses replied. 'Take off your sandals, for this is holy ground,' said God, 'I have seen the suffering of my oppressed people. I will set them free and lead them to a fruitful land that I promise to give them. I will send you to the Emperor of Egypt that you may lead them out to freedom.'

Exodus 3:1–10

Reflection

Seventeen centuries before Christ, Moses had a desert encounter with God which changed history. His people had become an oppressed minority in Egypt. He had been adopted by Egypt's queen and received a royal education, but had to flee when he took sides in a dispute between an Egyptian and one of his fellows. It has been said that for forty years Moses was a somebody who God made a nobody; for forty years (in the desert) he was a nobody who God made into somebody; for forty years (as his people's freedom leader) he was a somebody who knew that he was nobody.

Often in the Bible a person has to go into the desert to have a life-changing encounter with God. The actor Stephen Fry walked away from his London play, his job, his friends, to a lonely place where he could find his true self. He faxed his agent: 'I have been selfish. But I only have one life to lead. I desperately needed to get away and to rethink my life . . . for years now I have been incapable of saying 'no' and have allowed my work to become my life. I hope you will allow me a little space and solitude . . .' He, like many others, did not realise that Christianity makes provision for this need to get away, to rethink, to come face to face with our true selves. Some people call it 'desert spirituality'. It does not require us to take a plane to Morocco – we can create 'desert spaces' in our own area. For 'the desert' is any place where we learn hard lessons and real priorities, where we are simplified down to our true selves, until we are ready to meet the God of life and death.

Pause for thought

What is the nearest thing to a burning bush on my horizon?

Prayer

You, Lord, burn in this place;
your presence fills it.
Strip from me all that is not of you,
call me to whatever you will,
lead me wherever you will.

Today's step

I step
away from mere work
towards holy fire.

Spiritual breathing exercise

Fire in.
Cold out.
Holy ground.

MARCH 21

Sanctuary in the city

Bible reading

Do you not know that you are God's temple and that God's Spirit dwells in you? Any person who violates that Spirit will come to nothing. God's temple is holy, and you are that temple . . . Do you not know that your body is the temple of the Holy Spirit? You do not belong to yourself, you belong to God. Christ has purchased you at great price, therefore glorify God in body and soul.

1 Corinthians 3:16 ,17; 6:19, 20

Reflection

'I work in the city and I live in the fast lane,' someone says, 'how is it possible for a person like me to have a retreat?' The answer may simply be: 'Put it in your diary.' But even if you cannot go away to a retreat, you can learn to make an inner retreat. How? By turning your body and soul into a temple of the Holy Spirit.

We can do this by visualising our heart to be a little prayer room. We still its noises. We clean out its rubbish. We shut the door to distractions. We create a window that lets in the light, and out of which we may throw stressed reactions, prejudice, pride and all ill-will. We furnish this inner room with paintings, samples of creation and objects of beauty. Bible verses are strewn around it. We place an altar there, which symbolises the divine presence, before which we bow. We have a cross on the wall, which reminds us at all times to meet unwelcome assaults on our well-being with suffering love. Perhaps there is flowing water, to remind us to be immersed in the Spirit at all times.

Although there will be interruptions and jarring moments during the day, we practise coming back into our inner room as often as possible. Is this not what it means for us to be temples of the Holy Spirit?

Pause for thought

What else will I put in my inner place of retreat?

Prayer

God make my heart a little cell,
keep harm without, keep peace within.
God make my heart an altar
where I may gaze into your face.
God make my heart your home,
where I am content to be with you.

Today's step

I step
away from the fast lane
into God's presence within me.

Spiritual breathing exercise

Spirit in.
Speed out.
Dwelling.

MARCH 22

Pilgrims are blest

Bible reading

How I love going to places that are hallowed by your presence. My body and soul cries out to be in them . . . Blest are those who have set their hearts on pilgrimage. As they pass through the valley they make it a place of springs . . . They go from strength to strength, till each appears before God.

Psalm 84:5–7

Reflection

The purpose of pilgrimage is to tread in the shoes of Christ or his saints in order to make contact with the many rich experiences which are to do with being a pilgrim. Such pilgrimages draw us into deeper devotion to our Lord Jesus and will inspire us to mission. Members might seek out communities of prayer. The Community recommends pilgrimage to sites of the Celtic Christian tradition, such as Iona and Lindisfarne as well as to new 'places of resurrection'. Soul friends give guidance about different ways of making pilgrimage.[16]

We shall never find our lives' purpose by just drifting. Nor by climbing the ladder of success. Pilgrimage helps us to step off that ladder, to cease to drift, and to step forward intent to find God. We encourage everyone to make pilgrimage in some form. When we make pilgrimage we bless ourselves and others: a life-changing spiritual dynamic lies hidden in pilgrimage, for it challenges the lust to control which has eaten its way into human motives ever since the ill-fated attempt to build a tower that reached to heaven (Genesis 11:1–9). This desire to control is deep in all of us. In true pilgrimage we let go of having to be in control.

On some types of pilgrimage we also risk getting lost. We move away from our own territory on to that of others, where our language and customs may no longer be dominant. We discover that ours are not the only ways. We have to adapt. We may be dependent upon the help of others. We get in touch with our vulnerability. We need sources of security which are deeper than those we have left behind.

Pause for thought

What do I find most difficult to leave behind in order to go on pilgrimage?

Prayer

We release into your hands, O God
the work we shall leave behind,
the things we cling on to,
the problems that would pursue us,
the tasks left unfinished.
Hand of God, hold us.

Today's step

I step
away from what clings
towards what calls.

Spiritual breathing exercise

Your hold in.
My hold out.
Pilgrim.

MARCH 23

The annual pilgrimage

Bible reading

When you are settled in your land, travel once a year to the place God will show you. Offer to a priest best samples of your livelihood, and he will place these before an altar. There, recount together how God has led your people. Rehearse in your mind every good thing God has given you and give thanks. Before you do this, make sure you have given practical gifts to support the poor, orphans and those who without pay maintain the public worship of God.

Keep God's commands. Walk in God's ways. Listen to God's voice that you may be a holy people.

Deuteronomy 26

Reflection

Pilgrimage is at the heart of the Jewish religion out of which Christianity grew. The central experience of the Old Testament believers, which they constantly recalled, was the journey of the Israelite people for forty years through trackless deserts towards a land promised by God. They were to recall this journey every year at their Passover meal in spring. Tens of thousands would travel great distances to be at one of the great festivals, Jesus among them.

The Hebrew word for pilgrim means 'one who goes up'. This was understood in both a physical and a spiritual sense. Pilgrims from across the world had to go up from the surrounding plains in order to reach the heights of Jerusalem. They also lifted up their spirits in expectation of meeting God. The Psalms of Ascent (120–134) were pilgrim songs which pilgrims sang as they climbed the many steps leading up to the temple.

Most of the first Christians were converted while they were on a pilgrimage. Over three thousand converts were baptised while they were taking part in the Jewish Pentecost Festival in Jerusalem. They had journeyed there from places far and wide (Acts 2).

Pause for thought

What is God saying to you about pilgrimage?

Prayer

High king of land and sea,
wherever we go is yours.
You led our forebears by cloud and fire,
you lead us through the days and years,
you led your saints by sign and sail,
be our Pilgrim Guide ahead.

Today's step

I step
away from my routines
towards a pilgrim route.

Spiritual breathing exercise

Rendezvous in.
Scrabbling out.
Divine!

MARCH 24

Pilgrim places

Bible reading

When all the people had crossed the river Jordan into freedom God charged Joshua to ask twelve representatives, one from each tribe, to each carry on their shoulder a large stone from the river and erect these in their new land as a lasting sign. Thus in future years, when children asked their parents what these stones meant, they would reply: 'When our people brought the great scroll of God's commands during our march to freedom, the impassable river became shallow and we were able to pass over.'

Joshua 4:1–9

Reflection

Since the time of Christ it has been a once-in-a-lifetime ambition of many Christians to visit Jerusalem, the place of Jesus' death and resurrection, as well as other places in the lands of the Bible. In the third century, when Christians were in danger of staying in their comfort zones, radical followers of the gospel made journeying to gospel sites part of their discipline. The great centres of Christianity such as Rome and Byzantium (now Istanbul) soon also drew many pilgrims. Other places where saintly people wrought miracles or were martyred became pilgrim centres, and, in the Latin world especially, great Basilicas were erected.

In the Celtic Church only a few could pilgrimage to a world Christian centre such as Jerusalem or Rome. In practice most people made more frequent pilgrimage to holy sites nearer home. They might walk prayerfully round a number of holy places in a certain order. Sometimes these were known as sacred rounds. These would not take more than a day to complete. Visiting each cross or other holy stopping place in turn, the pilgrim said appropriate prayers.

This practice caught on with the English, too. The holy stopping places on the monastic trackway across Dartmoor between Tavistock Abbey and Buckfast Abbey are marked by a well-preserved series of named crosses.

Jesus taught God was everywhere, but he did not say that there was no value in special places. In fact, he urged people to find special places in which to pray. After his resurrection he made Galilee a place of rendezvous.

Pause for thought

What are, or could be, my special places?

Prayer

Dear Father God,
I have journeyed to this place and here I pause.
My life so far has brought me here,
my future stretches further than the eye can see.
If, thus far, my journey you have shared,
accompany me now.
Give wisdom, light and always joy
so that in thought, and gift, and love
my life shall be to fellow travellers
a witness to your presence in the world.[17]

Today's step

I step
away from the daily roundabout
towards the place of meeting.

Spiritual breathing exercise

Pilgrimage in.
Sloth out.
Light!

MARCH 25

New places of resurrection

Bible reading

I lift my eyes to the mountains. I ask myself, 'Where will help come from?' This is the answer: My help comes from the Eternal God who made earth and heaven alike.

God never lets us slip. The One who looks after us never sleeps. Because our Creator is our Shelter, created things like the sun shall not strike us down by day, not the moon by night. The Eternal God will shield us from all harm, and will always protect us as we come and go.

Psalm 121

Reflection

In Celtic lands pilgrimage to famous sites was popular, but pilgrimage could also be about meeting God in an untrodden place, in the elements, or on the edge.

There are allusions to pilgrimage in two saints of Ireland who lived even before Patrick: Ciaran of Saigir and Ailbe of Emly, both of whom are invoked in The Litany of Saints. Ancient Gaels, they looked out across the vast and trackless ocean to the 'eternal west, the setting of all the suns', to the place of the ever young. When they became Christians they continued this mindset, but they journeyed towards the Sun of suns. For the Romans, the sea represented a barrier to the advance of her legions. To the Celt it beckoned them to cross far frontiers defenceless, yet with the legions of heaven. With them we say:

We leave behind our ties: we journey with single hearts.

The sun shall not strike us by day, nor the moon by night: we journey in your shielding.

We look not to right or left, but straight towards your way: we journey in your truth.

The rough places shall be smoothed and the pitfalls shall be cleared: we journey in your power.

The proud shall be brought low and the humble shall be raised up: we journey in your justice.

The hungry shall be fed and the poor shall have good news: we journey in your love.

No final home have we on this life's passing seas: we journey towards our eternal home.

A special place is one which beckons and draws something out of you. This may be because in it nature renews you, history speaks to you, land or sea enfolds you, heaven draws near to you.

Pause for thought

Let your feet follow your heart until you find your place of resurrection.

Prayer

Lead us on our journey
to places of resurrection,
to dwellings of peace,
to healings of wounds,
to joys of discovery.

Today's step

I leave behind worries
and step towards the place of resurrection.

Spiritual breathing exercise

Intimations in.
Worry out.
Resurrection.

MARCH 26

False and true pilgrimage

Bible reading

People who trust in God will be like the mountains we pilgrims are approaching. Mount Zion will never be moved. As the mountains surround this pilgrim city of Jerusalem, so God encircles us. The powers of bad people surely have no power over us here. Do good, O God, to those whose hearts are set on you.

Psalm 125

Reflection

Pilgrimages can be done for wrong reasons. Unfortunately, both in medieval times and in today's tourist industry, people who want control or money have made an industry out of pilgrimage. In the Middle Ages abuses crept in; Martin Luther attacked the abuses – we cannot buy our way into heaven – and pointed out that pilgrimage was not commanded by Christ. A package tour to a pilgrim centre can sometimes be right, but beware that it does not kill the spirit of true pilgrimage.

In order to illustrate the difference between following the 'pilgrim package' and 'the pilgrimage of the heart' I share a personal experience in Jerusalem. The official tours tend to maximise trade for the rich and powerful, and marginalise the poor and oppressed, often in the garb of religious hyperbole. So I asked myself 'Where would Jesus go and what would Jesus do?' I felt that he would be among the poor, seekers, or friends. So I took a Palestinian bus from Damascus Gate to Bethany, to the site of Mary, Martha and Lazarus' house where they nurtured Jesus. There I meditated on how we may nurture God's servants today. I prayed in Lazarus' tomb for resurrection in tomb-like places in the world. Then I walked the hot and dusty road through Bethpage up to the Mount of Olives, to meet a Palestinian Christian and to discuss how we can support our brothers and sisters in Christ. Only then did I descend into the centre of Jerusalem.

I would like to be a person that cannot be bought, so I refrained from pilgrim practices that are born of that spirit.

Pause for thought

What distracts us from the heart of pilgrimage?

Prayer

Pilgrim God, who accepted such humbling
in your journey of trust on earth,
in my pilgrimage keep me on the paths
of listening and learning, reverence and respect,
simplicity and service
that I may not stray from your authentic steps.

Today's step

I step
away from trivia
towards the heart of true pilgrimage.

Spiritual breathing exercise

True ways in.
False ways out.
Trust.

MARCH 27

Things to do on a pilgrimage

Bible reading

I sing of faithful love. As I go forward I try to get rid of anything blameworthy. I look on nothing sordid, only on good things. I keep away from crime and strife. I create an atmosphere of respect. I make no room for deceit. Morning by morning I banish evil and dwell in the silence of God's presence.

Psalm 101

Reflection

You can, if you wish, go on to the internet and learn about or simulate pilgrimage to places throughout the world. This is no substitute for the real thing. For these lack the most fundamental ingredient of pilgrimage, which is to get up out of your seat and move away from your familiar surroundings. Nevertheless, if circumstances or health do not permit a physical pilgrimage, God can use a consecrated imagination to bring true blessing out of a simulated journey.

If we *can* make a physical pilgrimage, what do we do while we are walking? The psalm mentions singing, visual aids, good deeds, trust-building. While we are walking we could go through, or make up, an alphabet of devotion, for example: A = adore, B = believe, C = confess; we could go through the Lord's Prayer, memorise scriptures, prayers, hymns, share inspirations, reflect on the lives of holy people associated with the place which we approach.

When we come to a place we've never been to before, we cross a boundary, and, freed from our familiar routines, may become aware of God in a new way. By coming to a place of gathering one reinforces the sense of solidarity with fellow Christians irrespective of their different backgrounds.

Some bathe in healing waters, or light candles. In a Muslim Haj pilgrims throw stones as at the devil. Christians may find it therapeutic to get inner demons out of their system in such a way. At the end of the journey we are drawn to make an act of self-offering to God. It is good to spend time in prayer, silence, writing down of thoughts.

Pause for thought

Make a list of things you could do on a pilgrimage.

Prayer

Here am I at your service, O Lord,
to you belong the empires of the world.[18]

Today's step

I step
away from words
towards an action.

Spiritual breathing exercise

Action in.
Anxiety out.
On track.

MARCH 28

The benefits of pilgrimage

Bible reading

As the pilgrims make their way through Balsam Valley they make a little reservoir and – one more blessing – early rain falls and fills it. As they wend their way from one high place to another you reveal yourself to them. I had rather spend one day in your place than a thousand days in my own place without you. Just think of living on the threshold of your dwelling – this is infinitely better than living in the mansions of mammon. For you are like a protecting shield, a supporting rampart; you give grace and glory; you refuse us nothing good.

Psalm 84:6–11

Reflection

Some readers may find pilgrimage a new concept and be uncertain of its benefits. The following extract from the letter of a South African youth pastor who took a year to pilgrimage in Europe, working for his keep in each place, may encourage you to explore pilgrimage further.

> Lindisfarne was one of the more poignant steps on my journey. Praying one day on St Cuthbert's island, I had the sense of truly being in a coracle – that in truth I had actually pushed away from the shore of my life, and was now upon the vast sea with God. It was a momentous discovery for me because I had been in the mind set of wondering when, if ever, I would have enough courage to push away from the shore. Meantime my very act of pilgrimage had already thrust me out onto waters, and my life will never be the same again.

Sometimes we ask people in pilgrim groups 'What have

you appreciated in this pilgrimage? These are some responses:

> I've enjoyed watching pilgrims bless others by their presence, words or prayer.
> I've enjoyed people taking time to be outside themselves and help me work through rocky patches.
> It has enabled me to lean on others and give to others.
> I've learned to listen to the Holy Spirit and to be aware of God's presence.
> I've learned to be open to Christ in others.
> I've been given a sense of place.
> I felt hopeless. I feel embraced – even in the craziness of my life.

Pause for thought

Which of the following blessings do I covet?

Prayer

Blessing of discovery be yours
and blessing of rest.

Blessing of scenery be yours
and blessing of saints.

Blessing of meeting be yours
and blessing of solitude.

Blessing of friendship be yours
and blessing of thought.

Today's step

I step
away from bemoaning
towards blessing.

Spiritual breathing exercise

Appreciation in.
Apathy out.
Blessing.

MARCH 29

Pilgrimage helps you to trust

Bible reading

As once the eyes of a slave girl looked adoringly at the mistress who looked after and loved her, so our eyes look to you, our dear loving God. You feel such mercy for us. We suffer abuse; we are taken for granted, misrepresented and even are scorned behind our backs.

All this matters so much less, however, when we can gaze into the face of Eternal Love.

Echoes the pilgrimage Psalm 123

Reflection

Some members of *Christians Aware* expressed the meaning of their pilgrimage in this way:

> Trusting and needing each other: accepting the basic elements of God's created world, sun and rain, comfort and weariness, differences in nature and in human beings; travelling with purpose, aware of the goal; discovering people as people rather than as 'roles', since the blisters of bishops and bartenders feel much the same; seeing ourselves as only the latest members of a long line of pilgrims; risking the unknown, whether fellow-pilgrims or countryside; trusting God, who has led us far, and will lead us.[19]

We often fear to let go of our defences and our regular patterns lest someone should abuse our openness. We certainly should not be pushovers, and we need to create wise boundaries, but a closed person is a tragic person. A pilgrimage offers us a space where we can risk more than we otherwise might, for there are people and places to whom we may repair, opportunities to laugh at ourselves, to help one another along, to see things from someone else's point of view, to ask forgiveness for hurts, to be honest about what we feel, to celebrate differences and to find common ground.

Pause for thought

If I have withheld trust, how might I cease to withhold it on a pilgrimage?

Prayer

Risen Christ, you turned Mary's tears into joy;
turn our tears into joy.
Risen Christ, you turned the travellers' despair into hope;
turn our despair into hope.
Risen Christ, you turned the disciples' fears into boldness;
turn our fears into boldness.
Risen Christ, you turned an empty catch into fullness;
turn our empty routines into fullness.
Risen Christ, you turned Thomas' unbelief into trust;
turn our unbelief into trust.

Today's step

I step
away from mistrust
towards confiding.

Spiritual breathing exercise

Love in.
Fear out.
Trust.

MARCH 30

Inward and outward pilgrimage

Bible reading

When God brought back the first wave of our exiled people, who had been treated like prisoners, we lived in a dream. We sang and laughed until we had no voice left. Then other nations started to say, 'What great things God has done for them.' God certainly did great things for us and our joy overflowed. This inspired us to pray, 'Bring back wave after wave of our exiles, until they become like the torrent of our largest river.' Farmers who sow seeds in tears, because their work is so hard, start to sing once they reap. Our nation is like that farmer: she goes off weeping and comes back singing with a great harvest.

The pilgrim psalm 126

Reflection

The outward pilgrimages of the few can inspire inward pilgrimages of the many. For us all, the physical pilgrimage is an acting out for a short period of a journey that we need to make throughout our lives.

All of us may entrust our little daily journeys to God. An ancient practice is to make the sign of the cross over our hearts and faces when we set out. This seals us with Christ's victory over the destructive powers, takes away our fears, and helps us to be fully present to our journey.

It is thought that John Bunyan, who wrote the classic book, *Pilgrim's Progress*, spent much time behind doors, and travelled little. Yet he must have traversed the inward journey of the soul more than most. He tells how he flees the City of Destruction, overcomes the Slough of Despond, is guided through the Wicket Gate to the House of the Interpreter, ascends the Hill of the Cross where he loses his burden of sin, climbs the Hill of Difficulty and passes through two chained lions. He is rested in a lodge, has a painful battle with the devil, but meets a fellow pilgrim named Faithful who is imprisoned with him in Vanity Fair. Although they escape they succumb to the Giant of Despair and are held in Doubting Castle. After more ups and downs the celestial city comes into view, but they cannot reach it unless they pass the last obstacle, the River of Death. This they do.

Pause for thought

What key phrases describe your own Pilgrim's Progress?

Prayer

Lord, I will constant be, come wind, come weather.
There's no discouragement shall make me once relent
my first avowed intent
to be a pilgrim.

No demon or foul foe
will daunt my spirit.
I know I at the end
shall life inherit.
I'll not fear what folk say
I'll labour night and day
to be a pilgrim.[20]

Today's step

I step
away from doubt
towards truth.

Spiritual breathing exercise

Faith in.
Despair out.
Eternal City.

MARCH 31

Life-long pilgrimage

Bible reading

God said to Abram, 'Leave your country, your clan and your family home for a country that I will lead you to. I will make you a great people. I will bless those who bless you, and curse those who curse you. All clans on earth will seek to be blessed in the way I will bless you.

So Abram went as God directed, with his wife Sarah, his nephew, Lot, and his increasingly prosperous extended household. He went some distance, then stopped at the holy place at Shechem, the Oak of Moreh. In the area where Canaanites had camped for a time God showed Abram that his descendants would one day be given this for permanent settlement. Abraham built an altar in that place. From there he moved on to the mountains east of Bethel, and built an altar there, too. He made his way, stage by stage, to the Negeb.

Genesis 12:1–9

Reflection

Saint Columba is thought to have preached as follows:

> God counselled Abraham to leave his own country and go in pilgrimage into the land which God had shown him, the 'Land of Promise'. Now the good counsel which the Lord had enjoined here on the father of the faithful is incumbent on all the faithful, that is to leave their country and their land, their wealth and their worldly delight for the sake of the Lord of the Elements, and go in perfect pilgrimage in imitation of him.[21]

For many early Irish Christians, like Columba, pilgrimage became a symbol of a lifelong exile from home comforts, and a lifelong journeying, dependent upon providence, guided by the Spirit, fed by Christ. It was a kind of martyrdom – a laying down of one's life for God and to serve Christ in others. It is this lifelong pilgrimage that is the primary calling of followers of the Way of Life.

Pause for thought

What hinders me from holding on to nothing, and journeying on with God alone?

Prayer

Lord, for the rest of my life
I am willing to go anywhere,
and do anything for you.
Take me, shape me, lead me
until I reach beyond this world's shores.

Today's step

I step
away from the mortal
towards the immortal.

Spiritual breathing exercise

Advance in.
Hold-back out.
Eternal pilgrim!

APRIL 1

Rhythm

Bible reading

In the beginning, when God began to evolve the cosmos, God said, 'Let there be light.' God saw that the light was good, so God separated the light from the dark. God called the light Day and the dark Night. Evening came, and morning came, making one day.

Genesis 1:1–5

Reflection

The whole world cries out for the rhythm the Creator built into it, but which we have lost. Holistic gurus offer ways to find it and music bands sing about it:

> And the rhythm of life is a powerful beat,
> puts a tingle in your fingers and a tingle in your feet,
> rhythm in your bedroom, rhythm in the street,
> yes, the rhythm of life is a powerful beat.[1]

The word 'rhythm' comes from the Greek verb, *rheo*, meaning to flow. Dictionary definitions include phrases such as a measured flow, or pattern, or regular succession – of words, of musical notes, of actions, of strong and weak elements. There is rhythm outside us, in creation, there is a rhythm inside our bodies. There are rhythms and seasons of the soul. We wish to explore the mother of all rhythms, the rhythm of a human being who reunites with the God of rhythm.

> You fall out of your rhythm when you renege on your potential and talent, when you settle for the mediocre as a refuge from the call . . . Rhythm is the secret key to balance and belonging . . . It is the rhythm . . . of a poise which is not self-centred . . .

All life came out of the ocean; each one of us comes out of the waters of the womb; the ebb and flow of the tides is alive in the ebb and flow of our breathing. When you are in rhythm with your nature nothing destructive can touch you . . . To be spiritual is to be in rhythm.²

Pause for thought

What is the aspect of rhythm you most long for? What is the rhythm you have lost?

Prayer

Restore to me, O God your rhythms that I have lost:
the rhythm of rising and sleeping,
the rhythm of rest and work,
the rhythm of breathing and walking,
the rhythm of quiet and speech,
the rhythm of loving and losing,
the rhythm of light and dark.

Today's step

I step
away from contriving
towards embracing.

Spiritual breathing exercise

Acceptance in.
Pushing out.
Rhythm.

APRIL 2

The clash between 'progress' and rhythm

Bible reading

During their long march to freedom the community of the Israelites had to halt in a desert place. They were short of food and grumbled at their leaders, Moses and Aaron. Then God said to Moses: I will shower food out of the sky (this was in the form of quails). Tell the people to go out each day and gather enough for that day only . . . However, on the last day, tell them to gather two days' worth, so that they can keep the day of rest. This is to test them to see if they will follow my directions. Every sixth day, when they cook what they bring in, they will find it is twice as much as usual.

Exodus 16:1–8

Reflection

We cannot recover rhythm in society unless we unmask what is wrong in 'progress'. Progress, as most people think of it, involves creating ever more and 'better' products that ease our labour, widen our choices, and please our appetites. Most progress concerns wealth, health, information, technology and education. This kind of progress results in more and more of everything, faster and faster. This does not come without cost. The cost is borne in the psychological, social and spiritual areas of life. Progress results in increasing stress, complexity, speed, and fragmentation. In order to avoid the pain of these, we take refuge in addictions such as drugs, drink, sex, shopping, noise, internet pornography and escapism. Material progress takes no account of our physical, financial and emotional limits. The accelerating high-speed train of progress is on a collision course with the immovable rock of human limits.

Is it possible, not to abandon progress, but to redirect it? It would take a massive counter-revolution. This counter-revolution, though buried, already has a bridgehead. Bible scholars call it the sabbath principle. Ecologists call it sustainable development. In everyday language it means you and I say 'enough is enough'. Its fruit is the restoration of godly rhythm.

Pause for thought

If you were Moses today, what limits would you propose in your political party manifesto? As you are now, what limits do you need to create in your life?

Prayer

God of Monday and of Sunday,
you have created a world of limited natural resources
and you have created humans of limited duration,
and energy.
May we accept that we are mortal.
May we stop trying to be God.
May we live in a balance of input and output.
Save us and our world.

Today's step

I step
away from too much
towards enough.

Spiritual breathing exercise

Receiving, in.
Grasping, out.
Content.

APRIL 3

Bureaucracy stifles rhythm

Bible reading

As King David grew older the thought came into his mind to take a census. His commanding officers warned: 'What is the point of diverting our energies into such a big operation when your sight is still good enough to see that our population and our recruits are increasing, and when we pray that God will continue to prosper us?' The king took no notice, so the armed services spent over nine months conducting a census, clan by clan, in order to count up how many were eligible for military service. David then realised how wrong the whole thing had been and was stricken to the heart. A prophet named Gad came to him. Gad intuited that there would be consequences – either plague, famine or a military defeat – but that David could influence which of these they would suffer by interceding with God. Seventy thousand people died in a plague.

2 Samuel 24:1–15

Reflection

Bureaucracy robs us of rhythm. A dictionary defines bureaucracy as 'government by central administration, especially regarded as oppressive and inflexible'. But we are all like this, not just King David and modern officials. For we are insecure. So we concoct some activity that we think will justify our existence. There are always consequences. Bureaucracy stifles initiative, wastes time, builds up frustration, and robs people of rhythm.

But if we are caught up in the middle of it, what can we do? King David had the honesty and courage to face up to his wrong motives and to the fact that it would bring bad consequences. God and the military leaders warned him, though at first he took no notice. Can we point out to those who impose unnecessary paperwork, data-gathering, committees, reports, and talks about talks how these undermine the very people who have to deliver results?

When this bureaucracy results in a breakdown of good rhythms, can we take the trouble to point this out to a person who has some responsibility? And when the economic, social and health effects are felt in the nation's households, can we not merely pray in our churches for an end to the suffering, but can we also pray for an end to the godless patterns which caused it?

Pause for thought

On what do I needlessly expend energy which undermines good work-life rhythms?

Prayer

God of providence,
show us how to become a people of well-being.
May we not, through vain glory,
tamper with what is good in the work we inherit
nor, through handing down unnecessary regulations,
disrespect those who have to carry them out.
Embolden us to bless regulations that enable
and to remove those that disable.

Today's step

I step
away from the unnecessary action
towards the trust that enables.

Spiritual breathing exercise

Trust in.
Bureaucracy out.
Humanness.

APRIL 4

A rhythm recovery plan

Bible reading

As the Holy Spirit says: 'Today, if you hear God's voice above the clamour of your own voices, do not harden your hearts as your forebears did at the Rebellion during their desert march to freedom. God made clear then, and makes clear now, that people who depart from God's ways lose that elusive, essential quality called Rest. So make sure that none of you become desensitised through pretending to be what you are not.

Hebrews 3:7–13

Reflection

> We commit ourselves to 'a rhythm of prayer, work and recreation'.[3]

Today we suffer from choice overload. In 1980 there were 12,000 items in the average supermarket, today there are 30,000. We suffer from technology overload: through the internet, mobile phones, laptops. We suffer from activity overload: too many invitations, commitments, relationships, tangles. We suffer from expectation overload: through advertising, government, professional and work targets. Our economies and societies are run by driven people. The result is an unprecedented epidemic of stress. We become desensitised to God by pretending that we can keep up with all this without suffering the consequences – the loss of balance, well-being and rhythm.

P. J. Curtis[4] says that the search for meaning is really the search for the lost chord. When humans discover the lost chord, the world's discord will be healed.

In this way of life we dedicate ourselves to replacing the factors that cause this dis-ease with spaces that enable rhythm to be restored.

Poor Mr Micawber, who is arrested because he cannot pay his creditors, weepingly offers this timeless warning:

observe that if someone had twenty pounds a year for his income, and spent nineteen pounds nineteen shillings and six pence, he would be happy, but that if he spent twenty pounds one shilling and six pence he would be miserable.[5] That is a parable that applies to what we expend in time and energy. Even a small adjustment of margins can make the difference between an overloaded life that makes us captive, and a life with spaces that makes us creative.

Making spaces is the gateway to good rhythm. We create a space between our overload and our limits in each area of our lives. This space can be used for emergencies occasionally, and for replenishment routinely.

Pause for thought

What causes me most stress?
What stress factor could I replace with a space?

Prayer

Make me content with little things
and not have too much stuff.
May I cease to strive for this and that
and know when enough is enough.

Give me the steel to say 'no' when I ought,
give me the strength to be,
grant me to know the divine ins and outs,
the rhythm of Trinity.

Today's step

I step
away from 'one more thing'
towards 'one less thing'.

Spiritual breathing exercise

Being in.
Overdoing out.
Life.

APRIL 5

Margins

Bible reading

Lazarus was dying. His sisters Mary and Martha asked Jesus to come. Jesus loved them all dearly. When he received the message, however, he stayed where he was for two days. Then he informed his disciples that Lazarus had died and set off with them on several days' journey to the house. Lazarus had been buried four days by the time they arrived. First Martha, and later Mary, said to Jesus, 'If you had been here, our brother would not have died.' Jesus said, 'I told you before and I say it again, if only you will believe you will see the glory of God.' He spoke in a loud voice to the corpse, 'Lazarus, come out.' Out came the dead man. Jesus said, 'Take off his funeral bindings and set him free.'

John 1:1–44

Reflection

Pastors and church workers get just as swamped as everyone else, in fact more so, for other professions have unions who have clarified duties and agreed limits. People often say 'How can a Christian refuse to meet a need?' There is an ocean of need. No human being can meet it. Jesus, in his human form, was crystal clear about this. As Henri Nouwen[6] has pointed out, Jesus' creative absences often resulted, as in this passage, in a greater work of God than did his presences.

Why, then, do we find it so hard to say no? Is it because we need to be needed? We are an insecure people. The test-tube baby generation often does not know, at a continuous, bonding level, a father and a mother's love. So to be able, emotionally, to say no we have to seek our deepest identity in God.

Try imaging yourself as an infinitely loved child of God. And try saying 'no', not because you do not care, but because you know you cannot give what is needed unless you have a rhythm of taking in as well as giving out. To learn to say no in the spirit of Jesus is the means to new life.

Pause for thought

Try praying, alone, to the Father as Jesus prayed to him until you get a sense of what you should say yes to and what you should say no to.

Prayer

Father, Mother God,
I am your child.
Meet my need to be needed.
Help me so to love myself and others,
that I can say 'yes' out of love and 'no' out of love
and trust that you will bless the outcome.

Today's step

I step
away from dependence
towards adulthood.

Spiritual breathing exercise

God-pleasing in.
Man-pleasing out.
Purr.

APRIL 6

Flow

Bible reading

Jesus was standing around observing the celebrations on the last great day of the Festival of Shelters in Jerusalem, such as the ritual pouring of water, when he shouted out: 'If anyone is truly thirsty, come to me, and believe you me you will really get a full drink. This is what the Scripture said: "Out of the believer's heart shall flow rivers of living water."' He was referring to the Spirit, which those who believed in him would receive.

John 7:37–39

Reflection

There is a connection between natural water and the spiritual which someone who is familiar with the Holy Spirit can understand. At times something inside us is so strong that it flows like a creative river. How may we understand this? Natural springs of water flow until they meet up. The more they interconnect, the greater the flow. In human lives, as the different sources deep down where our mind and our emotions, our spirit and God's Spirit interact, so our whole lives flow.

The law of flow has been described like this: Everything is energy. When energy is static its power level is low. When energy flows, at a regulated acceptable level, then it is very effective in all areas. When energy flows, at full speed, creativity as well as destruction and damage could result. The flow of energy that is most effective, most productive, most prosperous is when the outflow of energy matches the inflow of energy. No strain, no draining, no leakage of energy is experienced. The flow of energy, at the correct level, enables blockages to be removed. Balancing the flow of energy keeps everything at its optimum performance. This also applies to personal emotions, health, relationships, finances, work, love, friendship – and everything else that has meaning in your life.

John S. Dunne[7] explores themes in John's Gospel of life passing through death, light passing through darkness, and love passing through loneliness. Christ lived this flow pattern, and so may we. As we allow ourselves to flow in these patterns we discover the deep rhythm of rest in the restlessness of the heart.

Pause for thought

What stops your flow?

Prayer

Help us pluck out by the roots
Adam's sinful greed in Eden
that proved so deadly to the world.
Help us to touch the tree of the Cross
that pours out immortality on the world,
that we may flow with the new river from paradise
by which all things are made alive.

Today's step

I step
away from resistance
towards divine movement.

Spiritual breathing exercise

Spirit in.
Static out.
Flow.

APRIL 7

The poetry of the soul

Bible reading

Remember the time when you were like dead people, subservient to human whim and the rebel spirit. But through God's great love in Christ we have been brought to life. Now we are like a poem written by God, a work of art. We are created in Christ for a life of good works, for a way of life which reflects God's purpose for us.

Ephesians 2:1–10

Reflection

'Ebb tide, full tide, let life's rhythms flow': This often-repeated phrase of David Adam's captures the apostle Paul's vision that those who harmonise their life with Christ are like a poem of God. A poem that has both rhythm and beauty.

But can city dwellers find such a rhythm and beauty in their daily routines? If we are out of process, we lose our flow. The Bible uses some striking words to describe this loss: 'the Fall', 'hardness of heart', ' stiff-necked', 'barriers', 'missing the mark', 'division', 'lost'.

Yet the answer to this question is 'Yes.' Listen to Denise Levertov as she captures the joyful surprise of morning for the commuter in the restless city:

> Each day's terror
> almost a form of boredom – madness
> at the wheel and
> stepping on the gas and
> the brakes no good –
> and each day one,
> sometimes two, morning glories,
> faultless, blue, blue sometimes

flecked with magenta, each
lit from within with
the first sunlight.[8]

Pause for thought

Where do you look for beauty, and where is the rhythm flowing today?

Prayer

O Lord God of the universe,
thank you that this morning is not simply an arbitrary unit
in a random sequence of days.
Thank you that there is design, purpose and order
in your universe, because you made it so.
Thank you that there is design, order and purpose
in human life, because you have willed it so.
Thank you that there is design, order and purpose
inherent in whatever happens to me today,
because such is your nature and your plan for me.[9]

Today's step

I step
away from the accelerator
towards the hidden beauty that slowly grows.

Spiritual breathing exercise

Purpose in.
Boredom out.
Poetry.

APRIL 8

We are rhythmic creatures

Bible reading

For everything there is a season, a time to begin and a time to end:

a time to be born and a time to die;
a time to plant and a time to root out;
a time to destroy and a time to mend;
a time to weep and a time to laugh;
a time to grieve and a time to dance;
a time to throw away and a time to gather;
a time to embrace and a time to keep one's own space;
a time for quiet and a time for speech;
a time to take the offensive and a time to let things be.

Ecclesiastes 3:1–8

Reflection

We are rhythmic creatures, breathing in, then out, walking on first one foot, then another, working and resting, waking and sleeping, living and dying.

> There's the rhythm of earth's seasons that makes our blood quicken or quiet, putting bright colour in our winter cheeks, or turning our arms brown as we dig in the summer earth. And there's a splendid rhythm to the Christian year, from Advent to Christmas, Christmas to Epiphany, Epiphany to Lent, and so on through Easter and Pentecost. Just chanting those seasonal names stirs in me the realisation that as I wheel around the sun, I am enacting the drama of Christ's incarnation and death and resurrection and ascension. I bind the liturgical seasons to me, tie them spiritually on my forehead and fingers and wrists, sing them, mourn them, celebrate them.[10]

Pause for thought

Breathe deeply, from the stomach.
In, out . . .
Breathe in God, breathe out stress.
Breathe in good, breathe out bad.
Practise this rhythmic praying as you walk.

Prayer

Help me to breathe in step with you.
Help me to know the time.
Help me to go with the flow.

Today's step

I step
away from artificial constructs
towards the season.

Spiritual breathing exercise

Season in.
Façade out.
In time.

APRIL 9

Rhythm of the seasons

Bible reading

My lover said to me: 'Look, the winter is past, the rains are gone. Flowers appear on the earth. The season of singing has come, the cooing doves are heard again. The fig tree shows its first fruit, the blossoming vines spread their fragrance.' My lover browses among the lilies. Turn, my lover, and be like a gazelle or like a young stag on the rugged hills.

Verses from The Song of Songs 2:11–17

Reflection

There is a rhythm of the seasons. Leaves have to fall. Seeds have to lie fallow. Shoots have to grow. Buds have to bloom. But in every case, they first have to let go. Loss is central to our condition. Along the way there are repeated losses, of innocence, relationships, securities, energies. As Rilke puts it, 'So we live, forever saying farewell.'[11] The 'farewell' is to people, states of being, the departing moment. The only path through and beyond this suffering is the relinquishment of the desire to control, to let be, to go with the wisdom implicit in the transience of nature.

'I don't want my leaves to drop,' said the tree.
'I don't want to freeze,' said the pool.
'I don't want to smile,' said the sombre man.
'Or ever to cry,' said the fool.
'I don't want to open,' said the bud.
'I don't want to end,' said the night.
'I don't want to rise,' said the neap-tide.
'Or ever to fall,' said the kite.

They wished and they murmured and whispered,
they said that to change was a crime.

Then a voice from nowhere answered,
'You must do what I say,' said Time.[12]

Pause for thought

What do you refuse to let go of that prevents you gracefully moving into the next season?

Prayer

God be in my day, and in my sleeping.
God be in my work, and in my resting.
God be in my gain and in my losing.
God be in my growth and in my fading.
God be in my life and in my departing.

Today's step

I step
away from resisting
towards embracing.

Spiritual breathing exercise

Flow in.
Control out.
Time.

APRIL 10

Prayer in the rhythms of the sun

Bible reading

I am distraught by the noise of those who violate me, by the clamour of those who pile troubles upon me. They prowl around the city day and night spreading fraud and frenzy. Even my friend who used to join me in the daily prayers is as bad as the rest of them. I long to get away from it all to some wild place. Despite all this I am determined to call upon God. Morning, noon and night I pour out my soul and God, everlastingly enthroned, always hears me.

Psalm 55

Reflection

The scholar Joachim Jeremias observes:

> It is probable from the last words of this injunction, 'and when you lie down and when you rise', that the custom of beginning and ending each day with the confession of one God is derived.[13]

Joshua called on the people to meditate on God's law day and night (Joshua 1:6–9). The Jews who settled in their new land prayed in the rhythm of the sun's rising, zenith and setting (see, for example, Psalm 55:17). Daniel continued to do this even when he was exiled in an alien culture where it was difficult to maintain (Daniel 6:10). 'The three hours of prayer were so universally observed among the Jews of Jesus' time,' writes Jeremias, 'that we are justified in including them in the comment "as his custom was" which is made in Luke in reference to Jesus' attendance at sabbath worship' (Luke 4:16).

The early Christians continued this practice of daily prayer (Acts 2:42, 46; 3:1; 10:3, 9). The Didache (a book of teaching by the first post-apostles generation) urged Christians to pray three times a day along the lines of Jesus' teaching on prayer. Early Irish Christians related the daily rhythm of prayer to that of the sun and the moon, but references in Adomnan's Life of Columba suggest that they measured time in standard hours, perhaps by a candle or water device.

Pause for thought

The sun daily speaks out the glories of God, yet would we be dumb?

Prayer

Morning
As the sun rises so I arise with you.

Noon
As the sun rides high at noon, so I pause,
and relax,
and become aware of your presence,
true and uncreated sun,
your rays warming and renewing me.

Evening
As the sun sets in the west
so I settle down with you.

Today's step

I step
away from frenzy
towards the sun.

Spiritual breathing exercise

Ray in.
Fray out.
Calm.

APRIL 11

A regular discipline of prayer

Bible reading

When you pray, don't keep babbling out incessant shopping lists, as so many people do, thinking that the more noise you make and the more words you spew out, the more likely God is to give you what you want. Your divine Father knows what you need before you ask him. This is how you should pray:

Our Father in heaven, may you be honoured. May your civilisation come, your will be done, on earth as it is in heaven. Give us today our daily supplies. Forgive us the harm we have done to you, as we forgive those who have harmed us. Steer us away from temptation. Deliver us from evil. For yours is the authority, the power and the majesty for ever. So be it.

Matthew 6:7–13

Reflection

> We commit ourselves to a regular discipline of prayer. Ways of praying will vary according to temperament. The Community encourages a renewal of all kinds of praying (Ephesians 6:18), and we are therefore committed to discovering new ways of praying, from liturgy to tongues, contemplative prayer to celebratory praise.[14]

There are many ways of praying that we may fruitfully practice; some of these we shall explore. But there is one way, according to Jesus, that we should not pray. The main point of Jesus' teaching in this passage from Matthew's Gospel is this: In our praying, do not pressure God into giving us our selfish desires; rather, align ourselves and our world with God.

Everyone may freely address their prayers to Father, which, in the Aramaic Jesus used, was Abba. This is an inclusive, primal word. Listen to a baby anywhere in the world. Its first gurglings, long before it can differentiate between its parents' genders, are 'Abab-abab-abab'.

What we know as the Lord's Prayer is a template for our prayer throughout our days and years, it is not just a prayer to say. It is possible to take each phrase as a springboard for hours of prayer. A good starting point in prayer is to bring every need, person, situation and place that concerns us and to pray 'You be honoured' in that person or group or place.

Pause for thought

What does my prayer most resemble: a shopping list or a dialogue with someone who knows better than me?

Prayer

May you be honoured in my heart, in my home,
in my homeland.
May you be honoured in the workplace, in the war zones,
in the world.
May your will be done, in my place of need,
in their place of need.
May your economy, your civilisation, come on earth
as it is in heaven.

Today's step

I step
away from shrill demands
towards childlike trust.

Spiritual breathing exercise

Your will in.
My will out.
So be it.

APRIL 12

Liturgy

Bible reading

On the Day of Pentecost about three thousand souls were baptised. They devoted themselves to the apostles teaching, fellowship, breaking of bread, and the prayers. Day after day they met in the temple. Peter and John were on their way up to the temple for the hour of prayer at three in the afternoon when a lame man was carried past.

Acts 2:41, 42, 46; 3:1

Reflection

Many people think that half the world's churches have liturgy – a prescribed form of worship – and the other half are free of it. That is not quite correct. The root meaning of the word liturgy is 'service', and every act of worship should set aside personal whims in order to better serve God and the needs of worshippers. God has built structure into creation, and many Free Church and Pentecostal Christians now value structure that makes for more sustainable worship.

The practice of daily prayers grew from the Jewish practice of reciting prayers at set times of the day: for example, in the Book of Acts, Peter and John visit the temple for the afternoon prayers. Psalm 119:164 states: 'Seven times a day I praise you for your righteous laws.'

This practice is believed to have been passed down through the centuries from the Apostles, with different practices developing in different places. As monasticism spread, the practice of specified hours and liturgical formats developed. Around the year 484, St Sabbas began recording the liturgical practices around Jerusalem. In 525, St Benedict of Nursia wrote the first official Western manual for praying the Hours. Already well-established by the ninth century, these canonical offices consisted of eight daily prayer events and three (or four) nightly divisions (called 'nocturns', 'watches', or 'vigils'). Building on the recitation of psalms and canticles from Scripture, the Church has added or subtracted hymns, readings from the saints, and other prayers.

Fresh, contemporary resources[15] often combine the printed words with optional spaces for silence, free prayer and creative activity. If the words are said from the heart, they connect us to God and to the many others who use them, and guard against a dominant personality taking over.

Pause for thought

Good liturgy is memorable, scriptural, and participatory. It unites us with Christians of all times. It is filled with song and ensures balance.

Prayer

We praise you, O God,
we acclaim you as Lord;
all creation worships you,
the Father everlasting.
To you all angels, all the powers of heaven,
the cherubim and seraphim, sing in endless praise:
holy, holy, holy Lord, God of power and might,
heaven and earth are full of your glory.[16]

Today's step

I step
away from the windbags of worship
towards the pearls of worship.

Spiritual breathing exercise

Practised harmony in.
Mindless froth out.
Worship.

APRIL 13

Tongues

Bible reading

While Peter was still speaking the Holy Spirit fell upon everyone who listened. The Jewish believers were astonished that the gift of the Holy Spirit had actually been poured out on non-Jews. They heard with their own ears these foreigners speak in 'tongues' and praise God's greatness. At this Peter asked: 'Is there now any good reason why someone should refuse to baptise these people, for they have received the Holy Spirit in the same way that we have?'

Acts 10:44–47

Reflection

Tongues is a language not understood by the speaker which bubbles up from their spirit. There are three kinds of tongues. Every Christian can enjoy this lovely gift for use in praise to God, either alone or in meetings when everyone praises God at the same time. Sometimes there is singing in tongues, or 'singing in the Spirit'. Secondly, some people have the gift of giving a *message* in tongues at a church meeting. The apostle Paul advised the Christians who did this in Corinth to focus on just two or three messages, and to make sure that each one was interpreted by someone who sensed the meaning. Thirdly, a few people are given a tongue which is in an existing foreign language, although they have never learned it, and which is understood by a person who normally speaks that language. That is what happened on the Day of Pentecost, (Acts 2).

> Pope John Paul II taught: 'It is in fact he (the Spirit) who . . . guides tongues, works wonders and healings . . . distributes and harmonises every other charismatic gift. In this way he completes and perfects the Lord's Church everywhere and in all things.'[17]

Many Catholics have received the gift of tongues in *Life in the Spirit* seminars. One says: 'Once while praying the rosary, I felt so exhausted I prayed in tongues while the others answered with the second half of the prayers. I didn't know what I was saying, but I experienced an immediate burst of energy. God promised: "He who speaks in a tongue builds up himself" (1 Corinthians 14:4).'

Another says: 'After thanking and praising the Lord for a time we run out of ways to express ourselves – our consciousness, memory, and vocabulary are limited . . . We need the Spirit's gift of praising the Lord in another language, *the gift of tongues* (1 Corinthians 12:10).'

Pause for thought

As we grow in God's love, we realise more and more the need for the gift of tongues. Try praying in tongues.

Prayer

Father, fill me with love for you and a desire to praise you. In Jesus' name, stir up the Holy Spirit in me to pray in another language. Remove all obstacles in the way of receiving this gift. Thank you. Amen.

Today's step

I step
away from pride
towards the sounds of the Spirit.

Spiritual breathing exercise

Child-likeness in.
Hardness out.
. . . (Tongues).

APRIL 14

Contemplative prayer

Bible reading

Leave everything quietly to God, my soul. God alone suffices. God is everything to me: my rock, my rescue, my refuge. For God alone my soul waits in stillness. Nothing now can throw me.

Psalm 62:1, 5

Reflection

Although praying and singing in tongues is a quantum leap forward in our praise-power, it is still limited. Finally, our praise turns to *silence* (Zephaniah 1:7; Revelation 8:1). We are so aware of God's glory that we are rendered speechless. This type of profound silence after praise in tongues is the ultimate praise of God by a person on earth.

> There is a contemplative in all of us
> almost strangled but still alive
> who craves quiet enjoyment of the now
> and longs to touch the seamless garment of silence
> which makes us whole.[18]

St John Cassian[19] wrote of the contemplative prayer of the desert Christians: 'It reaches out beyond all human feelings. It is neither the sound of the voice nor the movements of the tongue nor articulated words. The soul, bathed in light from on high, no longer uses human speech, which is always inadequate. Like an overabundant spring, all feelings overflow and spring forth towards God at the same time.'

A few are called to an intensive life of prayer as hermits or solitaries. Many of us develop a contemplative element in otherwise busy lives. St Cuthbert was like this at first, and a full time contemplative at last. The anonymous Lindisfarne monk who wrote about Cuthbert's busy time at

Lindisfarne observed: 'Cuthbert dwelt also according to Holy Scripture, following the contemplative amid the active life.' Yet in old age, according to Bede, he 'finally entered into the remoter solitude he had so long sought, thirsted after, and prayed for. He was delighted that after a long and spotless active life he should be thought worthy to ascend to the stillness of divine contemplation.'

The difference between planned and contemplative prayer can be likened to the making of a pond. The planned way diverts water from its source and pours it into the pond. The alternative locates the pond over a spring's source. The first way of praying begins in our efforts and ends in God. The contemplative way begins in God and ends in us.

Pause for thought

God made us human beings, not human doings.

Prayer

Today I weave these prayers across my head:
silence of knowing,
clearness of seeing,
stature of waiting.

Today I weave these prayers across my heart:
humility of listening,
depth of understanding,
peace of being.

Today's step

I step
away from doing
towards being.

Spiritual breathing exercise

Deep centre in.
Surface noise out.
Calm.

APRIL 15

Celebratory praise

Bible reading

King David convened a great gathering of the people to celebrate the placing of the ark that contained God's Commandments in a central consecrated place. He asked leaders among the Levites, who were responsible for public worship, to appoint music, singing and other group leaders. Three singers had to beat time with bronze cymbals; eight had to lead praise with lutes set for soprano voices; six had to use harps set for bass voices. Chenaniah was in charge of transport. There were two warders for the ark, and seven priests who sounded the bugles in front of it. David and others danced with all their might, wearing a kilt. Indeed, the whole people advanced in procession with festal shouts, blasts of bugles, trumpets and cymbals, beating time with lutes and lyres.

1 Chronicles 15

Reflection

Most churches have an organ, keyboard, or small worship band and one or two preachers and worship leaders, but which has anything approaching the great celebration of praise which King David prepared? Yet it would be sad if we went through life without ever experiencing anything like this. That is the value of the occasional big event, when many churches come together. All kinds of musical instrument sound their notes. Massed singers, singing groups with different styles, from Black Gospel to Cathedral Chant, each offer their best. Colour in decor and artwork, skill in sound recording and visual presentation, words of encouragement and prophecy abound. Solos and guest speakers, liturgical dance and signed language, poetry and prayer processions, banners and BBQ can all play their part.

Some Christians attend regular gatherings of celebratory praise, others never do. God's people in Old Testament times came together every seventh year for a great act of praise. Just as some people determine to go on pilgrimage once, at least, in a lifetime, why not determine that you will not depart this life without experiencing some great celebration, whether in a park, cathedral or hired auditorium? And if frailty should make this impossible, at least listen in to Handel's 'Hallelujah Chorus'.

Pause for thought

In which act of celebratory praise should I aim to join?

Prayer

We give thanks to our Eternal God.
We celebrate among the peoples God's exploits.
We sing and make music to him,
rehearse the wonders God has done.
We rejoice and glory in God's name.
We worship God and be strengthened.
We worship in the divine presence for evermore.[20]

Today's step

I step
away from the box
towards greater celebration.

Spiritual breathing exercise

Celebration in.
Half-baked worship out.
Joy.

APRIL 16

Praying with icons

Bible reading

We have not ceased to pray that you will be filled with spiritual understanding, and be able to give thanks to the Father who has made it possible for you to enter in to the Light that the saints share, and to transfer to the Kingdom of God's Son.

He is the icon of the unseen God, born pre-eminent, before created things. For through him all things were created, seen and unseen.

Colossians 1:9–16

Reflection

We stand in front of an icon of a holy person or angel who reflects the divine light and draws us towards God. We stand with our eyes open and let the icon 'look' at us. We do not make up our own thoughts, we simply allow the divine attribute to which the icon points fill us. Thus, if it is, for example, an icon of Christ in glory, we soak in the divine glory. We feel it so deeply that it possesses and transforms us.

Some express the devotion this evokes with a kiss, a bow, a sign of the cross, or a prayer of love.

Christians who use icons stress that these are 'windows' that lead us more deeply into the divine presence. They are not like idols, which invite us to worship something other than God. The New Testament describes Jesus as God's icon (Hebrews 1:3) and councils of the universal church in 692 and 787 agreed that God's incarnation in Christ makes it permissible to represent God in art. Now, 'to those whose heart is pure all things are pure' (Titus 1:15). God intends us to see the invisible through the visible (Romans 1:20).

If the Word of God has been seen, touched and proclaimed, and himself proclaimed God's kingdom through visual signs, then Christ could be preached visibly as well as verbally. God wishes us to pray through our eyes as well as through our mouths.

In its rules for icon painting the Orthodox Church has taken these points most seriously. It drew up rules: only the twelve main feasts of the liturgical year and some of the saints should be portrayed. An icon should point to two kinds of time, our everyday 'clock time', and the 'Eternal Now'.

Pause for thought

Let one divine quality seep into us until it suffuses us with the obedience of angels, the humility of Mary, the life of the risen Christ, or . . .

Prayer

As I gaze into your light,
may the obedience of angels be mine,
may the joy of saints be mine,
may the humility of Mary be mine,
may the suffering of the Cross be mine,
may the freeing of the imprisoned spirits be mine,
may the glory of eternity be mine,
. . . and may it also be theirs, for whom I pray.

Today's step

I step
away from this world
towards the world redeemed by Christ.

Spiritual breathing exercise

God-seeing in.
Self-centred seeing out.
Divine.

APRIL 17

Thanksgiving

Bible reading

We urge you, dear ones, to encourage the faint-hearted, help the weak, be patient with everyone. Do not retaliate when someone behaves badly to you, but try to do good to one another. Rejoice always, pray without ceasing, give thanks in all circumstances, for this is God's will for you.

1 Thessalonians 5:14–18

Reflection

Gratitude is the root of all virtue.[21]

A good proportion of readers who live in one of the world's top twenty economies should be able to give thanks for many things that contribute to 'the good life':

Car or public transport,
health service,
heating and lighting,
water and sewage disposal,
refuse collection,
choice of foods for purchase,
salary, unemployment/disability/pension income.

Thanksgiving is not just about thanking God for the end product which we buy in the shops; it is taking time, in our mind, to go through the whole process, tracing it back to the mysterious original sources given by our sister earth, and back further to the divine source of all.

Readers everywhere, even the most destitute, should try to move into a still-deeper level of thanksgiving when we give thanks for God's unfailing self-giving and eternal blessings freely offered to every soul.

Make a habit of thanking God for something whenever you feel a grouse coming on.

Pause for thought

What eternal blessings can you think of?

Prayer

Almighty God, Father of all mercies,
we your children give you humble and hearty thanks
for all your goodness and loving-kindness to us
and to all people.
We bless you for our creation, preservation
and all the blessings of this life;
but above all for your inestimable love
in the redemption of the world by our Lord Jesus Christ,
for the means of grace and for the hope of glory.
And we beseech you,
give us that due sense of all your mercies,
that our hearts may be truly thankful,
and that we show forth your praise,
not only with our lips, but in our lives;
by giving up ourselves to your service,
and by walking before you in holiness and righteousness
all our days;
through Jesus Christ our Lord,
to whom with you and the Holy Spirit
be all honour and glory, world without end. Amen.[22]

Today's step

I step
away from complaining
towards thanksgiving.

Spiritual breathing exercise

Gratitude in.
Grumbling out.
Bliss.

APRIL 18

Chanting

Bible reading

When they returned from exile to rebuild the temple in Jerusalem they appointed Levites from twenty years old upwards to supervise the work. When the foundations were finished the priests took trumpets and Asaph's clan took cymbals to praise God according to the liturgy of King David. They chanted their praises with this refrain: 'For God is good, whose kindness never fails'.

Ezra 3:10, 11

Reflection

We are committed to discover new ways of praying. Many of the psalms were sung as chants as people walked in procession; sometimes one side sang and the other responded. Monks have always chanted, and recently their chants have hit the popular music charts. Fabrice Fitch, an early music reviewer for *Gramophone* magazine, wrote, 'Hearing the monks of Stift Heiligenkreuz chant lunchtime prayer is a contemplative experience. As the 40 voices dance around the liturgy, the effect is hypnotic, akin to the repetitive rhythm of rowing.' The choirmaster, Father Simeon, explains that the call and response repetition allows the monks to meditate. 'It is an objective form of singing but it allows for subjective emotion.' Father Karl suggests that, whether we understand it or not, plainchant 'leads the soul through different stages of feeling; it makes you sad, it gives joy, it raises the soul to heaven.' Exactly the primal response that Tom Lewis[23] felt when he heard Stift Heiligenkreuz for the first time.

One 'miracle' remains for Father Karl to explain. In two weeks in February three monks died – the first deaths at the monastery in five years and an exciting experience for the younger brothers . . . 'Death is nothing we chase away,' says Father Karl. 'We are living for this; we want to go to heaven, to paradise. The young brothers all found the funeral liturgy joyful – we think that the monks arrived at their goal – and so we chose those songs for the CD and we call the album *Music for Paradise*.'[24]

Pause for thought

Keep singing one of the chants below, or make up your own.

Prayer

Lord have mercy, Christ have mercy, Lord have mercy.

Alleluia! Alleluia! Alleluia!

Veni Sancte Spiritus (Come, O Holy Spirit come)

O come let us adore him
O come let us adore him
O come let us adore him
Christ the Lord.

Today's step

I step
away from my own prayers
towards the primal rhythm of holy chant.

Spiritual breathing exercise

Chant in.
Chatter out.
Paradise.

APRIL 19

Praying with candles

Bible reading

Each evening the worship leaders light the golden lamps in the sanctuary.

2 Chronicles 13:11

No one lights a lamp and then hides it under a piece of furniture or in a cellar. They put it on a stand so everyone who comes in can see it. Nothing is hidden that shall not come into the light and be seen by all. Be like servants who are ready for action with their wicks lit.

Luke 8:16, 17; 12:35

Reflection

A woman with drug problems was converted to Christ during a Sunday morning church service. That church was closed on weekdays, and she found the long words of the Sunday sermon difficult. But in her heart she wanted to pray. She stumbled across a church of a different tradition. It was open every day and had a place where people could light candles. She learned to pray with candles. This was a Roman Catholic church, but if you enter the Presbyterian St Giles' Cathedral, in Edinburgh, you can pray with candles there, too.

Candles symbolise that our Lord is the Light of the World. Two candles represent the two natures of Christ who is fully God and also fully human. A beautiful meaning attached to candles used in worship is that the wax, which comes from the virgin bee, symbolises our Lord's body, born of the Virgin Mary; the wick symbolises his soul; and the flame symbolises his divinity, thus setting forth the mystery of the Incarnation.

Pause for thought

May the candle I light be more than itself.
May it be:
healing for sickness,
closeness for loneliness,
comfort in mourning,
self-respect when rejected,
love to share.

May it be a moment of shining
in a tiny bit of darkness;
a hope, a prayer, a blessing.[25]

Prayer

Candlelighter Lord,
this candle that I have lit –
may it be light from you to lighten my way
through difficulties and decisions.
May it be fire from you
to burn up my selfishness, my pride
and all that is impure within me.
May it be flame from you to warm my heart
and teach me love.
Lord, I cannot stay long in your house.
This candle is a little bit of myself that I offer to you.
Help me to continue my prayer in all that I do this day.

Today's step

I step
away from darkness
towards light.

Spiritual breathing exercise

Flame in.
Cold out.
Light.

APRIL 20

Praying with stones, beads or knots

Bible reading

Engrave these commands I give you in your hearts. Repeat them each time you get home and sit down together, when you walk along the road, when you lie down and get up. Tie them round you. Display them on your doors.

Deuteronomy 6:6–9

Reflection

In later Old Testament times the extended family would gather to say the 150 psalms which they had often heard read in the synagogue. Since they could not read, they put 150 stones in a bag, took out one stone at a time and tried to remember as much as they could. If they could not remember the psalm they might think good thoughts. Early Christian monks used beads or knots in a rope. Some of them said 'Our Father' together 150 times. Over the centuries this practice evolved in various ways for use by ordinary Christians.

Roman Catholics developed a string of 55 beads. This is called the Rosary, perhaps because praying this way is like being in a rose garden. The believer holds a large bead and says the 'Our Father', then holds in turn the ten smaller beads that follow and repeats the words the angel addressed to Jesus' mother; and finally holds another larger bead and repeats 'Glory be to the Father, and to the Son and to the Holy Spirit . . . ' This is repeated. When this is recited very often it becomes like background mood music and frees the mind to think about the life of Jesus. On one day, a person may think about the birth and childhood of Jesus, taking one episode for each ten beads. These are named the Joyful Mysteries. On another day they think about five episodes in the suffering and death of Jesus. These are named the Sorrowful Mysteries. Pope John Paul II introduced the 'Mysteries of Light' – Jesus' works in spreading God's kingdom on earth. Lastly, they think of the resurrection of Christ and of those most close to him, and of the coming of the Holy Spirit. These are named the Glorious Mysteries.

Some Christians use the Jesus Rosary. This is similar to the above, but all prayer is addressed to Jesus directly. The Swedish Lutheran Bishop Martin Lonnebo has introduced the Pearls of Life, a bracelet of different-coloured pearls including a desert, love, serenity, night and resurrection pearl. The largest is the golden God pearl. As we hold each pearl in turn we think and feel its meaning for us.[26]

Pause for thought

Try using a stone, bead or knot in a way that is new to you.

Prayer

Come into every heart, O Jesus,
knock, knock on our hearts.
Be patient and untiring.
We are still closed because
we have not yet understood your will.
Knock perseveringly.[27]

Today's step

I step
away from disordered praying
towards ordered praying.

Spiritual breathing exercise

Jesus in.
Muddle out.
Peace.

APRIL 21

Work is a gift from God

Bible readings

Every work that King Hezekiah undertook he did with all his heart and prospered.
2 Chronicles 31:21

Whatever your hand finds to do, do it with all your might.
Ecclesiastes 9:10

Work with enthusiasm, as if you were serving God, not mortals, knowing that we will receive pay-back from God for whatever good we do, whether we are at the top or the bottom of the ladder.
Ephesians 6:7, 8

Reflection

> We welcome work as a gift from God. Every member should engage in work, whether it be the routine activities of life or paid employment. Work motivated by values which conflict with the Way should be avoided as much as possible. In humility we accept what God gives us. If we have no employment and are not clear what our work is, then we seek the advice of our soul friend. We seek not to overwork, standing firm against all pressure to do so, because it robs ourselves, others or God of the time we should give to them.[28]

All human beings resemble God in certain ways (Genesis 1:26). It is our nature, like God's, to create. We are co-creators with God. Work reflects our divine calling, it is a blessing of creation, not a result of human sin. Sin has, however, marred and distorted the way work is experienced. The Christian's task is to redeem it. Curse will come upon us if our motive is to treat the world as a cake, from which we get a bigger slice for ourselves. Blessing, which selfishness denies us, is the true birthright of the world of work.

In a true understanding of work the owners of capital, managers and employees work together like fingers on a hand to serve the needs of the world, all aware that the hand is an instrument of God. This is not how work is usually thought of in the Western world. When a person says they are 'out of work' they usually mean they have no work for which they are paid wages. Every person has compassion, energy, talents which they put either to good or to poor use.

God calls us to undertake work that is valid and to do it with all our heart, as an offering to God.

'Labour without joy is base.'[29]

Pause for thought

Does our work go beyond good management into heartfelt participation?

Prayer

Your glory be seen in work that is done from the heart.
Your glory be seen in work that meets true needs.
Your glory be seen in communication
that ennobles the spirit.
Your glory be seen in beauty of form and friendship.

Today's step

I step
away from slapdash actions
towards heartfelt participation.

Spiritual breathing exercise

Heartfelt work in.
Careless work out.
Blessing.

APRIL 22

Each of us has some work to do

Bible reading

In the days when landowners employed servants to manage the affairs of their estates, they would look for a faithful and wise person to put in charge of each household's day-to-day running, such as making sure that good meals were served on time. If the owner made an unexpected return and found the housekeeper maintaining everything well, he and the servants would be happy, and he would promote the housekeeper to be in charge of all his estates. On the other hand, if the housekeeper assumed that the owner would not return just yet, and so mistreated the servants and neglected duties, the owner would in fact return unexpectedly, see the damage, and put the housekeeper under discipline – what a miserable end.

Matthew 24:45–51

Reflection

> Usefulness is the rent we pay for the privilege of living on earth.[30]

The point of Jesus' story is that each of us is given something to do, and each of us is meant to be alert, aware, so that we do our best, do what is appropriate in each situation. We may be resting or playing; in old age our work may be prayer or keeping plants watered – that does not matter. What does matter is that whatever is given to us, whether it be little or much, we do well.

Pause for thought

What, today or tomorrow, needs your best thought in order that you do it well?

Prayer

I do my work as to you, Lord,
I think my thoughts as to you.
I clean my room as to you, Lord,
I send messages as to you.
I shop and eat as to you, Lord,
I care for others as to you.

Today's step

I step
away from the shoddy
towards the best I can give.

Spiritual breathing exercise

Care in.
Carelessness out.
Happiness.

APRIL 23

Values in work

Bible reading

Moses gave this briefing to his people: When you cross the river into your new land, these specified leaders shall go to Mount Gerizim and proclaim blessings that will come to the people if they do right and obey God's commands. These other specified leaders shall go to Mount Ebal and proclaim calamities that shall befall the people if they do wrong and disobey God's commands. Here is an example of what you should enact: If you make an idol of something but conceal what you are doing the leader shouts: 'A calamity on that person.' And all the people reply: 'So be it.' Calamities will come on those who do not respect rights to life and property, the rights of the disabled, asylum seekers, spouses and animals. But if you listen to God's voice blessings will come upon your work and your produce, your trades and your finances, your enterprises and your cities.

Deuteronomy 27:11–28:14

Reflection

Most things may be used for good or for ill purposes. It is like that with capitalism. Capital, and profit, may be raised in good or bad ways and used to bless or curse the world. Christian social teaching says that profit should not be an end in itself, but a consequence of delivering a greater good. Most of our jobs are interconnected. They involve a chain of many elements – good, bad and indifferent. So we need discernment. Is the primary product something that meets a true need? Can I play my part in the process without being dishonest? If Jesus were in my shoes when I have to make a decision would he stay on the job, what would he decide, and how would he relate to colleagues, superiors, suppliers and customers?

Here is an example of the shared values of a business:

We give our personal best,
we take responsibility for identifying and developing skills,
we have as much responsibility for the worth and dignity of others as we do for ourselves,
we share knowledge necessary for others to achieve,
we follow through on tasks in a timely manner,
we communicate information and concerns in a clear and appropriate manner,
we communicate with kindness, openness and honesty,
we expect the best from one another,
we respect confidentiality,
we admit mistakes and honour commitments.

Pause for thought
Why not have a stab at writing a statement of values for your work situation?

Prayer
Provider of all, may employers, employees and shareholders work together like fingers on your hand,
stretched out for the common good.
Workday Christ, may I offer my best even when others fail.
Sustaining Spirit, may the wealth and work of the world be available to all and for the exploitation of none.

Today's step
I step
away from perfunctory practices
towards prayerful work.

Spiritual breathing exercise
Good values in.
Bad values out.
Quality.

APRIL 24

To work is to pray

Bible reading

Don't only work when your boss has an eye on you, like those people who live to curry favour, but work with simplicity of purpose, as an expression of the honour you give to God. Whatever the work you do, do it with all your heart, as something you do for God, and not for mortals. You can be sure of this, you will inherit a reward from God that is true payment. The One you ultimately serve is Christ, the Lord over all. God will bring to account any person who abuses their position. God believes in equal opportunity and fair employment.

Colossians 3:22–25

Reflection

When Noel Dermot O'Donoghue was a child in the south-west of Ireland every step in the working day had a prayer to go with it. He writes, 'The seedsman is his own priest. The work is equally labour and liturgy.'[31] We should try to hold to this ideal of praying over everything we do even if we feel trapped in work which is depersonalised, degrading or which misuses people or the created world. If we are trapped in such work, we may have to make decisions about leaving, confronting or patiently bearing it.

The word 'agriculture', which means 'cultivation of the land', retains the Celtic understanding of the intimate relation between human work and earth's work. Only when that relation, in high-tech industry, commerce, as well as in agriculture, is one of care and prayer, does either earth or human society experience the fullness of blessing that is inherent in them both.

Faith needs to be exercised. For example, I can act as if my workmates, bosses and customers are cherished fingers of God's hand even though they do not treat me or others in that way.

Pause for thought

May we do everything, whether it be programming the computer, making the tea, or carrying loads, with love.

Prayer

Worker Christ, as we enter our workplace,
may we bring your presence with us.
Grace us to speak your peace and perfect order
into its atmosphere.
Remind us to acknowledge your authority
over all that will be thought, decided
and accomplished within it.
Give us a fresh supply of truth and beauty
on which to draw as we work.[32]

Today's step

I step
away from careless work
towards mindful work.

Spiritual breathing exercise

Thoughtful in.
Slapdash out.
Worth.

APRIL 25

Long-term unemployment

Bible reading

I, Paul, a church leader who is now old and under house arrest, write this appeal to you, Philemon, a wealthy person who employs slaves, and who has become my spiritual child. I write to you about Onesimus, who escaped from your employment. He is a fellow Christian. After his escape he joined me here. He was not that much use to you, but he was enormously useful to me. Now I am sending him back to you, through his choice and mine, even though I shall miss him dearly. I appeal to you. He is now not just your slave, he is your brother. So, if you have regard for me, have regard for him, too. Welcome him back. I will pay you any compensation you think you should have, though, if you think about it, you owe me far, far more – your very self, your eternal life. Knowing you as I do, I am sure you will do even more than I ask.

Paul's Letter to Philemon

Reflection

You, or someone you know, may suffer from long-term unemployment. You may feel isolated, at the bottom of the social pile, the victim of neglect, vandalism and despair. You cannot imagine how you could go back to regular employment. Onesimus, who was forcibly employed as a slave without rights, ran away. He became a Christian and joined the worldwide Christian family where each person is treated as a brother or sister. Through Paul's mediation, we presume his former boss, who was a Christian, welcomed him back. There was a new sense of worth, a new relationship, a new motivation. That is possible today, too.

You feel useless, drained and that you cannot work? Hear these words of Jesus: 'My child, I made you. I love you. I have planted all kinds of seeds within you. Let me water one or two, and pour my sunshine upon them. I know what these seeds are, but I want you to tell me what *you* think they are. Confide in me a hope that you have not dared name. Share that hope with one of my friends. Talk through with your friend what you might do to make this hope come true. Take one small step, and then another. Your worth is not measured by your pay, but by the amount of love you give me. I know how much effort it takes you to take one small step. This means so much to me. It is of great worth.'

Pause for thought

Take that step.

Prayer

Bring to flower in your children the seeds that dormant lie:

in those who have none to encourage them
bring the seeds of confidence to flower,
in those who are trapped by their circumstances
bring the seeds of possibility to flower,
in those who find it difficult to learn
bring the seeds of understanding to flower,
in those at the bottom of the social pile
bring the seeds of empowerment to flower.

Today's step

I step
away from 'can't do'
towards 'can do'.

Spiritual breathing exercise

Belief in.
Despair out.
Hope.

APRIL 26

Rest

Bible reading

During the period Jesus was spreading the message of God's kingdom among the cities he prayed these words aloud while he was with his disciples: 'I thank you Father that you have hidden these things from people of arrogant intellect and revealed them to the childlike. Come to me, all you people who are weighed down with heavy loads and I will give you rest.'

Matthew 11:28–30

Reflection

> The hours of rest and recreation are as valuable as the hours of prayer and work. The Lord Jesus reminds us that 'the sabbath was made for humankind, and not humankind for the sabbath' (Mark 2:27). In the Scriptures even the land was given a sabbath in the seventh year (Leviticus 25:3–5). The need for rest was built into creation (Genesis 2:1–3). A provision for this kind of rest, which is both holy and creative, should be part of each member's personal Way of Life.[33]

In the Bible passage Jesus speaks to those who are overburdened. Why are we overburdened? For some, we have no choice; like slaves one task after another is forced upon us. For most of us we have a choice. We are over burdened because we allow ourselves to get caught up in too many tasks and tussels. Christ says that if we lay down our burdens and take his burden, he will give us rest. How can this be? Christ clarifies our priorities. We stop doing things and engaging in issues that do not advance eternity's agenda. We find a rhythm of prayer, work and rest.

Three enemies of physical recreation are lack of sleep, poor conditioning and obesity. Recreation begins with rest. Rest is not just a nice idea, it is a medical necessity and part of the divine pattern. The hours of rest and recreation are as valuable as the hours of prayer and work.

Many people exist through their work. When their work is taken away they have a feeling of non-existence or emptiness. So they fill up the void with new forms of work that do not flow out of their inner being. They disregard the law of laying down burdens.

Pause for thought

What conflict of interest do I need to give back to Christ?

Prayer

Christ of the gentle heart
I place myself under you.
I plan my diary by your priorities.
I direct my feet along your way.

Help me to
see clearly
act courageously
and move on calmly
day by day.

Today's step

I step
off the treadmill
under your supervision.

Spiritual breathing exercise

Christ in.
Yuck out.
Rest.

APRIL 27

Make rest a habit

Bible reading

And he came out and proceeded **as was his custom** to the Mount of Olives; and the disciples followed him. When he was settled there, he said, 'Pray that you do not succumb to temptation.' He went alone to a spot about a stone's throw away from them, knelt down and prayed.

Luke 22:39–41

Reflection

Apparently, Jesus had taken time out on the Mount of Olives with some regularity and with the awareness of the disciples. Even God rested, so why should we think that we can avoid a rhythm of restful withdrawal in our lives?

If someone were to look at your life right now and write about it, what text would surround the words, 'as was his/her custom?' Would it say, 'And he came out from work very late and tried to pray just before sleeping and dozed off as was his custom'? Or 'And she found herself constantly in a rush while never completing her 'to do' list as was her custom'? Or 'He slammed more coffee and just kept moving, but could never seem to find any peace or joy as was his custom'?

When the fourth-century hermit St Antony first lived in the desert he became listless and unfocussed. Then he noticed another hermit who for a period stood up in prayer, and then for another period sat down and worked at his rope-plaiting, and who repeated this rhythm. Antony felt this was God's angel sent to advise him. From that time he maintained a prayer-work rhythm.

'Rest' is a God-given principle for creation and human society, as well as for individuals. Churches sometimes fail to model the principle of rest. A vicar once explained that he had to work on his day off because there was no one else to do what was needed. A little later the curate confessed that he had had an affair with someone else's wife because there was no one to do what he needed. When those present expressed horror he explained that he had made up this story, because he wanted them to feel similar horror at the vicar breaking the fourth commandment as they did at him breaking the seventh commandment!

Pause for thought

Have you a weekly or a regular custom that safeguards a space for rest in your life?

Prayer

I place my soul and body under your shaping, O God.
Shape my times of rest.
Shape my times of zest.
Change the fretting moth that eats away my peace
into sweet rest in you.

Today's step

I step
away from godless calls
towards godly custom.

Spiritual breathing exercise

Order in.
Chaos out.
Sabbath.

APRIL 28

Exercise and diet

Bible reading

The child developed in body and spirit. *Luke 1:80*

Jesus walked ahead of the others on the way up to Jerusalem. *Luke 19:28*

I harden and master my body. *1 Corinthians 9:27*

Physical exercise has some value. *1 Timothy 4:8*

Reflection

Samson was a strong man only so long as he kept his vow to serve God with unshaven hair (Judges 16). Daniel and his God-fearing friends were stronger and in better condition than their other work colleagues when they followed their conscience as to their diet and ate no unhygienic meats (Daniel 1:15). The first apostles did hard, manual labour, such as fishing, which kept them strong and fit. Jesus did long-distance walking, and, like so many God-guided Bible people, climbed mountains.

Don't you realise that your bodies are temples of the Holy Spirit? asked the apostle Paul (1 Corinthians 6:19). To be good stewards of our hearts we need exercise three or four times a week. Those who don't like sports and gyms get this through fast walking or swimming. We need to renew muscles and sustain endurance. If we do not use them, in natural work or in exercises, we lose them. We should aim to be supple. Gentle stretching and flexibility exercises can be combined with meditation. Only some are called to be athletes, but all are called to be 'fit for purpose' as far as it lies with us.

Avoid too much fat, sugar and processed foods. Eat smaller portions more slowly. Enjoy fresh fruit, vegetables and whole grains. The occasional treat harms no one.

Pause for thought

If you are poisoning, neglecting or overloading your body, what can you do about it?

Prayer

God, make me fit for purpose,
alive in heart and limb.
God, stretch my creaking body
until it tingles and feels trim.

Put fibre in my being,
take flabbiness away,
strengthen what is weak,
keep binge and bulge at bay.

May my body be a temple
of your Spirit who is true,
a picture frame on earth
of eternity on view.

Today's step

I step
away from flabbiness
towards fitness.

Spiritual breathing exercise

Exercise in.
Flab out.
Fitness.

APRIL 29

Sustaining physical energy

Bible reading

If people build a house their own way, and not God's way, they waste their labour. If people try to create a secure city without God, their security systems are futile. If you overwork, get up too early and go to bed too late, until anxiety gnaws away at you, it is all in vain. God wants to give you sleep times.

Psalm 127:1, 2

Reflection

God endows us with physical energy and desires that, as far as we are able, we live in a way that replenishes that energy. Three factors drain us of energy: poor physical condition, lack of sleep, and obesity. When we fail to make provision for exercise, relaxation and sleep, we become depleted and overwhelmed. We then have no energy for our own needs or those of others. Although modern medicine has banished many ancient infections, 'diseases' of modern lifestyle increase; these are caused by our bad habits and poor choices. 'Progress' brings plenty and education, but not the inner discipline that is needed to sustain good physical health.

Dr Richard Swenson[34] prescribes actions that break the habit disorders of poor nutrition, poor exercise and poor sleep hygiene. When possible, retire to and rise from bed at the same each day. If you are wakeful in the night, to avoid becoming stressed, relax and read or pray until you become drowsy and sleep comes again. Take short naps once or twice a day, eat less packaged food. Put smaller portions on your table. Take longer to chew and savour each mouthful. Grow food or buy locally when this is possible. Drink plenty of water. Put smaller portions of food on your plate.

Exercise enough to sweat, whether it is brisk walking, swimming or something more strenuous. Thirty to forty-five minutes of sustained exercise three or four times a week is needed to keep the heart, lungs and blood vessels in good condition. If we do not use our muscles we lose them: so use them! Flexibility exercises keep us supple and give us good deportment.

Pause for thought

Review your exercise and diet.

Prayer

Grant me grace to
eat well
think well
and move well
until my body, mind and soul
are truly a temple of your Holy Spirit.

Today's step

I step
away from junk food
towards good food.

Spiritual breathing exercise

Exercise in.
Sloth out.
Well-being.

APRIL 30

Recreation

Bible reading

God took time to look at all that he had made, and how good it was! Thus on the sixth day the vast array that makes up the cosmos was finished. On the seventh God desisted from work. He used the seventh day to bless and honour the creation – that is why God refused to work.

Genesis 1:31–2:3

Reflection

In the parable of creation with which the Bible begins, the Creator rests on the seventh day. Not because the Creator was exhausted; the seventh day was a living, vibrating space for the enjoyment of what had been created. The intention of the created order has always been, not that we rest from work, but that we work from rest. We are more fruitful when we live according to God's patterns. That is the value of building in spaces for rest that bring renewal to our life and work.

> God gave ten commands to his people through Moses. The command to keep the sabbath largely defined Israel's life as a nation which preserved human dignity. When St Patrick was on extended mission work he rested on Sundays. He urged everyone, not just Christians, to observe Sunday rest. When some workers mocked him for his views he used the Irish word 'Mudebroth' – meaning 'The God who judges'. He told his mockers, 'However hard you work, you will achieve nothing.' That is what happened. A gale undid the building work they had begun.[35]

Continuous production lines and continual information overload threaten to steal our space and time. So rest is a moral issue. It is about not stealing time that belongs to another. To switch off the computer, to forego that journey, to delay shopping until the next day are not ends in themselves, they enable us to savour the wonder of life and of its Creator.

Pause for thought

How do you keep Sunday special? How do you make a personal day of rest?

Prayer

The glory of God in my working,
the glory of God in my thinking,
the glory of God in my speaking,
the glory of God in my eating,
the glory of God in my hearing,
the glory of God in my meeting.

Today's step

I step
away from fret
towards rest.

Spiritual breathing exercise

Relaxing in.
Pushing out.
Re-creation.

MAY 1

Live simply

Bible reading

'Think about this story-with-a-truth-in-it,' said Jesus. 'A farmer scattered seed in different places.

'One group of seed fell on the hard path. This is like someone whose head is so full of unsorted stuff that any bad guy can snatch away what God sowed in their heart. Another batch of seed fell on stony ground; but because it had no root it died in the scorching sun. This is like the seed that begins to grow in a person's heart, but as soon as opposition comes they cave in. A third lot of seed fell among weeds; it began to grow well, but the weeks choked it. This is like someone who lets frenetic pre-occupations and the lure of wealth take over their lives. A fourth group of seed fell on good soil, grew to maturity and bore varying amounts of good fruit. This is like the person who listens to God's word, cultivates it, and puts it into action. Their fruit will be everlasting.'

Matthew 13:1–23

Reflection

We wish to live simply that others may simply live.[1]

To live simply is to be authentic – to remain true to our origins in God. We cease to live simply when we swerve off course. Jealousy diverts our energy: we accumulate too much. Pride subverts our ego: we compete too much. Anger replaces love: we lash out too much. This splits our being and creates pain. To cope with the pain we cling, like limpets, to attachments. We become attached to persons, belongings, fantasies, addictive substances and habits. This complicates our lives no end. Confused thoughts and activities multiply.

In order to live simply we take time to nurture the divine seed within us, through meditation. We live simply for good. We are like the seed that grows deeper in the soil of wisdom and bears fruit. 'To live simply that others may simply live' was a slogan used by Christian Aid. It makes the point that, although to live simply helps us to walk more closely with God, it also frees up energies and resources that may make the difference between life and death for people in extreme poverty. We are one world. The surfeited lifestyle of folk in one country may mean no food, water or income for those in another.

Pause for thought
What can I give up that complicates my life and steals resources that are needed more by others?

Prayer
Help me
to live simply that others may simply live.
Free me from false attachments
that I may be
true to myself,
true to others
and true to you.

Today's step
I step
away from attachments
towards my true self in God.

Spiritual breathing exercise
I am.
You are.
Simple.

MAY 2

Don't compare yourself with others

Bible reading

Don't look down on anyone as if you were a judge in a court trying to find out all their faults; if you do that, others will treat you in the same way. The degree to which you write off others will be the degree to which they write off you. What you give out is what you receive. Don't be like someone who points out a speck in a neighbour's eye and offers to take it out, while all the time they have a log in their own eye! Don't be a hypocrite. Start with yourself. Take that log out.

Matthew 7:1–5

Reflection

> We wish to avoid any sense of judging one another; and God will make different demands of each of us.[2]

The story of two fourth-century spiritual fathers of the Egyptian desert helps us to see that the Holy Spirit can work in people of opposite types and that we should neither judge nor compare them. Arsenius, the senior educator in the imperial palace, embraced silence when he became a hermit even to the extent of refusing to talk to visitors. Moses, the dashing bandit, when he was converted and became a hermit, loved to feed and converse with guests. When a monk asked which of the two one should prefer, a wise abba described a vision he'd had of two boats sailing along the river Nile. Arsenius was in one, and total silence reigned. Moses was in the other, which overflowed with honey cakes and conversation. But the Holy Spirit poured from heaven in equal measure upon each of the boats.[3]

God may call one person to live simply by withdrawing from the world, and another person to pour their life into active service, which is what Dietrich Bonhoeffer meant by a 'Christian worldliness':

> By this worldliness I mean living unreservedly in life's duties, problems, successes and failures, experiences and perplexities. In so doing we throw ourselves completely into the arms of God, taking seriously, not our own sufferings, but those of God in the world – watching with Christ in Gethsemane.[4]

Pause for thought

Forget what others do, what does it mean for *you* to adopt a simple lifestyle?

Prayer

Christ of carefree compassion,
may I do on earth
what you have given me uniquely to do.
And keep me in the beautiful attitudes:
simple, caring and unjudging.

Today's step

I step
away from comparisons
towards the service to which I am called.

Spiritual breathing exercise

Calling in.
Comparing out.
Your style.

MAY 3

Steward your income

Bible reading

Be shrewd in the way you use money. If you make more friends through your use of it, you will have more friends to welcome you into heaven. If you handle even small amounts of money with integrity, you can be trusted to handle larger amounts. If you are dishonest in small amounts, you will be dishonest with big amounts. How can you be entrusted with eternally important responsibilities if you have not been a faithful steward of this world's currency? If you have not been faithful with investments that belong to another, how can God invest in you? You cannot serve two bosses – you will either hate one and love the other, or be attached to one and reject the other. You cannot serve both God and money.

Luke 16:8–13

Reflection

> Our common responsibility is to regularly hold before God (and as appropriate to share with our soul friend) our income, our savings, our possessions, conscious that we are stewards, not possessors of these things, and making them available as God requires.[5]

If we are of an age to work, we should do our best to find a job and do it well. This may mean a contract and a wage; or it may mean we give friends a hand in return for provisions. We may get any short-term job in order to finance some project; later, we find a longer-term job that best suits our temperament, talents and sense of call. Sometimes we have to accept a job we would not choose, but still we give it our best.

We try to earn what we need. If we live simply, our need is less and the pressures reduce. We do not buy things with money we do not have, unless, say, a mortgage repayment is based on a realistic proportion of a seemingly secure income. Debt is a major reason why many believers are not free to respond to the call of God on their lives. Some of us are addicted to spending as a way of shoring up our self-image. We cannot serve two bosses. We talk all these things through with our soul friend, including how we may find our self-worth in God rather than in things we buy.

Pause for thought

How can you best use whatever you have?

Prayer

God of providence,
help me to use what I have for the best.
Give me wisdom.
Give me prudence.
Give me flair.
May my investments in this earth bear fruit.

Today's step

I step
away from misuse of money
towards good use of money.

Spiritual breathing exercise

Thrift in.
Spendthrift out.
Good.

MAY 4

Steward your savings

Bible reading

The kingdom of God, said Jesus, is like this: A wealthy owner of a multi-national company took time out. He summoned three managers, and gave them responsibilities. To one he gave a large sum of money, to another a medium amount, and to a third a small amount, which he allocated according to their potential. When he resumed operations these three managers accounted to him for their use of the money. The first and the second had traded their money and doubled it. The third person, however, was so frightened that she might lose it that she had hidden it in a safe place. 'Well done,' the owner congratulated the first two, and offered them great opportunities. The third person lost her job.

Matthew 25:14–30

Reflection

Some of us have no money to save. We can, however, save things that give us nutrition, beauty or memories. Some of us cannot save because we are in debt. We can start now to reduce the debt, make a plan, spend less, and repay something as soon as we can. A mother's electricity was cut off because she did not pay her bills. I advised her to put her weekly allowance into three jars – one for food, one for electricity and the rest which she was free to spend or save.

The same principle holds for those who have the ability to handle larger sums of money. 'The kept dollar is a stinking fish,' said Andrew Carnegie, the great American philanthropist. 'It should be used either to make more money or to do good.' If we invest, make sure that we invest in what is ethical. Do not invest in a finance institution which makes profit by misusing the earth, abusing people, or whose debts are greater than their assets. If we have the talent to make profit, judge the profit by the good it does, not merely by its financial return.

Pause for thought

Pray over the money that is left after you have paid for essentials. How can you best invest it?

Prayer

Good be on you, gift from heaven.
Wisdom be on you, gift from heaven.
Restraint be on you, gift from heaven.
Thought be on you, gift from heaven.
The Blesser be on you, gift from heaven.

Today's step

I step
away from procrastination
towards wise investment.

Spiritual breathing exercise

Usefulness in.
Wasting out.
Well done.

MAY 5

Support God's economy

Bible reading

When you come across anything that belongs to another you are to restore it to its owner. You shall not misuse your powers to influence lawmakers in order to defraud the poor. Never take a bribe. Do not use aliens as cheap labour. Take stock every seventh year, and find a way for those who have little – and for the wildlife – to benefit from your six years of surplus. Provide good working conditions for everyone in the work chain.

Exodus 23:4, 6, 9–12

Reflection

We are stewards, not possessors.[6]

'There is enough in the world for everyone's need but not for everyone's greed,' said Mahatma Gandhi, yet global economics has become so complicated that many of us have abdicated our responsibilities. The term 'God's economy' is now being used as a call for us all to participate. In the Bible the word 'oikonomia' refers to a dispensation of good stewardship. An oikos means a household, and nemo means to manage. The whole global system is described as God's oikos in Ephesians chapter 1. We are called to manage it as stewards, as in Jesus' parables of the vineyard labourers (Matthew 20) and the unjust steward (Luke 16).

Emerging theologians such as Ched Myers apply aspects of the biblical sabbath principle to modern socio-economics. Myers states that 'God's people are instructed to dismantle, on a regular basis, the fundamental patterns and structures of stratified wealth and power, so that there is "enough for everyone". This emphasises the voluntary redistribution of wealth which replaces the "weakest must go to the scrap heap" creed of greedy market-driven economics. It is a modern application of the Jubilee Year principles instituted by Moses, when every forty-nine years debts were cancelled and property returned to its owners, and of the Sabbath Year when land was allowed to renew itself and slaves were released.[7] Christians of this generation have engaged in campaigns to end un-repayable debts that prevent responsible initiatives in Africa from succeeding.

Pause for thought

It is said that if multinational companies paid the tax due on their holdings in Africa, instead of placing their profits in tax havens elsewhere, no aid programmes would be needed. Can we morally challenge this if we ourselves are dishonest in our tax payments?

Prayer

God our provider, source of all,
re-awaken in us our dependence upon you.
Help us to share enough and care enough
so that everyone has enough.

Today's step

I step
away from dishonourable financial practices
towards good stewardship.

Spiritual breathing exercise

Sharing in.
Hoarding out.
Sabbath.

MAY 6

Steward our possessions

Bible reading

Do not accumulate possessions on this earth, where moths consume, rust corrodes and thieves break in and steal. It is much better to accumulate treasures in heaven where neither moth nor rust destroy and where thieves do not break in and steal. For where your treasure is, there will your heart be also.

Matthew 6:19–21

Reflection

Friends of mine had a spacious house full of nice things they had accumulated over the years. Then they visited India, and witnessed people who had nothing and yet lived with dignity. On their return, they scrutinised every item they possessed and asked themselves 'Do we really need this?' If the answer was no, they got rid of it.

Another friend has an ancestral home, packed with family heirlooms. She thought she could not vow to live a simple lifestyle if she owned such a home. But I drew out of her that she had been given this to steward for future generations and that she used it generously to provide hospitality. She had given up wearing jewellery and was quite willing, on her own account, to pass the house on to others – but to do so would betray a trust. So she, unlike others, could be at peace about having a second home.

When we have strong energies we may require all sorts of things in order to achieve legitimate goals. A lone parent with five children obviously needs more items in the house than others. Each child needs things to play and learn with that suit their age and aptitude. For such a family, a simple lifestyle might mean giving away items that have been outgrown, and sharing what they have with friends.

After children have 'left the nest', and as we get older, it is appropriate to scale down our possessions. We cannot take them with us when we leave this life. It is unkind to leave a mess for our next of kin to clear up.

Some of us give something away every time we are given something.

Pause for thought

Do a stock-check of your possessions in the light of eternity. Get rid of everything you do not need.

Prayer

O God, you have fashioned us for joy,
grant us to find it:
in the wild flower's beauty,
or a mother's love.
Our society is ever restless,
always craving one more thing to do,
seeking happiness through more and more possessions.
Teach us to be at peace with what we have.
To embrace what we have given and received;
to know that enough is enough
until our strivings cease
and we rest content in you alone.

Today's step

I step
away from acquisitiveness
towards eternal treasure.

Spiritual breathing exercise

Acceptance in.
Grasping out.
Contentment.

MAY 7

Set things in simple beauty

Bible reading

Balaam the seer saw the tented dwellings of the people of Israel stretching out in the desert below him. God's Spirit touched him until he uttered these lines: The oracle of the seer who hears God speak and sees a vision of the Almighty.

> How beautiful are your tents, O Israel:
> like glens that stretch far into the distance
> like gardens by a river
> like oaks planted by God
> like cedars beside a stream.
>
> *Numbers 24:2–6*

Reflection

> A simple lifestyle means setting everything in the simple beauty of creation. Our belongings, activities and relationships are ordered in a way that liberates the spirit; we cut out those things that overload or clutter the spirit.[8]

This may seem unrealistic, for surely in the vast kaleidoscope of human life there is room for extremes of taste, including those things that are dark and painful? Certainly. But whatever our taste, we apply the principle of purity. Plants and minerals are varied and unique, yet they do not fuss or try to be what they are not. A simple lifestyle does not mean that it is shoddy. Beauty is important. It is better to spend more on one item of beauty than on ten items of trash. The Shaker communities of USA, an off-shoot of Quakers, espouse elegant simplicity. Their furniture is still famed for this quality. Think about the rooms we live in. How can we position furniture, decorate or leave bare the walls, 'cure' problem areas, arrange their spaces, artefacts, colours in a harmonious way that is welcoming, relaxing, enriching?

The point is to have only what we need – and that may include things that feed our own and others' bodies, minds or spirits. How do we discern what choices to make? We may learn by asking advice from those who know about interior design, for example. But ultimately, we ourselves have this simple measure for each choice we make: Does it free or overload my spirit?

Pause for thought

Ask this question of each thing in your house; does it liberate or clutter my spirit?

Prayer

May our homes reflect your presence
coming through the personalities you have given us.
Grace us to express your peace and perfect order into them.
Remind us to acknowledge your authority
over all that will be thought, purchased and arranged.
Give us a fresh supply of truth and beauty on which to draw
as we relax, entertain, work and sleep.

Today's step

I step
away from the shoddy
towards simple beauty.

Spiritual breathing exercise

Quality in.
Rubbish out.
Beautiful.

MAY 8

Activities

Bible reading

Jesus likened the way we discharge our duties to a wise manager whom the landowner leaves in charge. When the landowner returns he finds the manager carrying out each duty, whether it is to do with food or finance, mindfully and at the appropriate time. That brings good to the manager. But suppose the manager is mindful neither of the landowner nor the staff, but treats them badly and gets drunk, he better beware. For the landowner will return unexpectedly and the manager will suffer dire consequences.

Luke 12:42–48

Reflection

There are three kinds of activity: primal ones such as food-gathering, eating and washing; chosen ones such as our paid jobs and creative interests; and those we bumble into because of invitations and fancies. Jesus only did what he saw his divine Father doing (John 5:19). Assess each of these types of activity in that light. Perhaps you may simplify your shopping habits by making lists; avoid unnecessary entanglements at work by exercising restraint, and decide which casual activities run you, and which you can do with serenity, still fully present to others. 'Christians should remember that the value of their good works is not based on their number or excellence, but on the love of God which prompts them to do these things.'[9]

If we are 'attached' to an activity, we make wrong choices. When two duties clash, we think through which of the two can best be delegated, postponed, missed with apologies, or honoured in some other way; and which most requires us, and cannot be repeated. We then do what gives us most peace. No two true duties conflict.

When we order our activities mindfully there is room for the spontaneous, inspired activity. I stayed with friends on the Isle of Skye. Their son ran to the top of The Maidens and back, showered, dressed in tartan, played bagpipes for thirty minutes, and joined us for breakfast. That was an inspired activity!

In the early 1900s Max Weber developed a model for the 'ideal organisation' based on the principle of 'division of labour'. The production of a product or service is divided into separate tasks, each performed by the person best suited to do it, and without unnecessary overlapping. The economist Adam Smith suggested that productivity would rise significantly when this principle was applied. This is an inadequate application of St Paul's model, where each person is like a member of the human body. Each is needed. Each has work to do. None should do what belongs to another.

Pause for thought

Which of your activities bring life, and which bring overload? What will you do about this?

Prayer

Lord, temper with tranquillity
our manifold activity,
that we may do our work for thee
with very great simplicity.[10]

Today's step

I step
away from mindless activities
towards mindful activities.

Spiritual breathing exercise

Right activity in.
Wrong activity out.
That's good.

MAY 9

Management of time

Bible reading

It's time to wake up you sleepy people, like someone who rises from the dead. God's promised Anointed One will make day dawn upon you. Look carefully at the way you journey through life. Live a life of purpose that measures true worth. Do not be futile and superficial: be wise, use your intelligence. Make the best use of time. Buy up each opportunity because there's plenty of bad stuff around.

Ephesians 5:14–16

Reflection

God gives us the authority to use the time available to us in the most productive way. It has been said that it is the busiest person that has time to spare. We can start by making a list of the things we do and numbering them in order of priority. In this way the urgent does not push out the important. We follow the law of delayed gratification: we do the most difficult things first, and then we have more space to enjoy the things we like doing.

We can treat waiting time – for example when we are in a queue, expecting someone, or even sitting in a loo – as an opportunity to read, think, write, phone, text or pray. We can listen to music or talks while we drive a car. We can address technical problems, for example on a computer, so that time-saving techniques can be used, such as group emails and ordered, accessible information. Some of us have the opportunity to delegate. We should delegate what someone else can do better than us so that we only do what we do best; however we should spend time with the person we delegate to so that they become enriched. You will never have so much authority as when you give it away.

Avoid meetings that waste time. If you are responsible, clarify the objectives, make sure only the necessary people are present, circulate the agenda with clear explanations beforehand. Plan time limits for each item. Include time to establish aims, ensure effective discussion, reach conclusions and minute actions to be taken. End meetings on a positive note, summarising decisions and actions to be taken.

Pause for thought

Spend time to save time.

Prayer

May each thing I do be without regret,
may each minute I spend be used for the best.
May each thought I have be without waste,
may each moment I'm in be in God's time.

Today's step

I step away
from time-wasting
towards time management.

Spiritual breathing exercise

Ordering in.
Frittering out.
God's time.

MAY 10

Relationships

Bible reading

Encourage one another. Build one another up, as you are doing. Get to know those who have oversight of you; show them warm appreciation. As for difficult people – the loafers and disorderly – take them seriously, speak to them personally, explain in what ways their behaviour is harmful. Encourage the faint-hearted, motivate the weak and be patient with the backward. Always keep your temper. Don't retaliate when you are attacked. Always aim to show kindness and seek the good of every one.

1 Thessalonians 5:11–15

Reflection

'If civilization is to survive, we must cultivate the science of human relationships,' wrote Franklin D. Roosevelt. Governments frantically try to treat the symptoms of social dysfunction by providing more police, teachers, social and health workers. But the underlying causes stem from a failure of relationships in the home. According to Britain's Emeritus Professor Richard Whitfield 90% of the prison population lacked the security of attachment to one person who really cared for them up to the age of three.[11]

We cannot love another person unless we first know that we are loved. That is why so many people cannot make good relationships. To be able to build friendship we have to be present to another, accepting them and wanting the best for them, resisting any compulsion to say something just to cover our shyness, being willing to say nothing, to listen, to search for something of interest to the other. From there, sooner or later, a friendship may grow. Each relationship is unique, and has a naturally different degree of closeness.

One key to creating and sustaining friendship is this: don't focus on what your friend fails to give you, but on what he or she does contribute. Never expect any one person to give you everything.

One of Jesus' most common greetings was Shalom Aleichem, which means 'peace be with you', and one of God's names revealed in the Bible is Jehovah Shalom. God's people are called to shalom, a profound and integrated peace expressed not just in inward tranquillity but also in outward relationships.

Pause for thought

Be an actual or potential friend to everyone you meet today.

Prayer

Eternal Friend,
renew in us the gift of friendship:
friendship without guile,
friendship without malice,
friendship without striving.
Friendship with insight,
friendship with warmth,
friendship with the light touch.

Today's step

I step
away from discouragement
towards encouragement.

Spiritual breathing exercise

Warmth in.
Indifference out.
Friendship.

MAY 11

Sexual relationships

Bible reading – a love song

Female lover:
O for a kiss from your lips;
your caresses are sweeter than wine.
People scent your fragrance from afar –
that is why the girls love you.
You are my king: take me to your bedroom
and there let us thrill with delight.
This love for you is the right thing.

Male lover:
How beautiful you are.
Your words enchant me.
Your cheeks glow.
Your breasts captivate me.
You are beautiful in every way, my love, you ravish my heart.

The Song of Songs 1:1–4; 4:1–9

Reflection

Sex is a beautiful gift of God to be celebrated and cherished. Loving sexuality offers an intimation of the holy. In order to cherish it we have to go to great lengths to avoid misusing it, for to do so causes profound damage. A struggle rages in most people between the desire to be decent and pure and hormonally driven urges. We live in an era of sexually supercharged stimuli, so we become confused as to what is good and what is deviant. Pornography is pervasive. If we have sexual intercourse with someone with whom we do not have a whole-life commitment we cease to treat that person and ourselves as sacred: we cease to be mindful. If we have been abused, we find it difficult to trust someone of the same gender as the abuser, or to see the beauty in ourselves. If we have been divorced, our confidence and sense of worth may have suffered a setback.

Wherever the place we are at, know this: there is no pit so deep that our Saviour cannot enter it and lift us out. If we find ourselves downloading pornographic images, if we stimulate our appetites through bits of persons' bodies, or if we despair of our ability to truly love – a good corrective is to pray for that person whom we are using as a sex object, to meet our need for intimacy by opening our deepest cravings to the divine caresses and to share our needs with another.

Sexual love is most precious when its fullest genital expression is saved up for a relationship that is sealed before God and others as a sacred trust.

Pause for thought

Learn to use your sexual organs as the Creator desires.

Prayer

Root of our Desire,
thank you for the sap that rises in our bodies
and the feelings of attraction between two people.

Ocean of Mercy,
wash through us, until distorted desire ebbs away.

Divine Lover,
teach us to hold the other in our heart
and not to possess them;
but to grow in tenderness as a plant grows.

Today's step

I step
away from denial
towards delight.

Spiritual breathing exercise

Healing love in.
Cheap love out.
Tenderness.

MAY 12

Marriage

Bible reading

Some religious purists put a test question to Jesus: Is it OK to get a divorce whatever the reason?

'Have you not read in the Bible,' Jesus replied, 'that from the beginning God made people to be male and female. That is why a male and a female leave their father and mother and become joined – they become one flesh. They are no longer two, they are one. No one should try to split apart what God has joined together. Moses permitted divorce because he recognised how hard human lives are. But that was not the original intention.'

Matthew 19:3–8

Reflection

Sexual engagement, the reciprocity of marriage and the creativity of parenthood are fundamental sources of engagement with God. Marriage is a communion of love in which the two partners give all of their being – not just this or that part – to the other, within the love of God. The relationship between a husband and wife is like that between Christ and his spiritual family (Ephesians 5:22–33). Thus the marriage is animated by a tender, cherishing love that lays down its life for the other.

According to Dr John Gottman, a leading marriage researcher, the quality of a couple's friendship is five times as important as physical intimacy. He was not able to crack the code of saving marriages until he started to analyse what went right in happy marriages. He found that, even if couples had arguments, it was their development of friendship when they were not fighting that tipped the balance.

Definitions of marriage vary from one culture to another. In modern Western culture some perceive it as a merely external relationship which only rich people can afford – hollow and hypocritical. They respond by having sex with anyone whose company they enjoy. Others try to model a relationship of integrity but without a public label. Followers of this way of life heed Jesus' teaching and try to restore marriage to its original place in God's plan. In this, an unmarried man and an unmarried woman join themselves (sexually, practically, emotionally and spiritually) and become one flesh, with an unconditional commitment to offer this relationship to their partner alone. True marriage gives the other space – it is not entrapment, but glorious freedom, as the prayer below makes clear.

Pause for thought

Think of the fruits of such a marriage.

Prayer

May we always be together in the silent memory of God.
But may there be spaces in our togetherness,
and may the winds of the heavens dance between us,
and love be a moving sea between the shores of our souls.

May we sing and be joyous together, but let each be alone,
Even as the strings of a lute are alone
though they quiver with the same music.[12]

Today's step

I step
away from half-love
towards whole love.

Spiritual breathing exercise

Communion in.
Co-habitation out.
Love.

MAY 13

Single for God

Bible reading

The disciples said to Jesus: If what you say is true it's better not to marry! Jesus replied: It *is* better not to, but in practice not everyone can live that way – it is only for those who have been given the capacity. There are three kinds of unmarried people: those who have been born incapable of marriage, those who can't marry because of what others have done to them, and those who have chosen to be single for the sake of God's kingdom. Let anyone practise this who can.

Matthew 19:10–12

Reflection

God calls many of his people to be single, some for a period, and others for life. The apostle Paul wrote 'It is better not to marry' (1 Corinthians 7:1). Celibacy is one of the gifts of the Holy Spirit. Few understand the great honour it is to serve God in this way. Marriage is not the only route to wholeness. Jesus Christ, the supreme specimen of a whole human being, chose to remain single. Britain's sixteenth-century Queen Elizabeth, who looked set to be overthrown by all kinds of sexual and state affairs, dedicated herself to be a virgin queen for her people's sake, ruled for forty years, and achieved great things, as even her opponents recognise. Robert Schuman, France's Foreign and Prime Minister, dedicated himself to be as a priest, but to serve in politics. He became an architect of a European Union that could leave national feuds behind. Those who choose to be single for the sake of God's kingdom can make their love available to all equally, and receive back flows of affection.

Others of us, however, want to marry and are in pain that we cannot. This may be because we have been abused, castrated, divorced, passed over, widowed, because we cannot relate well or are physically or psychologically barren. We must not pretend that all is well. Embrace the wound, seek healing, and remain open. To love people and to be loved we have to be vulnerable.

A single woman, devoted to God but regretting she had not married, received a vision that she had a baby. The baby was the fruit of a great calling. She became one of that noble line of women who do not accept that non-marriage means non-fulfilment, that women have potential far beyond their expectations and that many barren ones do become spiritual mothers of their people (Isaiah 54:1–3). Something similar applies to men.

Pause for thought

How do we know whether we are called to be single or married? Ask what most liberates your spirit.

Prayer

Lord, help me as a single adult
to be at home with my sexuality,
to acknowledge my need for companionship,
to find contentment in your will,
to share my vulnerability,
to be a channel of your love.

Today's step

I step
away from regrets
towards my Christ-calling.

Spiritual breathing exercise

Acceptance in.
Rejection out.
Christ fulfils.

MAY 14

Handling our temptations

Bible reading

Ask yourself some questions. What lies behind your discords? Do they not arise from your desires that are like a war going on inside you? You want what others have – your desires remain unfulfilled – so murderous thoughts fester inside you. Because you have no inner contentment you are an angry and disgruntled person.

You only have to ask God, except that when you do ask you have mixed motives – you really want a selfish lifestyle. You are like an unfaithful partner – someone who breaks their vows to God. Don't you realise that by befriending this greedy, driven world you put yourself at odds with God?

There is deep truth in the Bible verse that says God's Spirit has been put within you and God passionately yearns to have you. The good news is that God gives the power of the Holy Spirit to cure you of these divided tendencies.

James 4:1–5

Reflection

> A man who has not passed through the inferno of his passions has never overcome them.[13]

Bishop Basil of Caesarea taught young males who fell prey to lust: 'When you see the most beautiful woman in the world, go with your mind to her grave a few days after she has died. Such a terrible odour and putrid flow comes from her body, such that all the latrines in the world don't smell as bad. Behold what you were lusting after!' He would also say, 'Death, death, death! The coffin, the shovel, the spade, the pickaxe . . .' Perhaps we need not go to that extreme, but we may all find it helpful to look upon someone whom we lust after from the perspective of their deathbed and ours.

Irish Christians before and at the time of Aidan advised continence during the three Lents and on Saturday and/or Sunday night. This practised them in self-discipline and made them available to God alone.[14]

Pause for thought

Hold your desires before God: hand them over to God.

Prayer

Holy Spirit,
come with power into my divided tendencies.

Holy Love,
one by one, I give these divided affections to you.

Holy Dove,
make of them what you will,
take them where you will.

Today's step

I step
away from temptation
towards integration.

Spiritual breathing exercise

Deepest love in.
False frenzies out.
Content.

MAY 15

Clothes and furniture

Bible reading

The angel showed me the new Jerusalem, descending from God out of heaven, all ready like a bride adorned for her husband. Its sheen resembled some rare jewel, clear as crystal. The angel measured everything carefully with a golden measuring rod. The city is transparent, like glass. The main building blocks are adorned with all kinds of precious stones. Its light is the glory of God. To it people of worth bring their glories and treasures. Nothing false enters it.

Revelation 21

Reflection

> We are not seeking a life of denial for we thoroughly rejoice in the good things God gives us. Our clothes and furniture should reflect God-given features of our personalities. There is a time to feast and celebrate as well as to fast. Our commitment is to openness. We stand against the influence of the god of mammon in our society by our lifestyle, by our hospitality, and by regular and generous giving.[15]

In order for our clothes and furniture to reflect God-given features of our personalities we need to know something of our personalities. Try the following exercise. Don't take time over it; answer the first word that comes into your mind. Which 1) season of the year 2) day of the week 3) colour 4) shape (e.g. square, circle, oval, rectangle, spiral) 5) plant 6) mineral most reflects your personality? Ask someone else to say what they think best reflects you.

Think about colours. It is often thought that the following colours draw attention to these qualities: white – light;

black – anger; red – passion; yellow – happiness; green – fruitfulness; blue – stability; purple – nobility. Which colours calm you or make you come alive? Think about the quality and shape of the materials used in your furniture. Wood breathes, plastic does not – does that matter to you? Think about balance. Do you need much space and a minimal number of objects? How can you make best use of natural light? What artefacts do you enjoy looking at? Are they arranged so that 'they give their best', or are they just dumped any old how? Whether we own a large house or sleep on a mat in a hut we can arrange ourselves and our surroundings in a mindful way.

Pause for thought

Look in a mirror. Feel good or make a change.

Prayer

God of order and beauty,
help us to clothe our bodies and our homes
with beauty appropriate to the season.
Give to us a sense of balance and of order,
with room for spontaneity.
Show us what bubbles and what brings calm,
what brings energy and what brings charm.

Today's step

I step
away from jaded imitation
towards creative arrangement.

Spiritual breathing exercise

Mindful arrangement in.
Mindless arrangement out.
Shalom.

MAY 16

A time to feast

Bible reading

Some people came to Jesus and said, 'The followers of the Pharisees and the followers of John the Baptiser are keeping a fast – why don't your followers do the same?' 'Can friends at a wedding feast go on a fast while the bridegroom is still with them?' Jesus asked them, 'As long as they have the bridegroom with them they cannot fast. A time will come when the bridegroom is taken from them – then they will fast.'

Mark 2:18–20

Reflection

There is a time to feast and a time to fast, but how do we know which we should do and when?

In the Bible significant occasions such as weddings are marked with a feast, and it is good if we celebrate special anniversaries. In Jesus' parable of the runaway son who came to his senses and returned home, the whole extended household held a welcome-home banquet. It is good to celebrate significant comings and goings. The most significant event in the world is Jesus' resurrection, which took place on a Sunday. Christians mark every Sunday as a day to celebrate 'the presence of the Bridegroom'. That is why Sundays are excluded from seasons of fasting such as Lent, and why a tradition of inviting guests to join in the best meal of the week – Sunday lunch – has grown up.

In the Christian Church the climax of great seasons such as Christmas, Easter and Pentecost are traditionally called Feasts. These are appropriate times to pull out all the stops in worship as well as in homes – special music, banners, processions, arts, as well as food and maybe entertainment. Natural seasons such as harvest and yule lend themselves to warming suppers or dance. Midsummer in the northern hemisphere perhaps calls for a beach barbecue. In some branches of the Church every service of Holy Communion is called a celebration, and the priest who presides is called the celebrant. Another name for this service is Eucharist, which means 'thanksgiving'. In the Celtic tradition all life is to be celebrated, for the cosmic Christ is at its heart.

In Jewish teachings the taste of the food is an expression of the divine in the food. Eating is a means through which one can draw closer to God. We must give eating enough space for this to happen. Each time I eat I acknowledge this is a choice to live again and celebrate my existence.

Pause for thought

It has been said that the kingdom of God is a party. Plan to celebrate something worthwhile.

Prayer

Divine Birther,
may the whole world celebrate your existence.
May every race add colour to the celebration.
May every soul join with the song of creation.
May the birds sing,
may the trees clap,
and may we taste and dance.

Today's step

I step
away from stale routine
towards festivity.

Spiritual breathing exercise

Celebration in.
Staleness out.
Goodness!

MAY 17

A time to fast

Bible reading

In the church at Antioch there were prophets and teachers. While they were worshipping God and fasting, the Holy Spirit told them to dedicate Saul and Barnabas to a special work to which God had called them. After fasting and prayer they laid hands on them and sent them off . . . When Saul and Barnabas had appointed elders for each new church they entrusted them to the One in whom they had come to believe with fasting and prayer.

Acts 13:1–3; 14:23

Reflection

'We are consumption junkies, goodies-sniffing moral down-and-outs, inhabiting our cardboard cities of the soul.'[16] Our excessive consuming has not just harmed us physically; we die psychically when we ingest too much. We close down our souls when we cannot raise our bodies.

'Diet is a point of power in my life, something under my direct influence and control . . . With eating, less really does mean more. It's the Law of Nutritional Frugality.'[17]

No individual on the path towards wholeness eats poorly, we take joy in simpler foods; we refuse to be slaves to the materialistic system.

Christian fasting is denying ourselves something physical in order to live more deeply in the power of God's Spirit. Some Christians control their diet so that they are fit to live life to the full. It is a Christian tradition on a Friday to refrain from eating meat, or anything solid, until 3pm, so that we are mindful of Christ who was on the Cross until that time. People in the time of Saint Aidan practised this on Wednesday, too. Many Christians abstain from luxury during the forty days of Lent. Others fast altogether from food when they feel called to dedicate time to prayer. It is said that the Prophet Muhammad advised people to reserve one third of their stomach for food, one third for liquid, and one third for a space.

Wise fasting is not physical denial, it is tempering one aspect of our being in order to release other aspects. It is not physical decline, it is physical responsibility, leading to emotional, relational and spiritual advance.

Pause for thought

We may fast, not just from food, but from anything that threatens to take us over, from TV to shopping, from internet surfing to phone calling. What do you need to fast from?

Prayer

Forgive us for
grasping at things we do not need,
clinging to projects that distract us from you,
accumulating worries that hold us back from your path.

Help us to acquire what no money can buy:
a free spirit,
a wise mind,
a beautiful attitude,
a serving heart.

Today's step

I step
away from too much
towards true being.

Spiritual breathing exercise

Access in.
Excess out.
You're here.

MAY 18

An open lifestyle

Bible reading

Philip said to Nathaniel, 'We have found the one whom Moses and the prophets spoke about. Come and see.' When Jesus saw Nathaniel coming towards him he said, 'Here comes a truly open person.' He said to Nathaniel, 'Heaven will be opened to you, and you will see divine messengers attending to the one you have come to see.'

John 1:45–51

Reflection

Our commitment to openness means that we are open to the good in every person and situation, we are not open to subterfuge and ill-intent. This requires a humble, honest and childlike spirit. It is possible only when we are secure in our origins in God. We do not say one thing and do another. We explain why we do things. We speak and write plainly. We do not talk down to people or falsely talk things up. We do not use six words when one will do. We look other people in the eyes. If the time is right, we open our door to a genuine person. We are transparent in our relationships. We treat each person the same, without taking sides.

We have no skeletons in our cupboards. We may have had them, but we have acknowledged them and dealt with them. We admit we have struggles, weaknesses. We are not unwise – we do not cast our pearls before swine – but neither do we hide our light under the table. Our life is like an open book that any discerning person may read.

Jesus chose Nathaniel to be one of his twelve apostles because he could 'read' him even before he had spoken to him. Nathaniel was like an open book. Jesus was able to recognise this quality of openness because he himself was open with us. He shared his home and his heart, his time and his thoughts, his temptations and his tears, his prognoses and his prayers with those who were most truly open to him. An ancient Celtic poem suggests: 'If there be a guest in your house and you conceal anything from them, it is not the guest that will be outside it, but Jesus, Mary's Son.'

Pause for thought

We close up when we have something to hide, want to control, or become over busy. What prevents you being as open as Jesus?

Prayer

Lord, make my life an open book
that good persons may read.
Take from me a judging heart
and a spirit that bangs doors shut.
Weed out falseness.
Help me accept my weakness.
May my light shine.

Today's step

I step
away from closure
towards the opening.

Spiritual breathing exercise

Barriers down.
Doors open.
Jesus.

MAY 19

Against the influence of the god of mammon

Bible reading

No one can serve two chiefs. They will either hate one and love the other, or be devoted to one and be against the other. You cannot serve God and Mammon – that is untrustworthy material riches. Therefore I tell you, stop being perpetually worried about material acquisitions. Life is greater than food, and the body greater than clothing.

Matthew 6:24, 25

Reflection

Mammon is the Aramaic word Jesus used for riches. This word was retained when the Bible was translated into other languages. Medieval writers used it as the name for the devil of covetousness. Today it is used to refer to a worldwide mindset that makes a god of 'the money market'. Shaped by this mindset, we accumulate all kinds of obligations. More people expect something back from us. Stress increases. We rush through life as if everything depends upon us. We forget that everything on this earth can be taken from us in a moment, that we have here no eternal home.

How can we stand against the influence of the god of mammon in our society? We can live a lifestyle that is sustained by something deeper and longer-lasting than possessions. To belong is not to own, it is to recover awareness of our origins in God, who has placed priceless treasures within and around us. 'The sacred duty of being an individual is to gradually learn how to live so as to awaken the eternal within you,' writes John O'Donohue[18]. 'We are God's work of art, created in Christ Jesus to live the good life as from the beginning God meant us to live it,' writes the apostle Paul to Christians in Ephesus. He contrasts this with their former lifestyle: 'When you were ruled entirely by your own physical desires and your own ideas' (Ephesians 2:10, 3).

Pause for thought

Visualise the origin of your life as a blank artist's canvas. Forget, for the moment, the blots and mistakes that may later have marred it. Invite the risen Christ to show you what he has painted upon it: for example, a calling, a habit, a virtue, a talent, a coming together with another. What is incomplete? What might be the next brush strokes?

Prayer

Divine Artist,
you uniquely shape our characters,
endow us with gifts
and pattern our lives.
May your inspired fingers work upon us
that we may become your work of art.

Today's step

I step
away from the acquisitive in me
towards the eternal in me.

Spiritual breathing exercise

Eternal treasure in.
Fleeting treasure out.
All yours.

MAY 20

Goodness is more interesting than greed

Bible reading

Someone in the crowd yelled at Jesus, 'Tell my brother he's got to give me my share of our dad's inheritance.' 'Who made me your executor?' said Jesus. Then he talked to them. 'Keep clear of covetousness in every shape and form, for a person's life does not consist in possessions, even if they have more than they need.' He told them this parable: A rich man gained big returns. So he knocked down his storage facilities and built bigger ones, and decided to eat, drink and live for pleasure. But God said to him: 'You fool. This night I will take your soul; then who will all these possessions be for?' It's like that whenever a person stores up worldly treasure for themselves but is not rich in the eyes of God.

Luke 12:13–21

Reflection

We stand against the influence of the god of mammon in our society by making goodness more interesting than greed. When we do something that is wrong there is a fleeting feeling of excitement, but this is quickly followed by a long-lasting let-down feeling. In contrast there is no end to the unexplored possibilities for good, at a physical, social, intellectual, scientific and spiritual level. These good possibilities stretch every muscle, expand our hearts, our imagination, our minds, our capacity for courage, creativity and love.

In fourth-century Egypt, where mammon held sway, Antony and his fellow monks considered it a spiritual disaster to accept passively the tenets and values of their society. They escaped from the sinking ship and went into the desert to model a way of life that had few material but many spiritual pleasures. Those who saw Antony after his many years in desert solitude described him as balanced, gentle and caring. He had become radiant with God's love. Solitude had made him a compassionate man.

God is present in cities as well as in deserts, but in the cities of the Old Testament people are so driven by lust of power, pleasure and money that they do not seek God there. It is in the simplicity and solitude of the desert that people hear God. In the desert we see things as they are, not engineered or packaged. The new monasticism movement may be today's equivalent of those desert experiments. And the desert can come to the city.

Pause for thought

What treasure should you forsake, and what should you ask for?

Prayer

Make me rich in your eyes, dear God.
Help me to take freely of the treasures of heaven.
Clothe me in the virtues whose attractions increase.
Feed me with food that never goes bad.
Adorn me with beauty that never fades.
Free me to stride through the courts of mammon,
uncluttered by its enticements,
content with you.

Today's step

I step
away from deceitful riches
towards eternal treasure.

Spiritual breathing exercise

Priceless pearls in.
Prideful piles out.
Treasure.

MAY 21

A lifestyle of service

Bible reading

Two fisherman's sons had joined Jesus' band of twelve disciples. Their mother begged Jesus to give them top places in his coming kingdom – one on his right and the other on his left. 'You do not know what you are asking,' Jesus replied to them. 'Can you drink the cup that I am going to drink?' 'We can,' they replied. 'Very well,' said Jesus, 'you shall drink my cup, but as for places at my right and left, these are not mine to allocate; these belong to whomever my Father has prepared them.' . . . When the other ten disciples heard about this they were indignant. Jesus called them all together and said, 'Whoever wants to be great among you must be your servant, and whoever wants to be first must be your slave – just as the Son of the human race did not come to be served, but to serve.'

Matthew 20:20–27

Reflection

James was one of these two brothers. Was he wrong to desire to be great? Jesus' answer suggests that a desire to be great can be good if it is divorced from the desire to be above others. These two brothers' eagerness to do anything to be 'in there' with Jesus was half-sighted; they had not thought through the consequences or the cost, but Jesus senses that they will, in fact, stick with it, even when they realise that he will not dethrone the Roman imperial power in their lifetime, as they probably expected, and even if it involved suffering. In fact James was perhaps the first in the roll-call of disciples who were killed for their faith.

If we really want to be at the top, there is no alternative but to go to the bottom.

A few weeks before he was assassinated, Mahatma Gandhi had a conversation with his grandson, Arun. He handed Arun a talisman upon which were engraved the 'Seven Blunders' out of which, said Gandhi, grows the violence that plagues the world:

Wealth without work.
Pleasure without conscience.
Knowledge without character.
Commerce without morality.
Science without humanity.
Worship without sacrifice.
Politics without principles.

True greatness lies in living to banish these plagues from the world.

Pause for thought
How can you find your greatness by making someone else great today?

Prayer
Teach me to serve you as you deserve;
to give and not to count the cost,
to fight and not to heed the wounds,
to toil and not to seek for rest,
to labour and not to ask for reward,
save that of knowing that I do your will.[19]

Today's step
I step
away from short-term ambition
towards long-term ambition.

Spiritual breathing exercise
Service in.
Status out.
Greatness.

MAY 22

A fun lifestyle

Bible reading

A merry heart does good like a medicine. *Proverbs 17:22*

'Imagine this, friends,' Jesus said to some self-righteous mutterers. 'One of you has a hundred sheep. One of them gets lost. Do you forget about it just because you want to keep the ninety-nine? Nope, you set off until you find that lost sheep. What do you do when you get home? You have a party of course. You bang on every neighbour's door and say, "Heh. I've found my lost sheep. Come round and help me celebrate!" I tell you this,' Jesus said, 'there'll be more celebrations in heaven over one sinner that converts than over ninety-nine respectable people who think there's nothing wrong with them.'

Luke 15:3–7

Reflection

Jesus' love of humour is repeatedly revealed in his parables. Jewish readers get this, but many Western translators have ruined the original feel. God must have a sense of humour, G. K. Chesterton[20] pointed out, otherwise why would he have created so many fun creatures? He also said, 'Angels fly because they take themselves lightly.' Heaven is full of joy, lightness, delight.

The Bible is riddled with puns, clever wordplay, and caricature stories designed to make people laugh at themselves. The patriarch Isaac's name comes from the Hebrew word for laughter because of the joy and disbelief his birth brought to his aging parents, Abraham and Sarah.

Chesterton also said, 'The test of good religion is whether or not you can joke about it.' I used to loathe TV comedies that poked fun at my profession, until someone said, 'If you can't laugh at yourself there is something wrong with you.' Laughter does good like a medicine, says the proverb. Research bears this out. Cancer patients who were sent on a weekend of movie comedies improved more than those who received more conventional treatments.

Not all laughter is good. G. K. Chesterton said laughter is the shriek by which fools recognise themselves. But humour is linked with an ability to see things from different angles, to accept unpalatable or unconventional things, and to realise that we are but mortals. It also helps us, and the people we are with, to relax and to bond. 'Whom the gods would make bigots, they first deprive of humour,' wrote James M. Gillis.[21]

Laughter is healing. Finding humour in our struggles does not mean we do not take them seriously.

Pause for thought

In some places laughter clubs have been established. Prove that you don't need to join one. Laugh long and loud now.

Prayer

As nature laughs in spring,
restore laughter to our lives.
When we become complaining and sour-faced
put something funny into our minds.
Help us not to take ourselves too seriously
and to enjoy the world with you.

Today's step

I step
away from the doleful
towards the mirthful.

Spiritual breathing exercise

Smile in.
Frown out.
Ha ha.

MAY 23

All out

Bible reading

My eager desire and unflagging expectation is that I will be ashamed of nothing that I attempt, but that with unfailing courage, speaking out freely, my body and my whole being may honour Christ in everything I do, even if it is in dying for him. For to me to live is Christ, and to die is gain. If I am meant to go on living here on earth – that for me means a life of fruitful service.

Philippians 1:20–22

Reflection

In 1927 a collection of spiritual messages of Oswald Chambers was published under the title *My Utmost for His Highest*. It has never been out of print. Something in us is stirred at the thought of giving our utmost. A rugby player can give his utmost to his rugby, but only for a short space of time – it is not a whole life for the whole of life. A religious fanatic can become a Bible basher or suicide bomber in the name of god fashioned after their own image, but they remain closed to the highest nature of God and of their own divine calling. To give our utmost for God's *highest* requires us to put mercy above justice, thoughtfulness above reflex actions, serving people above bulldozing them, creating greatness above settling for smallness.

What is God's highest?
Catching each divine whisper.
Going the extra mile.
Returning to solitude
when there are blandishments to do otherwise.
Developing one's talent and putting it to use
to benefit the world.

Embracing pain and limitation without complaint,
seeking the best for whoever cares for me.
Learning from the shock of new ideas.
Tasting with joy some new delight of God's universe.
Performing faithfully a mundane chore.
Stretching my brain to master some fresh thinking.
To run with the calling.

Pause for thought

What level do I live on? How can I go up a level?

Prayer

We give you worship with our whole life.
We give you praise with our whole tongue.
We give you service with our whole body.
We give you love with our whole heart.
We give you honour with our whole desire.
We give you our best thought, our deeds, our words,
our will, our understanding, our relationships,
our intellect, our journey, our end.[22]

Today's step

I step
away from half-heartedness
towards whole-heartedness.

Spiritual breathing exercise

My utmost in.
Second-best out.
Your highest.

MAY 24

Giving hospitality

Bible reading

Two followers of John the Baptiser heard him point out Jesus as 'The Lamb of God'. They went after him and asked where he was staying. 'Come and see,' Jesus replied, and they stayed with him that day.

John 1:38, 39

Reflection

Inviting people to our homes can be a blessing to them and to us. Sharing meals features strongly in the life of Jesus. In the fellowship of a meal the deepest things of the heart are often shared.

Hospitality is a matter of honour in the Old Testament (cf. Genesis 19:8; Judges 19:23), and in the early Christian Church (e.g. Titus 1:8). Many biblical stories of hospitality repay study. Abraham promptly and with simplicity offered three complete strangers hospitality (Genesis 18). Bishop Clement of Rome concluded that Rahab, who gave shelter to two reconnaissance officers (Joshua 2) was saved, although she was a prostitute, by 'faith and hospitality'. It was normal for a Jewish home in the time of Jesus to set aside a room for hospitality; the visitor would be offered a bed, a meal, and a wash. 'Remember to welcome strangers to your home' (Hebrews 13:2).

Hospitality is more, however than just allowing someone into our home, it is a principle of the kingdom of God which everyone is called to apply in some way or other. In the New Testament the church is described as the household, or home, of God. Every aspect of church life is meant to be an experience of hospitality. The guest is the unseen Christ.

We saw a stranger yesterday,
we put food in the eating place,
drink in the drinking place,
music in the listening place,
and with the sacred name of the triune God
he blessed us and our house,
our cattle and our dear ones.
As the lark says in her song:
often, often, often goes the Christ
in the stranger's guise.[23]

Pause for thought

Food? Drink? Music? What can I make available to someone who needs it?

Prayer

I would prepare a feast and be host to the great High King,
with all the company of heaven.
The sustenance of pure love be in my house,
the roots of repentance in my house.
Baskets of love be mine to give,
with cups of mercy for all the company.
Sweet Jesus, be there with us, with all the company of heaven.
May cheerfulness abound in the feast,
the feast of the great High King,
my host for all eternity.[24]

Today's step

I step
away from the shut door
towards the opening door.

Spiritual breathing exercise

Welcome in.
Barriers out.
Accepted.

MAY 25

Hospitality of the heart

Bible reading

Jesus said: Whoever welcomes you welcomes me, and whoever welcomes me welcomes the one who sent me. Whoever welcomes a prophet will receive a prophet's reward, and whoever welcomes a good person will receive good reward. Whoever gives even a little child a drink of water in the spirit of friendship with me – anyone who does this kind of thing will receive more than they have given.

Matthew 10:40–42

Greet one another in a way that is honouring.

Romans 16:16

Greet one another with a gesture of love. *1 Peter 5:14*

Welcome the person who is weak in faith. *Romans 14:1*

Reflection

A person who is free of false attachments, and who finds their well-being in their Source, greets each person they meet, outwardly or inwardly. For another person is not a threat, she is a joy. We acknowledge her as a person of worth, who shares with us the dignity of being human. People have different ways of expressing this: a bow of the head, a spoken greeting, a smile. In cultures where this is appropriate, eye contact is good.

In our hearts we say to the other person: You are welcome. I recognise that you, like me, have needs. You, like me, should have a space on this earth that we share. Welcome to this moment when we touch each other.

Hospitality of the heart means that I clear out self-concerns so that I have a space in my heart for the other person, however briefly. It may be a smile, a greeting, or a phrase such as 'Can I help you?' It may be a listening ear or an inclusion in information or in the group I am with.

Fear of our welcome being abused often prevents us from living a lifestyle of greeting. We do not have to succumb to abuse. We say, in one way or another: If you abuse me I will not get drawn in. I will pass on. But still I will bless you in my heart.

Pause for thought

Practise welcoming, inwardly or outwardly, each person you meet today.

Prayer

God bless the stranger at the door,
God bless the baby on the floor,
God bless the shopper, piled with goods,
God bless teenagers masked in hoods,
God bless the sombre city gent,
God bless the crone, lined and bent,
God bless us all – one family,
love-encompassed in Trinity.

Today's step

I step
away from aloofness
towards another.

Spiritual breathing exercise

Welcome in.
Withholding out.
Touching place.

MAY 26

Receiving hospitality

Bible reading

Jesus commissioned seventy others and sent them out in twos to prepare the way in every place he was to visit. He briefed them: 'The first thing you should say in each house you visit is "Peace to this house." If people of peace live there your peace will remain on the house; if they do not, it will return to you. Stay in the house of peace as long as you stay in that area. Eat and drink whatever they give you. People who work deserve their pay. Heal those who are suffering. Keep saying, "God's kingdom has come to you."'

Luke 10:1–10

Reflection

Do-gooders put people off. We all know someone who smothers people with so-called hospitality, but who will not allow them to help, and who will not receive from them. Let us beware of doing good in order to shore up our fragile ego, keep ourselves in control or our vulnerabilities at arm's length.

Jesus' mission method was to send out teams who were not self-sufficient. They needed to ask for a bed and a bite. They did not push themselves on people who were not willing to receive them; they gave a peace greeting and only made their request if they received a genuine peace-greeting back. 'Good karma' we say today. Of course, that was in a culture where this was understood, but the principle can be applied in any culture. St Patrick began his mission to Ireland by seeking the hospitality of a pagan. Aidan and Hilda used Jesus' form of mission in seventh-century Britain.

It is an important part of a Christian lifestyle to ask for things we need, for it means that we are in touch with our real nature as limited, vulnerable, interdependent human beings.

Pause for thought

Some of us find it very hard to ask for something we need, whether this be a material or a spiritual need. Ask for something you need today.

Prayer

You are the Potter, I am but clay.
You have made me to need others,
when I am born and when I die,
and when I am tempted, in the false flush of pride,
to go it alone.
I now hold out my hand, with palm open to receive.
Help me receive through one of your children I pray.

Today's step

I step
away from self-sufficiency
towards the person who can help me.

Spiritual breathing exercise

Asking in.
Pride out.
Shalom.

MAY 27

A giving lifestyle

Bible reading

The person who sows sparingly will reap sparingly. The person who sows generously will receive generous amounts in return. Each person should give whatever God puts into their heart, not grudgingly, or out of a false sense of duty. God loves someone who gives cheerfully. And God is well able to provide for all your needs if you give yourself for the good of others.

2 Corinthians 9:6–8

Reflection

> It is impossible not to notice that, in some of the poorest parts of the world, most people, most of the time, appear to be happier than we are. In homes constructed from packing cases, and palm leaves, people engage more freely, smile more often, express more affection than we do behind our double glazing, surrounded by remote controls. Perhaps one of the reasons is that they have less to lose by letting people into their lives. The more wealth we possess, the more isolated we become. We retreat to gated communities, hire guards and install CCTV. The rich lock themselves in, and lock everyone else out.[25]

The cure for meanness is to give generously. This New Testament principle was carried forward in the early Church's practice of alms-giving. Muslims have made this one of their seven pillars, but too many Christians have neglected it.

The principle of giving away one tenth of our income, including profit from our savings, did not end when Jesus' ways superseded the laws of Moses. Abraham tithed before Moses' law was brought in (Genesis 28:22), Jesus tithed after it and encouraged tithing.

Tithing was continued by the early Christians, except that they thought it should be increased to whatever they could afford to give away. Giving our 'first fruits' or dividends to God is part of faith (Acts 5:2).

In some countries, such as the UK, it is possible for every tax-payer to give to charity through their employer's pay scheme so that the tax they would have paid is also given to the charity.

An organisation such as 'Stewardship' can be the intermediary; this enables you to give to specific needs from your Stewardship fund as and when you are so inspired.

Pause for thought

Is there a good reason why you should give away less, or more, than ten per cent of your income?

Prayer

God of generosity and order
wean us from the selfish pursuit of gain.
Inspire us to administer our money
in the power and wisdom of your Spirit
for the good of the world,
the sustaining of those who serve you without salary
and above all for your glory.

Today's step

I step
away from prayerless use of money
towards prayerful use of money.

Spiritual breathing exercise

Tithing in.
Shilly-shallying out.
Gift.

MAY 28

Regular and generous giving

Bible reading

About the money collected for the relief of God's people: do this the same way as I directed the churches in Galatia to do. On the first day of each week let each of you put aside an amount that is in proportion to what you have received and save this up so that no collections need be taken after I arrive among you. When I arrive I will send on representatives whom you approve, with credentials, to carry your donation to Jerusalem.

1 Corinthians 16:1–3

Reflection

It is well known that the apostle Paul organised a collection from the Greek churches of Achaia and Macedonia for the benefit of the impoverished churches of Judea. It may seem extraordinary that he should have devoted so much space in his letters to this mundane matter, referring to it in Romans 15, 1 Corinthians 16, and 2 Corinthians 8, 9. But Paul did not see it as a mundane matter. On the contrary he saw it as relating deeply to the grace of God and the unity of the Holy Spirit.

I have studied 'Christian Stewardship' material used by various Christian Churches in Britain. The most compelling leaflet I have seen depicts someone being baptised by immersion. Every part of their body is submerged under water, except for one arm – this is desperately held above the water grasping a bulging purse. The last thing to be baptised is our money.

There are two principles to do with giving in the Bible. The first is the principle of planned giving to specified, ongoing ministries. For example, the Levites and others who sustained the temple and its worship were paid through the proportionate, routine gifts of the people. Many churches run on this principle today. Regular, ordered, proportionate giving is part of baptising our money. The second is the principle of 'faith ministries'. I think it was the missionary Hudson Taylor who said, 'God's work, done in God's way, will not lack supplies.' When someone launches out in faith to serve God and the poor, this as often as not touches the hearts of people who give over and above what they have already planned.

Giving is a gift of the Spirit that some people have in a special measure. These are the people who should be given jobs as treasurers. They get huge delight in tracing and telling about the good fruits that a gift has brought.

Pause for thought

What is my total income after tax? What proportion do I give, and to whom?

Prayer

Help me to
gain money honestly,
spend a little wisely,
save some prudently,
and give generously.[26]

Today's step

I step
away from profligacy
towards planned generosity.

Spiritual breathing exercise

Giving in.
Meanness out.
Glow.

MAY 29

A now lifestyle

Bible reading

The time to awaken to present reality is now. Let us live as if darkness has already gone, and live the present fully clothed in light. Let everything we think and do be fully present to the light of day.
Romans 13:11–13

In whatever situation I am in I know how to be content: in poverty or plenty, in struggle or success.
Philippians 4:11–13

Reflection

It is easy to become bored with a person, a situation or with life as a whole. We can respond to this problem in two ways. The first way is to rush into the pursuit of trifles – into anything so long as it is new and catches our fancy. Some people spend their lives doing this. It is not, of course, an answer at all; it is merely a temporary distraction. The second way to respond is to become fully present, so that the meaning, energy, colour and adventure with which, all unseen, the present moment is filled become available to us.

This is sometimes called 'the sacrament of the present moment'. We can be 'fully present' in all sorts of ways. Perhaps the words of someone speaking to us are like water off a duck's back. Then we decide to become fully present to that person, and we become aware of their unique history, future and present, of the wonder of a life. Or perhaps we are mindlessly reciting familiar words; then we imagine that *we* are the author. Boredom flees; emotions flow; encounters, tears, healings come.

In order to cultivate this attitude we may keep certain boundaries, for example times when calls are not answered, so that we can be fully present to one another. In a balanced life we are fully present to both the light and the shade. I like sun, sport, good films and fun. Left to myself, I avoid conflict, illness, loss, yet these, too, are part of life. A life that tries to avoid these is superficial. I aim to be fully present to each in their season.

When we visit friends we sometimes think, 'What gift can I take?' and the fuss involved can drain us of time, energy and money. There is no single right or wrong approach to this, for cultures vary. However, if the process of finding a gift distracts us from being fully present, why not bring the best gift of all, yourself?

Pause for thought

Is there someone you could say this to: 'I thought my best gift would be myself, fully attentive to you'?

Prayer

What can I give him, poor as I am?
If I were a shepherd I would bring a lamb;
if I were a wise man I would do my part,
yet what I can I give him –
give my heart.[27]

Today's step

I step
away from half-attention
towards full attention.

Spiritual breathing exercise

Presence in.
Distractions out.
You are here.

MAY 30

Ever ready

Bible reading

Be like people on active service who are always dressed for action. Always be switched on, like lights. Or be like staff at a large private wedding function, ready to open the door the moment the host returns. Happy are those whom the host finds alert to their duties. I tell you something you should really take note of: when the host returns she herself will put on staff uniform, sit them down at table, and serve those diligent staff. This may not be the moment the tables are cleared, it may be a bit later, or much later. Whenever it comes, happy those staff whom the host finds ready.

Luke 12:35–38

Reflection

We embrace a lifestyle of readiness – alertness to any call of duty. Some people develop alertness by exercises that free up the joints, promote the flow of blood and greater understanding of the body's mechanics of movement. By developing flowing movements we help to improve balance and mobility, repattern habitual tendencies, release innate energy – in other words, to be wakeful persons.

Baden-Powell gave the motto 'Be Prepared' to the Boy Scout movement, and urged boys to practise preparedness. He once told how the war General Lord Allenby was riding to his house after a field day when his little son shouted to him, 'Father, I have shot you, you are not half a Scout. A Scout looks upward as well as around him – you never saw me.' There was the boy, sitting up in a tree overhead; but far above him, near the top of the tree, was his new governess. 'What on earth are you doing up there?' cried the General. 'Oh, I am teaching him Scouting,' she said.

We want to be Christians who are not derailed by opposition, a downturn in fortunes, a sudden change of circumstances or boredom, and who are ready to seize every God-given opportunity. Christ is the ever-new source of our inspiration.

Pause for thought

Where have you become slack, blinkered or inconsiderate? How can you become more alert?

Prayer

We come to you, God of surprises, alert and watchful.
Awaken in us awareness of our origins in you,
and the needs of the world,
that droplets of eternity may fall from us on this earth.
Make us sensitive to the motions of your Spirit –
in our souls, in the faces of others,
and in the meetings we did not expect.

Make us prepared, like a samurai warrior, for the next move.
May we move with you, attentive and supple,
alert to opportunities and pitfalls.
Make us aware of your presence in each waking moment.
Keep us ready, even in the depths of night
and the evening of life
that we may relish the coming privilege
of sitting at table with you and being served by you.

Today's step

I step
away from inattention
towards readiness.

Spiritual breathing exercise

Alertness in.
Indifference out.
Communion.

MAY 31

Authenticity

Bible reading

Out of his prayer Jesus was prompted to ask his disciples, in private, who people thought he was. They cited various famous types of people. 'But who do you think I am?' he pressed them. Peter answered, 'You are the Anointed One from God.' Jesus very sharply insisted that they tell this to no one, whoever they might be.

Luke 9:18–22

Reflection

'If Jesus had hired a top PR person he could have avoided execution and cruised to a comfortable lead in the public opinion ratings,' some wag suggested. This passage reveals why Jesus did nothing of the sort. His life was one hundred per cent the opposite of 'spin'. It was totally authentic.

He may have needed to know what people were saying about him in order to know how to frame his message and his timetable. When one person realised Jesus' true role (that of messiah) Jesus asked him to keep quiet. He wanted people to recognise his true nature for themselves, not because someone else said so.

Jesus embraced the worst, he came to terms with death, and was thus freed to be true to his calling – a role model; of unconditional, suffering love.

The biographer of the Church of Scotland minister George McLeod says 'he was keeping strict controls on access to his innermost core, where the puritan carefully policed the passionate. The language of one's innermost feelings was not in the McLeod family lexicon . . . he had the McLeod reputation of omni-competence to protect and uphold.' After a breakdown George had a transforming experience, which enabled him thereafter to model a Christianity which helped people to become more fully human.

Pause for thought

What does it mean for you to cut out pretence and self-advertisement and to be wholly true to your calling?

Prayer

You are the refined molten forge of the human race.
Purge me of all that is false and unreal.
Forge my character until I am true –
true to myself, to others, to you.

Today's step

I step
away from putting on an act
towards being myself.

Spiritual breathing exercise

Pretence out.
Calling in.
God.

JUNE 1

Creation is an expression of God

Bible reading

In the beginning was the Word. The Word was God. Through the Word everything came into being. Not one thing in all creation came into being apart from the Word. The origin of life is in the Word. The Word is the light in every human being. The Word is the One who created the world, entered the world, and came among the Word's own.

John 1–14

Reflection

> We look upon creation as a sacrament, reflecting the glory of God, and seek to meet God through his creation, to bless it and celebrate it.[1]

Writing of the above words from John's Gospel, Philip Newell observes that 'John is listening to the universe as an expression of God. It is spoken into being by the One from whom all things come. It comes directly from the heart of God's being. And in it we can hear the sound of the one heartbeat.' Newell reminds us that Irenaeus, the leader of the early Celtic church in Lyons, drew upon John's understanding through John's disciple, Bishop Polycarp: 'Irenaeus speaks of creation coming out of God's substance. It is not as if the elements of creation are fashioned out of a neutral substance. It is not as if creation is set in motion from afar. The matter of life comes forth directly from the womb of God's being . . . The whiteness of the moon, the wildness of the wind, the moisture of the fecund earth is the glow and whiteness and moistness of God now. It is the very stuff of God's being of which we and creation are composed.'[2]

Orthodox Christian teaching clarifies that the created world is not God, but it reflects God and is God's energy.

Pause for thought

If creation is a unique expression of God, how dare we disdain or wantonly destroy it?

Prayer

For the glory of creation streaming from your heart,
we praise you.
For the air of the eternal seeping through the physical,
we praise you.
For the everlasting glory dipping into time,
we praise you.
For the wonder of your presence beckoning from each leaf,
we praise you.
For setting us, like the stars in their courses,
within the orbit of your love,
we praise you.

Today's step

I step
away from contempt for the earth
towards contemplation of earth.

Spiritual breathing exercise

Wonder in.
Disdain out.
Presence.

JUNE 2

The cosmic Christ

Bible reading

Christ is the firstborn of all creation. In Christ all things were created – the entire cosmos and the non-material world alike – all exist through, in and for Christ. Christ existed before all these things, but these all subsist in Christ – it is in and through Christ that they cohere and are held together.

Colossians 1:15b–17

Reflection

Have you been introduced to the cosmic Christ? It is a tragedy if you have not. The infinite being who birthed the cosmos has not treated it as a clockmaker might treat a clock, leaving it to tick away somewhere on its own. The aspect of deity which we know as Christ has entered into the stream of created life, and holds it together in some way that intimately connects it to the being of God.

Irenaeus wrote: 'The Creator of the world is the Word of God and this is our Lord . . . who in an invisible manner contains all things created, and is inherent in the entire creation . . . That is why he came to his own in a visible manner, and was made flesh, and hung upon a tree, that he might sum up all things in himself.'[3]

The apostle Paul understood that the cosmic Christ was present in the raging waters of the Red Sea and in the water that came out of the arid mountain when Moses' thirsty refugees from Egypt fled across that sea to the safety of another land (1 Corinthians 10:1–4). Those are just two examples of the presence of Christ in moments of grace in the unfolding earth story.

I love to gaze at Father John Giuliani's icon of the cosmic Christ. Christ is imaged as an impressive Native American in whose body are contained mountains, beasts, plants, breasts and sky, and in whom all creation finds fullness.[4]

Pause for thought

The purpose of God's incarnation in Jesus is to birth the cosmic Christ in us. This puts us in touch with more than the wildest science fiction films can imagine.

Prayer

Glory to you, the vital force
that vibrates throughout the cosmos.
Glory to you, the infinite mind that understands the cosmos.
Glory to you, the fertile birther
that conceives each element of the cosmos.
Glory to you, the purest love
that comes to live in one small corner of the cosmos.
Glory to you, the gatherer of planets and peoples,
space and time,
the climax of the cosmos.

Today's step

I step
away from God-in-the-box
towards the cosmic Christ.

Spiritual breathing exercise

Cosmos in.
Blinkers out.
Christ.

JUNE 3

Moments of grace in the unfolding cosmos

Bible reading

God said, 'Let there be lights in the skies to separate day from night, to mark out the sacred seasons, the days and the years; let them shine from space to shed light on earth. So God made two great lights, the greater light to rule the day and the lesser light and the stars to rule the night. This was the fourth 'day'. Then God said: 'Let the waters teem with shoals of living creatures, and let birds fly over the earth.'

Genesis 1:14–20

Reflection

There are moments of grace in the unfolding life of the cosmos. Such a moment occurred when the star out of which our solar system was born collapsed in enormous heat, scattering itself as fragments in the vast realms of space. Another was the appearance of the first living cell. Then another cell capable of using the oxygen of the atmosphere with its immense energies appeared: photosynthesis was completed by respiration. At this moment the living world as we know it began to flourish until it shaped the earth anew. Daisies in the meadows, the song of the mockingbird, the graceful movement of dolphins through the sea, all these became possible at this moment. We ourselves became possible. New modes of music, poetry, and painting, all these came into being in fresh forms against the background of the music and poetry and painting of the celestial forms circling through the heavens.

In human history there have also been such moments of grace. Such was the occasion in northeast Africa some 2.5 million years ago when the first humans stood erect.

There were other moments of grace. Such a moment was experienced when humans first were able to control fire; when spoken language was invented; when the first gardens were cultivated; when weaving and the shaping and firing of pottery were practised; when writing and the alphabet were invented. Then there were the moments when the great visionaries were born who gave to the peoples of the world their unique sense of the sacred, when the great revelations occurred.[5]

Pause for thought

If Christ was in these moments of grace, do we need to enlarge our mental picture of Christ?

Prayer

Infinite birther.
Thank you for moments of grace
in the unfolding life of the cosmos,
for the explosion of a star
and the creation of our solar system,
for the cooling aeons and the birth of our planet,
for the seed of life and the emergence of plants,
for the evolution of creatures
and the dawning of human consciousness,
for our ability to make a fire, a wheel and a computer.
But far more than these all we thank you for yourself.

Today's step

I step
away from an ego-centred view of the cosmos
towards an eco-centred view of the cosmos.

Spiritual breathing exercise

Cosmos-centering in.
Homo-centering out.
Christ.

JUNE 4

Matter matters

Bible reading

The earth and everything it contains belongs to God, the world and all who live on it. For it was the Eternal Source who created its firmness when all was flux and flow.

Psalm 24:1, 2

The Word of God became a human being.   *John 1:14*

Then I heard all the living things in creation – everything that lives in heaven and on earth, and under the earth, and in the sea, proclaiming: To the One seated on the throne . . . be all praise, honour, glory and power, for ever and ever.

Revelation 5:13

Reflection

George McLeod, the founder of the Iona Community used to ask the question, 'What is the matter?' 'Matter is the matter,' was his answer, meaning that too many spiritual people are deluded into thinking that spirit is opposed to matter, and that we can therefore treat the created world as something to disregard. In fact, Christianity is the most material of religions.

In the first place, it believes that the material out of which the world is made should be treated with respect because it is created by God. In the second place, it believes that the incarnation of God in a human form makes all created life sacred in the most profound way possible.

This truth is expressed most beautifully in Orthodox and Celtic prayers: At the birth of Christ 'earth gave him a cave'; at Christ's baptism 'the uncreated enters the stream of human life and the world is charged with the grandeur of God'. The real reason why early Church leaders critiqued the Gnostic writers was their denial of the presence of God in the natural creation. Irenaeus went so far as to teach that through the resurrection of Christ there would be a new heaven and earth (Revelation 21:1), and a new human body, and therefore 'neither the substance nor the essence of creation will be annihilated, although "the fashion" of the world passes away'.[6]

Pause for thought

O Human Being
have regard for yourself.
You have within yourself
heaven and earth.[7]

Prayer

You are the Rock from which all earth is fashioned.
May we give precious earth its worth.
You are the Food from which all life is fed.
May we give precious life its worth.
You are the Source from which all matter is forged.
May we give precious matter its worth.

Today's step

I step
away from over-spiritualising
towards matter.

Spiritual breathing exercise

Spirit through matter in.
Matter versus Spirit out.
Union.

JUNE 5

Creation is the divine milieu

Bible reading

The God who made the world and everything in it is in control of heaven and earth, and does not dwell in humanly made shrines or need anything we humans can provide. It is God who gives everything, including life and breath, to everyone . . . It is in God that we live and move and have our being.

Acts 17:24, 25, 28

Reflection

This truth that the divine presence is in all of creation and not just in churches was reflected upon deeply by Pierre Teilhard de Chardin[8]. He called creation 'the divine milieu' and wrote:

> From the ultimate vibration of the atom to the loftiest mystical contemplation; from the lightest breeze that ruffles the air to the broadest currents of life and thought (Christ) ceaselessly animates, without disturbing, all the earth's processes. And in return Christ gains physically from every one of them. Everything that is good in the universe is gathered up by the Incarnate Word.[9]

This insight does not devalue the work of Christ on earth. In Orthodox Christian thinking the highest privilege of the lower forms of creation is to serve Christ in his incarnate form:

> The destiny of the earth is to receive the body of the Lord for the repose of the Great Saturday; and the destiny of stone is to end as the sealed tomb and as the stone rolled away before the myrrh-bearing women. Olive oil and water find their fulfilment as conductors

of grace to regenerated humanity; and the wheat and the vine culminate in the Eucharistic cup. Everything refers to the Incarnation and everything leads to the Lord . . . there is nothing in this world which has remained a stranger to his humanity and has not received the imprint of the Holy Spirit.[10]

How can this be? The great Church teacher Maximus[11] taught that God has planted in each created thing a characteristic 'thought' which is God's intention for it and which draws it towards God, the Whole.

Pause for thought

I bow in wonder before God in whom all things move and have their being.

Prayer

May we love you in your earth and in every grain of sand.
May we love you in your skies and in every ray of light.
May we love you in the animals
and in everything that breathes.
May we love you in your plants and in every leaf that greens.
May we love you in your creation
and in the symphony of the whole.
May we love you for yourself, and in your infinite Being.

Today's step

I step
away from a hollow vision of creation
towards a holy vision of creation.

Spiritual breathing exercise

God through all in.
God-in-a-box out.
Milieu divine.

JUNE 6

Creation is a sacrament

Bible reading
What can be known about God is plain for all to see. Ever since the world was created God's invisible attributes, everlasting power and divine being have been quite perceptible in what God has made.

Romans 1:19, 20

Reflection
William Shakespeare found 'tongues in trees, books in the running brooks, sermons in stones and good in everything'. A Stoney Indian named Tatanga Mani, in his autobiography, comments on the white man's education he received:

> Oh yes, I went to the white man's schools. I learned to read from school books, newspapers, and the Bible. But in time I found that these were not enough. Civilised people depend too much upon man-made printed pages. I turn to the Great Spirit's book which is the whole of his creation. You can read a big part of that book if you study nature. You know, if you take all your books, lay them out under the sun, and let the snow and rain and insects work on them for a while, there will be nothing left. But the Great Spirit has provided you and me with an opportunity for study in nature's university: the forests, the rivers, the mountains, and the animals which include us.[12]

Among modern white people Newtonian mechanics have been somewhat superseded by the quantum physics of Werner Heisenberg[13], who famously told his students to see the world as made of music, not matter. His work suggests that the physical world is made up not of individual parts but of an essential 'process and movement' with particles 'dancing' from order to disorder and back again. This vast diversity of movement happens within a common unity. Nature is made up of precise numerical patterns and there is an ordered, harmonic interconnectivity between these patterns holding the very fabric of the universe together.[14]

Pause for thought

Look and see.

Prayer

Great Spirit,
you nod and beckon to us through every stone and star.
Your life surges towards us in every greening leaf.
We hear you in the quiet pools and storm-tossed waves.
We are touched by your beauty in birdwing and blossom.
We come to you.

Today's step

I step
away from surface
towards meaning.

Spiritual breathing exercise

Nature in.
Masks out.
God.

JUNE 7

Creation feels God's sorrows

Bible reading

Jesus was nailed to a cross-shaped tree. From midday to three o'clock there was an eclipse of the sun and darkness reigned over the land. About three o'clock Jesus cried out in a loud voice and died. There was an earthquake. Rocks and tombs split open; the bodies of long-buried people came out of the tombs and were seen in the city. The heavy curtain which separated the inmost sanctuary of the temple from the people was torn in two. A Roman military officer who witnessed all this said of Jesus: 'He came from God all right.'

Matthew 27:45, 50–54

Reflection

In death as in life the Gospels portray Jesus as being in harmony with nature. At the moment of his death earth responds by shaking violently and the sun hides its light. Irish monks preserved a legend that one of their pre-Christian kings asked his Druid advisor what was the meaning of the sun's eclipse. 'The meaning,' he replied, 'is that in some place far away the son of the High King of all has been put to death, and the sun averts its gaze.' An early Saxon poem sums up the events described by Matthew in the poignant phrase 'all creation wept.' There will be a future coming when not just the earth, but moon and stars will also be shaken, so intimately linked are they to their Source.

Mystics have seen animals also suffering alongside the crucified Christ. A most powerful vision of the whole of creation suffering with Christ in his crucifixion is that of Dame Julian of Norwich: 'All creatures that can suffer pain suffered with him. The skies and the earth failed in their nature for sorrow at Christ's death. For it is in their nature to know him for their God, who sustains their well-being. When he failed, it was fitting for them, out of kindness, to fail with him, in the measure that belongs to them, for sorrow at his pains.'[15]

The Gospels imply and the Christian Creeds proclaim that for three days after his death Christ descended into the depths of the earth. Gerrard Winstanley[16] wrote: 'The body of Jesus is where the Father is, in the earth, purifying the earth, and his Spirit is entered into the whole creation, which is the heavenly glory where the Father dwells.'[17]

Pause for thought

If creation can weep, where have I hidden my tears?

Prayer

O Son of God,
it was you, the glory of creation, who was scourged.
It was you, the refined molten metal of our human forge,
who died for us.
It was you, the creator of the bright sun and the steadfast earth
whose death caused the light to fade and the soil to tremble.
O Immortal One on the Cross, do one more miracle for us,
change our hearts.

Today's step

I step
away from moaning
towards mourning.

Spiritual breathing exercise

Creation's sorrows in.
Surface distractions out.
The Crucified.

JUNE 8

The new creation

Bible reading

In that day the wolf will live with the lamb, the young goat will share the leopard's lair, the calf, the lion and the bear will graze together and a little child will look after them. The infant will play by the hole of the cobra, and the young child put her hand into the viper's nest. No hurt, no harm will be done, for the land will be as full of the knowledge of God as the ocean beds are full of sea. The Messiah, the offspring of King David's father Jesse, will be a sign to all and the nations shall seek him out.

Isaiah 11:6–10

Reflection

Old Testament prophets look forward to a time when harmony will reign within the world of nature, and between humans and the rest of creation. The New Testament tells us of the One who brings this about by inaugurating the new creation. The Gospels portray Jesus as having a unique power of communion with the animals, plants and the elements. In Luke's account of Jesus' birth he is amid cattle, sheep and straw. In Mark's account of Jesus' desert testings he is amid the wild beasts. In the Gospel accounts of Jesus walking on water, and stilling the winds and waves, he is portrayed as the One who can uniquely overcome the forces of chaos that threaten to overwhelm us. Jesus demonstrates that God's power is present to him on earth as it was in creation. These stories suggest that Jesus is not interested in merely subduing the forces of nature, he is trying to evoke a response from them just as he seeks a response from people.

New Testament writers compare Jesus to a lamb. Lambs are those vulnerable and innocent creatures we see gambolling in the fields, suckling at their mothers' breasts, and then slaughtered for us to eat – and in religion they were sacrificial offerings – symbols of humans asking God to forgive. The Bible ends with the vision of the world's peoples reclining at table with the Lamb who sits on the throne – surely the ultimate fulfilment of Isaiah's vision.

Pause for thought

Country people used to imagine that on Christmas Eve the horses and oxen knelt to Jesus in their stables, and even the bees gave out a special buzz. What do you imagine?

Prayer

May the rains fall on our land
and the cows grow fat.
May the children take the wisdom of the ancestors
and build on all that is good.
May time stand still
as we gaze upon the beauty that is around us.
And may the love in our hearts
envelop all those whom we touch.[18]

Today's step

I step
away from the consumer mentality
towards the creatures.

Spiritual breathing exercise

Communion in.
Disregard out.
New creation.

JUNE 9

Meet God through creation

Bible reading

This word from the Eternal God came to Jeremiah: 'What do you see?' 'I see,' said Jeremiah, 'a shoot growing out of an almond tree, which we know as a "wake tree".' God said to him: 'You have seen well. I am wakeful over my word, to carry it out.'

Jeremiah 1:11, 12

Reflection

We are called not only to speak to nature, but to let nature speak to us, for it is God's mouthpiece. God spoke to Jeremiah through a tree, to Moses through a bush, and to three wise magi through a star. The lad who became the famous Brother Lawrence[19] was converted by gazing at a tree. Meister Eckhart said, 'Anyone who truly knows creatures may be excused from listening to sermons for every creature is full of God, and is a book.'[20]

To become still. To listen. To be touched. That is the divine intention for us – that creation be a physical reality bringing us in a special way into the presence of the divine.

A Dakota author states that to the Indian the duty of prayer is more necessary than daily food. He wakes at day break and steps into the water's edge, rubbing water over him. Then he stands erect, and meets the advancing sun, the new sweet earth and the Great Silence alone in prayer. Whenever a hunter comes upon a scene that is strikingly beautiful or sublime – a black thundercloud with the rainbow's glowing arch above the mountain, a white waterfall in the heart of a green gorge; a vast prairie tinged with the blood-red of sunset – he pauses for an instant in an attitude of worship.[21]

JUNE 9

The earth lifts its glass to the sun, and light – light is poured.

A bird comes and sits on a crystal rim, and from my forest cave I hear singing.

So I run to the edge of existence and join my soul in love.
I lift my heart to God and grace is poured.

An emerald bird rises from inside me
and now sits upon the Beloved's glass.

I have left that dark cave forever.
My body is blended with his.
I lay my wing as a bridge to you
so that you can join us singing.[22]

Pause for thought

Become aware of something in nature that draws your attention. What does God say to you through this?

Prayer

Great Spirit,
the birds sing: what song do you wish to awake on my lips?
The clouds open: what do you wish to open in my heart?
The stones know; what do you wish me to know in my mind?
The plants come into bloom:
what do you wish to bring to flower in our time?

Today's step

I step
away from plastic
towards the elements.

Spiritual breathing exercise

Natural in.
Unnatural out.
Spirit.

JUNE 10

Touch the earth

Bible reading

God speaks to a mortal: When I created the earth, where were you? Has any human measured the earth? Do you think you could grasp earth by its four corners and shake out what's wrong? I could. Earth stands out clearly in all its colours. Can you put your arms round earth's girth? If so, tell me. Do you think you have been around so long that you could witness the making of earth? The mortal (Job) answers: My self-importance has gone, I now know I am small compared to you.

Job 38:4, 5, 18, 21; 40:3, 4

Reflection

A Native American chief[23] wrote of his people: 'The Lakota loved the earth and all things of the earth, the attachment growing with age. The old people came literally to love the soil and they sat or reclined on the ground with a feeling of being close to a mothering power. It was good for the skin to touch the earth and the old people liked to remove their moccasins and walk with bare feet on the sacred earth. Their tipis were made upon the earth and their altars were made of earth. The birds that flew in the air came to rest upon the earth and it was the final abiding place of all things that lived and grew. The soil was soothing, strengthening, cleansing and healing . . . For the old Indian, to sit or lie upon the ground is to be able to think more deeply and to feel more keenly . . . and come closer in kinship to other lives about him.'[24]

Are we humans still part of nature, or has the human race grown too far apart to recover its connectedness, with its power to destroy now more developed than its power to partner? We now have a veto of life and death over much of life on earth. Global capitalism has a dynamic of its own which seems inimical to nature and immune to human control. Yet could the collapse of faulty infrastructure of capitalism, and a re-wilding of the globe's exhausted landscapes be part of God's answer?

However that may be, each of us may reconnect with the earth by taking ten minutes each day to contemplate God's creation and to acknowledge our earthiness.

Pause for thought

Why not find a way to 'earth the earth' in our consciousness by carrying, wearing or praying with a stone? Or by making a practice of repeating these words: 'From earth I come: to earth I go'?

Prayer

Earth, teach me stillness.
Earth, teach me humility.
May I allow myself to be
softened by rain,
dug deep by providence,
planted with wisdom's seeds,
replenished by rest
and made into a hospitable bed for others.

Today's step

I step
away from the synthetic
towards the earth.

Spiritual breathing exercise

Earth in.
Airs out.
Jesus.

JUNE 11

We bless creation

Bible reading

Bless the Holy One, all you works of God
to whom be highest praise and glory for ever!

You skies and clouds , bless the Holy One,
you sun and moon, bless the Holy One,
you, showers and rain, bless the Holy One
to whom be highest glory and praise for ever.

You breezes and winds, bless the Holy One,
you cold and heat, bless the Holy One,
you summer and winter, bless the Holy One
to whom be highest glory and praise for ever.

All that grows in the ground, bless the Holy One,
all that swims in the waters, bless the Holy One,
all birds that fly in the air, bless the Holy One
to whom be highest glory and praise for ever.

Bless the Holy One all creation,
bless the Holy One all the human race,
whose love is everlasting.

Selected from the Septuagint version of the Book of Daniel 3:51–90

Reflection

Because everything that God has made, including ourselves, is interconnected, we respond to it. We either wish it well or ill. To bless is to wish it well. In the Bible's second creation account God invites Mr Earth (Adam) to name each bird and animal. Naming is a way of blessing by honouring that which is distinctive in another. It is good also to bless the soil. At a midsummer earth blessing these words are sometimes used:

How beautiful is the soil that God has made. Frail seeds blown by gentle winds become garlands of colour flowering in crevice and cranny.

How mysterious is the soil that God has made. Its deeps bring forth minerals with which we bring buildings, energy and ornament to our lives.

How fruitful is the soil that God has made. It brings forth crops of wheat and wood, of fruits and nuts, of roots and berries.

How hospitable is the soil that God has made. Even the birds who soar above the highest mountain must return to earth to find food. The earth provides a bed for the ocean, and a floor for humankind.

How like a mother is the soil that God has made. It contains us and feeds us, it warms us and holds us.

Pause for thought
Become aware of one plant or creature you feel drawn to. Bless it.

Prayer
Nurturing God, bless this soil, the soil on which we live and work and make community. In your mercy may it bring forth goodness to nourish and renew the whole community who shares it.

Today's step
I step
away from raping the earth
towards blessing the earth.

Spiritual breathing exercise
Blessing in.
Misusing out.
Shalom.

JUNE 12

We celebrate creation

Bible reading

You shall go out with joy. The hills shall burst into song in front of you. And the leaves of the trees shall clap their hands.

Isaiah 55:12

Burst into song, mountains, forests and all trees.

Isaiah 44:23

Praise God:
sun, moon and shining stars;
fire and hail, snow and mist;
mountains and hills, orchards and cattle;
all peoples and rulers, young and old
whose splendour transcends earth and skies.

Psalm 148

Reflection

> Now we're learning from the new sciences that the universe has actually been constructed as a We. Everything in creation – oceans, whales, mountains, humans, eagles, roses, giraffes and viruses – is a dance of subatomic particles. No single creature can disengage from the dance of creation without jeopardising the eternal beauty of that dance.[25]

We can celebrate creation in our hearts, songs, prayers, arts and decorations – and through our senses.
We see beautiful scenery, a rainbow.
We hear a baby's cry, birdsong.
We taste water, food.
We smell the fragrance of flowers, foods.
We touch a pet, a friend.
We marvel at how God creates within us.

In our eating we are linked with those who have prepared our food, we are grateful for plants and animals who lived and died for this eating to be possible. In our churches we may bring tokens of creation's goodness into worship and explain how these speak to us of God.

This is just a foretaste. When Betty Eadie had her out-of-the-body experience of the next world she experienced music coming from water: 'the water was praising God for its life and joy. The overall effect seemed beyond the ability of any symphony or composer here.'[26]

Pause for thought

Taste and see how good is God!

Prayer

Glad Bringer of brightness,
day's blessing, rainbow's embrace,
teach our hearts to open as the buds open
and to welcome in your grace.
Teach us to dance with the playful clouds
and to laugh with sun's smile on our face.
The earth is yours, may it bring forth its produce,
the birds are yours, may they bring forth their songs,
our work is yours, may it bring forth its yield.
May all that has been made stir within us
creation's song of praise.

Today's step

I step
away from complaining
towards celebration.

Spiritual breathing exercise

Savouring in.
Sourness out.
Celebrate!

JUNE 13

The goodness of creation

Bible reading

When God began to form the universe the world was a void enveloped in darkness. But the Spirit of God was hovering over the waters that covered it . . . God formed every kind of living creature, and also every kind of bird. God saw that it was good . . . God saw all that he had made, and how good it was!

Genesis 1:1–4, 21, 22

Reflection

We affirm God's creation as essentially good.[27]

When you go barefoot, you feel the touch of the ground. Some of the rivulets are warm to the step. They've flowed long on sun-warmed surfaces. Others are icy; freshly sourced in the spring. They're the ones to drink from. And you tread on the earth so much more gently barefoot. You don't dig in as with hard-heeled boots when stepping down the slopes; you softly contour your toes and grip the land, like an embrace. You lean forwards rather than backwards; you see better what lies beneath your feet. You pass, unharming, over emerald sod and yellow-flowing tormentil with its golden mandala-shaped petals. You realise, afresh, why we evolved toes, their function in giving balance. You experience a harmony of body, soil and soul. You become more . . . incarnate.

I walk on like this for two or three miles. Not far away, the high Cuillin rise. We walk on, all of us, until, to our amazement, three eagles ascend and wheel over the mountains' silhouette. They draw us back, together, into a space that now is different; different now, as we too lift and soar on eagle wings.[28]

Creation does, of course, grow. It is incomplete. It is a work of God in progress. There are evils that spoil it, but in its original essence it is good.

Pause for thought
Become aware of the goodness of some part of creation you can see now.

Prayer

In the flavour of a fruit,
in the flowing of a stream,
in the feeling of a sunset,
may we know that you are good.

Today's step

I step
away from trash
towards goodness.

Spiritual breathing exercise

Appreciation in.
Disparagement out.
Goodness.

JUNE 14

The elements: earth

Bible reading

Jesus passed a man who had been blind from birth. He spat on the earth and made mud with the saliva. He smeared it on the man's eyes and told him to bathe his eyes in the nearby healing pool of Siloam. The man did so, and went home with his sight restored.

John 9:1, 6, 7

Reflection

> What is the meaning of the beautiful story of Jesus healing a blind man by putting mud made with his saliva on the man's eyes, and then telling him to bathe in the pool of Siloam (John 9:1-7)? Is it that Jesus took the man back to primordial reality and mixed his own, life-creating spittle with the clay of the earth to bring the man into the fullness of creation?[29]

In both Western and Eastern tradition there are four material elements – earth, water, air and fire – and a fifth, the ether, which represents the spiritual world.

David Tacey writes: 'We are more than human beings, we are cosmic beings, "formed from stardust", and when we catch a glimpse of this deeper belonging, we suddenly feel "at home" in the universe, and we desire to work for the good of the whole, rather than strive only to satisfy the part. The paradox of spirituality is that in serving the whole the part is truly satisfied. This is the testimony of saints and martyrs throughout history, and we can experience this for ourselves today.'[30]

Pause for thought

Holy people draw earthly things to them.[31]

Prayer

When all was prepared, you formed human beings from the soil. You breathed your life into them. May we never forget that we are mortal creatures; from earth we come, to earth we go.

We offer you the earth and the vegetables that grow from it.
We offer you the earth and the minerals that lie under it.
We offer you the earth and the creatures that move over it.
We offer you ourselves who make our home upon it,
for all creation is yours and we want to be enriching it.

Today's step

I step
away from self-sufficiency
towards earth.

Spiritual breathing exercise

Touch in.
Trash out.
Good earth.

JUNE 15

Water

Bible reading

The poor and needy search in vain for water. But I, the Almighty, will not leave them desolate. I will make rivers flow in barren hills, I will turn deserts into pools of water, and the thirsty ground into water springs. Then the cedar and olive trees will grow, the fir and the cypress side by side, so that people may see and understand that the hand of providence has made this possible.

Isaiah 41:17–20

Reflection

Human beings are some three-fourths water. Planet earth is more than three-fourths covered in water. Water sustains life, but water is more even than that. It is the facilitator of life. In the emergence of the cosmos, the appearance of water was the crucial hinge that facilitated the emergence of biological life. Water's unique molecular structure was the 'womb' making a space in which life could form.

Water is a substance that communicates the spiritual. It is an enchanted halfway space between the spiritual and the physical. Water is ethereal. It can be a mist suspended in the air. Water can create buoyancy, which requires faith. It can be overwhelming. Water can wash us clean and let us start anew.

Could it be that God orchestrated the amazing role and power of water so that we would not get too far away and disconnected? The sacramental character of water is writ all through Christian Scripture. The psalms speak often of waters. When Israel's people were devastated in their exile, they were drawn to sit down by the waters of Babylon and there pour out the sorrows of their soul (Psalm 137). People who are oppressed by the weight of injustice feel they can tell their story to the waters that flow on to somewhere else, free, with energy, and beyond control.

Water is, for people in this awful psychological space, a reservoir. Water's substance as tangible but fluid is a medium to hold the memories which are too deep for concrete expression. Only water can carry this formless pain's weight and give memory a space. Water is specially suited to allow God's presence without demanding a specificity beyond the strength of the grieving. (Inspired by a talk by Tim Clayton.)

Pause for thought

Come to the living waters and drink.

Prayer

Lead me to a still pool of water.
Revive my dryness,
soak my soreness,
refresh my tiredness,
wash my filthiness,
bathe my woundedness.
Immerse me in your love.

Today's step

I step
away from what is parched
towards living water.

Spiritual breathing exercise

Flowing in.
Dryness out.
Filled!

JUNE 16

Air

Bible reading
It is God's breath that made the skies clear . . . It is God's breath that produces the ice that freezes over the lakes . . . If God withdrew his breath all human beings would instantly expire and return to dust.

Job 26:13; 37:10; 34:14, 15

Reflection
This most excellent canopy, the air.[32]

Without air, everything would die. Yet, because we cannot see it, we too often take it for granted. According to one encyclopaedia properties of air include temperature, density, heat, thermal conductivity, and kinematic viscosity! The molecules of two different elements, nitrogen and oxygen, make up about 99 per cent of the air. Oxygen is the life-giving element in the air. It helps plants make food. Oxygen supports fire and other chemical changes in matter. Air is essential to the pumps that make possible our essential services. It is essential to aeroplanes, and to everything that breathes.

In Chinese understanding *chi* is linked to air; it is a life force or energy. In the Bible air is linked to breath. The breathing of God is the Spirit of God. Key words such as *aspire, conspire, inspire, perspire,* and *spirit*, all derive from the Latin *spirare* – to breathe.

It takes 10 trees to provide one person's lifetime consumption of oxygen.

The poet Gerard Manley Hopkins wrote a poem comparing the Blessed Virgin Mary to the air we breathe:

> Wild air, world-mothering air,
> nestling me everywhere,
> that each eyelash or hair
> girdles;

this needful, never spent,
and nursing element;
my more than meat and drink,
my meal at every wink;
this air, which, by life's law,
my lung must draw and draw
now but to breathe its praise,
minds me in many ways
of her who not only
gave God's infinity
dwindled to infancy
welcome in womb and breast,
birth, milk, and all the rest
but mothers each new grace . . .

Pause for thought

A meditation of the mystic Neil Douglas-Klotz on the Aramaic words of Jesus which we translate as 'Blessed are the poor in spirit' begins: 'Happy and aligned with the One are those who find their home in the breathing.'

Prayer

O Breath of God come sweeping through us
renewing thought and will and heart.
O Breath of God refresh, revive us
and fit us now to play our part.

Today's step

I step
away from what is lifeless
towards fresh air.

Spiritual breathing exercise

Your breath in.
Staleness out.
Eternal life.

JUNE 17

Fire

Bible reading

The heavens bespeak the glory of God;
the firmament ablaze, a text of God's works.
Dawn whispers to sunset,
dark to dark the word passes; glory, glory.
All in a great silence, no tongue's clamour –
yet the web of the world trembles
conscious, as of great winds passing.
The bridegroom's tent is raised, a cry goes up: he comes!
Rejoicing, presiding, his wedding day.
From end to end of the universe, his progress.
No creature, no least being, but catches fire from him.[33]

Psalm 19

Reflection

The sun's ceaseless revolutions surely speak about divine Principles of heat and keenness, the exuberance of their intense, tireless activity, and their permeating of those below, kindling them and firing them to their own heat, and purifying them by an all-consuming flame and by the unhidden, unquenchable, radiant and enlightening power, dispelling and destroying the shadows of darkness.

The amount of solar energy reaching the earth's surface in one minute is greater than all the other types of energy used by everyone in the world during one year. Wisdom seems to say 'tap into it'. In Ottawa I met a man who is doing just that. Dave has developed a host of inventions, especially solar energy equipment that maximises heat and light generation. Dave wants to write a book entitled *The Sun and the Son*. He says, 'The Son created the sun so that we can all have plenty of energy. All it needs is to get those photons into the right places. The Son can show us how to do this.'

The universe is not something just 'out there', however. We carry within us the energy that fashioned the stars. It is significant that light was the first creation. It existed outside of time and space. It is our link with the eternity that preceded the cosmos. It can become matter but is not confined to matter.

Hildegaard of Bingen[34] wrote that 'All living creatures are sparks from the radiation of God's brilliance, and these sparks emerge from God like the rays of the sun.' Pseudo-Dionysius the Areopagite in his *Celestial Hierarchy* described the seraphim as 'those who kindle or make hot'.

Pause for thought

Seek this fire, this purifying ardour, for yourself.

Prayer

I arise today in the brilliance of the sun:
its fire to warm us
its beams to light us
its rays to cheer us.

I arise today in the power of the Sun of suns:
the Sun of truth
the Sun of life
the Sun without end.

Today's step

I step
away from the gloom
towards the glow.

Spiritual breathing exercise

Sun in.
Dark out.
Light.

JUNE 18

Oil

Bible reading

A harvest comes out of the depths of the earth when engineers blast their way down, drilling channels, exploring for hidden yields that are worth a fortune. But where is wisdom to be found? That is not so easy to find.

Job 28:5, 10–12

Reflection

> There is no substitute for energy. The whole edifice of modern society is built upon it: it is a basic factor, equal with air, water and earth.[35]

Most human eras, such as the stone age, lasted for millennia and most civilisations have lasted for over four hundred years. It looks as though the Oil Age may be the shortest in history. The human race became industrialised and rich when it discovered the temporary delight of fossil fuels. This enabled us to move from human and horse power to machines, vehicles and aeroplanes; it enabled us to light and heat workplaces at all hours, to create metal and drugs, and to expand from a population of one billion in 1820 to over six billion today.

The oil is now about to run out. Even during its peak discovery years, the world consumed two barrels of oil for every barrel discovered. Planes will be grounded. Shops will be empty. Hospitals and banks will close. Without a miracle, five-sixths of the world's population will lie dead. What went wrong? What can we learn?

God put the oil there. We learned how to extricate and turn it into energy, but we did not consult God as to how we should steward it. Even in 1999 the USA Energy Secretary Bill Richardson stated: 'Oil has literally made (USA) foreign and security policy for decades . . . it has provoked the division of the Middle East . . . the Arab Oil Embargo; Iran versus Iraq; the Gulf War. This is all clear.' We built a civilisation on the premise of unending growth – growth that depends upon energy.

Pause for thought

Now we have to prepare, as did so many people in the Bible, to live God-guided lives in a period when the society we have known crumbles.

Prayer

God bless the oil and the good things it has made possible.
God forgive us for grabbing it
and wasting it without wisdom.
God help us as we reap the harvest of our misdeeds.
God guide us as we seek to harness the energies
of sun and wind and water –
and make us wise.

Today's step

I step
away from oil
towards wisdom.

Spiritual breathing exercise

Conserving in.
Guzzling out.
Enough.

JUNE 19

Trees

Bible reading

God's trees drink their fill, the cedars of Lebanon which God sowed. There the birds build their nests; on the high branches the stork makes its home. You bring on darkness, and night falls, when all the forest beasts roam around. How countless are your works, O God, all of them made so wisely!

Psalm 104:16, 17, 20, 24

Reflection

The story of Easter Island is a parable for our time. It seems this island of verdant trees was first settled some four hundred years before Christ. By 1600 total deforestation had caused massive and irreversible degradation to the environment. It became a desert. What happened? The islanders cleared the trees for agriculture, dwellings, and for their great stone sculptures, and gradually used up what was available to them for food and wood, without any thought as to how these needed to be stewarded and replenished. They continued to do this even when it must have become obvious that they were nearing the end of their limited resources. Without trees, the island was finished. Without forests, our planet is finished.

St Kevin[36] swore that the branches and leaves of the trees bowed down to him and sang sweet songs when he prayed there. He warned those who threatened to cut or burn the wood that they would reap what they sowed and their life, too, would be cut short if they did this.

Father Amphilochios[37] of Patmos was noted for his love of trees. 'Do you know,' he used to say, 'that God gave us one more commandment, which is not recorded in Scripture? It is the commandment *Love the trees.*' Whoever does not love trees, he was convinced, does not love Christ. When hearing the confessions of the local farmers, he assigned to them as a penance the task of planting a tree; and through his influence many hillsides of Patmos, which once were barren rock, are now green with foliage every summer.[38]

Pause for thought

Plant a tree, save a tree by using less packaging, or simply go to a tree and become present to it.

Prayer

Let me not spoil one leaf nor break one branch.
Let me not blunder, plunder, pollute, exploit,
but rather see and hear,
and touch and taste and smell,
and in my sensing know you well, Creator God.[39]

Today's step

I step
away from excess packaging
towards a tree.

Spiritual breathing exercise

Trees in.
Waste out.
Glory.

JUNE 20

Spoiled!

Bible reading

God placed a man and a woman in a great garden, to care for it, and told them: 'You can eat fruit from anything you like except this one tree, whose fruit would destroy your innocence.' A sly serpent said to the woman, 'Did God really command you not to eat of that tree? Try it and see – it will be good for you.' So the woman took the forbidden fruit, and so did her husband. Then they became self-conscious about being naked and started to cover up and hide from God. God said: 'The result of this is that there will be conflict between you and nature, even child-bearing will become a pain, the land will become resistant and your work will no longer be a pleasure.'

Genesis 2

Reflection

In the novel *The Shack*[40] Mack asks, 'I know you are the Creator, but did you make the poisonous plants, stinging nettles and mosquitoes, too?' Mack was informed that God created what he considered 'the bad stuff', but that 'when I created it, it was only Good, because that is just the way I am.' 'Then why has so much of the "Good" gone "bad"?' asked Mack. He was told: 'You humans are truly blind to your own place in the Creation. Having chosen the ravaged path of independence, you don't even comprehend that you are dragging the entire Creation along with you . . . So very sad, but it won't be this way for ever.'

Headteacher Richard Dell writes: 'We all have things to relearn. We are too much trained in the technical and mechanical; too much conditioned by the processes of logic. For generations we have been divorced from the moods and movements of the seasons, from the intricate rhythms of nature, from the story held in the flight of a bird, from the meaning contained in the flight of a butterfly's wing. We have all but lost our place in our own planet's book of life. We have become like spiritual orphans in our own dying lands, trapped for the sake of our own sense of security, ensnared for no other reason than to deny the existence of our inner demons . . . when all the universe, the entire multi-dimensional cosmos itself only awaits our cry for help.'[41]

Pause for thought

Do you feel this?

Prayer

Creator of our earth, the trees
the water, animals and humans –
out of wet mud you have fashioned a wonderful world
and what beautiful men and women!

We drink in your creation and cannot get enough of it,
but we forget the evil we have done.
Tear us away from our sins.
This wonderful world fades
and one day our eyes snap shut.
Then all that is not from you is over and dead.[42]

Today's step

I step
away from disobedience
towards God.

Spiritual breathing exercise

Sharing in.
Me-first out.
Restoring.

JUNE 21

An inconvenient truth

Bible reading

There was a violent earthquake.
The sun went black and the moon turned red.
The stars fell on to the earth
as figs fall from a tree in a gale-force wind.
The sky looked like a paper scroll being wound up.
Mountains and islands were displaced.
All the world's top people, as well as the ordinary population,
hid among rocks and caves and cried out for mercy.

Revelation 6:12–16

Reflection

Today we dumped another 70 million tons of global-warming pollution into the thin shell of atmosphere surrounding our planet, as if it were an open sewer. And tomorrow, we will dump a slightly larger amount, with the cumulative concentrations trapping more and more heat from the sun. As a result, the Earth has a fever. And the fever is rising. The experts have told us it is not a passing affliction that will heal by itself . . . The consistent conclusion, restated with increasing alarm, is that something basic is wrong. We are what is wrong, and we must make it right.[43]

How do we make a habit of cherishing creation? Indigenous people suffer from the insensitivity of modern, industrialised nations that destroy power spots to make superhighways, burn rainforests to make houses, and put state parks and recreation areas on ancient burial grounds. This destructive style of relating to the world is manifest not only in air and water pollution, but in how you repress your own nature by failing to develop the second attention that experiences the earth as mysterious and alive.[44]

Money is not wealth. True wealth is good land, healthy animals, flourishing forests, clean water, honest work, abundant creativity and human imagination . . . The purpose of money was and should be to serve the human and the Earth community. However, it appears the original purpose has now been reversed. Now people and the planet are put into the service of money.[45]

Pause for thought

How may we escape retribution before it is too late?

Prayer

Help us to know that the earth does not belong to us,
we belong to earth.
Help us to know that we did not weave the web of life,
we are merely a strand in it.
Help us to know that whatever we do to ourselves,
we do to the earth.
Help us to know that whatever befalls the earth
befalls the sons and daughters of the earth.

Today's step

I step
away from denial
towards truth.

Spiritual breathing exercise

Developing in.
Dumping out.
Shalom.

JUNE 22

Respect nature

Bible reading

God says: The time will come when I will give back to the land I love her vineyards, and turn her 'Big Valley' into 'Gateway of Hope'. I will make an unalterable treaty with world wildlife – the animals, birds, and insects under the earth. I shall be to the earth like a lover who vows to give faithful love and tender care. Then my cosmic spiritual energies will respond to the earth, and the earth will respond to the grain, wine and oil, and the land will say, 'You are my God.'

Hosea 2:17–25

Reflection

> We therefore respect nature, and are committed to seeing it cared for and restored.[46]

We are milking the world dry without any thought. Treat the world as a garden. Respect nature by increasing biodiversity in our gardens and on our rooftops, in our cities and parks, our forests and oceans. New Zealand has taken a lead in establishing marine reserves: where can we take a lead?

Efforts to localise economies are happening at the grassroots all over the world, and bringing with them a sense of well-being. A young man who started an urban garden in Detroit, one of the USA's most blighted cities, said: 'I've lived in the community over thirty-five years and people I'd never met came up and talked to me when we started this project. We found that it reconnects us with the people around us – it makes community a reality.' Another young gardener in Detroit put it this way: 'Everything just feels better to people when there is something growing.'

Respect nature in our holidays. Eschew mindless package tours. Save up for fewer but longer visits. Stay in a place long enough to respect it. Tourism can honour the countryside, learn about its history, respect local traditions and the environment. Walk or cycle, sit and touch and see.

Pause for thought

The continued destruction of the natural environment is, essentially, a spiritual problem which we, when guided by our deepest spirituality, seek to change.

Prayer

Creator God,
help us to give all creatures their due respect.
Teach us how to conserve, to share, to enjoy,
to tend the earth with care,
to develop agriculture that truly enhances,
to guide science along wise and considerate ways,
to restore the lands that have been ravaged,
until we, the earth and you blossom in a relationship of love.

Today's step

I step
away from indifference to the created world
towards commitment.

Spiritual breathing exercise

Tending in.
Trampling out.
Restore.

JUNE 23

Earth-care

Bible reading

Jesus began to tell stories about earth which had an eternal message. A landowner planted a vineyard, protected it with a wall, watered it with good irrigation, and erected a watchtower. Since the landowner had other concerns, he leased the vineyard to well-qualified tenants. At harvest he sent staff to collect his share of the produce, but the tenants beat them up. This happened three times. Eventually the landowner was so concerned he sent his only son, thinking they would surely not harm him. But they did worse. They thought that if they killed the son, no one else would be sent to bother them, and they could do what they liked with the vineyard. So they killed the son. The landowner, however, did come. The tenants were sentenced under the law, and the landowner gave the vineyard to foreigners.

Mark 12:1–9

Reflection

The vineyard was planet earth. The tenants were Jesus' tribe, the Jews. The landowner was God. The son was Jesus. The point of the story, which Jesus told to his disciples days before he was killed, was that just because God had called the Jews to care for the earth, did not give them a right to abuse this call without consequences. Others – foreigners – would be entrusted with the work. And what is the work with which we all are now entrusted? Care of the earth. There will be consequences for us if we continue to neglect the earth and abuse those who till and farm it.

An old holy Wintu woman used to say that the Indians never hurt anything. When they use rocks, they take little round ones for their cooking, but everywhere the Whiter Man touched the earth, it is sore.

Pause for thought

Touch the earth lightly, tenderly, today. Clear up a mess or attend to something good.

Prayer

Here be the peace of those who do your sacred will,
here be the praise of God by night and day,
here be the place where strong ones serve the weakest,
here be a sight of Christ's most gentle way.

Here be the strength of prophets righting greed and wrong,
here be the green of land that's tilled with love,
here be the soil of holy lives maturing,
here be a people one with all the saints above.[47]

Today's step

I step away
from mis-use
towards tender care.

Spiritual breathing exercise

Tend.
Care.
Love.

JUNE 24

An earthed lifestyle

Bible reading

What you sow does not come to life unless it dies. There are different kinds of created bodies. Humans have one kind of flesh, animals another, birds another and fish another. There are celestial bodies and earthly bodies; each has their own kind of splendour. The same principle applies to the resurrection of dead bodies. The body that is 'sown' is perishable, it is raised imperishable. It is sown a natural body, it is raised a spiritual body. That is why the Scripture writes: The first Mr. Earth became a living being, the last Mr. Earth became a life-giving spirit. The spiritual did not come first, but the natural. The first human was of the earth, and so are all of us who are of the earth. The second human came from heaven, as are all those who bear the likeness of the One from heaven.

1 Corinthians 15:36–40, 44–49

Reflection

> In the Indian the spirit of the land is still vested; it will be until other men are able to divine and meet its rhythm. Men must be born and reborn to belong. Their bodies must be formed of the dust of their forefather's bones.[48]

Humility is about being rooted in the earth. Every human being has to eat and sleep. Every human being is completely dependent upon others when they are born, and probably when they die. Jesus, the Peoples' Son, was born among farm animals and schooled at a workman's bench. He used his brain to the full, but was not up in the clouds. He had his feet firmly on the ground.

He calls us to be willing to get our hands dirty, to care for others, to make relationships.

If you are a practical person and work most easily with your hands rather than with paper, know that God is with you in this and you can be close to God. If you are a person to whom ideas and talk come easily, work at body-mind balance; take pains over practical things, be earthed.

Pause for thought

Count to two before saying or doing anything superficial. Use the space to connect with something real.

Prayer

May I be grounded, like the earth.
May I be real, like the elements.
May I be true, like the fire.

Today's step

I step
away from the clouds
down to earth.

Spiritual breathing exercise

Reality in.
Unreality out.
Earthed.

JUNE 25

Ecologically aware

Bible reading

In the aeon that the Eternal God made heaven and earth as yet no plant had sprung up, for the Eternal had not yet sent rain and there was no human to till the soil, though a mist rose from the earth and moistened its surface. Then the Eternal evolved a human from the earth, breathing life that resulted in a living soul. Far in the east, in the land of Eden, the Eternal planted a garden, with all kinds of delightful trees, where he placed the human being to till it and look after it.

Genesis 2:1–9, 15

Reflection

The concept of the 'biosphere' which emerged widely in the 1980s understands that everything that makes up the earth and the 'envelope' of substances that surround it, are a living, interconnected whole, and one part affects the other parts.

In 1973 Arne Ness[49] introduced the concept of 'deep ecology'. Its central tenet is that the human species is a part of the earth and not separate from it. A process of self-realisation or 're-earthing' is used for an individual to intuitively gain an eco-centric perspective. The notion is based on the idea that the more we expand the self to identify with 'others' (people, animals, ecosystems), the more we realise ourselves. Deep ecologists believe that:

> The whole system is superior to any of its parts.
>
> The well-being and flourishing of human and non-human life on earth have value in themselves regardless of the usefulness of the nonhuman world for human purposes.

> Humans have no right to reduce this richness and diversity except to satisfy vital human needs. Present human interference with the nonhuman world requires a radical change of policies.

How sad that Arne Ness perceived the Judeao-Christian tradition as being against these values. He wrote 'The arrogance of stewardship [as found in this tradition] consists in the idea of superiority which underlies the thought that we exist to watch over nature like a highly respected middleman between the Creator and Creation.' There is no hint of this arrogance in the earliest biblical creation story, above. Dominion is not domination; it is an eschatological sign of the perfect kingdom of God.

Pause for thought

May we discard superiority that abuses, and embrace a calling that enhances the earth.

Prayer

Bless us with humility towards nature and other people.
Bless us with good encounters with nature
in all types of weather, terrain and seasons.
Bless us with wisdom in our care of animals and plants,
that we may steward creation
with regard to each thing's intrinsic value.[50]

Today's step

I step
away from de-earthing
towards re-earthing.

Spiritual breathing exercise

In with the web of life.
Out with independence.
Aware.

JUNE 26

Good eco-habits

Bible reading

Like ice that cools a strong drink, so is a person who can be trusted. If you are able to obtain some product such as honey, eat only what you need. If you binge you will vomit. Do not rush here, there, and everywhere: if you outstay your welcome people will turn against you. A person who does not know when enough is enough is like a town with holes in its protective walls. When we are overfed we disdain simple food, but to a hungry person even some bitter-tasting food seems sweet. If you tend a tree well you will get its fruits. If you are farmer, you gather the grass and stack the hay first, and then your sheep will provide you with wool for your clothes, and your goats with milk. A grasping person stirs up envy, but the person who trusts God thrives.

Proverbs 25–28

Reflection

Here are some simple steps to reduce your 'carbon footprint':

In the home:
1. Use energy-saving light bulbs and switch off when you are not using them!
2. Switch everything off by the mains and don't leave it on 'standby'. A TV left on standby still uses around 80 per cent of the energy used when it is playing.
3. Lower your thermostat by 1–5 degrees, and if necessary put on an extra layer of clothes.
4. Recycle and compost.

In the car:
1. If your journey is less than two miles – walk.
2. Change gear sooner. A car travelling at 45mph in fifth gear produces less than 50 per cent of emissions that a car travelling at the same speed in fourth gear produces.

3. Accelerate slowly – therefore producing fewer emissions.
4. When travelling long distances, travel slower. The most economical legal speed both for the environment and fuel consumption (therefore your wallet!) is in the mid-50s mph.

In the shops:
1. Reduce food miles by buying locally.
2. Buy organic! The amount of pesticides used on soft skin fruit can be so harsh that a seed planted from one of these fruits with no pesticides used in its growth can produce fruit still full of pesticides!
3. Buy 'bags for life'.
4. Go for the least packaging possible.
5. Grow your own.

Pause for thought

Let's all play our part. You can make a difference!

Prayer

Help us, God of the whole created world, to:
buy wisely,
use energy carefully,
travel prayerfully,
eat mindfully,
exchange thoughtfully.

Today's step

I step
away from waste
towards good stewardship.

Spiritual breathing exercise

Stewardship in.
Waste out.
Eco.

JUNE 27

Pray for all creatures

Bible reading

God causes spring waters to flow that quench the thirst of wild animals and enable birds to nest in nearby branches and sing.
Your work, O God, satisfies the needs of the earth
so that grasses grow on which the cattle feed.
The earth is full of your creatures, teeming beyond number, living beings both large and small:
They all look to you to give them their food in due season. When you open your hand, they are satisfied with good things.

Psalm 104

Reflection

If God's mercy is poured out upon the animal world, surely we, who are made to reflect the divine mercy, should pour out our mercy, beginning with our prayers? The Universal Prayer Circle for Animals believes that 'animal cruelty and exploitation are symptoms of a deeply embedded and misguided cultural belief system that maintains that human beings have the right to commodify, exploit, enslave, and kill whomever society deems "less than human".' Together we may address the cause of animal suffering by spiritually embracing the world with an energy field of compassion and reverence for all beings: 'Compassion encircles the earth for all beings everywhere.'

Surely, when Jesus said, 'how blest are the merciful', he longed for us to have hearts overflowing with mercy towards every person and every creature on this earth?

The famous story of Saint Kevin of Glendalough, whose prayers for God's creatures were put into practice in an unforgettable way, is well captured in this poem by Seamus Heaney:

And then there was St Kevin and the blackbird.
The saint is kneeling, arms stretched out, inside
his cell, but the cell is so narrow, so
one turned-up palm is out the window, stiff
as a cross beam, when a blackbird lands
and lays in it and settles down to rest.

Kevin feels the warm eggs, the small breast, the tucked
neat head and claws and, finding himself linked
into the network of eternal life,
is moved to pity: Now he must hold his hand
like a branch out in the sun and rain for weeks
until the young are hatched and fledged and flown.

Pause for thought

Kevin lived his prayer for a blackbird. Think of a creature you wish to pray for.

Prayer

Hear our humble prayer, O God, for our friends the animals, especially for animals who are suffering; for any that are hunted, or lost, or deserted or frightened or hungry; for all that must be put to death. We entreat for them all your pity, and for those who deal with them we ask for a heart of compassion, gentle hands and kindly words. Make us true friends to animals and so to share the blessing of the merciful.[51]

Today's step

I step
away from nonchalance towards creatures
towards pity for them.

Spiritual breathing exercise

Praying in.
Creature-neglect out.
Mercy.

JUNE 28

Stand against violation of creation

Bible reading

Someone had a fertile vineyard. He dug and planted it, protected it and put in a grape press. He expected to have delicious grapes, but in fact he only got sour grapes. Think about this – what more could the vineyard owner have done? God says: 'I am that person, and you, the people, are the vineyard. Therefore the vineyard will be trampled down.'

Isaiah 5

Reflection

Human beings are part of a whole called by us 'The Universe', a part limited in time and space. We experience ourselves, our thoughts and feelings, as something separated from the rest – a kind of optical delusion of consciousness. The delusion is a kind of prison for us, restricting us to our personal desires and to affection for a few persons nearest to us. Our task must be to free ourselves from this prison by widening our circles of compassion to embrace all living creatures and the whole of nature in its beauty.[52]

Weaver-God Creator sets life on the loom,
draws out threads of colour from primordial gloom.
Wise in designing, in the weaving deft,
love and justice joined the fabric's warp and weft.

Called to be co-weavers, yet we break the thread,
and may smash the shuttle and the loom instead.
Careless and greedy, we deny by theft,
love and justice joined, the fabric's warp and weft.

Weaver-God, Great Spirit, may we see your face,
tapestried in trees, in waves and winds of space.

Tenderness teach us, less we be bereft,
of love and justice joined, the fabric's warp and weft.

Weavers we are called, yet woven too we're born,
for the web is seamless; if we tear, we're torn.
Gently may we live, that fragile earth be left,
with love and justice joined, the fabric's warp and weft.[53]

Pause for thought

What practical action can you take? If you are not sure, ask at your local 'green' shop.

Prayer

God forgive us
for polluting waste dumped by rich nations
on lands of the poor,
for the lust of the few to own and control life forms,
for turning your gifts of water and life itself
into products for gain,
for turning the sowing of seed from a sacred duty
into a crime,
for destruction of biodiversity,
God, change our hearts.

Today's step

I step
away from mis-use of creation
towards good stewardship.

Spiritual breathing exercise

Tending in.
Plunder out.
Trust.

JUNE 29

Stand against cruelty to animals

Bible reading
It was the sabbath – the day when people rested from work including on their farms. Jesus, however, saw a sick man and healed him. He realised that some legal purists were about to condemn him for working on the sabbath, so he got in first and asked them: 'Which of you, if your donkey or ox falls into a hole would not at once pull him out even if it is the sabbath day?'

Luke 14:1–5

Reflection
In Jesus' society it was taken for granted that everyone helped an animal in trouble. In our society a few unhappy people are cruel to pets, but many buy products that have involved cruelty to animals without even thinking about it.

Compassion in World Farming was founded to end all cruel factory farming practices, such as intensive farming which prevents animals from enjoying natural conditions. As a result of such campaigning the European Union now recognises animals as sentient beings, capable of feeling pain and suffering, and landmark agreements have outlawed the barren battery cage for egg-laying hens, narrow veal crates and sow stalls. A few supermarkets refuse to stock cosmetic products that have involved cruel tests on animals. Discriminating shoppers buy free-range eggs and chickens. Organisations such as the World Wildlife Fund seek to preserve and extend reserves where wild animals may roam safe from human predators. But there is much more to do.

Pause for thought
Review your shopping habits in the light of animal-friendly criteria.

Prayer

Mother, Father, All that is, Source of life and love,
thank you for your miracles – for this planet, for this Life,
for our next breath.
Thank you for truth, for beauty, for innocence –
and for the animals.
Thank you for their being here with us – in the forest,
in the field, in the sea, in the sky, in our yards,
and in our homes.
Thank you for their presence on this planet.
If it were not for them, we would be here alone –
and how sterile and sad our lives on this earth would be.
Thank you for the truth of the animals,
for their profound beauty, for their innocence,
for their love – and for their witness.
We ask your forgiveness – and that of all non-human
animals to whom we have caused harm through our actions
– either directly through anger or thoughtlessness,
or indirectly through our purchases and consumption.
Help us to see that the light in their eyes is your light.
Help us to see that their love and trust of us
is your love and trust of us.
Help us to not betray that trust.
Help us to love you through loving your creation
and your creatures –
and to remember who we are.[54]

Today's step

I step
away from cruelty or neglect
towards mindfulness of animals.

Spiritual breathing exercise

Compassion in.
Cruelty out.
All are yours.

JUNE 30

A modern Noah's ark

Bible reading

When God realised that human beings were hell-bent on destruction and had a mind for nothing but squabbling God felt enormously sad that he had made all the wonderful creatures of earth only for this to happen. However, he came up with a rescue plan. There was one person who was still close to God – Noah. God informed Noah that a huge flood would almost wipe out the inhabited world, but that Noah was to build a vast barge – an ark – big enough to hold his family and a male and female of many species of animal and bird. The flood indeed deluged the world. But after many weeks it began to subside, and the people and animals in the ark started to live on earth again as God intended.

Genesis 6, 7

Reflection

In Christian tradition the church is likened to Noah's ark. The main part of a church building is called the nave, whose root is the Latin word navis, which means ship. Nothing less than a vast Noah's ark operation is called for from today's church. Operation Noah – faith communities coming together to tackle climate change – is a good beginning. It was founded by Christian Ecology Link (CEL) and the Environmental Issues Network of Churches Together in Britain and Ireland. It exists 'because God's creation faces the most urgent peril, which, to be averted, requires a rapid and radical transformation of our economy and culture – towards livable, supportable lifestyles'. Its slogan is 'shop less, live more, save the earth'. Local groups commit to increasing renewable energy use and do litter picks.

Christian Ecology Link provides an informed daily prayer guide on green issues. A Rocha is a Christian nature conservation organisation with a focus on science and research, conservation and education. In Britain Green Church Awards are given to congregations who do some of the following: use the church as a centre for environmental action and awareness, promote community energy saving, set up community composting, recycling schemes, transport-sharing, or help people on low incomes insulate their homes.

Pause for thought

Choose one action, from all those mentioned in today's reflection, that you will take.

Prayer

Birther,
the planet is pulling against you,
it is falling apart,
it is becoming deluged.
You do not want this.
So we come close to you.
Show us what to stop doing.
Show us what to start doing.
Show us how to build together
a worldwide Noah's ark for today.

Today's step

I step
away from squabbling about unimportant matters
towards saving the planet.

Spiritual breathing exercise

Earth-saving in.
Squabbling out.
The ark.

JULY 1

Making a whole new world

Bible reading

The serpent was more cunning than any other creature in the great park where God had placed the man and the woman. It said to the woman, 'God didn't really say that anything should be out of your reach.' The woman told the serpent: 'We can eat from any tree except for the one in the centre; if we touch that we will die.' 'Life will still go on,' said the serpent, 'you'll see. Why shouldn't you be like God?' So the woman ate some of the forbidden fruit and so did the man. Then they realised they were naked and covered themselves. In the cool of the early evening they heard the sound of God walking in the park. They said, 'We hid from you.'

Genesis 3

Reflection

Wholeness. It's what draws many to this way of life: trying to piece together life in a coherent whole, recognising we are part of something greater than we, but unable to make the connections.

The hunger for wholeness shouts our own fragmentation, that we are a wounded people who live in a wounded world. There is a fundamental woundedness at the heart of creation. Wounded people wound others. Abused people abuse others. Wounded communities abuse their members.

In order to address this we need to look back again to the wounding which we know as the story of The Fall of Human Beings in the third chapter of the Book of Genesis. It is worth noting that neither apples nor sex, two items popularly associated with the story, have any mention. The state of this couple as naked and not ashamed speaks of a vulnerability and childlike dependency. Their recognising the sound of God walking in the garden after their disobedience hints that it was familiar to them, that perhaps God came to them at the end of each day to instruct them about this new world God had put in their hands. It is important to note that there was not a prohibition about a tree of knowledge, as if human curiosity and a desire to learn was a wrong thing. It was a particular, moral knowledge that would shortcut their relationship of dependence upon God that was advised against which, according to the serpent's words, would move them from the role of dependency to equality with God. So long as the first humans remained in relationship with God, then all subsidiary relationships were whole and well. The temptation to be like God, to break the subservient role, was a test that the humans failed.

Pause for thought

How do I try to shortcut my dependence upon God?

Prayer

God, Source of our Being,
I acknowledge that we are fragmented.
Our communities are hurting.
Give me courage to look at the wound
at the heart of everything,
the wound we run away from,
the wound we hardly dare name.

Today's step

I step
away from fragmentation
towards wholeness.

Spiritual breathing exercise

Wholeness in.
Fragment out.
Healing.

JULY 2

A broken, blameful society

Bible reading

God said to the woman, 'What have you done?' She replied, 'It's the serpent's fault – he misled me.' 'Childbirth will become a pain to you, and your husband will become dominating,' God told her. The man said, 'It's her fault; she gave me the forbidden fruit to eat, and it was you who gave her to me.' God said: 'Because you listened to your wife more than to me your relationship with the earth will become pain and trouble, everything will become hard, the soil and the work of tending it.'

Genesis 3

Reflection

One can almost hear the fracturing of relationships throughout the whole created order. The first visible fracture is within human nature. Their eyes being opened to their folly, they are ashamed of their vulnerability and seek to cover it by their rudimentary clothing. The second is the sign of their broken relationship with God: they hide. The next fracture is that between people, the blaming. Adam seems better at this than Eve, for he seeks to pass on the blame to both Eve and God in one sentence! The final fracture indicated is normally referred to as God's curse of the ground. But this is probably not an accurate label. It seems not so much that God is placing a curse where none existed as simply pointing out that Adam, being in authority over creation, is now a curse on creation. 'Cursed is the ground because of you.' The systems of creation still function. Adam's body continues to work, his intelligence to reason. The land is still fertile, the earth holds together. Adam and Eve even maintain a community of sorts, but now it is disordered, involving domination and held together by a biological function that was ever intended to be secondary to the fellowship of human beings in wholeness.

As we look upon the story of creation through this lens the full breadth of the fracture begins to show itself. Even the concept of 'total depravity', never a part of Celtic Christian spirituality, makes a sort of sense – not as the utter ruin of the *imago Dei*, but the declaration that there is no part of existence that has escaped being wounded by sin. As nothing has escaped the Fall, so no part of our life is free from the fragmentation of a wounded creation. However, what began in Adam is being reversed in Christ. In Jesus a new humanity is offered, and the members of the old may enter. This new creation is a work in progress and involves taking the stories of wounded creation into the redemption of Christ.

Pause for thought

Think of a story of wounded creation and place it before Christ.

Prayer

I confess that we wound one another.
Our world is disordered.
Accompany us on a journey towards wholeness.

Today's step

I step
away from blame
towards blessing.

Spiritual breathing exercise

Fellowship in.
Disorder out.
Shalom.

JULY 3

Fractured society

Bible reading

Cain, the son of Adam and Eve, made an offering to God of some crops. His brother Abel made a more costly offering from his livestock. Realising that Abel was closer to God than he, Cain became jealous, and they quarrelled. 'Why quarrel?' God asked Cain. 'If you have integrity, all will be light between us.' Cain, however, killed his brother. 'Where is your brother?' asked God. 'Why should I be concerned, am I my brother's keeper?' Cain replied. 'Your brother's blood cries to me from the ground,' God said.

Genesis 4

Reflection

In ancient times Cain said, 'Am I my brother's keeper?' In the seventeenth century the philosopher Descartes said, 'I think therefore I exist.' This led Westerners to equate their identity with one piece of themselves, their mind, instead of with their whole being in relation to the whole world. As a result of this split in the Western psyche most people perceive themselves as isolated egos 'inside' their bodies. Each individual has been split up further into innumerable separate compartments, according to their beliefs, aptitudes, feelings which are engaged in endless conflicts and which generate confusion and frustration. Science was separated from religion, the sacred from the secular, money from morality. This fragmentation is surely the primary cause of the ecological and social crises that now threaten the very fabric of the world. It has divorced the consumer from the producer, and has alienated us all from nature.

> Things fall apart; the centre cannot hold;
> mere anarchy is loosed upon the world,
> the blood-dimmed tide is loosed, and everywhere

the ceremony of innocence is drowned;
the best lack all conviction, while the worst
are full of passionate intensity.[1]

The hand is a complete unit only as long as it is attached to the body. When it is severed from the body it may appear like a hand, but it loses the hand's powers. Similarly, humans are part of a Whole. If we are severed from this, the illusion that we are complete cannot survive the reality of experience. Only when everything is in organic relationship with the Whole do the parts become whole in themselves.

Pause for thought

'In Christ all things hold together' (Colossians 1:16–18). Out of Christ all things fall apart – they literally go to pieces.

Prayer

Ground of all being, all peoples come from you,
may we honour one another and seek the common good.
Reconciler of all people,
employers, employees and shareholders
are like fingers on your hand,
may the wealth and work of the world be available to all
and for the exploitation of none.
Unity of the world, from you all peace, all justice flows;
may we cherish the web of life and respect the rule of law.

Today's step

I step
away from fragmentation
towards fusion.

Spiritual breathing exercise

Reconciliation in.
Severance out.
All one.

JULY 4

Independent or interdependent?

Bible reading

Listen to this message from the true, universal and eternal God who stretched out the galaxies and made planet earth and everything in it, who gives breath and life to every person who walks this earth: I called you for a purpose, to be a servant nation; I have taken you by the hand. I have formed you in order that you may rescue my children, bring light to all nations, open blind eyes, free the oppressed and release those who are shut up in dark prisons.

Isaiah 42:5–7

Reflection

> We renounce the spirit of self-sufficient autonomy, and are committed to a much more holistic approach which was the strength of the Celtic Church.²

On July 4 the USA celebrates its independence. When it was a colony of the British Empire it was not a natural part of a greater whole, it was subservient. Its Declaration of Independence marked a fine achievement of the human spirit which honoured God as the source of a nation's well-being. However, the temptation to act as if there is no need to relate to the greater whole is great. How good, therefore, that on this day up to 25,000 gather for a Rainbow Family Prayer for World Peace. Most of this Rainbow Family refer to this as *Interdependence Day* and, for the first week of July, all live in primitive conditions by choice, in State forests, and rely upon one another. On the morning of Independence Day participants pray, meditate, or are silent.

> With a good conscience our only sure reward, with history the final judge of our deeds, let us go forth

to lead the land we love, asking God's blessing and help, but knowing that here on earth God's work must truly be our own.³

Pause for thought

Let readers outside the USA pray the following prayer with those who live inside it.

Prayer

Great God, the inspiration of every generous impulse, we thank you for those pilgrims of faith who came here in their frail barque across mountainous seas and greeted their new world in your Name. May this nation, conceived in liberty and dedicated to the proposition that all people are created equal, find its truest destiny in serving this earth. Save us from a freedom of speech so empty that we have nothing worth saying, from a freedom of worship so futile that we have no God to adore, from freedom from want and fear with no creative idea as to how to use our plenty for the well-being of the world.⁴

Today's step

I step
away from self-sufficiency
towards interdependence.

Spiritual breathing exercise

Service in.
Subservience out.
Freedom.

JULY 5

Heal the split

Bible reading

Jesus and his apostles sailed across the Lake of Galilee to Gerasene. As Jesus stepped out he was met by a split personality possessed by many demons. Jesus ordered the unwhole spirit to leave him but he shrieked, 'Jesus, Son of God, leave me alone.' 'What is your name?' Jesus asked. 'Legion' he replied, implicitly recognising that he had his legion of demons. The demons begged Jesus not to send them over the clifftop. A large herd of swine were grazing nearby. Jesus allowed them to leave the man and enter the herd – who promptly rushed into the lake and drowned. When residents turned out to see what it was all about, they found the man clothed and in his right mind. Those who witnessed this healing reported it back in town, but the farmers were more concerned about losing their pigs than about a person being healed and they asked Jesus to stay away from their area.

Luke 8:26–37

Reflection

This true story of Jesus healing a split personality is also a parable for our times. Echoing the sin of Adam and Eve, which is the perennial sin of the human condition, we want to be independent of God, the source of our wholeness. We want to be self-sufficient in order to keep our pigs, make our money, feel superior to others, live our lives insulated from the sufferings of the less fortunate.

> For an individual to be 'well', they must be in balance, both with themselves, and in relation to their society and the natural world. Each individual is a part of the great Circle of Life. If they live as if they are separate

from it, then disaster will inevitably follow – not as some form of retribution from a judgemental God, but because they are singing out of harmony with the Whole, and jarring clashes of disharmony will result.[5]

Pause for thought

The greatest wound a human soul can experience is the lack of *sobornost* with Christ. When a soul is not united with Christ's soul, it is fragmented.[6]

Prayer

Dear Father, Mother, Source of my being,
the precious robe with which you birthed me
is torn into shreds,
love has been scattered.
Yet I long for you, and you long to gather together
the fragments of my life.
You know who I am.
Snatch me from the maze.
Restore me to my right mind.
Heal my wounds.
Return me to fellowship with the human family
and make me one with you.

Today's step

I step
away from fragmentation
towards wholeness.

Spiritual breathing exercise

Mending in.
Splitting out.
Whole.

JULY 6

Healing the soul of a people

Bible reading

If you set people free from crippling debt, share your food with the hungry and never turn away from fellow mortals in need, then light shall dawn upon you with healing for your wounds . . . The Eternal God shall guide you until you are like a well-watered garden. Your children shall rebuild the ancient ruins and on the old foundations you shall rise again. Then you shall be called Repairer of Broken Walls, and Restorer of Streets with Homes.

Isaiah 58

Reflection

When a nation's soul is sick and is preyed upon by the purveyors of greed, power and apathy it becomes too weak to engender the depth of responsibility necessary to build social and environmental cohesion. Wherein lies its healing? Dmitri Lvov[7], points to three pre-conditions for building a sound national identity: integration with the land, spirituality and community empowerment. He discerns a biblical principle: 'The profit of the earth is for all', and urges that profits from land ownership and rent are invested in the community. Community trusts in some countries, for example Scotland, are doing just that.

According to Irish history it took figures such as St Brigid to 'turn back the streams of war' that such founding figures as Chuchulain had set in motion. It may have been the Christian theology of forgiveness that caused the early Celtic world to embrace the new religion so dearly. And for my money, if 'Celtic spirituality' means anything, it means showing how a culture ripped apart by violence can again be made whole. That is what makes it a suitable metaphor for what the world needs deeply today. For no place is more sacred, no peoples more worthy of honour, than those who have made beauty blossom anew out of desecration.[8]

Each nation has a birthright and a womb. Much of that womb is the very nature of its land.

> I cried: Here is the real Scotland,
> the Scotland of the leaping salmon,
> the soaring eagle, the un-stalked stag,
> and the leaping mountain hare.[9]

Pause for thought

How would you describe the birthright of your land?

Prayer

I pray to you for the place of desecration:
bring forth from it beauty.
I pray to you for the hard and barren place:
bring forth from it generosity.
I pray to you for the greed- and guilt-laden place:
bring forth from it forgiveness
and let eternal life bloom.

Today's step

I step
away from hoarding
towards healing.

Spiritual breathing exercise

Restoring in.
Resistance out.
Rebirth.

JULY 7

Healing wounded communities

Bible reading

Jesus upbraided the towns where he had worked many miracles but where there had been no repentance. 'The worse for you, Chorazin and Bethsaida,' he said, 'if the miracles that took place in you had taken place in Tyre and Sidon, they would have long ago repented. I tell you it will be better for Tyre and Sidon in the day of judgement than for you. And O, Capernauam – you think you're the tops? – far from it. You will sink into oblivion.'

Matthew 11:20–23

Reflection

The wounds we humans inflict upon each other build up with the passing of time. Each succeeding generation has the opportunity to heal these wounds, but more often we simply add to them, fixing ourselves in repetitive patterns of destruction and condemning the next generation to suffer the consequences. But the chains that bind us to the wounds of the past may be broken.

The character of the founders of a community (or city) and the purposes for which the community was founded form a substantial part of that community's character, and of the wounds it carries from generation to generation. Russ Parker[10] speaks of his home city of Liverpool as a city unloved and unwanted. It was a centre of slave trade and a home for unwanted refugees – the Irish in the nineteenth century and Asian immigrants in the twentieth.

How then, do we hear the story of our own city or village? First, we must research it. Why was it founded? Why was it founded *there*? Why was it founded *when* it was? What have been its moments of blessing or of shame? Second, we must *walk* our city. It is not enough to drive quickly through the places of hope, ambition, fear or despair. The community is best seen on foot. On foot you can see what has been abandoned, where the areas of vitality are, what parts of your city are loved and unloved. As you walk, pray over the places as well; listen to what God has to say about these areas. Finally, observe. Who is moving into your community – and out? Listen to the debates in business and government. In short – listen to the story of your city.

Pause for thought

Listen to your local community.

Prayer

God who weeps over the city,
may we know the abandoned places,
may we sense the destructive patterns,
may we feel the hurting groups.
May we confess the ravages and rage.
May we embrace the hopes and despairs.

Today's step

I step
away from disinterest in the city
towards its heart.

Spiritual breathing exercise

Prayer in.
Indifference out.
Healing.

JULY 8

Healing wounded cities

Bible reading

The words of Nehemiah, steward of King Artaxerxes of the Persian Empire: I learned that some of my fellow surviving exiles had returned to our province. Jerusalem is broken, its city gates have been burned down. I wept and fasted for several days and prayed to God: I confess the sins my people committed. I include myself and my family in this. We have not obeyed your laws. That is why you scattered us among the nations. But you also promised to gather us to you again in Jerusalem, which was designed from the start as your dwelling place. Hear my prayer. Give me success in my endeavour to return and rebuild.

Nehemiah 1

Reflection

Once the story of your city is told, you will know what to celebrate and where you need to repent. Repent? What if you are new to the city? What if you are a victim of the woundedness of the city? Where does repentance come into this? There is another principle of healing wounded history to which we need to attend which is sometimes called 'representational confession.' Drawing on the examples of Daniel and Nehemiah we see those who identified with their community and confessed to God its failures to live into God's purposes. Not all can take the role of confessor. First there must be a connection between the person and the community. Daniel and Nehemiah were Jews, confessing the sins of the people of the covenant. Second, there must be access to the one offended by the sin, to God himself. Through the intercession of Christ, a Christian has access to the Throne of Grace.

But when all such conditions are met, of what use is this practice in healing the wounds of a community? It is, in the end, only the beginning, but a necessary beginning nonetheless. It opens the door to harder work, to addressing the divisions in the community. To undertake this work requires a commitment to involvement in the life of the community. To undertake this work also moves us to call other Christians into the work.

Pause for thought

What do you need to specifically confess on behalf of the place where you live or lived?

Prayer

I confess on behalf of . . .
these sins that mar its life . . .
these areas that have been neglected . . .
these unjust deeds that have been inflicted . . .
these integrities that have been violated . . .
Show me what harm can be restored
and the place where I may begin.

Today's step

I step
away from defeatism
towards repentance.

Spiritual breathing exercise

Faith in.
Filth out.
Healing.

JULY 9

Conflict resolution

Bible reading

Remember that once you were regarded by Jews as shut out of the privileges of 'the Commonwealth' – the people who had a right to all the promises – devoid of hope and of God.

Now, however, you who once were far away have been brought near through God's outpoured Gift in Christ. For Christ is the Peacemaker who in his person has brought together the two divided peoples. In his own person he has created a new, united human family.

Ephesians 2:12–15

Reflection

The world is full of intractable warfare, explicit and implicit. Following the 9/11 2001 attack on the USA Trade Centre, invasions of Iraq and Afghanistan triggered unrelenting warfare rooted in age-old tribal conflicts. In the African, Chinese, Indian and Russian spheres of influence power struggles for precious resources exacerbated by tribal hostilities cause intractable disputes.

Such warfare is not always open conflict. Bitterness is also a kind of warfare. It is found in the racial divides between indigenous people and settlers within many countries. The problem is history – wounded history – unhealed and unresolved. There is no magic bullet for healing wounded history. The stories of the people, stories of tragedy, injustice, brutality and victimisation are passed on to each generation. The disease of sin in the depths of human nature ensures that each generation will be able to add to the stories that get passed on.

Many Christian groups have begun to address the problem of wounded history. Acts of corporate repentance and statements of forgiveness have been issued. Sometimes there has been a failure to understand that an act of repentance is but the beginning of a process that will take a long time and whose costs will be high both for the wounders and the wounded. This work of healing wounded history is not the sign that the kingdom of God will be realised instantly, but that the kingdom of God is at work.

So how do we proceed? I seek out someone who distrusts or fears me solely because I belong to a particular group. I ask to hear their story, which is often that of many others. I admit the truth the story tells: I cannot defend, justify or dispute; I listen and affirm. This costs time and emotional energy, for there is no reason, at first, why the other should trust me. I must expect to be tested, for this person has probably been betrayed before.

Pause for thought

Take your companion's wounds and your wounds and place them on the Cross of healing.

Prayer

Before your Cross, O Christ,
I recollect one story of wounding.
I ask for your mercy upon this wounded person and people.
I ask your forgiveness for me and my people.
I ask for the healing of the wound
and the birth of our common humanity.

Today's step

I step
away from the tornness
towards togetherness.

Spiritual breathing exercise

'What' is right in.
'Who' is right out.
Jesus.

JULY 10

Integrate the parts

Bible reading

Age after age, O God, your have been our home. From eternity you are God. You lay bare all our secrets before you. You sum everything up. Teach us to put together our days that we may take this to heart. Let your love dawn upon us so that the whole of our lives may become an act of praise. Look on us with mercy, that all that we do may be fruitful.

Psalm 90:1, 11, 12, 14, 17

Reflection

> We encourage the ministry of Christian healing. We not only lay hands on the sick and pray for their healing, we also 'lay hands' on every part of God's world to bless it and recognise its right to wholeness in Christ.[11]

Wholeness means there are no split-off areas in our lives, it is the full realisation of our humanity. In this realisation all the jigsaw pieces are present and known, the kaleidoscope shapes resolve into a pattern, and relationships are complete as they were in the primordial Garden. There we can be naked as were Adam and Eve – we need no boltholes for renegade parts of us or for renegade phases of our lives.

As we grow in wholeness the past ceases to be disconnected from the present. 'Church' is not just about one day of the week, Sunday, it is about the whole of the week. Theology is not just about one restricting subject, God; true theology spells the death of isms, for it relates all things to the Source. A Christian organisation is not just about producing certain products, it goes about its work in a godly way. A Bible college hired outside caterers to replace the believers who had previously cooked. In disconnecting the cooking from the ethos which their studies pointed to, the college lost its wholeness.

'Call' has many facets because the whole of life coheres around it. If we are to make ultimate sense of our lives, all the disparate elements in us have to be integrated around it. 'Call' is about the whole of our life – work life, spiritual life, family, relationship with the earth, recreation, use of time, money, energy.

Pause for thought

What is still disconnected?

Prayer

Great Spirit, bring to harvest the fragments of our lives,
penetrate the storehouse of our memories,
making them whole and holy.
May the light that shines out from your face
flood the world with goodness
and gather into one
a divided and broken humanity.

Today's step

I step
away from the breaking
towards the mending.

Spiritual breathing exercise

Joining in.
Splitting out.
Wholeness.

JULY 11

Wholeness links emotions and intellect

Bible reading

Persons who do not affirm the wholesome teachings of Christ, and teachings which value good and God are stupefied by their own conceit and woefully ignorant. They are addicted to disputes and strife about words which engender envy, quarrels, abuse, slander and suspicious attitudes.

1 Timothy 6:3, 4

Reflection

Wholeness means that reason cannot be divorced from relationships. Intellectuals schooled in the rationalism of recent centuries tend to make an opposition between 'feeling' and 'reasoning'. They do not wish to muddy logic with emotions such as pity. Emotion takes individual circumstances into account. It is not objective. The truth is that reality is grounded in God whose nature is love. Rather than a commitment to truth excluding love, only the presence of real love enables us to see the truth. Really seeing the truth, like really loving, depends upon our ability to see ourselves, others and God as more than an extension of our own needs and fantasies.

Wholeness means that we cannot divorce private from public morality. People in public life who betray a spouse sometimes pretend that what they do in private is their own affair, and has no bearing on how well they do their job. But trust and honour are indivisible.

Caroline Myss and Norman Shealy observe human patterns that can contribute to a person's illness. Those same patterns may also contribute to a nation's malaise.

The patterns run as follows:

Unresolved or deeply consuming psychological or spiritual stress.
Negative belief patterns.
Inability to give and/or receive love.
Lack of humour and the inability to distinguish serious concerns from the lesser issues of life.
Ineffective exercise of the power of choice; inability to hold dominion over the movement and activities of one's own life.
Poor nutrition and exercise.
Absence or loss of meaning in one's life.
Tendency towards denial: not acknowledging what it is that is not working in one's life.[12]

Pause for thought
If we wish to journey from fragmentation to wholeness we must learn to relate the part to the whole.

Prayer
Lead me from that which is partial
to that which makes whole.
Lead me from that which is false to that which is real.
Lead me from that which is self-centred
to that which is good.
Lead me from that which fades to that which endures.

Today's step
I step
away from false projection
towards the Ground of Being.

Spiritual breathing exercise
Honesty in.
Dogmatism out.
Reality.

JULY 12

Body, mind and spirit

Bible reading

Jesus was in a crowded house in Galilee. The power of God was present for healing. Some people placed a paralysed man in front of him. When Jesus saw their faith he said, 'My friend, your sins are forgiven.' The only concern of some legal purists, however, was to question Jesus' right to forgive a person's sins. 'Why do you have such a mind-set?' Jesus asked. 'Which is easier, to say to this man "Your sins are forgiven" or to say, "Get up and walk"? So that you may know that I have authority, I say to this man "Get up, take your stretcher, and return home."' The man immediately stood up and praised God, as did those who witnessed it.

Luke 5:17–26

Reflection

Body, mind and spirit fairs and bookshop sections multiply – but sometimes they only scratch the surface. Healing is not mere first-aid, though that can be a contribution, nor is it even just a physical cure. To cure eczema in a Hitler who then goes on a killing spree, eaten up with the cancer of hate, achieves little. Healing is to make whole. It is to engage in the journey away from fragmentation towards wholeness. It may be engaged in at ever-deeper levels throughout our lives.

Ninian, who introduced Christ's ways to parts of Britain in the fifth century, understood this. The Church in his time was either non-existent or at a low ebb and there is no evidence of any healing ministry. Then Ninian established a great Christian community at what is now Whithorn, on the south-west coast of Scotland. The local ruler, Tudwal, felt his influence waning as Ninian's grew and started to persecute Ninian. However, he contracted a serious disease which damaged the crown of his head, and spread to the eyes, causing blindness. 'The man who opposed the light of the truth lost the light of the flesh' declaimed Ninian's biographer Aelred, suggesting perhaps a cause-and-effect psychosomatic condition. The man repented and asked Ninian to visit him. Ninian, full of love, gently rebuked him for his wrong actions, then 'with healing hand touched the sick man's head and traced the sign of saving life on his blind eyes'. To cut a long story short, he was healed. He was healed in body and soul. He cherished Ninian and gave him close personal support thereafter. That is holistic healing.

Pause for thought

Think of someone to whom you can be as Ninian was to Tudwal.

Prayer

May illness depart from our eyes.
May weakness depart from our eyes.
May soreness depart from our eyes.
May hardness depart from our eyes.
May sourness depart from our eyes.
May lewdness depart from our eyes.
In the name of the All-seeing Healer.

Today's step

I step
away from the breaking
towards the mending.

Spiritual breathing exercise

Faith in.
Hardness out.
Whole.

JULY 13

Joined-up living

Bible reading

Former refugees had returned to their occupied territory, but were oppressed by their fellow Jews. Then started an outcry. Some said, 'We have to sell our homes or fields to you in order to stay alive, and on top of that you require us to pay interest. Some of our daughters have been sold to you and we have no money to buy them back.' When I, Nehemiah, heard this I was very angry. I confronted the leaders of my people: 'I have done everything in my power, without charge, to buy back our people from exile, and yet you now sell them for gain. You are doing wrong. Will you not live in awe of God?' They were silent. Eventually they answered, 'We will restore everything as you say.'

Nehemiah 5

Reflection

Nehemiah restored his people to their land, but their relationships were still not restored. They were not joined up. Wholeness in business requires money to be harnessed to morality. Bill Jordan[13] told conference delegates that the world's 40,000 multinational companies, concentrating billions of dollars in a few hands, now controlled the global economy far more effectively than governments. 'Individually, most companies are run by decent people who would defend their principles,' he says, but individual morality was not being reflected in collective decisions because of 'intense and intensifying competition'. This force of global competition now seemed 'intent on dismantling the effectiveness of workplace standards'.

Awe of God affects business, medicine, art, everything. After the second world war some Christians in Germany founded the Evangelical Academy of Bad Boll. They realised that Nazism had been able to plunge the country into ruin because disciplines such as law and medicine had been divorced from the civilising spiritual sources. Yet this divorce continues in most Western countries.

An artistic person goes to great lengths to create furnishings, paintings and flowers of beauty in her flat. But as soon as she leaves she is confronted by an ugly jungle of concrete, buildings, road signs which lack symmetry or taste. She may shut herself off from this world and seek inspiration only from her little home. A person committed to a whole world will press planning and other authorities to take seriously this need. The way of Christ is written into the whole of creation, it is designed to work his way; it is written into the structure of our beings.

Pause for thought

Fear separates. Love connects.

Prayer

Divine Light encompassing me,
penetrate my soul, my mind and my body.
Cleansing, healing soul-light,
shine out into my business dealings,
shine out into all dealings,
shine out into the architecture of life.

Today's step

I step
away from a-morality
towards the grain of Christ.

Spiritual breathing exercise

One world in.
My world out.
Awe.

JULY 14

The link between holiness and wholeness

Bible reading

The Eternal God said, 'Be holy as I am holy . . . Honour your father and mother . . . leave sufficient leftovers for the poor and incomers. Treat each person with equal respect . . . Challenge someone who is wrong without blame or bitterness . . . Do not degrade your own or your children's bodies. Always be honest in court or commerce, for I am your holy God.'

Leviticus 19

Reflection

There is a link between wholeness and wholesomeness. There is a link between wholesomeness and holiness. There is a link between these and the biblical concept of shalom. Shalom is sometimes translated as 'peace', but it means much more than that. It is about wholeness, harmony, between oneself, one's neighbour, one's environment and one's God. The above passage links God's holiness with the divine concern that people in every area of life be honoured.

The neuroscientist Susan Greenfield points out that a baby's brain is the passive recipient of myriad chaotic sensations, but gradually it begins to organise them, building up associations, ignoring immediate sensations in favour of over-arching concepts so that meaning, memory, knowledge and personal identity are constructed over time. She warns that cyberspace kids, blitzed with information from anywhere, may never acquire the capacity to see things in context. The brain may become the plaything of any fashion or ideology. Teach such a child holiness, and they will relate their myriad sensations to the Whole.

The most direct way of infusing everyday surroundings with the Sacred is through cleaning. 'Sacredness is experienced in the qualities of purity, orderliness, balance and renewal – all these can be achieved through cleaning.' Let this come in life and religion; church and society; rich and poor; money and morality; work and worship; the earth and humans; politics and prayer; body and soul; the mystical and practical; science and religion; service and love; architecture and the Spirit; technical and personal; youth culture and parent culture; masculine and feminine.

Pause for thought

Healing is not mere patching up, it is patterning together.

Prayer

God of wholeness, may our hospitals not be centres of disease but homes of healing.
May they not treat cases but help persons.
May nurses and doctors, cleaners and chaplains,
administrators and ambulance drivers
increase their compassion.
May many grow well, others die well, staff work well,
and may we all harness our work
to that of the Great Physician.

Today's step

I step
away from a mere part
towards the whole.

Spiritual breathing exercise

Holy in.
Unwhole out.
Whole.

JULY 15

The place of pain in wholeness

Bible reading

The persecuted apostle Paul wrote to Church members in Colosse: I am suffering on your behalf, but that makes me happy. I look at it like this: Christ suffers hugely on account of his commitment to help us – I want what I suffer for the Body of Christ (the Church) to make up what remains to be completed of Christ's afflictions for the sake of his body.

Colossians 1:24

Reflection

To be holistic requires us to integrate pain into the whole scheme of things. I do not see pain as an enemy that is alien to life as it is meant to be. I think of a chrysalis coming out of a caterpillar's skin. Without this painful struggle the beauty could not emerge.

We should neither seek nor glorify pain. But the apostle Paul speaks of a sorrow that leads to change of heart, and of a pain 'that God is allowed to direct' (2 Corinthians 7:9). When we keep our pains in our own hands and deal with them on an entirely human level they make us bitter, cynical and full of complaints. They lead to death – the death of hope, meaning and purpose. When we bring God into our pains and allow him to guide them then he turns them from what seems senseless suffering into spiritual character. The pain itself may have come from an evil source, but the question is not so much where it came from but where is it going? This is determined by whether we have a spiritual perspective on issues and see the pain as fitting into an eternal plan.

Sometimes it is right to revisit a memory that causes us distress: a humiliation, rejection, loss, abuse or neglect that still festers and causes dysfunctional behaviour patterns. To understand what causes us pain can lead to redeeming actions. In Canada I met a First Nation harp player. He once asked, 'Why did these (white) people do such bad things to my people? I need to understand them.' He came to Britain. There, despite the surface media trash, he journeyed until he discovered Celtic music. We help to bring healing when we try to understand those who have hurt us. Do not write them off, and even draw from the best and deepest in their tradition.

Pause for thought

Reflect upon something that causes you mental pain, and seek to understand those who contributed to it.

Prayer

Life-giver, Pain-bearer, Being of Love,
you hold in your hearts our name,
and the hurts we cannot bear to speak of.
You journey with us through pain
until you reconcile all that we have rejected in ourselves
and no part of your creation is alien to us.

Today's step

I step
away from triumphalism
towards understanding.

Spiritual breathing exercise

Acceptance in.
Denial out.
Christ-heart.

JULY 16

Healing starts with oneself

Bible reading

Jesus performed healings in the villages. Then he went to his home town. 'Isn't he Joseph the carpenter's son?' they said. Jesus said, 'I suppose you will quote this proverb to me: "Physician, heal yourself".' Later he was at a dinner party. All sorts of socially unacceptable people came to it. The religious moralists complained to members of his team that he ate with such people. Jesus answered them: 'Sick people need a doctor, healthy people don't. I have not come to call people who have no needs, I have come to call those who do.'

Luke 4:22, 23; 5:29–32

Reflection

Jesus did not, of course, believe that any of those people really had no needs. His point was that self-righteous people who do not admit to needs cannot receive healing. A man said to me: 'These evangelists who spend so much energy spreading their message in other continents do not realise that they have an inner continent that has not been evangelised.'

Each of us has a continent of inner wounds. Our first task is to become aware of them and bring these to Jesus. It is now possible to watch the effect of emotions on the stomach wall. When angry the stomach becomes swollen with blood. When depressed its lining becomes grey. Bitterness causes the bile duct to work overtime. Anxiety can lead to ulcers, weight loss, and so on. The relationship between the emotions and the body is intricate. We may pray for healing of the physical symptoms, but we may also invite the Healing Christ into the emotions.

> One of the qualities that you can develop, particularly in your older years, is a sense of great compassion

for yourself. When you visit the wounds within the temple of memory, the places where you made bad mistakes and now feel such regret, you should not blame yourself. Sometimes you have grown unexpectedly through these mistakes. Frequently, in a journey of the soul, the most precious moments are the mistakes. They have brought you to a place which you would otherwise have always avoided. If you visit this configuration of your soul with forgiveness in your heart, it will fall into place itself. When you forgive yourself, the inner wounds begin to heal. You come in out of the exile of hurt into the joy of inner being. This art of integration is very precious. You have to trust your deeper, inner voice to know which places you need to visit.[14]

Pause for thought

Take time to visit the places mentioned in the prayer before you pray.

Prayer

I bring to you, Healer of my soul:
unvisited places that have no name for love;
abandoned places that lie untended;
stunted places that long to grow again;
resentful places that await forgiving touch;
fearful places that need you as a coach;
defeated places where fresh belief can come.

Today's step

I step
away from licking wounds
towards healing of wounds.

Spiritual breathing exercise

Healings in.
Hurts out.
Healer.

JULY 17

Heal others

Bible reading

Jesus gave the twelve apostles authority to drive out demons and heal diseases, and he sent them out to proclaim the kingdom of God and to heal the sick... After this the Lord appointed seventy-two others and sent them ahead of him. He told them, 'heal the sick who are there...'

Luke 9:1, 2; 10:1, 9

Make disciples from all peoples and tell them to do as I have commanded you to do.

Matthew 28:19, 20

Reflection

Jesus not only healed people himself, he mandated his followers to continue a healing ministry. For several generations after the twelve apostles Christians continued to lay hands on sick people and to anoint them with oil, as James had advised (James 5:14). After the Church became a state religion in 353 healing ministry receded, and became a clerical ritual, though provision was made for people called exorcists to look after those with learning difficulties. Martin of Tours (d.397) and his recruits prayed for the sick, and even raised one or two from apparent death.

> The Fathers of the Church considered it normal that believers would ask God not only for the health of their soul, but also for that of their body...
>
> In the course of the Church's history there have been holy miracle-workers who have performed wondrous healings. The phenomenon was not limited to the Apostolic period...
>
> There is abundant witness throughout the Church's history to healings connected with places of prayer...

Every member of the faithful is allowed to pray to God for healing . . .
In prayer meetings for healing . . . the only thing to do is to entrust oneself to the free decision of the Holy Spirit, who grants to some a special charism of healing in order to show the power of the Risen Christ. Yet not even the most intense prayer obtains the healing of all sicknesses. So it is that St Paul had to learn from the Lord that . . . the meaning of the experience of suffering can be that 'in my flesh I complete what is lacking in Christ's afflictions for the sake of his body, that is, the Church' (Colossians 1:24).[15]

Pause for thought

What limits Jesus' healing power in us?

Prayer

Jesus, Master Physician of all times, your divinity did not require a PhD. Eagerly, you resurrected the dead, restoring the health of the sick. Be it physical or spiritual torment, none were a great obstacle to you, for your loving power is omnipotent. I ask for your abounding healing love; maintain my body and soul so I may fulfil my daily functions. Then a world will be conquered by you, and all afflictions will be dissipated![16]

Today's step

I step
away from defeatism
towards healing.

Spiritual breathing exercise

Health in.
Disease out.
Healed.

JULY 18

Heal the person as well as the body

Bible reading

Do you not know that your body is the temple of the Holy Spirit? You do not belong to yourself, you belong to God. Christ has purchased you at great price. So, then, honour God and bring glory to God in your body.

1 Corinthians 6:19, 20

Reflection

> Your body is, in essence, a crowd of different members who work in harmony to make your belonging to the world possible.[17]

If we work in medicine we treat the person, not an organ that is divorced from the person. Nor do we treat a person, even if they are hooked up to a machine, as if they are divorced from those close to them.

> A doctor says he was trained to look on patients as 'biological machines'. Such was the 'obsession to find the disease that we never looked at the individual to see God in him and to feel the potential for his health,' he says. He learned a different way when his house and his clinic were destroyed by bombs, and he hid in an underground shelter for ten days with many others. Under that stress, people had migraines, some became paralysed, some had wounds from flying glass. He had no medical tools, but he could give them 'a human heart, a human touch'. So he let God's compassion flow into them through his hands. Now, he is able once again to use the tools of science in his medicine, but no longer is his medicine crabbed by the arrogance that divorces the gifts of healing from their source.[18]

Godfrey was a fitness fanatic. His gym world and his marathon world gave him a buzz. He jealously guarded them and kept them separate from his other worlds. When he became holistic he decided to integrate his exercise with the rest of his life. He cycled or walked to work, did more gardening, and invited fellow runners to meet socially.

St Gregory Palamas (fourteenth century) writes: 'The spiritual joy that comes from the spirit into the body is not at all corrupted by communion with the body, but transforms the body and makes it spiritual.'

Pause for thought

To live apart from God affects our mental and physical well-being, and this has a chain effect upon our environment.

Prayer

Eternal Source of Life, you are the core of my being.
Flow through my body like a life-giving river.
Wash and transform the negative conditions
in my heart, mind, body and circumstances
with light, love and grace.
By day and by night may your Life flowing through me renew every cell of my body after your indwelling image.

Today's step

I step
away from negativity about my body
towards affirming my body.

Spiritual breathing exercise

Spirit in.
Poison out.
Temple.

JULY 19

We can all play our part

Bible reading

Large crowds came to Jesus, and brought to him people who could not walk, or see, or hear or speak. Jesus cured them and the crowds praised God. Jesus called his disciples and said, 'I feel sorry for these people, for they have now been with us for three days and have nothing to eat. I do not want to send them off hungry, or they may faint on the way.' 'Where could we buy enough food to feed all these people in this deserted place?' his disciples asked. 'How many loaves have you?' Jesus asked. 'Seven, and a few small fishes,' they replied. Then Jesus directed the crowd to sit down, took the seven loaves and the fish, gave thanks, broke them and handed them to the disciples to distribute among the crowds. Everyone ate as much as they wanted, and they even collected seven baskets full of leftovers.

Matthew 15:30–37

Reflection

Many churches now have healing ministry in some form. Those who are not part of such a ministry may feel 'I could not possibly engage in such healing'. The twelve apostles, it seems, did not share in Jesus' healing ministry on this occasion out in the desert. But they did carry out Jesus' request to gather what food they had and to share this with others. We can all be part of a healing chain.

When St Cuthbert was on the way from Melrose to Lindisfarne one of the king's bodyguards asked him to visit his house. There they found a servant very ill. Cuthbert blessed some water and asked someone to give it to him to drink. Water was poured down his throat three times. He went into a deep sleep and woke up cured. On another occasion the local sheriff was very ill. Someone gave him a piece of bread they had with them which Cuthbert had blessed. When the sheriff ate it he was cured.

Pause for thought

As we share the scraps we have, Jesus works more than we can imagine. Share our scraps of love, thought, gifts, time, presence, prayer. Notice how the recipients respond. That, too, is a form of healing. Everyone can take part in it.

Prayer

We come to you as we are, with our hurts and our hungers.
We come to you whose love restores us.
Encircle us and others:
heal our ailments;
renew our weary frames;
make us whole.

Today's step

I step
away from unbelief
towards giving whatever God shows me.

Spiritual breathing exercise

Provision in.
Unbelief out.
Praise God.

JULY 20

A nation's healing ministry revives

Bible reading

After his resurrection Jesus appeared to his eleven apostles and told them, 'These signs will accompany those who believe: in my name they will drive out demons and speak in new languages. They will pick up serpents and if they drink anything deadly it will not hurt them, for they will lay their hands on the sick and they will get well.'

Mark 16:14, 17, 18

Reflection

The above verses come from an ending to Mark's Gospel which was added to later editions. Perhaps the reason for their inclusion was discussion in the Church as to whether Jesus intended his healing ministry to be continued in each generation.

A story about Samson, the sixth-century British church leader, reveals that healing ministry had then died out, and was regarded as the province of pagan practitioners. The brothers at Illtyd's great Christian community were weeding the crops on a sunny day when a poisonous snake bit one of them in the groin. It had all the signs of being fatal, and the brothers were weeping, and expecting him to die. Samson, moved by the Holy Spirit, asked Illtyd's permission to pray for the brother's recovery, because, said he, 'my father is informed and able to set this brother free from this death of pain'. Illtyd initially thought Samson was returning to the magic healing arts taught by some father figure of the pagans. Samson, however, echoing Jesus' words in John's Gospel, 'I only do what I see my Father doing', explained that he had only one father, the same father God as Jesus. Deeply touched, Illtyd sent him to the dying brother.

Samson asked the brothers to leave. He and one experienced priest made the sign of the cross on the poisoned snake bite. From noon to 3pm he prayed, often aloud, and washed the wound with water mixed with oil. The brother was restored. In order that Christ, rather than himself, should be the focus of this healing, he went straight into a vigil. Samson's biographer notes that his healing ministry flowed out of his wonderful love for all. This marked the revival of healing ministry in the British Church.

Pause for thought

What do you have faith for?

Prayer

Give us faith that heeds your call to heal.
Give us eyes that see your healing rays.
Give us speech that transmits your healing words.
Give us hands that bring your healing touch.
Give us grace to give to you the glory.

Today's step

I step
away from unbelief
towards your healing power.

Spiritual breathing exercise

God's powers in.
Human powers out.
Healing.

JULY 21

A great healer in the early English Church

Bible reading

Jesus and his team went with James and John to the home of Simon and Andrew. Simon's mother-in-law was ill. Jesus went to her, held her hand, and raised her up. The fever departed and she began to serve them.

That evening the people brought to Jesus the sick and demon-possessed. The whole town crowded round the door and Jesus healed many people of different kinds of disease, and drove out demons.

Mark 1:25–34

Reflection

Cuthbert, who died in 687, was one of the first indigenous leaders of the Church of the English, and he modelled healing in an outstanding way. Through his persistent prayers he restored to health many who were sick, he cured some that were afflicted by unclean spirits, not only when present by praying, touching, commanding and exorcising, but also when absent either by prayer alone or even by predicting their cure.

The plague struck while he was at Melrose monastery, and he was expected to die. However, when he was told that his brothers had spent a whole night in prayer for him he said, 'Then what am I lying here for? God will certainly have heard the prayers of so many good men.' He got up, and day by day his strength returned. His prior, Boisil, prophesied that he would never again be struck by the same disease.

Abbess Aelfflaed at Coquet Monastery became so crippled she had to walk on all fours. 'How I wish I had something belonging to dear Cuthbert,' she sighed, 'I know for certain I should be quickly healed.' Soon after someone arrived with a linen cincture sent by Cuthbert. She put it on and next morning could stand up straight. In a plague village Cuthbert restored a dying boy to health and prophesied there would be no more plague deaths in that village. On his own deathbed, though sick himself, his servant was healed of diarrhoea the moment he touched Cuthbert.

Pause for thought

What prevents such healings?

Prayer

Jesus, you healed a mother of her sickness:
heal those who have caught an infection.
Jesus, you restored the troubled to their right mind:
restore those whose minds are fragmented.
Jesus, you raised the dead:
raise up those who have been struck down.

Today's step

I step
away from disease
towards the divine healer.

Spiritual breathing exercise

Health in.
Sickness out.
Jesus.

JULY 22

Heal our blindness

Bible reading

Towards the end of their last long walk from Galilee to Jerusalem Jesus and his disciples reached Jericho and drew a large crowd. As they were leaving a blind beggar began to shout, 'Jesus, have mercy on me!' Many told him to shut up, but he shouted all the more. Jesus became still. 'Call him here,' he said. The man jumped to his feet and came to Jesus. 'What do you want me to do for you?' Jesus asked him. 'I want to see,' the beggar replied. 'Go on your way,' Jesus told him, 'your faith, not mine, has healed you.' The man immediately realised he could see, and followed them along the road.

Mark 10:46–52

Reflection

Can we reach out to another person in a healing way when we ourselves carry a crushing burden, and need all our strength to face an imminent crisis? If we rely on our own strength: no. If we draw sustenance from our divine Father and Mother: yes. Jesus was nearing the end of his long march south to face desertion, betrayal, trial, torture and death in Jerusalem, and he knew it. Yet, at perhaps the last main stop before Jerusalem a blind beggar, oblivious to Jesus' needs, cried out for his help. Those around Jesus, understandably, thought his cry for help was out of place and they tried to shut him up. Jesus made no knee-jerk response. He stood still in the crowd. Did he listen to his divine Father? Did he draw sustenance from the divine milk of kindness? Then Jesus asked the man a question. When someone comes to us for help it is often good to ask them to clarify what they want. This man wanted to see. Jesus did not heal him. He neither laid hands on him nor prayed aloud for him. He released the beggar's sense of possibility and responsibility: 'Go – your faith has made you well.'

Bishop Cogitosus recorded that St Brigid of Ireland (born 452) cured one nun of blindness, but encouraged all her sisters to make the sign of the cross over their eyes so that they would see as God sees. Most blind people who are prayed for remain blind. But each of us, when we are asked for help, can become present to God, to the person in need, and we can speak one word of life that heals. We can do this even when we are at the end of our tether, because we invite Jesus to do it, not ourselves, and we invite the needy person to co-operate with the healing Jesus.

Pause for thought

Next time your bio-rhythms are low and you get an unwelcome request for help how might you respond?

Prayer

Jesus,
when I am weak, remind me that your strength
can reach another through my weakness.
Open my eyes to notice what you notice.
Open my mouth to speak one healing, life-giving word.

Today's step

When there is clamour I will step into stillness
and then step towards the person God lays on my heart.

Spiritual breathing exercise

Help me.
Help the other.
See.

JULY 23

A healed creation

Bible reading

Even the cities will become deserts . . . until the Spirit is poured upon us. Then things like this happen: deserts become orchards, and orchards grow like forests. All who live there will be upright: the effect will be that fairness and harmony reign and dwellings are secure. Even when there are setbacks, everyone will gladly set to work sowing seed wherever there is water, and honouring the creatures by letting them roam free.

Isaiah 32:14–20

Reflection

The reading from Isaiah is one of many prophetic passages that glimpse future possibilities. Such glimpses culminate in the vision of a new creation (Isaiah 65:17; Revelation 21:1).

> Our aim is that 'the whole created order may be reconciled to God through Christ' (Colossians 1:20).[19]

The theologian Hans Kung said, 'The kingdom of God is a healed creation.' Jesus promised that the gentle shall inherit the earth (Matthew 5:4) but many might say that they haven't noticed it. It is true that those who are driven by success, sex and security will trample on you as they rush on, but the earth itself will not take to them. Once they have passed, they are gone, and the place knows them no more. The one who cherishes a place, and calls forth its love, stays in its heart, whether they stay for a short or long time. That person truly inherits the earth.

We are called
> to 'widen the space of our tents' (Isaiah 54:7) in order to embrace all God's creation,
> to discover the different faces of God in people of all faiths and cultures and to recognise how God is at work in their lives,
> to understand and express ourselves in the language and symbols through which the people of today make known their desires and their dreams,
> to leave our safe places to be with those who are asking for a deeper meaning in life,
> to hear the call to flexibility and mobility in order to go beyond.[20]

Pause for thought
Allow healing to flow from your heart into all creation.

Prayer
Holy Spirit,
breathe upon the cosmos.
May it share in Christ's resurrection
and grow with the birth pangs of his kingdom.
May I, even in the middle of its groanings and pains,
be an instrument of its healing,
and breathe peace upon it this day.

Today's step
I step
away from the things that consume me
towards a new, healed, creation.

Spiritual breathing exercise
Cosmic healing in.
Crummy pursuits out.
Your creation.

JULY 24

Heal jealousy

Bible reading

Where do your quarrels and bad attitudes come from? Can't you see that they come from passions that war inside you – your cravings, your deadly jealousy of what others have and you don't have? You don't get what you want because you don't ask God for it. Or, if you do ask, God doesn't give it because you ask for the wrong things . . . God resists the proud but gives grace to the humble.

James 4:1-3, 6

Reflection

The term 'green with envy' reflects the ancient belief that jealousy leads to an overproduction of bile.

> O! beware my lord, of Jealousy;
> it is the green-ey'd monster which doth mock
> the meat it feeds on.[21]

Jealousy is a primitive force in the personality that is opposed to, and therefore mounts destructive attacks upon, parts of the object felt to be good. Healing is two-pronged. First, to accept that no two people are the same, to focus on thanking God for another, and asking for growth in our own unique being. Second, to forgive those who make us feel diminished.

A son who had been crippled with jealousy of his father, wrote to thank his mother for keeping the marriage together until the spell of jealousy, fear, resentment and hatred was broken. He wrote, 'These had bound me so tightly that I could not really love. With the spell broken and myself free emotionally, I now turn to take care of my soul . . .' He had matured and he had forgiven.

Pause for thought

Look at the palm of your hand. No other hand in the world has that pattern marked in it. Kiss it. Be glad that you are not another. Be glad that you are you.

Prayer

Help me, O Healing One,
to stop dwelling on what the other achieves that I don't.
As I look on the pattern in the palm of my hand,
I thank you that this is uniquely me.
May I grow in confidence, love, and creativity
according to the design you have for me.
I forgive the one who makes me feel inferior.
Meet their need; help them find their best course.
Heal and have mercy on us all.

Today's step

I step
away from comparison
towards growth.

Spiritual breathing exercise

Growth in.
Envy out.
Freedom.

JULY 25

Heal a human wreck

Bible reading

Peter and John were on their way to the temple for three o'clock prayer. A man who had been lame from birth was being carried along in the crowd before being left at the entrance gate where he would beg. This man asked Peter and John to give him something. Peter and John gazed intently at him, and asked him to look them in the face. 'I have no silver or gold to give you,' said Peter, 'but what I have I will certainly give you. In the name of Jesus Christ of Nazareth, get up and walk.' He grasped the man's hand and helped him up. At once his feet and ankle bones grew stronger and steady. He went with them into the temple, leaping, walking and praising God.

Acts 3:1–8

Reflection

How may we also be such channels of healing? Another John was a young man whom Hilda trained at her Whitby monastery, but he became very busy when he was made Bishop of Hexham in 687. In order to keep close to God he built a prayer centre in a secluded spot some three kilometres from Hexham. He dedicated this to Michael, angel-force leader, and spent time there with a few others, especially during Lent. One Lent he asked his prayer team to seek out some poor, sick fellow in the locality and invite him to stay in their guest hut. They invited a lad who was covered in scurvy, had lost his hair, and had been dumb from birth. After a week or so John had the lad over, held his chin and asked him to put his tongue out. He made the sign of the cross on his tongue. John then asked him to put his tongue in again and to say the word 'yes'. This the lad did. So John asked him to repeat after himself each letter of the alphabet, then words, and then sentences.

The lad was so overjoyed that he could speak that he spent all day and most of the night speaking out loud the thoughts of his heart. John asked their doctor to treat the scurvy and continued to pray for him. His skin was gloriously restored, he grew a beautiful crop of hair, and a youth who was ugly and destitute turned into a handsome, fit young man.

Pause for thought

Visualise someone who has a life-long defect after they have been healed.

Prayer

Healing power of Christ,
penetrate the brittle shell of the ones for whom we pray.
Where they are no longer present to others –
attract them to your gaze.
Where they are down and out –
grasp hold of them and raise them up.
Where they are fettered, set them free to leap and praise.

Today's step

I step
away from the sickness of self-absorption
towards the face of Christ.

Spiritual breathing exercise

Awakening in.
Withering out.
Leap.

JULY 26

Heal abuse

Bible reading

Jesus went through towns on his preaching mission accompanied by the twelve apostles and also some women who had been healed of various conditions. These included Mary, of Magadala, from whom seven demons had been cast out, Joanna, the wife of King Herod's head of staff, and many others who ministered to their needs and provided for them financially from what they owned.

Luke 8:1–3

Reflection

Rape or abuse of a woman by a man is devastating. This varies in degree, of course, with each person, and no two persons' healing process is the same. Generally these four phases are part of a healing process: First the victim needs to come out of trauma or denial and get in touch with feelings such as anger and worthlessness. Second, the victim enters into a contrasting context where there is love, trust, and enjoyment of life. Sooner or later this will allow unacceptable, buried parts of the story to come to the surface, to be relived, and shared with another person. This will come gradually over a period. Fourthly, some kind of line needs to be drawn, so that the victim may move on. Sometimes a ritual in the presence of a priest or pastor is helpful. If there was an abortion or miscarriage, the child may be given a name and symbolically given a Christian committal. The power of the man, or men, over the victim may be broken in visual and verbal prayer, and the greater power of the divine love may be invoked. Tears often accompany these stages and bring a measure of release.

Although one tradition holds Mary of Magdala to be a former prostitute, the Gospels do not state this and Orthodox Christians believe she was not. It is equally possible that her healing was as a victim of abuse. A lovely legend says that following Jesus' resurrection, when he appeared to her first of all, she used her position to gain an invitation to a banquet given by Emperor Tiberius. When she met him, she held a plain egg in her hand and exclaimed, 'Christ is risen!' and she proclaimed the gospel to the entire imperial house.

Pause for thought

No condition is so bad that Jesus cannot bring healing.

Prayer

Source of Love, God of Tender Beauty, Bearer of our Pain, you accept what we hardly dare name.
You know all, even more than we can recall.
May we find no part of creation alien.
Embrace in your heart what we have rejected in ourselves.
Your reflection is in our deepest core.
Flow through every cranny of our being and our memory like a pure, life-giving stream
that we may daily grow more whole.

Today's step

I step
away from self-rejection
towards your embrace.

Spiritual breathing exercise

Loving in.
Loathing out.
Growth.

JULY 27

Healing wells

Bible reading

Isaac went to live near the Well of the Living One Who Sees. He departed to live in the valley of Gerar. The Philistines had choked with earth all the wells there that his father Abraham had dug. Isaac restored these wells, and gave them the names his father had given them. The women quarrelled over a well which provided plenty of running water, so he named this Quarrel. They dug another well and also quarrelled over that, so he named it Feud. When they dug another well over which they did not quarrel he named it Room – 'for surely God has made room for us now so we can be fruitful here.'

Genesis 26:17–22

Reflection

We learn of Celtic Christians being divinely guided to discover a well when a water supply was needed, using well water to bless pilgrims, bathing in wells and being healed, using wells as waymarks of God's deeds, and establishing churches beside wells. Adomnan's *Life of Columba* describes a poisonous well which Picts 'worshipped as a god' and which 'was converted by the saint into a blessed well'. St David is reputed to have done something similar at Glastonbury where he came to a well full of poison, blessed it, and caused it to become warm; it was called the Hot Baths.

The well at Ffynnon Enddwyn in Wales became famous when St Enddwyn was cured after bathing in it. John of Tynemouth wrote in 1350 that the waters from the well on Ramsey Island, 'when drunk by sick folk, convey health of body to all'. A man suffering from a swelling in his stomach drank from it, vomited out a frog, and was cured immediately! It was said that God caused wells to come to light for the needs of David and Teilo, and that this well water tasted as pleasant as wine.

Even water taken from a well can be used for healing. In Iona Columba once saw a threatening rain cloud moving towards Ireland, and he knew that it would bring a life-threatening sickness to a particular district there. So he sent one of his monks to sail over to Ireland saying: 'Take this bread I have blessed in the name of God, dip it in water and then sprinkle that water over both the people and their livestock in that place, and they will soon recover their health.' The monk, Silnan, landed and found six men in one house who were already near to death. When he sprinkled them as Columba had said they were restored to health. News of this spread and many people came to Silnan with their livestock. These were all sprinkled and were saved from disease.

Pause for thought
Touch water and meditate in its healing properties.

Prayer
You are the Well of heaven.
When we visit wells of the earth,
the way to you is opened.
Touch us. Refresh us. Heal us.
Flow over us and make us whole.

Today's step
I step
away from dry spots
towards a well-spring.

Spiritual breathing exercise
Your water in.
Dryness out.
Well.

JULY 28

Healing through art

Bible reading

A new heaven and a new earth. The city shone and sparkled as if it was made from diamonds and gold, and decorated with precious jewels in every colour of the rainbow. Through the middle of the city flowed a river as clear as crystal. On either side of the river grew groves of the healing tree of life. The gates of the city stood open, welcoming everything that was good. The city was lit with the glory of God.

Kathy Day, echoing words from Revelation 21:21–22:5

Reflection

We renounce the spirit of self-sufficient autonomy, and are committed to a much more holistic approach which was the strength of the Celtic Church. We 'lay hands' on every part of God's world to bless it and recognise its right to wholeness in Christ.

Kathy Day is a single mother and explorer of this way of life. Out of the ugliness of certain human experiences was born a desire to create beauty. Kathy reads a piece of inspired writing, visualises it, and creates a representation of what she visualises, using silver paint on twigs, from which hang many-coloured objects, surrounded perhaps by candles planted in moss, and stones enscribed with prayers.

A work of art can open us up to other worlds, other dimensions, other times and ways of understanding. It can be rewarding to treat a cultural tour like a pilgrimage, and to become fully present to just one period, or one place.

Wendy Beckett, the art critic and nun, was interviewed about an exhibition of paintings of the apostle Paul. She was asked, 'Can you understand such paintings without having a faith?' 'Anyone can understand who does not want to be small, but who wants to grow,' she replied.

Pause for thought

Have a conversation with the artist within you.

Prayer

Divine Artist,
the world is your canvas,
and we your prime exhibits.
Bring to flower the artist you have planted within us
and transform art to become a panorama of healing.

Today's step

I step
away from what is stagnant
towards the artist within.

Spiritual breathing exercise

Rigid ways out.
Art in.
Grow.

JULY 29

Become more fully human

Bible reading

Happiness is the person who shuns unloving ways,
who is not attracted by apathy or sarcasm,
but finds delight in your teaching,
testing it out by day and by night.

Such people are like great red gums
growing by the riverside,
flowering every season, defying drought,
and constantly putting forth new growth.

Not so unloving people;
they are like grass in a willy-willy[22].
When pressure is on they can't take it,
nor can they stand the company of good folk.

Those who love have their taproots in God;
the unloving are rootless.
The Lord can work with loving people,
but the unloving work their own ruin.[23]

Reflection

> We seek to become more fully human as we grow in Christ.[24]

I want to know what you ache for, and if you dare to dream of meeting your heart's longing.

It doesn't interest me how old you are. I want to know if you will risk looking like a fool for love, for your dream, for the adventure of being alive.

I want to know if you have touched the centre of your own sorrow, if you have been opened by life's betrayals or have become shrivelled and closed by fear of further pain! I want to know if you can be with JOY, mine or your own; if you can dance with wildness.

I want to know if you can see beauty even when it is not pretty every day; and if you can source your life on the edge of the lake and shout to the silver of the full moon.

YES![25]

Pause for thought

What interests you?

Prayer

Christ of this continent,
let us not be frightened
by the feel of your energetic presence,
but rather courageous, strong and hopeful.

Christ of waiting,
let us wait for wisdom,
to draw us into the Intimate,
Christ-heart of this land.

Christ of brokenness,
let us be held,
in the bosom of our waters, deserts,
mountains and bushlands,
always searching for beauty
in the midst of chaos and despair.[26]

Today's step

I step
away from the unreal
towards the real.

Spiritual breathing exercise

Humanity in.
Withdrawal out.
Being.

JULY 30

A life fully lived

Bible reading

I pray that the real you will receive such strength from the immense divine resources, that you may be deeply rooted in love and big enough to grasp the breadth, length, height and depth of that love, which far surpasses mere head knowledge of God; so that every part of your being may be filled with the divine presence; that your physique, too, may be flooded with God, who is able to work in and through you far beyond anything one can imagine. To God be glory for ever.

Ephesians 3:16–21

Reflection

> We believe that 'the glory of God is seen through a life fully lived' (Irenaeus).[27]

Archimandrite Sophrony[28] saw in his mentor, Father Silouan, some of the qualities of 'a life fully lived', qualities that we, too, may aspire to:

> Simplicity stamped the Staretz' outward manner but his demeanour did not mask his aristocracy of spirit. Even the most perceptive intuition brought into contact with Father Silouan, whatever the circumstances, could have found nothing ignoble in him. He did not know what it was to spurn or disregard. He was a really noble spirit in a way only a Christian can be noble.
>
> He was absolutely fearless and free but without any hint of self-assurance. Though afraid of nothing, he lived in awe before God, genuinely fearing to grieve him if only by an ugly thought. He was that rare and beautiful combination of courage and exceptional meekness.

Anger as a passion had no place in his heart, yet for all his astonishing gentleness, rare unassumingness and docility, everything that was false, evil, ugly he opposed absolutely.

Back-biting, pettiness, narrow-mindedness and the like found no place in him.

A rare, strong will but devoid of obstinacy; simplicity, freedom, probity and valour together with gentle goodness; humility and obedience without a trace of sycophancy – Father Silouan was a man in the original sense of the word, made in the image and likeness of God.

The world is beautiful – the creation of a mighty God. But there is nothing more beautiful than a human, a true human, a child of God.[29]

Pause for thought

A half-lived or a fully lived life – which do I choose?

Prayer

I would be true, for there are those who trust me.
I would be pure, for there are those who care.
I would be strong, for there is much to suffer.
I would be brave, for there is much to dare.[30]

Today's step

I step
away from half-hearted living
towards whole-hearted living.

Spiritual breathing exercise

The noble in.
The ignoble out.
A life.

JULY 31

Let your light shine

Bible reading

You are the light of the world. A hill-top town cannot be hidden from view: a lamp on a stand can't be hidden beneath a piece of pottery – its light will leak out to other parts of the house. No more should you try to hide your light. Let it shine out so that everyone can see the good you do and attribute the glory to God.

Matthew 5:14–16

Reflection

Our deepest fear is not that we are inadequate. Our deepest fear is that we are powerful beyond measure. It is our light, not our darkness that most frightens us. We ask ourselves, 'Who am I to be brilliant, gorgeous, talented, fabulous?' Actually, who are you *not* to be? You are a child of God. Your playing small does not serve the world. There is nothing enlightened about shrinking so that other people won't feel insecure around you. We are all meant to shine, as children do. We were born to make manifest the glory of God that is within us. It's not just in some of us; it's in everyone. And as we let our own light shine, we unconsciously give other people permission to do the same. As we are liberated from our own fear, our presence automatically liberates others.[31]

A Palestinian completed non-violent conflict training. 'I would like to thank you in a way we Sufi Muslims do when we want to express special appreciation for something,' he said to the Jew Marchall Rosenberg. He locked his thumb on to Rosenberg's, looked him in the eye and said, 'I kiss the God in you that allows you to give us what you did.' He then kissed Marchall's hand.

Pause for thought
Don't withdraw. Don't push. Shine.

Prayer
This little light of mine,
I'm going to let it shine.
I'm going to let it shine,
Ev'ry way, ev'ry day.

Today's step
I step
away from cover-up
towards being natural.

Spiritual breathing exercise
Shining in.
Hiding out.
That's good.

AUGUST 1

Take us where the Spirit wills

Bible reading

A man of influence in the Jewish religious establishment, named Nicodemus, plucked up courage to arrange a meeting with Jesus, albeit at night. He began by saying, 'We believe you must be a teacher sent from God, otherwise you would not be doing these miraculous good deeds.' Jesus responded, 'A person can not experience God unless they are born again.' 'Surely a mature person cannot possibly re-enter their mother's womb?' countered Nicodemus. 'I tell you,' said Jesus, 'unless a person is born both of water and of the Spirit they cannot enter God's kingdom. A physical birth is just that; a spiritual birth is of the Spirit. The wind blows where it wants to. Although you hear its sound, you do not know where it comes from or where it will go. It is like that with every one who is born of the Spirit.'

John 3:1–8

Reflection

> We allow God to take us where the Spirit wills, whether by gentle breeze or wild wind.[1]

To be open to God is to grow. The faith tradition we receive on our entry into the Christian community depends for its authenticity and effectiveness on personal experience . . . It calls us to have the courage, even the recklessness, to open ourselves to the unknown, the unfathomable and truly mysterious dimension of the tradition . . .

> We need to see faith as openness. The effectiveness of what we do depends on the quality of our being. To be open implies qualities: such as being still – because we cannot be open to what is here if we are

always running after what we think is there; such as being silent – because we cannot listen or receive unless we give our whole attention; such as being simple – because what we are open to is the wholeness, the integrity of God.[2]

Pause for thought

Let the Son of God grow in you,
for he is formed in you.
Let him become immense in you
and may he become a great smile
and exultation and perfect joy.[3]

Prayer

O Spirit be free in me.
Let me not bind you through fear
of where your disturbing power will lead.
Burst through this brittle shell,
shake me to the foundations,
strip me to the core,
and lead me day by day.

Today's step

I step
away from the closed heart
towards the God-opening.

Spiritual breathing exercise

Openness in.
Obstinacy out.
Born anew.

AUGUST 2

Gentle breeze

Bible reading

The fruit of the Holy Spirit (the work which the Spirit's presence within accomplishes) is love, joy, peace, forbearance, kindness, goodness, faithfulness, gentleness, self-control. There is no law against such things. Those who belong to Christ Jesus have put an end to their godless nature with its runaway passions, appetites and cravings. If we live by the Spirit, let us also journey by the Spirit's guidance, going forward, keeping to the Spirit's course for us, controlled by the Spirit.

Galatians 5:22–25

Reflection

When Paul listed gentleness as one of the nine fruits of the Spirit he used the Greek word *praotes*. This word overflows with meanings; it is far removed from some current images of gentleness as unreasonable sweetness, powerless passivity, or timidity. Plato considered gentleness to be 'the cement of society'. Aristotle defined it as the mean between being too angry and never becoming angry; the gentle person expresses anger for the right reason and duration and in the right way. It is the characteristic needed when exercising discipline (Galatians 6:1), facing opposition (2 Timothy 2:25), and opening ourselves to hearing God's Word without pride (James 1:21).

Gentleness has soothing qualities such as politeness, kindness and courtesy; yet it is also a fire storm of indignation, kindled by the wrongs and sufferings of others.

In early Britain women, children and lone men feared to travel the land. Yet, according to the historian Bede, within a generation of Christianity coming to Northumbria, a child could run from one end of the kingdom to the other without being molested. I believe that if enough of us pass on the secret of how to turn rage into gentleness, it can happen again. For, in the words of Francis de Sales: 'There is nothing so strong as gentleness, there is nothing so gentle as real strength.'

A noble lady gave food and a resting place to a traveller. Before he departed she asked him if there was any service she might make him. 'There is one,' the man replied, 'tell me the secret of your exceeding gentleness.' At this the lady mused for long with eyes downcast; then she answered softly as one awaking from a lovely dream: 'There is no secret – only – only I am always at his feet, and he is always in my heart.'[4]

Pause for thought

Prayer is the seed of gentleness in the absence of anger.[5]

Prayer

Come as a gentle breeze
that cools in the heat of the day
come as a tender presence
that softens our hardness of heart.
May we breath Christ's gentle spirit
over each person we meet in this world.

Today's step

I step
away from hardness
towards tenderness.

Spiritual breathing exercise

Jesus in.
Rage out.
Gently.

AUGUST 3

Wild wind

Bible reading

Praise God Almighty whose spacecrafts are the clouds, who rides on the wings of the wind, whose messengers are wind, fire and flame. You are the greatest, the mighty elements form your majestic array.

From Psalm 104:1–4

Reflection

The Bible begins with the image of God's Spirit swirling through the flux and flow of the cosmos. There is wildness of energy at the beginning of life that gives rise to creativity – is it entirely different for us? In certain eras parts of the church have domesticated this wild Spirit of God. But not always. Many Celtic centres of mission were situated in wild places, and God-intoxicated adventurers did apparently wild things which in fact had the mark of the original wind, or breath of God. The swirling passionate energy of a man and a woman gives rise to conception.

Can we have creativity without turbulence? What are our turbulences? Yes, we have seen destructive potential of wildness, but what is its creative potential?

Our tradition is to believe in a leader of the angel force-field named Michael. In the Hebrides' tradition he rides a white, elemental horse with a flaming sword slaying a dragon. It is a wild horse – it has no saddle or bridle. He rides, not to subdue the wind, but to subdue the dragon – the destructive potential.

Pause for thought

Repeat silently the words from Psalm 104, 'You ride on the wings of the wind.' Ask God to forgive you for the ways in which you have caged the wild Spirit.

Prayer

Wild Spirit of the living God,
breathe the breath of heaven's lion
into this timid soul of mine.
Shape me by the touch of the crucified lamb,
so that I carry the Cross
with the dignity of a crown.
Wrap my fears in the faith you have in me,
and help me to lean into your blowing winds,
stand in the gaps of your calling,
fall under the weight of grace,
speak to mountains in your name,
go quietly to the secret place of prayer,
give away my gifts that others may grow
and in steps hardly noticed,
be changed forever into your likeness
through Jesus Christ my Lord.
Amen.[6]

Today's step

I step
away from the timid and tame
towards the wild matrix of your will.

Spiritual breathing exercise

Full-living in.
Half-living out.
Wild Spirit.

AUGUST 4

Wildness

Bible reading

Do you know how the wild mountain goats breed? Can you control the times when the hinds calve? They bend down, the womb opens, out drop their lusty offspring, thriving in the open – they run off and don't return to the herd. Who gave the wild donkey his freedom to roam where he wills, making his home in the steppes or the salt marshes? He scorns the traffic and other town noises, instead he delights to scour the hillsides for any green thing to eat. Would a wild ox be content to be domesticated by you? . . .

Job 39:1–9

Reflection

A true worship of God cannot be contained within the four walls of a church nor restricted to the boundaries of a religious tradition. It is true that wildness can be destructive, but we also know that wildness is at the heart of our God-given creativity, like the passion which lies at the beginning of a human life's conception, which perhaps reflects something of the passion that was at the heart of the birthing and the redeeming of the cosmos. If we deny these depths of wildness within us they will turn into destructive rather than creative energy.

We may also explore wildness around us. In 2006 Christopher Somerville set out to explore whether he could find just five hundred wild places left in Britain and Ireland. As he journeyed, he came to realise that he must redefine wildness. He learned to enter a disused quarry near Birmingham and discover its wild orchids, or to search for an ancient beech wood in sight of London or find dripping brick tunnels full of bats. Once he embraced this way of looking at things he found the wild waiting around almost every corner. When he thrust himself forward to find the wild, it eluded him. It was like a pearl of great price, hidden in a field, waiting to be found, in a railway siding jungle of buddleia, or even in the crack of a pavement stone.

Pause for thought

Where is the wild revealing itself to you?

Prayer

Great Spirit,
be wild and free in me.
Batter my proud and stubborn will,
blow me where you choose,
break me down if you must,
refashion me as you will.

Move me powerfully away
from the games I play
in order to try and tame you.

Lead me into the wild places:
the places of dream or scream,
the long dark tunnels
or the wide, sunny vistas

to speak to lions,
to move mountains,
to bear tragedy,
to mirror you.

Today's step

I step
away from the cocoon
towards the challenge.

Spiritual breathing exercise

Wildness in.
Closet out.
God's Breath.

AUGUST 5

Wind-swept coracles

Bible reading

A hurricane swept down and our ship was caught in the storm. Eventually we gave up all hope of being saved. But Paul urged them to keep up their courage. He told the crew: 'The ship will be destroyed but not one of you will lose your life, for last night an angel of the God I serve said, "Do not be afraid, Paul. You must stand trial before the Emperor and God has graciously given you the lives of all who sail with you."'

Acts 27:14, 20–24

Reflection

> The Celtic Christians had such faith in the leading of the Spirit that they gladly put to sea in small coracles, and went where the wind took them.[7]

The Anglo-Saxon Chronicle for 888–900 records that 'three Irishmen came to King Alfred in a boat without any oars from Ireland, whence they had stolen away because they wished to go on pilgrimage for the love of God they cared not where'. Those three monks were among the great number who for over a period of five hundred years set out to wander across the face of Europe, from Iceland to Italy and even as far as Kiev.

They seem to have taken the words of the second-century Irenaeus literally, when he defined the true search for God as starting from 'roadlessness', a state of complete trust in the direction of God rather than that of a human decision.

Pause for thought

How about abandoning yourself to the 'next wave' that God sends?

Prayer

Shall I abandon, O King of Mysteries, the soft comforts of home? Shall I turn my back on my native land, and my face towards the sea?

Shall I put myself wholly at the mercy of God, without silver, without a horse, without fame and honour? Shall I throw myself wholly on the King of kings, without a sword and shield, without food and drink, without a bed to lie on?

Shall I say farewell to my beautiful land, placing myself under Christ's yoke? Shall I pour out my heart to him, confessing my manifold sins and begging forgiveness, tears running down my cheeks?

Shall I leave the prints of my knees on the sandy beach, a record of my final prayer in my native land? Shall I then suffer every kind of wound that the sea can inflict?

Shall I take my tiny coracle across the wide, sparkling ocean? O King of the Glorious Heaven, shall I go of my own choice upon the sea?

O Christ, will you help me on the wild waves?[8]

Today's step

I step
away from fear and inaction
towards the horizon God puts before me.

Spiritual breathing exercise

Faith in.
Hold-back out.
I'm moving.

AUGUST 6

All may voyage

Bible reading

Have no fear, for I will be with you when you pass through the waters. You shall not be overwhelmed in river torrents; when you pass through fire you will not be burned, for I will deliver you . . . I the Majestic One, your Maker, who opens a road through the sea, a path through the mighty waters . . . I have formed you for myself.

Isaiah 43:2, 19, 21

Reflection

When I arrived in Christchurch, New Zealand/Aoroteara, I discovered that the focus of its cathedral was the ships of its founding pilgrim fathers from Canterbury, depicted on the mosaic floor. In the town square outside the focus was the large sculptures of the twelve ships in which the earlier Maori settlers arrived at the island 'of the long white cloud'. These were icons of a heroic past that now seemed remote to contemporary people. I addressed a meeting there as follows:

Voyaging need not be something only of the past. We invite those who have heard the call of God's untameable Spirit to set sail in the ocean of God's love. We say, 'be ready for the Spirit to lead you into wild, windy or well-worn places in the knowledge that God will make them places of wonder and welcome. In stillness or storm, be always vigilant, waiting, sharing, praising, blessing, telling. Sail forth across the ocean of God's world knowing both the frailty of your craft and the infinite riches of your God.'

This then, is the journey:
from the head to the heart;
from the city of learning

to the field wide open to the sun and rain;
from music dots on paper
to the sound of a Chopin nocturne;
from the structure of words
to the mystery beyond their meaning;
from the smallness of a manger
to the Love that holds the universe in being.[9]

Pause for thought

Imagine your life as a boat. What does it look like? Where is it going?

Prayer

Jesus who stopped the wind and stilled the waves,
grant you calm in the storm times;
Jesus Victor over death and destruction,
bring safety on your voyage;
Jesus of the purest love, perfect companion,
bring guarding ones around you;
Jesus of the miraculous catching of fish,
and the perfect lakeside meal,
guide you finally ashore.[10]

Today's step

I step
away from the place that is stagnant
towards the place that beckons.

Spiritual breathing exercise

Looking forward in.
Looking back out.
Sailing.

AUGUST 7

What do we leave behind?

Bible reading

Since we are surrounded by crowds of people who witness to us of Christ, let us strip all the excess baggage that hinders us in running the race that God has coursed out for us, and also the sins which trip us up, and run with determination, our eyes fixed on Jesus, the goal and the source of our faith.

Hebrews 12:1, 2

Reflection

Surely we can't leave everything behind? We leave behind things that we want to control, worry about or cling to. We do not leave behind memories and good experiences – these we carry in our hearts and they are strength for the journey. Other resources, too, are needed for the journey – love of friends, knowledge, skills. How may we 'look to the things unseen?' We may look out for the risen Christ – his hands beckoning us, his voice whispering to us, or his presence preparing a welcome, or we may look out for a divine test, as yet only dimly perceived.

Pause for thought

What plans, points of view and relationships are you meant to leave behind because they are egocentric? Lay them at God's feet and experience how the present becomes presence.

Prayer

Teach us to leave behind the things that tie our spirits down and learn again to be your pilgrim people.
Though fasting from the frenzied feeding of false desires,

through study of your Word, meditation and acts of service
restore the clearness of our seeing
and free us to share your generous love with all.

Today's step

I step
away from that which is finished
towards that which is unfolding.

Spiritual breathing exercise

Your concerns in.
Self-concerns out.
Christ's athlete.

AUGUST 8

Open to the Spirit

Bible reading

Those who had been scattered by persecution preached Christ's Word wherever they went. Philip proclaimed Christ in a city in Samaria. When the crowds saw the miracles he did they paid close attention and many were healed . . . When the apostles in Jerusalem heard of this, they sent Peter and John to them. When they arrived they laid hands on them and prayed that they might receive the Holy Spirit, because the Holy Spirit had not yet come upon any of them; they had simply been baptised in to the name of the Lord Jesus.

Acts 8:4-7, 14–17

Reflection

> We desire this kind of openness to the leading of the Spirit.[11]

There was a remarkable expectation about the personal experience of the Holy Spirit in the first Christians as this episode in the Acts of the Apostles illustrates. When Philip preaches in Samaria, the Jerusalem church sends two apostles, Peter and John, to check things out. When they arrive, they start laying hands on the new converts that they might receive the Holy Spirit. These converts had already received Christian baptism; how, then, did the apostles recognise that they had not 'received' the Holy Spirit? Was it that they had acknowledged Jesus with their heads and mouths, but did not show the fruits of the Spirit, such as love and joy, in their feelings and actions? Was it that they showed no signs – such as the gifts of tongues, prophecy or healings – of the freeing up of the Spirit?

This mood of expectation became muted in later times. One reason is that the experience of the Spirit can be rather messy, upsetting a more settled order of church life. Nonetheless, even in the most tightly organised era of the Church, there are ample records of outbreaks of the fullness of the Holy Spirit. This way of life invites us to live once again with a biblical level of expectation, looking for the Spirit of God to manifest in works of power, mercy and love in every situation.

We must never, however, mistake signs of the power of the Spirit with spiritual maturity. God pours out the Spirit without measure regardless of age, background or mental stability; we can be no more proud of the power of the Spirit than a well-educated person can be proud of having mastered the alphabet.

Pause for thought

Invite the Holy Spirit afresh, and unconditionally, into your life.

Prayer

Holy Spirit, you have anointed your servants
from the Day of Pentecost until now.
Anoint us as you will for the callings you will.
Here we wait, alert and open,
praying that you will come to us.

Today's step

I step
away from head-only knowledge
towards the Spirit within.

Spiritual breathing exercise

Fullness in.
Half-belief out.
Holy Spirit.

AUGUST 9

The spirituality of waiting

Bible reading

I wait for the Lord and put my hope in his word. I wait for the Lord more eagerly than sentinels in a city's watchtowers wait for the dawn. Put your trust in the one with whom is love and a wealth of saving power.

Psalm 130:5–7

Reflection

The idea of waiting is alien to the diseased form of capitalism that has come to dominate our society. The 'how to grow rich quick' mindset focuses on some thing it wants, and never lets up until it gets it, no matter what else it overrides. President Barack Obama recognised this flaw in himself as a chronic restlessness; 'an inability to appreciate, no matter how well things were going, those blessings that were right there in front of me. It's a flaw that is endemic to modern life.'[12] However, Obama came to accept his limits and mortality. He thinks it was out of this acceptance came the idea of running for the senate.

Waiting is not useless, it is a period of taking stock, becoming aware of flaws, of things in oneself that need to be processed and brought to God, of what is germinating.

Saint Bernard of Clairvaux advised people to be reservoirs, not channels. Channels let the water flow away until there is not a drop left. The reservoir is first filled, and then, without emptying itself, pours its overflow, which is replenished, over the fields which it renews. Waiting with God, as distinct from empty wasting of time, enables us to accomplish far more good than if we are burning ourselves out in 'good works' which become ever more dry. For God fills the reservoir with love and a wealth of saving power.

Pause for thought
Wait. Take time to assimilate the life of God which nourishes.

Prayer
From the depths of my heart,
from the scope of my vision,
from the greatness of my body,
I want to know you Lord.

I ask myself and want to know
him who made me, you the Creator,
but where will I get an answer,
eternal God of all hope?

I also seek to understand
why Jesus, who came to defend me,
accepted to die on the Cross,
eternal God of all power.

Here I am before your throne.
I ask the Holy Spirit
that he might sanctify me.

I bow before you
to implore your pure Spirit
that he might purify my thoughts.

I sit at your feet
so that the Spirit of truth
might reveal these things to me.[13]

Today's step
I step
away from gush
towards the reservoir.

Spiritual breathing exercise
Waiting in.
Whizzing out.
Renewal.

AUGUST 10

Openness

Bible reading

Jesus' friends once asked him, 'In God's set-up, who's the greatest?' Jesus drew a little child into the circle. 'Look,' he said, 'you won't even get into God's set-up unless you change your entire way of thinking and become like children. The person who humbles themselves and becomes like this child – that's the person who is greatest in God's set-up. But if you put barriers in the way of a little child you are sunk. At all costs, guard against putting up barriers.'

Matthew 18:1–7

Reflection

Openness means that we refuse to close our hearts to God's presence, God's possibilities, in anyone, anything, any situation. It pre-supposes that we seek to discern and do only God's will, and that we will be shown God's will only as we begin, however falteringly, to journey with the Spirit.

Openness is the opposite of possessiveness; it requires a childlike spirit. Adults close up, and build thick and complex defences, because they fear the hurts caused by a thousand devouring egos. Some adults continue to take risks in business or leisure pursuits while they are 'climbing' in life, but they become hard and retire into comfort zones once they have achieved their aim. Phrases such as 'I keep myself to myself', 'charity begins at home' or 'my home is my castle' reflect this tendency to close up.

Is there a way to remain open to the possibility of good in every situation while remaining closed to the misuse of love? This is possible if we believe, not only in the reality of evil, but also in a universal God of love who permeates each person. Thus, when another person misleads or misuses me, I say 'no' to the wrong they would do, yet I remain open to that which is of God in them. I reject the wrong in them rather than the person they are.

Pause for thought

Jesus urged adults to be childlike, not by throwing tantrums but by trusting him enough to come at his call. In what way can you become more childlike today?

Prayer

Child of heaven, defenceless love,
in order to come to us
you had to travel far from your eternal home.
Give us your childlike spirit,
help us to move out of our places of comfort
to the little child, to the straying sheep;
to have an eye for those who are overlooked;
to learn from those who, though least in this world's eyes,
teach us to trust.
Teach us to notice the little things,
to serve you in the least of your children
and in the prayer of the humble heart.

Today's step

I step
away from barriers in my heart
towards Jesus.

Spiritual breathing exercise

Welcomes in.
Shutters out.
Jesus.

AUGUST 11

The open road

Bible reading

Be this the song of those whom God has called:
some wandered in wild and lonely places,
for they could not find a home.
Faint with hunger and thirst,
they cried to their Eternal Source,
who led them to a place of welcome.
Let them thank their God for the wonders he shows them . . .
Some crossed the sea in ships.
They saw God's marvels in the deeps.
They soared to the skies with the waves
and crashed down into the depths.
God stilled the storm and brought calm.
Let them give thanks among the people
for the kindness and wonders of God.

Psalm 107

Reflection

All sorts of people walk to 'thin places'. Some come with prayer, as pilgrims. Some come with wonder, as nature lovers. The difference between these two kinds of people is not so great as at first may appear. For God is in the nature and in the prayer. Walt Whitman's famous poem 'The Song of the Open Road' captures this, verse after verse beginning with the French 'Allons', meaning 'Let's go' or 'Come on'. Here is an excerpt:

> Allons! Whoever you are, come travel with me!
> Travelling with me you find what never tires . . .
> Allons! We must not stop here,
> however sweet these laid-up stores,
> however convenient this dwelling,
> we cannot remain here.

However sheltered this port
and however calm these waters,
we must not anchor here . . .

Pause for thought

Have I stopped somewhere when I should have continued?

Prayer

You who are heroic love,
alive in every leaf and lane,
beckon us through star and stone,
to stride across our petty ways,
in pursuit of the endless adventure.

Today's step

I step
away from the couch
towards the road.

Spiritual breathing exercise

Adventure in.
Sloth out.
Song.

AUGUST 12

Endless adventure

Bible reading

It was by faith that baby Moses' parents hid him for three months after his birth, refusing to be daunted by the king's decree to kill Hebrew baby boys. It was by faith that Moses himself, when a grown man, chose to share the burdens of God's oppressed people rather than the pleasures of Egypt's palace. It was by faith that he led them out of Egypt, walked through the Red Sea as though it were dry land, even though the pursuing Egyptians were drowned in it.

Hebrews 11:23–29

Reflection

> Men are most alive when they have an adventure to live, a beauty to win, and a battle to fight.[14]

Commitment to a pattern is wise as far as it goes, but it is a springboard for hearing the Spirit, not a straitjacket. Hence the call to be open to the Spirit. There is a deep wisdom which prudent people can miss but babes may find.

Celts emerged from Europe's heartlands but the Roman troops pushed them to the western fringes of Britain, Ireland and Gaul (France). Celtic Christians believe God likes to take us to the edges of life. Jesus allowed himself to be pushed to the edges of society. That is why he could communicate to so many ordinary people. Often it is only when we are willing to go to edges that we truly meet others, for many who are on edges of loneliness, anger, despair or adventure recognise and reach out to another who is on an edge. This is how the truly precious things of life are passed on – at the edges. And at the edge we see horizons denied to those who stay in their comfort zones. We are called to mould the kingdoms of the earth so that they reflect the kingdom of heaven. The edge is in fact always the centre of spiritual renewal.

So when the road is rough – keep close to the Unseen Companion.

When the seas rage – keep close to the Calming Companion.

When you don't know where you are going – keep close to the Steering Companion.

When you are stuck – step out again with the God of Adventure.

Pause for thought

Be open and receptive to every sign of the will of God, in every motion and sound, within and without.

Prayer

You whose Heroic Love comes in a thousand ways:
may I be
the clay that laughs in the hands of the potter,
a sail borne by the wind,
a tree earthed in the soil,
a dancer in tune with the rhythm.

Today's step

I step
away from mediocrity
towards the endless adventure.

Spiritual breathing exercise

Courageous heeding in.
Couch-potato out.
Your adventure.

AUGUST 13

Learning to listen

Bible reading

Samuel, the boy assistant at Shiloh shrine, was worshipping with Eli the priest. In those days visions or words from God were rare. One day, however, when Samuel was lying near the sanctuary lamp on night duty, God called, 'Samuel, Samuel.' He answered, 'I'm here,' and, not knowing who was calling, ran to Eli. Eli told him he had not called him and he'd best go to sleep again. However, this happened a second, and then a third time. Then Eli realised it must be God speaking. He told Samuel: 'If you are called again, say, "Speak, Eternal One, your servant is listening."' God did call, 'Samuel, Samuel.' 'Speak, your servant is listening,' Samuel replied. God said, 'I am about to do a mighty thing in the land . . .'

1 Samuel 3:1–11

Reflection

Listening is a skill that has almost been lost, and which takes many years to acquire. At the age of thirteen I became a Christian. Three years later I nearly became an atheist. Why? The people I read about in the Bible listened to God: the Christians I knew did not. Communists in those days had a passion, a philosophy and plan to change the world without God and certain Bible heroes had a passion, philosophy and plan to change their world with God. The Christians I knew merely told people, 'All you need is Jesus,' failing to take into account that Jesus said, 'You have ears – why don't you listen?'

Then I met some Christians who did listen. They used to say, 'God gave us two ears and one mouth – why don't we listen twice as much as we talk?' That set me on a life-long quest to discover the art of listening. I found that this faculty has become a victim of endless sound-bites that don't come from God, and of capitalism's 'hidden persuaders' who misinform our unconscious thinking in order to sell their products. The story of Samuel, however, gave me hope, for he, also, grew up in a society in which listening was a lost art.

The problem is not that God stops speaking, but that we no longer recognise God's voice. The Samuel experience was a turning point in a nation, and it can be a turning point for us.

Pause for thought

Think of an inner thought or voice which has returned several times. What makes you think it might, or might not, come from God?

Prayer

Lord, you know me by name,
more intimately than anyone else.
Help me to notice,
from among the countless thoughts that cross my mind,
the thought that comes as a gift
from someone who knows me from the inside.
In other words, help me to recognise your voice.

Today's step

I step
away from the sound-bites
towards the word that knows my name.

Spiritual breathing exercise

Communing words, in.
Shrill noises, out.
God.

AUGUST 14

Listen to our dreams

Bible reading

After the wise astrologers from the east had offered their treasures to the child with his mother they returned to their country by a different route, having been warned in a dream not to go back to King Herod. After their departure God's angel appeared to Jesus' father Joseph in a dream. 'Get up,' the angel said, 'flee to Egypt with the child and his mother and remain there until I tell you, for Herod intends to search for the child and destroy him.' So Joseph took the child and his mother and journeyed by night into Egypt.

Matthew 2:12–14

Reflection

Dreams can be a door into the recesses of the soul. They remind us that there is a life within us that we do not make happen and cannot contrive. Like Jesus when he spent testing time in the desert, we meet in our dreams both wild beasts and angels. For this reason some people block out dreams; but, like the biblical theme of the least being the vital element, the disregarded dream is, as the rabbis liked to put it, like a letter from God that is unopened.

Early Christian leaders thought that God wants us to learn from dreams. 'Almost the greater part of humankind get their knowledge of God from dreams' wrote Tertullian in the third century. 'When our heart spontaneously presents hope to us, as happens in our sleeping state, then we have in the promise of our dreams a pledge from divinity' wrote the fifth-century bishop Synesius of Cyrene.

If we invite the Holy Spirit to accompany us as we recall and learn from them, dreams can bring increased discernment. They take us into a more conscious awareness of how we are perceiving life. They can be a warning or be like a lighthouse beckoning us with deeper possibilities through those times when everything seems to crumble. Today's Bible reading gives examples of both kinds. Dreams can move us out of our constricted view into other facets of reality.

When we wake from a dream, the most important thing is to pay attention to our feelings, and reflect on these with Christ, inviting him to relate our feelings, whether of fear or hope, to gospel themes of grace, healing, reconciliation and love.

Pause for thought

Place a pen and pad beside your bed, write down the next dream you remember, and talk it through with God.

Prayer

Divine dream-weaver,
may your holy angels guard our sleep.
May they watch over us as we rest
and hover around our beds.
Let them reveal to us in our dreams
visions of your glorious truth.

Today's step

I step
away from the closed mind
towards the dream-giver who restocks our minds.

Spiritual breathing exercise

Dream-heeding in.
Dream-rejecting out.
Angelic.

AUGUST 15

Cultivate inner silence

Bible reading

In the vision I saw a door open into heaven. The voice I had first heard said, 'Come up here, I must show you what will take place.' At once I was in the Spirit . . . The Lamb at the centre of the throne will be their shepherd and guide them. When the Lamb opened the seventh seal there was silence in heaven for about half an hour.

Revelation 4:1; 7:17; 8:1

Reflection

> We seek to cultivate an interior silence that recognises and sets aside discordant voices, to respond to unexpected or disturbing promptings of God, to widen our horizons, to develop 'the eye of the eagle' and see and hear God through his creation.[15]

Out of the silence of eternity leapt the Word of God, and in the new heaven and earth the silence is restored. Only one who is immersed in silence ('the language of the age to come' according to St Isaac the Syrian) is able to receive or generate a word which is life-giving and which echoes the original Word of the Creator.

> Souls of prayer are souls of deep silence. That is why we must accustom ourselves to deep stillness of the soul. God is the friend of silence. See how nature, the trees, the flowers, the grass grow in deep silence. See how the stars, the moon, and the sun move in silence. The more we receive in our silent prayer, the more we can give in our active life. Silence gives us a new way of looking at everything. We need this silence in order to touch souls. Jesus is waiting for us in the silence. It is there that he speaks to our

souls. Interior silence is very difficult but we must make the effort to pray. A soul of prayer can make progress without recourse to words by learning to be present to Christ. In silence we find a new energy and a real unity.[16]

Stillness and silence are great educators. Silence has the power to force us to dig deeper into ourselves. Silence involves a discovery of underlying motives. Jesus would spend a whole night in the silence of mountain or desert. 'Great things are fashioned in silence' wrote Thomas Carlisle.

Pause for thought

Be still.

Prayer

In the silence I become aware of you, O God.
In the silence I adore you.
In the silence my sins stand out and are washed away.
In the silence my problems fall into their rightful place.
In the silence I become a grateful person.
In the silence, O Lord, we become one
and I catch the whispers of your heart.

Today's step

I step
away from clamour
towards silence.

Spiritual breathing exercise

Stillness in.
Babble out.
God.

AUGUST 16

Put aside discordant voices

Bible reading

Today, if you want to hear God's voice, do not harden your hearts as your forebears did that time in the desert at Massah. Though they had seen me at work, they were a trial. For forty years I had to put up with a people full of discord. I said to myself: 'Their hearts stray all over the place. They have been strangers to my ways. They have forfeited the peace that should be theirs.'

Psalm 95:8–11

Reflection

Why could Adam and Eve walk and talk with God so naturally? The answer is that to do so is the most natural thing in the world. It is instinctive. Unfortunately we humans erect an array of barriers which come between us and God. We then call this the norm.

> The man whispered, 'God speak to me'
> and a meadowlark sang.
> But the man did not hear.
> So the man yelled, 'God speak to me'
> and the thunder rolled across the sky.
> But the man did not listen.
> The man looked around and said, 'God show me a miracle!' and new life was born.
> But the man did not know.
> So the man cried out in despair, 'Touch me God and let me know you are here!' whereupon God reached down and touched the man.
> But the man brushed the butterfly away
> and walked on.[17]

A thousand voices shout at us. We listen to the most urgent or alluring, the ones that appeal to our pride or comfort, or we listen to the loudest and most annoying and block out the rest. Divine whispers are lost.

Jesus calls us to restore the naturalness of listening to God. That is why he is called The Second Adam.

Michael Mitton has put these words into God's mouth:

> My world suffers because of lack of wisdom;
> wisdom is not gained by talking but by listening.
> The fool speaks and plans and fills all silences.
> The wise one is prepared to look foolish
> by remaining silent until they hear a word from me.
> This incessant talking
> has cut my people off from the living word.

Pause for thought

Set aside discordant voices and wait for the deeper tones of the Spirit.

Prayer

Word of God, out of the silence of eternity
you ceaselessly speak to your children.
Teach us to listen,
not to the discordant babble of a sick society,
but to the treasures of truth in the depths of silence.

Today's step

I step
away from discord
towards God's chord.

Spiritual breathing exercise

Your way in.
My way out.
Concord.

AUGUST 17

The Seven Cs

Bible reading

Light shall dawn for you and God will speak to you. If you rid yourself of contempt for the oppressed, cynicism and ill-will, and if you care for those in need, then you will receive illumination. The eternal will guide you always, refreshing you from ever-renewed sources of inspiration.

Isaiah 58:8–11

Reflection

In earlier times the many seas of the world were reduced to seven – seven is symbolically the perfect number – starting with the Red Sea and ending with the Indian Ocean. The Seven Cs are a bit like that. The oceans of elements that make up discernment of God's will are focussed on seven elements, each beginning with C: Common Sense, Circumstances, Creation, Convergence, Conscience, Conviction, and 'the Click'.

Common sense enables us to do the right things 'on the hoof'. God has given everyone a sense of what is right, or appropriate, in practical, social and everyday matters. Circumstances often help us to know the framework in which we have to operate: when external circumstances fit the gravitation of the soul like a hand in a glove we call this synchronicity. Something in creation can trigger a 'God thing' in our soul, for creation is a sacrament through which God speaks to us. Conscience tells us which things we should avoid because they are wrong. Conviction is that deep inner sense which calls us to say 'yes' to something. Convergence is when these other factors, and the advice of wise friends, come together. Finally, there is the inner 'click' that a course of action is right.

In order to gain the discernment that the seven Cs make possible, we have to be attentive to them each day. This is an art. It can become enjoyable and deeply satisfying. It can make the difference between life and death.

Pause for thought

Think over the past week. How many of the 'Cs' do you think have figured in it?

Prayer

Carpenter Christ, give me common sense,
and save me from a life of nonsense.
Help me to discern where circumstances
herald rather than hinder your unfolding purpose.
Speak through nature, prick my conscience,
and make me aware of what I am on this earth for.
Then, Lord, prompt me to take the next step.

Today's step

I step
away from nonsense
towards divine sensing.

Spiritual breathing exercise

Guiding in.
Straying out.
Click!

AUGUST 18

Write the thought down

Bible reading

A message came from God to Jeremiah: 'Write down every word I have spoken to you, for the time is coming when I will restore my people. Here are some words to start with: "This is a time of dreadful anguish for this people . . . but you will come through it and then I will raise up a leader in the spirit of the great King David."'

Jeremiah 30:1–4, 9

Reflection

'Memory is weaker than the palest ink' says a Chinese proverb. Significant thoughts that God gives us are easily submerged under the avalanche of images, noises, activities and data that daily overload us. If we take time, in silence, to write these thoughts down, they become like signposts which stay standing and to which we may return.

Moses wrote down 'all the words of the Lord' (Exodus 24:4). Joshua wrote down God-given guidelines in the Book of God's Law (Joshua 24:26). Samuel wrote down God's rules for a king (1 Samuel 10:25). God told Isaiah to write the prophetic name he was to give to their future child on a large board (Isaiah 8:1) and so on.

What should *we* write down? If we are busy, we may start by writing down the things we must do in order of priority. By doing this we create mental space for thoughts that are of longer-term importance to emerge, or which, though little, are spiritually vital.

Perhaps a person or a failing flashes through our minds – by writing these down we change an unexamined negative pattern, and make ourselves accountable.

There is a place also to write down feelings, mental pictures, poems, drawings which limber us up to hear God more clearly because they put us in touch with problems that need healing or passions that need outworking.

Occasionally, a crystal-clear thought comes out of the blue. When I taught Humanities a few hours each week in a College of Building I had the thought 'Go to the Principal and ask him to invite a Christian musical to the college.' As a result the President of the Student Union listened to God: it did not matter that the musical never came.

Pause for thought

Write down the thoughts that come to you after reading this.

Prayer

Holy God who speaks words of life
make me a ready writer.
Speak through my confusion.
Help me to write honestly and simply,
and to name and carry out your priorities for today.
Grace me to catch your soothing tones,
your quiet intimations,
your stirrings in my soul,
and your bold commands.

Today's step

I step
away from fluffy thoughts
towards committed words.

Spiritual breathing exercise

Pinpoints in.
Vacuities out.
You speak.

AUGUST 19

Respond to promptings

Bible reading

God longs to show you compassion. Those who wait for God will be blessed. There will be no more tears. Though your supplies may be scant, your Teacher will never leave you. As soon as you cry out to him he will answer you. When you swerve to the right or to the left, you will hear a voice behind you whispering, 'This is the way, walk in it.'

Isaiah 30:18–21

Reflection

'I have been thinking,' writes Ruth Carvosso, 'how much everyone needs time apart from the rush and pressures of everyday living; and what a difference it makes when we can take time to note when God wants to speak to us, and when to listen for what he wants to say – and then to act upon it. God's time is certainly very different to ours. I am conscious that this work needs to be sown and then takes time to root, grow and flourish until it has fulfilled God's purposes – and then gives way to other "new things".'

God speaks in more than one way, so it is important we keep our ears open in more than one way. Yesterday, perhaps, we read our Bible and God spoke to us through it. Today, maybe, something wells up from inside us, or we are uneasy about something. It is important to give time to this, in order to discern what God might be saying. We should not focus on a stipulated Bible passage that does not speak to this, or which crowds out the time we need to listen in this way. It is also important to heed the inner voice that warns us to slow down or avoid going in a certain direction.

A seed can only take root and bear fruit in a person prepared to receive it. Everything depends upon our capacity and willingness to listen, to be transformed. If we are ready to open ourselves to be, to do, to go as God directs, we shall be free.

Pause for thought

Whatever our human conditioning, open our hearts so that the Holy Spirit, little by little, can wean us from wrong ways and guide us into divine ways.

Prayer

Thank you that you are a God who speaks.
Grace me to accept that I am hard of hearing.
Help me to attune my ears to your promptings
at the crossroads of each day
and in the movements of my soul.

Today's step

I step
away from obstinate attitudes
towards divine whispers.

Spiritual breathing exercise

Open ears in.
Blind pursuits out.
'This is the way.'

AUGUST 20

Widen our horizons

Bible reading

My thoughts are not your thoughts, says the Infinite One, and my ways are not your ways. As heaven is higher than earth, so are my thoughts and my ways vaster than yours. As rain and snow come down from the sky and do not return to it until they have watered the earth, enabling it to bud and fruit and provide seeds and food, so is the word that comes out of my mouth. It will not return to me empty, but it will accomplish the purposes for which I sent it.

Isaiah 55:8–11

Reflection

We can listen to God for our cabbage patch, or for a continent. It is our choice. God will speak to us about our cabbage patch, but if we follow this way of life we allow God to widen our horizons. We may shrink from this, but we need not fear for, in William Faber's[18] immortal words:

> There's a wideness in God's mercy
> like the wideness of the sea,
> there's a kindness in his justice
> which is more than liberty.
>
> For the love of God is broader
> than the measures of man's mind;
> and the heart of the Eternal
> is most wonderfully kind.

God speaks through visions. A vision needs to be sufficiently clear and concrete to act as a beacon. President John F. Kennedy had this. In 1961 he told of his vision to put a man on the moon by the end of the decade. He held out a vision of service overseas and launched the Peace Corps. Martin Luther King laid before his nation not a vague ideal of racial harmony but concrete visions of how black and white Americans might live together.

God puts into some people's brains whole eras and their needed foundations; into others God puts the vision of mountains to climb. From beginning to end the Bible tells of people who listened to God: each had a different horizon. Noah was told to preserve something. Abraham was told to discover something. David was told to prepare something, and Solomon to build. Elijah was told to anoint someone, and the shepherd Amos, like many others, was told to say something. For each of them, obedience to God's voice brought them to a wider horizon.

Pause for thought

What is God saying to you?

Prayer

Stretch my heart, Lord
and broaden my mind.
Open my eyes, Lord
that I may find:

fresh horizons,
a holy grail,
a noble challenge
a height to scale.

Today's step

I step
away from the cramped and confined
towards divine vistas.

Spiritual breathing exercise

God's thoughts in.
Petty thoughts out.
I see!

AUGUST 21

Perceiving with eagle eye

Bible reading

Saul, from the clan of Benjamin, was searching with his servant for his father's lost donkeys when they also became lost. 'Let us visit the seer in the town near here,' said the servant, 'perhaps he will tell us the way we should take.' In those days prophets were called seers. As they entered the town Samuel came towards them. The previous day God had revealed to Samuel, 'I will send you a man from the clan of Benjamin. Anoint him leader over my people.'

1 Samuel 9

Reflection

Our reflection on January 17 referred to that aspect of 'the eye of the eagle' that can gaze into the dazzling light in the heart of God. That is the contemplative aspect. An eagle also looks down upon earth until it spots something needful which no other bird can see. This is the perceiving aspect.

In early Old Testament times people with especially sharp godly perception were called seers. Often, as in today's Bible reading, they were shown something precise and practical. Today, Scots call such people 'canny'. Carved on the wall of the Scottish Parliament are these words of Robbie Burns: 'O wad some Pow'r the giftie gie us/To see oursels as others see us!/It wad frae money a blunder free us/And foolish notion.'[19]

The modern tragedy is that our vision has become so restricted. In his book *The Eye of the Eagle*, David Adam meditates on an early hymn, 'Be thou my vision', which some believe was written by the sixth-century Irish bard Dallan Forgaill. He observes that we are always wanting to analyse, but to dissect living things is fatal. Celtic

Christians, instead of always looking at secondary causes, looked at the unseen strands that, through the Prime Mover, unite all things and vibrate with the presence. Adam recalls reading a book entitled *How to Improve Your Vision Without Glasses*. It offered a system of daily exercises such as 'How to increase your range' and 'Do not miss out on the small things, they are often important.'

Pause for thought

Observe a small thing and learn from it.
Extend your vision today.

Prayer

All-seeing God, be my vision.
Be the light in my eye,
and the bright beam before me.
Be the thought in my head
and the theme of my sleep.
Be the shape in the gloom
and the piercing of darkness.
All-seeing God, may my vision be yours.

Today's step

I step
away from looking backwards
towards looking further.

Spiritual breathing exercise

Observing in.
Blinkers out.
Eagle eye.

AUGUST 22

The sounds of God in creation

Bible reading

The voice of the Almighty thunders over the waters.
The God of glory thunders through mighty waters.
The voice of the Almighty is powerful.
The voice of the Almighty is awesome.
The voice of the Almighty strikes with flashes of lightning.
The voice of the Almighty shakes the desert.
The voice of the Almighty twists the trees
and strips the forests.
And all the people gathered for worship cry, 'Glory!'

Psalm 29

Reflection

God speaks to us through the elements. The seventh-century Bishop Chad ran to the church and lay prostrate when there was heavy thunder and lightning – he took these as a summons from God.

God also speaks to us through creatures. Jesus advised us to listen to God through the birds and sheep. In Western societies we can also learn about God from dogs. Owen Wilson's character in the film *Marley & Me* says, 'A dog has no use for fancy cars or big homes or designer clothes. A dog doesn't care if you're rich or poor, clever or dull, smart or dumb. Give him your heart, and he'll give you his.' David Frankel, the director of that film, adds, 'There's something wonderful about the way dogs live in the moment. They don't look back. They don't yearn. They don't want what they don't have.'

Where the human body is limited, a creature may fly, run or squeeze through. When the human mind is in a groove or limited by shyness, so that we cannot be fully present to another, there are creatures that can transcend such blocks. Creatures may make us aware of a quality God wants to give us, and of the immense range of life-changing forces which, when placed in the divine hands of love, can bring undreamed-of transformation.

Pause for thought

Observe a creature. Ask God to show you through that creature a quality he wants you to have.

Prayer

Creator of love,
make us aware that you are present in every cell of creation
and in every cell of our being.
May we hear you in the movements of the sky
and in the soul's every sigh.
May we hear you in the passing of a fly
and in a poor creature's cry.
When our pets race and dart,
may we catch the beatings of your heart.

Today's step

I step
away from aloofness to animals
towards your voice in their play.

Spiritual breathing exercise

Creatureliness in.
God-almightiness out.
Um.

AUGUST 23

To discern is better than to copy

Bible reading

One sabbath day Jesus was teaching in a Jewish synagogue. A crippled woman who had been bent double for eighteen years was there. Jesus called her forward, laid his hands on her, and told her she was set free. Immediately she straightened up and praised God. The officer in charge at the synagogue, however, was upset because Jesus had healed on the sabbath. 'There are six days for work,' he told everyone, 'so come on one of those days if you want to be healed.' Jesus responded: 'You hypocrites. Each one of you would untie your ox or donkey on a sabbath so they could drink water – then why should this child of Abraham not be set free on the sabbath from what bound her?'

Luke 13:10–17

Reflection

If, when we read the Gospels, we merely try to copy the external acts of Jesus, we will probably be disappointed. If, however, we learn from and apply the motivations, we will grow in discernment. In this passage Jesus teaches in the synagogue. You may be called to be a cab driver, not to teach in a synagogue; the fact that Jesus taught in a synagogue, or trained as a carpenter, tells us about his calling, not yours. Jesus noticed a woman who was bent double, and sensed she could be healed. You are called always to be sensitive to others and to God's healing power, though you may never see a woman who is bent double. The fact that Jesus healed this particular woman but left others unhealed is his business, not yours. Jesus' action triggered a theological dispute about the sabbath. The subject of disputes today may be quite different, but the principles

Jesus teaches are timeless: the Spirit is more important than the letter and to meet a need that cannot be postponed is God's work.

If we are to discern what we should do, and how we should be, we need to use both our hearts and our heads as we read the Gospels. We need to become sensitive to the place and the people where we are, to sense the greatest need of the moment an the motivations of those who use their duties as a means of control.

Pause for thought

Apply these principles of sensitivity to place and person today.

Prayer

Father, Mother,
free me from unthinking, jaundiced ways of looking at others.
Sensitise my heart to detect
the uppermost need of the moment.
Sharpen me to reach out and not flinch at the reactions
of those who will feel insecure.
So help me God.

Today's step

I step
away from copying externals
towards understanding inner dynamics.

Spiritual breathing exercise

Discerner in.
Copycat out.
Unbind.

AUGUST 24

Knowing the right time

Bible reading

After John the Baptiser had been arrested, Jesus went into Galilee. There he proclaimed the Good News from God. 'The time has come,' he said, 'and God's kingdom has come close to you.'

Mark 1:14, 15

Reflection

Despite the fact that his mission was the most important in the world, Jesus did not rush in where angels fear to tread. He did not begin his public launch until the leader of the great reform movement, his cousin John, was put in prison. The old leaves need to fall before the fresh buds begin to replace them.

Fifteen minutes after the old year ended I knelt on the cold, dark ground of the holy island of Lindisfarne, which is known as a cradle of Christianity to the English. I unmistakably 'heard' God say that he wanted a cradle which is rooted deeper in the soil, deeper in the soul of the people, deeper in the supernatural, than mere top-down centres of Christianity, a cradle required by the kairos of our time. 'This cradle,' the inaudible voice continued, 'which has been lost sight of, is to be re-discovered; from it there will be a birthing of a new way in the Church, which has a significance far beyond anything that one person can comprehend.'

In the theology of the Greek New Testament the word *kairos* means an appointed time in the purpose of God. It is more generally an opportune moment for decision. The Greek word *chronos* is used for a length of time, and *aion* refers to an era, past, present or future. *Kairos*, however, is about being the right people in the right place at the right time, hearing and responding to God in such a way that it proves to be a turning point. There can be kairos moments in little as well as large matters. Each of us can have kairos moments if we grow in discernment. Remember, big doors swing on little hinges.

Pause for thought

What has reached its peak or is completed? What is coming to birth? What is God saying?

Prayer

Show me, Lord, that for which the time has come,
be it small or great.
Show me what lies in this moment.
Show me what you are bringing to a head,
or bringing to an end, or bringing to birth.
And I will obey.

Today's step

I step
away from inopportune involvements
towards synchronicity.

Spiritual breathing exercise

God-lines in.
Sidelines out.
Kairos.

AUGUST 25

Prophecy

Bible reading

Eagerly desire spiritual gifts, especially the gift of prophecy. Everyone who prophesies helps to strengthen, encourage or comfort people. Those who speak in tongues build up themselves, but those who prophesy build up the whole church. If unbelievers visit the church and find everyone speaking in tongues, they will understand nothing and be no better off. However, if they visit and find people prophesying, they will realise that God understands the deepest motivations of the heart; they will fall down in penitence and acknowledge that God is really among you.

1 Corinthians 14:1, 3, 23–25

Reflection

> Essential to this kind of openness is a proper affirmation of the gift of prophecy.[20]

What is prophecy? It is to bring a new angle to something from God to people, from heaven to earth, from the real to the unreal, from the true to the false, from the clear light of day to the cloud of confusion. Prophecy reveals something previously hidden. It can cut to the nub of a situation or a person, it can suggest a new direction, or a way to break a logjam.

The prophetic word can come from our creative and communicative God in a variety of ways. It can come through pictures, visions, dreams. Jesus' parable of the vineyard is an example. It can come through intuitions and inklings. It can come through words, either audible or like tele-print in your mind. It can come through Bible reading, life experiences, tongues with interpretation, preachers, songs, prayers, and the lives of past people who heard and spoke God's truth. And it can come through quakings. Members of the Religious Society of Friends are known as Quakers because they sit in silence unless they inwardly quake so much that they can no longer refrain from speaking out.

In such ways our Lord draws us into a greater understanding and experience of his character, love and greatness. Often we can then pass on the words God has given to us in order to encourage or motivate someone else. The potential blessing is great. If handled carefully we can avoid the pitfalls and abuses of the gift.

Pause for thought

Focus on one of the ways God can speak listed above. Write down anything that is given to you.

Prayer

Speak, Lord,
in stillness or storm,
in circumstance or sign,
in Scripture or word,
in conscience or heart,
in encounter or art.
Stir up the gift in me.

Today's step

I step
away from the closed imagination
towards the word that speaks.

Spiritual breathing exercise

Heavenly stuff in.
Selfish stuff out.
Bullseye.

AUGUST 26

All may prophesy

Bible reading

Deacon Stephen of the Jerusalem church addressed his fellow Jewish accusers in court with a survey of God's dealings with their people: '. . . Moses was rejected by his fellow Hebrews who said "who made you a judge over us?" Later God revealed something new about his nature to Moses: "I AM the God of your forebears Abraham, Isaac and Joseph" and called him to deliver the people from Egypt. Moses went up Mount Sinai and received living words from God to pass on. After their departure from Egypt, however, his fellow Hebrews turned to idols and rejected Moses . . .'

Acts 7

Reflection

The apostle Paul says all may prophesy, and should be eager to do so (1 Corinthians 14:31, 39). Moses rejoiced at the thought that all God's people might prophesy (Numbers 11:29). Moses is a fine example of how God teaches, speaks to and helps us develop a more sensitive ear, and a more tender heart which is ready to obey God. In the book of Acts, especially chapter 7, we find a good summary of how God moulded and changed Moses into the great prophet he became. In verse 38 we find a good definition of the prophetic gift – Moses 'received living words to pass on'.

The young Moses grew up in Pharaoh's palace with all its education and privileges. As he grew older he became more aware of his own bloodline. Moses had a strong sense of identity as a Hebrew and of God's calling on his life. God had anointed him as a leader and a prophet. At 40 years of age Moses had much expectation of how God was going to use him. But he began to feel impatient and decided to give God a helping hand. He murdered the Egyptian and was forced to flee into the desert. And there he had to stay for 40 years. He probably felt his calling, his dreams, his future, were all shattered. He was a broken man. But the desert proved to be the place that God used to prepare Moses and to hone his listening ear and prophetic gifting. Everything he had in Egypt was now gone. It was only Moses – and God. When the Lord spoke to him 40 years later through the burning bush, he was a different man.

Pause for thought

Pause in silence. Wait for the living word that God speaks.

Prayer

Speak, Lord in the stillness
while I wait on Thee.
Hushed my heart to listen
in expectancy.[21]

Today's step

I step
away from substitutes that drown out God's voice
towards the God who speaks.

Spiritual breathing exercise

Your voice in.
Idols out.
I hear.

AUGUST 27

How not to prophesy

Bible reading

Any prophets who presume to speak a word from me which I never commanded them to speak, or who speak out of their attachments to something other than Me are as good as dead. If you ask, 'How can we know what words have not really come from God?' – take note of what rings true and what comes true. There is no need to be pushed around for fear of a prophetic person who speaks out of their own ego.

Deuteronomy 18:20–22

Reflection

Some types of people get a thrill from prescribing what others should do. Other types get a thrill from prophesying. And some hopelessly mix the two up. Beware of such people!

A visitor burst into a retreat house kitchen and declaimed, 'There is a spirit of slavery in this place.' A suitable answer was, 'I don't feel enslaved. In fact I feel free enough to ask you to leave my kitchen and allow me to watch TV in my free time.' A man announced to an unsuspecting lady, 'God has given me guidance that we are to marry.' To which a suitable reply was, 'What a pity God hasn't given me the same guidance.'

My former church had meetings led by Quakers to which charismatic church members came. One such member, no longer able to bear the silence, announced, 'I have a picture of a large ship.' 'Oh,' said another, rather chatty member, 'a ship is a picture of the church.' 'That's a shame,' said the first, 'because the ship sank.' To which the wise Quaker response was – silence.

St John of the Cross warned spiritual guides against placing too much value on mystical experiences, visions and suchlike. He pointed out that these are not signs of holiness; they may be a sign that the person who receives them has a vivid imagination. The abandonment of the will to God should always take priority over these other things.

Pause for thought

Weigh and check out what you want to say before you say it. Weigh and check out what someone has said to you in God's name.

Prayer

God of the prophet Moses, man of meekness,
may we not use the gifts of the Spirit
unless they bear the fruits of the Spirit.
May we not say things that bolster our self-esteem
unless we first esteem the other more highly than ourselves.
May we not speak a word we have been given
unless we are willing for it to be weighed by others.
May we not speak at all out of season.

Today's step

I step
away from ego prescriptions
in awed silence towards any true prophetic word.

Spiritual breathing exercise

Costly word in.
Cheap words out.
God's-eye.

AUGUST 28

How we may prophesy

Bible reading

No prophecy of Scripture sprang from an individualistic interpretation of the truth. No such prophecy came just because the person who uttered it wanted to say something. People who honoured God spoke under the inspiration of the Holy Spirit. There were, however, false prophets in those days, as now. These dishonestly twist truth to suit their own agenda. In doing this they deny Jesus and sow the seeds of their own downfall.

2 Peter 1:20–2:1

Reflection

We may learn about how to prophesy from Moses, who is one of the greatest prophets and 'the most humble man on the face of the earth' (Numbers 12:3). He had no desire to hog the limelight. His longing was for all God's people to be able to move in the gift of prophecy (see Numbers 11:29). This longing of Moses is a foreshadowing of the promised outpouring of the Holy Spirit on the day of Pentecost.

What does all of this mean to us? It means that God is interested in shaping and moulding our character – just like Moses. It also means that the Holy Spirit – the prophetic Spirit – is now available to us and dwelling within us as believers in the Lord Jesus Christ.

The world is full of noise and disturbance. As God's people in God's world we can learn to listen to him, and share his word just like Moses did. Prophecy is receiving living words or visions from God and passing these on in order to strengthen, encourage and comfort others (1 Corinthians 14:3).

Some are called to prophesy to nations, others to churches. Prophecy includes: words of knowledge – for example facts about a person not obtained by normal means. This may have little guidance in it, but the fact that it has been given can touch or move the person concerned. An example of a word of knowledge in Scripture is John 4:16–19.

I encourage people to find a place to listen quietly to God for 20 minutes, and then to share anything God may have said through Scripture, creation, a mental picture, or a voice.

Pause for thought

Look up for vision. Look down for humility. Look to the other for connection.

Prayer

Great Creator of the gleaming moon and falling stars,
great Saviour of the miraculous birth and rising from death,
great Spirit of the seers and sacred words,
come into our minds,
come into our mouths,
until we become your message and sign.

Today's step

I step
away from the noise of proud spirits
towards your Spirit.

Spiritual breathing exercise

Living words in.
Empty words out.
Life.

AUGUST 29

Interpret and apply prophecy

Bible reading

If all prophesy at a church meeting – giving inspired witness and interpreting the divine purpose – and unbelievers come in, they become aware of the secrets of their hearts – their sins and needs. Let two or three prophets speak – those inspired to preach or speak – while the rest attentively listen and weigh what is being said.

1 Corinthians 14:24, 25, 29

Reflection

When we receive a prophecy, what should we do with it? First of all, decide who it is for. Is it for yourself, another individual, a group (e.g. a house group, church, organisation), or a nation? Second, decide whether it needs to be shared. If not, use it for intercession or put it on file to await confirmation. Confirmation might come by events or by others having similar convictions.

If it is for an individual, does it pass the test of 'Is it true, necessary, kind, timely?' Are you the one to share it, or should you share it with the person who has care for them? You might write the prophecy down and offer it to a mature Christian; perhaps, if it is in a church context, to someone in oversight.

The person who prophesies gives the raw material and need not be mature. The next stage is interpretation. A person who interprets generally does need to be mature. Sometimes it is helpful for a group to discuss the meaning of a prophecy.

The application of a prophecy is the third stage. If it is for a church, those in oversight need to approve it.

A Scotsman came on one of our retreats. Our warden, Jean, prayed over him. She had a picture of a white cloth with a red cross on it. He associated this with the English flag of St George, and thought, 'Oh no, Lord, do you want me, a Scot, to minister to the English?' Then he crossed the road and met me for the first time. I happened to be wearing a badge which consisted of the St George and the St Andrew flags crossed. He commented: 'I had never seen anything like this before, it was such an unlikely coincidence. I prayed, and I felt God was saying there is a reconciliation and healing needed between the Scots and the English, and I am to be part of this.' That is an example of the prophecy, the interpretation and the application coming together.

Pause for thought

Weigh something that has been said to you in God's name.

Prayer

God of wisdom
give us good judgement.
Help us to distinguish:
that which confuses from that which brings light;
that which brings peace from that which brings strife;
that which brings reality from that which cloaks it;
that which builds love from that which feeds distrust.

Today's step

I step
away from impetuous reactions
towards prayerful assessment.

Spiritual breathing exercise

Prayerful thought in.
Quick judgements out.
Edify.

AUGUST 30

Visions

Bible reading

Peter stood up on the day of Pentecost and explained to the gathered crowd what was happening by quoting the prophet Joel – 'In the last days, God says, I will pour out my Spirit on all people. Your sons and daughters will prophesy, your young men will see visions, your old men will dream dreams. Even on my servants, both men and women, I will pour out my Spirit in those days, and they will prophesy.'

Acts 2:17, 18

Reflection

We live in the age of the Holy Spirit, and visions continue to come. In the nineteenth century St Seraphim of Russia conversed with the young Nicholas Motovilov in the snow-clad forest:

> Noah conversed with God. Abraham saw God and his days and was glad (cf. John 8:56). The grace of the Holy Spirit acting externally was also reflected in all the Old Testament prophets and saints of Israel. The Hebrews afterwards established prophetic schools where the sons of the prophets were taught to discern the signs of the manifestation of God or the angels, and to distinguish the operations of the Holy Spirit from the ordinary natural phenomena of our grace-less earthly life. Symeon who held God in his arms, Christ's grandparents, Joachim and Anna, and countless other servants of God continually had, quite openly, various divine apparitions, voices and revelations which were proved true by miraculous events. Though not with the same power as in the

people of God, nevertheless the presence of the Spirit of God also acted in the pagans who did not know the true God, because even among them God found for himself chosen people.[22]

Pagans and Muslims meet Jesus in their dreams. A Martin Luther King has a dream. A Solzhentsyn envisages the power of 'one word of truth' to topple tyrant regimes. And so on.

Pause for thought

What is your vision?

Prayer

God, our Vision,
impelled by the visions you entrust to us,
may we break through the brittle shell of our unbelief
and move, untrammelled, towards the heavenly horizons.

Today's step

I step
away from the blinkers
towards your vision.

Spiritual breathing exercise

Seeing in.
Shut-eyes out
I see.

AUGUST 31

Prophetic warnings

Bible reading

The year that Barnabas and Saul were with the church at Antioch some prophets came from Jerusalem. One of them, named Agabus, warned, through the Spirit, that the entire Roman empire would suffer a severe famine. (This happened under the reign of the Emperor Claudius.) Each disciple decided to help their brothers and sisters in Judea to the best of their ability. They sent their aid through Barnabas and Saul.

Acts 11:27–30

Reflection

The Bible gives many examples of prophetic warnings. Often some kind of disaster is forecast if the people refuse to heed God's ways. Joseph was given warning of seven years of famine, and managed to persuade the ruler of a foreign power to make plans to survive this. In today's reading Christians were able, because they heeded a prophecy, to help their poorer brothers and sisters back home before it was too late.

In the time of Columba, the sixth-century founder of the Iona Community, Berach, who was planning to sail the always risky journey from Iona to Tiree, asked Columba to bless this journey. Columba looked at him long and hard: 'Take special care not to cross the open sea today in a straight course, otherwise you will meet an enormous monster who will terrify and well nigh overwhelm you. Go in a zigzag around the smaller islands.'

Berach set off, but, since everything looked fine and it seemed so much easier to go direct, he disregarded Columba's advice. Some time after this an immense whale rose up like a mountain in front of the crew, opened its jaws, gaping, full of teeth. They let down the sail in terror and rowed back for their lives. In future, they weighed God's prophetic words more carefully.

Baithene had to make a similar journey, but unlike Berach, his impulses were in harmony with God. On the morning of their departure Columba told Baithene and his crew about the whale, but gave no advice. 'That beast and I are both under God's power,' said Baithene. 'Go in peace,' said Columba, 'your faith in Christ will defend you from this peril.' They did see the whale and the crew was terrified, but Baithene himself was without fear. He raised both his hands and blessed the sea and the whale. At that precise moment the whale plunged under the waves and they did not see it again.

Pause for thought

Do not rush in where angels fear to tread. Become present to what is ahead. Do not heed fears, but do heed warnings.

Prayer

Stop us, dear God,
from rushing in where angels fear to tread.
Rebuke our headstrong ways.
Deflect us from foolhardy paths.
Alert us to meet a crisis that requires us to be prepared.

Today's step

I step
away from thin ice
towards the warning sign.

Spiritual breathing exercise

Heeding hearts in.
Headstrong ways out.
Provision.

SEPTEMBER 1

Overcome evil with good

Bible reading

Hate whatever is evil. Hold on to whatever is good. Do not punish those who commit evil deeds by committing an evil deed in return. Take great care to do what everyone can see is right. If your enemies are hungry, feed them; if they are thirsty, give them a drink. In doing this you will make a mark for good that they cannot ignore. Do not be overcome by evil: overcome evil with good.

Romans 12:9, 17, 20, 21

Reflection

The world can be divided into two groups of people: Those who see the enormity of the world's ills and say 'there is nothing I can do', and those who say 'with the help of God I will do what I can'. It has to begin with ourselves.

We overcome evil with good at different levels. We start with the evils within ourselves. With Jesus as our helper we go to the root of such things as pride, envy, greed, self-rejection, misplaced anger and ask the Holy Spirit to replace them with their opposite virtue. Perhaps we are dominated by the drive for success? The focus of our spiritual initiative is to replace this with service. Perhaps we are dominated by confusion, hostility or disillusion with ourselves? As we spend time praising God the foul stench of defeat is swept away. Defeatism blankets us? We take one step to overcome something. We are conditioned by lies? We wield the sword of truth. We fall prey to gossip? We turn away and meditate on Scripture. We are hurt by others and disengage? We reach out to them and communicate love. Relationships are tarnished? Talents are unused? Inspirations are shelved? Wounds are unhealed? Duties are neglected? Actions are postponed? Thinking is dissipated in trifles? Time is frittered away? The 'adult' within us can intercede for our inner tyrant, child, or procrastinator.

Pause for thought

It is better to light one candle than to curse the darkness.[1]

Prayer

Eternal God,
your goodness is stronger than evil;
your love is stronger than hate;
your light is stronger than darkness;
your life is stronger than death;
victory is ours through you who love us.

Today's step

I step
away from something that I know is not right
towards something that I know is of God.

Spiritual breathing exercise

Good in.
Bad out.
God.

SEPTEMBER 2

Overcome bad mindsets

Bible reading

Although we live in the world, we do not wage war in the way our world does. We harness spiritual forces in order that strongholds, false arguments and every proud obstacle that sets itself up against the knowledge of God comes to nothing. We take every thought captive and make it obey Christ.

2 Corinthians 10:3–5

Reflection

We overcome evils in the mindset of an organisation, locality or people. When fear, hostility or mistrust increase in a group, we try to anticipate negative actions and replace them with positive dynamics.

We nail lies that dominate the mindset of our society. Dominant lies in the period when this was written are that: big is beautiful; more means better; speed means good; know-how means wisdom.

Most of the world's population either dominates others, or succumbs to a victim mentality. Those with a victim mentality decide that because we, or our group, have been neglected, mistreated or lied to, all we can do is to react negatively – by complaining perhaps, by violence or by inertia. God, however, calls us to overcome evil with good. Nobody had more reason to succumb to a victim mentality than Jesus, who was betrayed at the deepest level possible.

The theologian Walter Wink developed a critique of 'the powers'. He observed that power is the will to be. Each power has an emergent characteristic, which is its ethos, or soul. Each power takes outward expression in institutions, governments and processes. The outward forms are shaped by their inner spirituality. When the spirituality is good, the soul of the power is honoured, and diversity and differences are valued. But when powers become idols they take over and become demonic. We need to unmask the means by which these powers cause degradation. They can be redeemed by connecting them to their original, God-given organising energy.

Pause for thought

What opposes God in a set-up that you are connected with?

Prayer

Power of powers,
a household divided against itself cannot last.
Bring the proud walls tumbling down.
And from the rubble let there grow up
lovely little plants of truth, goodness and love.

Today's step

I step
away from domination
towards transformation.

Spiritual breathing exercise

God's thinking in.
False axioms out.
Jesus.

SEPTEMBER 3

Overcome unseen spirit forces

Bible reading

Be strong in the Lord and in God's mighty power. Put on every item of the Divine armour so that you can combat the devil's schemes. For our greatest struggle is not against the obvious physical opponents, it is against the dark powers, rulers and authorities, and against the spirit forces of the Otherworld. That is why it's so important that you put on all of God's armour, so that when the crunch comes, after you have done everything in your own power against the evil forces, you can remain standing.

Ephesians 6:10–13

Reflection

> The Community affirms a worldview that recognises the reality of the supernatural and of struggle between the spiritual forces of good and evil.[2]

We address evils that lurk in the unseen world. Certain well-meaning people, thinking that anything that is not materialistic must be good, forget that some spirits are bad. Thus spiritual people can end up as captive to wrong spirits as others do to material possessions.

As well as those who believe that the 'powers' Paul here refers to are the accumulated dynamics of institutions or nations that have become oppressive or demonic, traditional belief is that they refer to demons. Other voices reject as unsound those forms of spiritual warfare which demonise people, treat them as enemies, or promote triumphalism or war.

These insights are not mutually exclusive. Perhaps we should heed a warning of C. S. Lewis[3]. The first mistake is to give the devil undue prominence. There is one God, not two. The devil is not equal to God. This world belongs to God and ultimately will be reclaimed. The second mistake is to ignore the devil altogether, for he is 'like a prowling lion, seeking whom he may devour' (1 Peter 5:8).

The person who writes off spiritual warfare as something that provokes violence and creates enemies has missed the point. The point is that military war is the inevitable consequence of the selfishness of peoples. Only if we engage in the moral and spiritual equivalent of war can we cure the causes of military war. How foolish of us to live as if we are the measure of all that is wrong in the world, or that we can combat multi-layered evils on our own.

Pause for thought

Take thought. Be aware.

Prayer

Save me from the arrogance of self-sufficiency.
Open my eyes to see what you see.
Strip naivety from me.
Help me to face up to evil.
Deliver us from evil.
For yours is the power and the glory for ever.

Today's step

I step
away from self-sufficiency
towards your forcefield.

Spiritual breathing exercise

Struggle in.
Blandness out.
Victory.

SEPTEMBER 4

Christ the Victor

Bible reading

The Lord Jesus Christ gave himself for our sins to rescue us from this evil age.
Galatians 1:4

Christ disarmed the powers and authorities, making a public spectacle of them, triumphing over them by the Cross.
Colossians 2:15

As in Adam all die, so in Christ shall all be made alive. Christ is the first fruits, then, when he comes, those who belong to him. When he has overcome every dominion, authority and power he will hand the kingdom over to God the Father.

1 Corinthians 15:22–24

Reflection

There are a hundred and one theories of the atonement, that is, of the meaning and effects of Christ's death. Some of these were only invented in recent centuries. An interpretation that deserves to be taken with the utmost seriousness is called, in Latin, *Christus Victor*. This does not disconnect Christ's death from his birth or from his resurrection or from his eternal role. It recognises that every single element of Christ is part of a unique victory process. For the apostle Paul this victory process affects not only individuals, but is set forth as the drama of the whole world's salvation.

Irenaeus[4] set out Paul's statements in a famous book entitled *Recapitulation*. He reminds us that the purpose of Christ's incarnation, trials, miracles, death, resurrection, ascension into heaven, and sending of the Holy Spirit is that he might deliver us from three evils – sin, death and the devil. It is his total life that does it. This victory of Christ over evil is an eternal victory, in the present as well as in the past.

No wonder that Columba of Iona could write:

> The Judgement Day of the Lord shall come . . .
> The brightest sign and standard of the Cross
> shall stand forth.
> The stars will fall like figs from a tree.[5]

No wonder that the Northumbrian poet could picture Christ thus:

> Then the young warrior, God Almighty,
> stripped himself, firm and unflinching.
> He climbed upon the Cross, brave before many, to redeem humankind.[6]

It is through Christ the Victor that we, too have victory over every kind of evil.

Pause for thought

Is there anything I cannot do if I allow Christ to do it through me?

Prayer

I bind to myself for ever by power of faith
Christ's incarnation,
his baptism in river Jordan,
his death on Cross for my salvation,
his bursting from the spice-strewn tomb,
his riding up the heavenly way,
his coming at the Day of Doom.[7]

Today's step

I step
away from defeat
towards the Victor Christ.

Spiritual breathing exercise

Strength in.
False triumphalism out.
Victor Christ.

SEPTEMBER 5

Discernment of spirits

Bible reading

Some Jews who cast evil spirits out of people began to do this in the name of the Lord Jesus. They would say 'I command you in the name of Jesus, whom Paul preaches.' On one occasion seven brothers were engaged in this practice when the evil spirit answered, 'Jesus I know, and I know about Paul, but who are you?' Then the man with the evil spirit sprang at them and overpowered them with such force that they rushed out of the house, wounded, with their clothes torn from their backs.

Acts 19:13–16

Reflection

These professional exorcists used the name of Jesus but did not have the spirit of Jesus: and the spirit in the man they were exorcising knew this!

It is important to distinguish between a sickness and an evil. Sickness is a condition, but evil is a behaviour. Sickness happens, but evil is inflicted. Sickness should be treated, but evil must be fought.

'Discernment of spirits' refers to the appraisal of the spirit within a person, a place, or a bodiless being. Jesus knew what was in people; he could read their thoughts (e.g. Matthew 12:24–28). He could also 'read' places (cf. Matthew 11:20–24). Jesus taught that there is a kingdom of evil spirits ruled over by 'Satan' (Matthew 12:24–28) who is the 'Prince of this world' (John 12:31), 'a murderer . . . and the father of lies' (John 8:44).

The pure in heart keep their focus on God, they do not go chasing after real or imagined demons. But they do spot a lying spirit. Paul asserted that some people 'will obey lying spirits' (1 Timothy 4:1) and John urges Christians to 'test the spirits' (1 John 4:1). Demons are like actors on a stage, tempting, deceiving, prowling like a lion to devour us, but they cannot control that which is of God in us.

In sixth-century Britain the ailing Bishop Dubricius wanted a boy named Moninus to look after him. The priest Samson advised: 'The net cast into the sea receives all the fish it can get, but later, on land, the fisherfolk separate the good from the bad.' On a subsequent occasion Samson perceived a blackamoor like a little boy sitting on the lad's left shoulder with his mouth turned towards his ear, indicating a conversation taking place between the devil and the lad.

Contemporary Christians debate the degree to which spirits are manifestations of psychic elements within or beyond a person. Either way, we need to discern them rightly.

Pause for thought

Try and discern the spirit of a person or a place today.

Prayer

I arise today in a Mighty Power.
The power of the One who is Three
The Creator, the Christ and the Spirit.
In their name I say:
lies: perish;
confusion: depart;
demons: flee;
people: bow before your God.

Today's step

I step
away from deception
towards discernment.

Spiritual breathing exercise

Jesus in.
Lying spirits out.
All is well.

SEPTEMBER 6

Overcome destructive spirits

Bible reading

Don't trust every spirit, dear friends, but test them in order to find out whether or not they are from God, for the world is full of false prophets. Here is a simple way to test them: every spirit that acknowledges that the Divine Christ actually became a human being comes from God, but the spirit that denies this fact does not come from God . . . You, dear children, come from God and have overcome the false spirits, because the one who is in you is greater than the one who is in the world.

1 John 4:1–3

Reflection

When we read a newspaper or watch the small screen our minds are too often filled with something negative: an accusation, murder, act of violence or self-aggrandisement. Subtly but inevitably we soak it in and become part of the negative mindset. Unless, that is, we exercise our right to overcome evil with good. There is a character assassination: we pray for the accused and the accuser to leave the past behind and embrace their best. There is a gruesome killing: we pray for the sick mind that committed this crime to be healed. There is violence in the streets: we pray for the mindless attackers to learn mindfulness through restorative justice, and we pray for the injured, the medical staff and the fearful to find inspired ways of responding.

While Abba Macarius[8] was travelling from Skete to Terenuthin he took night shelter in a pyramid where mummies of deceased pagans had been laid to rest. He used one of these for his pillow. The devils began to call out from the other bodies as if calling to a woman: 'Lady, come with us to the baths.' Another demon, as if he were the ghost of a woman, cried out from the body Macarius was using as a pillow: 'This stranger is holding me down and I can't come.' Macarius, far from being frightened, pummelled the corpse, saying: 'Get up and go swimming if you are able.' Hearing this, the demons cried: 'You win!' And they fled in confusion.[9]

Pause for thought

'This stranger is holding me down': what spirit of our age is holding you down?

Prayer

Almighty God of the invincible forcefield,
repel these alien invaders.
Disarm these hidden persuaders.
Evaporate these false imaginations,
and fill with your loving fragrance the places they vacate.

Today's step

I step
away from taking the 'safe' option
towards God's best.

Spiritual breathing exercise

Divine Christ in.
Lying spirits out.
Ah!

SEPTEMBER 7

Equipped for breakthrough

Bible reading

Put on truth as your belt, goodness as your chest cover, peace-making as your shoes, life-saving as your helmet, and in your hand the Sword of the Spirit, which is God's Word. Above all make sure you take faith as your shield, for this can deter every flaming missile hurled at you. Pray in the Spirit on every occasion.

Ephesians 6:14–18

Reflection

Truth means that we are honest and do not tell lies. We have no hidden agendas or underhand ways. We tell things as they are. We do not twist what people say or misrepresent other viewpoints. It means that we scrutinise the false conditioning and fashionable fantasies, the delusions and distortions that threaten to drown out reality, good and God. Many of us have imbibed a false image of God: that, too, we bravely face up to.

Peace does not just mean the absence of war. Nor does it mean polite niceness that never confronts the roots of violence. God makes peace with a hostile world by embracing us, becoming one with us, and taking the violent consequences of our selfish ways upon himself. The link between peace-making and footwear is that we have to take Christ's peace to others, rather than vainly wait for something just to happen.

Nowadays everyone has to wear a protective helmet whenever they go near a potentially dangerous site. We live in a dangerous world. From God's point of view every person and every thing needs salvaging in some way. The head is the control centre of the body. So it is vital to hold in our heads this need for salvation, and the One who is the world's Life-saver *par excellence*.

We seek to wield the words of God in appropriate and life-giving ways. Like a sword. One edge of the sword is Christ, the Eternal Word; the other edge is the written word of Scripture, and the point of the sword is the particular word the Spirit puts into our mouth at the appropriate moment.

Pause for thought

Be without fear in the face of your enemies. Be brave and upright. Speak the truth. Safeguard the helpless. That is your oath.[10]

Prayer

Make me true, for there are those who trust me.
Make me right with you – all else is treachery.
Life-saving – hold that in my head;
peace-making please, wherever I tread.
Your Word to sharpen me and give a cutting edge;
faith and prayer, these to you I pledge.

Today's step

I step
away from human reaction
towards divine pro-action.

Spiritual breathing exercise

Vigilance in.
Negligence out.
Breakthrough.

SEPTEMBER 8

Seize the initiative with God

Bible reading

When the Philistines learned that David had been anointed king over all Israel, they rallied their maximum forces to hunt him down. David talked to God about this, and defeated them. The Philistines invaded a second time. This time God told David not to go straight towards them, but to hold back and go in a circle until he reached the balsam trees. As soon as he heard rustling like the sound of marching in the tops of the trees he was to lead his troops into battle. David did as God said, and achieved a comprehensive victory.

1 Chronicles 14:14–17

Reflection

The Bible is a record of a struggle between good and evil. The soul of a nation is often at stake. God always reveals a strategy to overcome evil with good. It varies from place to place. We are called to keep alert, to sense what God is doing, to discern the critical issues, the right timings. Sometimes we are to wait, to build; but there is a time to seize the initiative.

During the conference that launched the Community of Aidan and Hilda in 1994 a woman inwardly heard a rustling of trees. This reminded her of how the God-honouring King David, when Philistines threatened to exterminate his people, was warned by God not to follow conventional military tactics: instead, when he heard the trees rustling he was to lead his troops from another angle. Was God guiding us to confront the enormous needs of our world from another angle, through the Way of Life God had given to us?

Christians learn lessons from accounts of military battles in the Old Testament, even though they understand that Christ does not want us to use military means to advance God's kingdom.

Pause for thought

Think of some bad situation you have to confront. Don't rush in. Talk to God first. Where do you hear a rustling?

Prayer

I arise today with the legions of God around me,
with God's sounds to distract ill-doers.
With God's to winds impel good-doers.
I arise today
in dependence on the Father,
in the daring of the Son,
in the direction of the Spirit.

Today's step

I step
away from headstrong rush
towards the heartstrong revelation.

Spiritual breathing exercise

Hearing in.
Haste out.
Advance.

SEPTEMBER 9

Redeeming the powers

Bible reading

When Cyrus was emperor of Persia a revelation about the nature of the real conflict at the heart of empire came to the Jewish exile Daniel, who worked in the emperor's court. For three weeks he mourned and went without meals. Then he saw a vision of a strong and mighty person. 'Do not fear, Daniel,' he said, 'the angel of the power of Persia thwarted me, but Michael, one of the chief angels, came to my aid, and will deal with the guardian angel of the Persian rulers. I am here to let you know what will befall your people . . . his kingdom shall be shattered . . . but everyone who is enrolled in the book of life shall shine like stars for ever.'

Daniel 11

Reflection

Prophets engaged with the angels of a nation. So may we, in our prayers, our ceremonies, our emails to the media and our daily conversations.

There is a story in Bede about the bishop who was abandoning Kent after the king died – he slept overnight in the church in Canterbury and in a vision was beaten by an angel for deserting his post. When he showed the new (pagan) king his wounds, the king converted and the Kentish mission was saved.

Martin Buber observed that every nation has a guiding characteristic which he calls its genius, its supreme faculties. If that nation makes an idol of these, and worships its own essence, it falls apart and dies. But if it uses what God has given it for the benefit of the world it flourishes.[11]

Pause for thought

Pray for the soul of your own or another nation.

Prayer

Great and awesome God,
ever faithful to those who love you,
we have done wrong, and turned against your ways.
We have not listened to those who spoke your truth.
Because you are just you have brought disaster upon us.
Yet now, drive this from us,
listen to our heart cries, forgive us our sins,
for deeper than all our disobedience
is the fact that we belong to you,
and so does our sacred place.
Re-build it, Lord, as your place.[12]

Today's step

I step
away from what is godless in my nation
towards what is of God in it.

Spiritual breathing exercise

Humble nation in.
Haughty nation out.
Restoring.

SEPTEMBER 10

As Cuthbert stormed the gates of heaven

Bible reading

When Jesus had finished praying a disciple said, 'Teach us to pray'. After he had responded Jesus added this story by way of an answer:

If a pal who is ravenous after a long journey unexpectedly arrives in the middle of the night and you lack provisions, you knock up a friendly neighbour and ask him to lend you some bread. He replies that it is too late, the front door is locked, and he does not want to disturb his wife and children who are fast asleep. However, if the neighbour keeps on knocking and won't take no for an answer, he will in the end give him what he asks for simply because he persists. It is like that with God. The one who asks will always receive. The one who searches will find, and the door will always be opened to the one who keeps knocking.
Luke 11:1-9

Reflection

> As Cuthbert and others 'stormed the gates of heaven', so we also need to engage in and to become familiar with intercessory prayer.[13]

When Cuthbert arrived in Farne Island 'our soldier of Christ entered, armed with "the helmet of salvation, the shield of faith, and the sword of the spirit which is the word of God". All the fiery darts of the wicked one were quenched, and the wicked foe was driven far away together with the whole crowd of his assistants.

Moreover not only the creatures of the air but also of the sea, yes, and even the sea itself, as well as air and fire did honour to him. For if a person faithfully and wholeheartedly serves the Maker of all created things, it is no wonder that all creation should minister to their directions.

. . . He had learned how to lay bare before those who were tempted the many tricks of the ancient foe, by which the person who lacks human or divine love may easily be trapped. But whoever goes strengthened by unwavering faith passes, with God's help, through the enemy snares as if they were spiders' webs. "How many times," Cuthbert said, "have they tried to kill me. But though they tried to frighten me away by one phantasmal temptation after another, they were unable to mar my body or my mind by fear."[14]

Pause for thought

How and for what do you storm the gates of heaven?

Prayer

I knock on your door, Lord, and ask for bread,
not for myself but for these your desperate ones . . .
I storm your gates, Lord, and plead for mercy,
not for myself but for these your feuding ones . . .
I persist through the hours
not for myself, but for these your sheep for whom you died.

Today's step

I step
away from quiescent etiquette
towards unremitting appeal.

Spiritual breathing exercise

Persistence in.
Desertion out.
Heaven.

SEPTEMBER 11

Christ intercedes through us

Bible reading

In the past the Law required Israel to have many priests to offer sacrifices to take away peoples' sins. In fact the Law never succeeded in doing this, and the priests were prevented by death from continuing in office. Now, however, Jesus has become the Guarantor of a better agreement. He holds his priesthood for ever. He is able to completely and for ever save those who come to God through him, since he always lives to intercede with God and intervene for them. He is the High Priest perfectly adapted to our needs. The old priests only foreshadowed what was to come: Jesus is the real thing – the successful mediator.

Hebrews 7:21, 19, 22–26, 8:5, 6

Reflection

Christ ever lives to intercede with the Father on behalf of all people. His intercession is a ceaseless outpouring. His self-giving in life and death was historically enacted only once, but is always a spiritual reality. The idea that because only Christ made the complete break-through between humans and God, none of us need intercede, is nonsense. Because of what Christ has done we are now in him. We are a part of the Body of which Christ is the head. As we unite ourselves to him, we do what the Head does. We are therefore called to intercede.

No initiative to change what is wrong can succeed unless it begins in a Godward movement of the heart – and that is intercession. Intercession is not just something we say, nor even just what we do – it is an outpoured life. Every Christian is called by God to intercede, that is, to come between a person or situation and bring them to God. Adam (the representative of the human race) was appointed to be an intermediary between God and the created world, in order to protect and bless it. He was a go-between – the first intercessor (Psalm 8:6; Genesis 2:15). That is our calling, to represent people, creatures, groups, before God.

In outpouring of prayer Christ ceaselessly seeks to bring every person to the Father. His life outpouring, his prayer outpouring – there is no difference. Life and prayer are one. And Christ, who is the Head of his universal Body, calls us to pour out our lives, our prayers, in union with his – having the same spirit, the same understanding, the same feelings of compassion. And like our Head this is ceaseless.

Pause for thought

Prayer moves the Hand that moves the world.

Prayer

God save the people:
save us from our hardness,
save us from our deafness.
God save the people:
save us from our vileness,
save us from our 'niceness'.
God save the people:
save us from our nemesis,
save us from ourselves.

Today's step

I step
away from the wastelands
towards the gap.

Spiritual breathing exercise

Soul-pouring in.
Selfish pouring out.
With Christ.

SEPTEMBER 12

Go-betweens

Bible reading

Abraham had a dialogue with God about the corrupt city of Sodom. 'If fifty good people live there will you save it from its downfall?' he asked. God said, 'I will spare it if there are fifty people who do right.' 'And what if there are forty-five?' asked Abraham. 'I will spare it.' 'And if there are forty?' Abraham persevered. 'For the sake of those forty I will spare the city,' God said. Eventually, Abraham asked God if he would spare the city if only ten right-living people lived there. 'For the sake of those ten, I will not let the city be destroyed' said God.

Genesis 18:23–32

Reflection

The word intercede literally means go-between (in Latin *cedere* means go and *inter* means between). We stand between God and some place or person in need. We go from the one to the other. A famous example of someone who intercedes for their city is this passage about Abraham.

Prophets tell us that God looks out for persons who will come between the oppressed and the oppressor: 'I looked for someone who would build up the wall that protects my people, and who would stand in the gap on behalf of the land' (Ezekiel 22:30). In older translations the word used for such a person is intercessor.

A go-between is only needed if there are two sides who have become estranged. What are the two sides who need us as go-betweens? On one side is God and the forces of good – 'the kingdom of heaven'. On the other side are the forces that, consciously or unconsciously, are ignorant of or opposed to God or who, though they desire God, are out of touch with themselves and unable to 'get on side'.

Pause for thought

What godless gap do you feel called to stand in and intercede?

Prayer

God of outpouring mercy,
pour into us your love of the whole human family.
Move our hearts with compassion to cry mercy
for a world lost in illusion, greed and war.
Deliver us from praying our own agenda,
that we may seek your best for all.
Renew us in your Spirit with the passion to intercede.

Today's step

I step
away from my agenda
towards the cries of the people.

Spiritual breathing exercise

Them in.
Me out.
We.

SEPTEMBER 13

For what should we intercede?

Bible reading

The apostle Paul writes to Timothy: Here is my commission to you. First of all offer requests, prayers, intercessions and thanksgivings on behalf of all people: for rulers and others who carry responsibilities, so that our common life may be peaceful and pervaded by a sense of God and our responsibility to reflect God's ways. This is without doubt the right sort of thing to pray for, for God's purpose is that all people should be restored and come to realise the truth.

1 Timothy 2:1–4

Reflection

Abraham prayed for a city[15], Moses for a people[16] and Hannah for a child[17]. Hezekiah prayed against imperialist domination[18]. Solomon prayed for pilgrims[19]. Mordecai prayed for targets of state terror[20]. Psalmists prayed for peace[21] and the poor[22]. Jeremiah prayed for nation-building[23]; Daniel for the healing of the land[24]. Many people prayed for God's ways to be enthroned in their lands[25]. Jesus taught us to pray for those who don't know God[26] and for those who persecute us[27]. Jesus prayed that his friends' faith would not fail[28] and for unity[29]. Paul urged that we should intercede for rulers and leaders in every walk of life[30] and that Christians should pray for one another[31]. James asks us to pray for the sick[32]. God may call us to intercede for something different still.[33]

Intercession should be understood as prayer through visualisation, verbalisation, and action. Scientists at Essex University have invented a device that measures the effects of imagining something. When a person imagines a particular action, even something as simple as moving their hand from right to left, neurons in the brain produce activity that sends a small white bar buzzing across a computer screen. Prayer visualisation works.

Certain people are called to make intercession their priority, or to intercede for a particular cause, but all Christians are meant to share in some way in Christ's work of intercession.

Pause for thought

The Holy Spirit pleads within us, and shows each of us what and who to pray for and when.

Prayer

Guide the nations.
Give your counsel to our Government.
Grant us honest financiers,
whole health workers, wise educators;
raise up those who have fallen,
support the weak, envision our writers
and revive your Church.

Today's step

I step
away from me-centred praying
towards world-centred praying.

Spiritual breathing exercise

True needs in.
False needs out.
Your kingdom come.

SEPTEMBER 14

The power of circling prayer

Bible reading

Listen to my cry for help, my King and my God.

I lay my requests before you . . . Let all who take refuge in you rejoice. Spread your protective covering over them. For without a doubt you encircle God-honourers with love, like a shield.

Psalm 5:2, 3, 11, 12

Reflection

Ninian[34] provides us with examples of how to overcome evil with good through intercession. As the Roman Empire's guardians of law and order departed from Britain's shores, crime, poverty and 'turf wars' increased. Ninian identified some of these, and took action. The 'colony of heaven' he established at the place now called Whithorn was a safe place and a source of provision for hungry visitors, but bandits threatened this. So, before going away, Ninian gathered the cattle to one place, marked a circle around them in the soil, and prayed a Caim (circling) prayer. Perhaps he used such words as these: 'Circle this spot, dear God: keep harm without, keep good within.'

Cattle stealers did arrive, but as they reached the circle marked in the soil, they experienced some mysterious seizure. This was so severe that their leader became paralysed, and they dragged him into the bushes fearing he was dead. Ninian found them there, befriended them, offered them regular hospitality as an alternative to stealing, and prayed for their leader, who was restored to life. Those men were no longer a threat to society. The story of what happened no doubt turned others away from similar paths.

Ninian's local ruler was corrupt. He tried to undermine Ninian's work. One day he became ill. He had heard that Ninian's prayers were powerful, so he sent a message asking

Ninian to come and pray for his recovery. Ninian, repelled neither by resentment nor fear, but compelled by love, did so, and the ruler recovered. From that time he became an ally, and society as well as the faith communities took a step forward.

Pause for thought

What should you circle in prayer?

Prayer

Circle this place O God
and keep these good things within:
- eagerness to learn,
- flowering of talents,
- experience of beauty,
- warmth of friendship,
- respect for all,
- care for the planet.

Circle this place O God
and keep these bad things without:
- low self-esteem,
- confusion,
- prejudice,
- stealing,
- fear.

Today's step

I step
away from negligence
towards encircling.

Spiritual breathing exercise

Prayer in.
Indifference out.
Well-being.

SEPTEMBER 15

Develop faith

Bible reading

Jesus' disciples could not cure a boy with a mental condition but Jesus did cure him. 'Why were we unable to cure him?' they asked. 'Because you have so little faith,' Jesus told them. 'If you only have faith as minute as a mustard seed, you will find nothing is impossible. You could say to this hill "Move over" and it would.' This kind of condition only gets cured through prayer and fasting.

Matthew 17:14–21

Reflection

The father of Bishop Samson, the sixth-century Briton, had been healed of a serious illness. As a result his family turned to God and began a mission.

While on a journey they came to a place which a notorious serpent had burned. Full of apprehension, they discussed what to do. Samson reminded them of Jesus' promise: 'If you have faith even as small as a mustard seed you can tell this mountain to move and it will.' 'Wait here, calmly,' he told them, 'while I go off and try to hear from God on this matter.'

Samson saw the fire-spitting serpent afar. He approached it, reciting scriptures such as, 'The Lord is my light and my salvation.' With huge swishing and hissing the serpent grabbed its tail in its teeth and tossed a lump of earth almost in Samson's face. Samson made the Caim Circle Prayer and placed a cross in the ground. The serpent hissed and reared up as if it had been pierced with a sword, and gathered itself into a ball, savagely biting its tail with its teeth. Samson continued to quietly sing psalms, holding his staff firmly in the ground. The others arrived. 'Come nearer,' Samson said, 'so that you may develop faith in faith.' They witnessed the serpent slowly uncoil and slither along the ground until it came to Samson's staff. Repeatedly it did the same thing, but never could it raise its head or go beyond the staff. This continued through the day, and Samson used the time to instruct and build up their faith with advice such as, 'Those who believe in the Creator ought not to fear the creature.' Eventually, as twilight came, Samson spoke to the serpent: 'We have a long journey, but you have no longer to live. In Jesus' name I command you to die now!' At once the serpent raised its head, as if making a final bow, cast forth all its venom, and lay down dead.

Pause for thought

Today practise having faith for some tiny little thing. Tomorrow have faith for something just a touch less small.

Prayer

Lord, I have not much faith, and I can't help it.
But help me to use the little faith I have,
so that it grows day by day.
May I daily increase in trust and in valour.

Today's step

I step
away from flight
towards God's might.

Spiritual breathing exercise

Faith in.
Withdrawal out.
Jesus.

SEPTEMBER 16

The power of a parent's intercession

Bible reading

Hannah was infertile. Year after year she and her husband visited the shrine at Shiloh where she refused to eat and wept before God. One year she prayed to God: 'Do not overlook me; if you will regard my misery and give me a son, I will dedicate him to you for the rest of his life. He will be vowed to you, and no razor will touch his head.' At first the priest thought she was drunk as she poured out her soul with tears. But when she explained what she was praying the priest said, 'Go in peace. May God grant your request.' Hannah went home. She conceived, and named her baby Samuel, which means 'because I asked God for him'.

1 Samuel 1:1–20

Reflection

Hannah is one of a noble line of barren women who ceaselessly begged God for a child whom they promised to hand back to God. Would that every infertile woman's prayers were answered thus. There is a mystery here. But just as it would be wrong to claim that every such request will result in a child, it would also be wrong to minimise the power of these mothers' intercessions.

Monica was a fourth-century Christian in North Africa. Though the wife of a non-Christian, Monica prayed that her family might eventually all come to Christ. Her most promising son, Augustine, ignored his mother's warnings, and took a wrong turning. He joined the Manichees who taught that matter was not good, and that you could therefore do what you liked with your body. He lived with a woman not his wife and fathered a child. Monica determined never to stop praying that he would turn to God.

When Augustine went to Italy to teach, Monica, by then a widow, followed him there. In Milan she attended Bishop Ambrose's church and rejoiced when Augustine was befriended by him and eventually became a Christian.

In his *Confessions* Augustine wrote of his grief for the mother 'who for years had wept over me, that I might live in your [God's] sight.' He also wrote, 'She never let me out of her prayers that you, O God, might say to the widow's son, "Young man, I say to you arise."' She died a happy woman for she had seen her prayers answered, and both her husband and her son had become believers.

Pause for thought

Have you ever interceded with fasting and weeping?

Prayer

Eternal God,
the light of the minds that know you,
the joy of the hearts that love you
and the strength of the wills that serve you:
grant us so to know you that we may truly love you
and so to love you that we may fully serve you,
whom to serve is perfect freedom.[35]

Today's step

I step
away from perfunctory prayer
towards heart-crying.

Spiritual breathing exercise

All-out prayer in.
Casual prayer out.
Birth.

SEPTEMBER 17

Intercession through the arts

Bible reading

In the vision I saw the Lamb of God on the throne, the angelic creatures and the elders. Each had a harp and each held golden bowls of incense – these were the prayers of God's holy people . . .

Then I saw an angel with a golden censer. He was given much incense and the prayers of all God's holy people to offer up to God on the altar of gold in front of God's throne.

Revelation 5:6, 8; 8:3, 4

Reflection

> A poet must assume the burden of his people's doom
> and dare to break their living tomb.[36]

In other words, a poet must intercede with those forces that would bring death to a nation, free the well-springs of life, and speak to the soul of a nation.

Those who pledge to overcome evil with good therefore need also to pledge, from the outset, not to stay in life's deceptive cocoons. I love God's will. I notice that when numbers of people combine to do God's will, there are pleasurable results. Harmony tends to replace strife. Creativity tends to replace sterility. Healing tends to replace hurts. Without realising, I am now in love with the pleasurable effects of God's will. But actually, it is God's will that I love God in poverty as well as in plenty, in opposition as well as support, in disappointment as well as in blessing, in death as well as in life.

> Prayer for others is very beneficial to the person who prays. It purifies the heart, strengthens faith and hope and arouses love for God and our neighbour.

If you make a habit of praying for the salvation of others God will give you an abundance of spiritual gifts, the gifts of the Holy Spirit. The Spirit itself makes intercession for us with groanings which cannot be uttered.[37]

Pause for thought

Visualise your prayers as incense, offered as works of art, reaching the throne of God.

Prayer

Give to me thoughts greater than my own thoughts,
prayers deeper than my own prayers.
Give to me the arts of prayer – prayers that rise like incense,
beautiful objects that catch your attention
and thoughts that penetrate to the Throne.

Today's step

I step
away from the humdrum
towards the glories fit for the Throne.

Spiritual breathing exercise

Glory prayers in.
Shoddy thoughts out.
Enthroned.

SEPTEMBER 18

Turning back epidemics

Bible reading

The refugees from Egypt ran out of bread and water and grew weak in the desert. They turned on their leader, Moses. Then poisonous snakes appeared and bit the people. Many died. Mortified, the people confessed their wrong attitudes to Moses. So he prayed for them.

God told him to make a bronze snake and place it on a pole; he promised that any person with snake-bite who looked at the pole would live. This is what happened.

Numbers 21:4–9

Reflection

Columba, the sixth-century abbot of Iona, set aside a day in the woods for sustained prayer combat. As he began to pray an oncoming wave of deathly black creatures relentlessly attacked with iron darts, desiring to wipe out him and many in the Iona community. Columba linked this experience with the threat of oncoming plague. His biographer, Adamnan, writes:

> But he, single-handed, against innumerable foes of such a nature, fought with the utmost bravery, having received the armour of the apostle Paul. The contest was maintained on both sides during the greater part of the day, nor could the demons, countless though they were, vanquish him, nor was he able, by himself, to drive them out from his island, until the angels of God, as the saint afterwards told certain persons, came to his aid, when the demons in terror gave way.[38]

On his way back Columba informed some brothers that Iona would now be spared the plague, but it would invade the monasteries in the region of Tiree. This came only too true. Two days later Columba added a postscript, whose lesson for us is: Don't leave the combat to somebody else. Baithen, the leader of one monastery in the Tiree region, had called his community to all-out fasting and prayer, and as a result only one brother there would die of the plague. This, too, came to pass exactly as Columba had foreseen.

Jesus models how a human being can look the worst-case scenario in the eye and remain victorious in spirit. His being lifted up on the cross-piece on which he was crucified was likened to Moses lifting up the bronzed snake. Those who look at Jesus will live, as did those who looked at the snake.

Pause for thought

Jesus not only models for us how to overcome the ultimate enemy, death, but his indestructible spirit. Lift up a prayer emblem that in this spirit we may overcome all things.

Prayer

Lord, plagues new and old afflict our world
and threaten its existence.
We have brought them upon ourselves.
Have mercy and forgive.
Help us to amend our ways.
Save us, O Christ, for you surely came for this hour, too.

Today's step

I step
away from acquiescence
towards the combat.

Spiritual breathing exercise

Fire of faith in.
Fiery darts out.
Turn-round.

SEPTEMBER 19

Overcoming evil is breathtaking

Bible reading

Jesus went into the Ten Towns region. Some people asked him to lay hands on a man who could not hear and could hardly talk. Jesus took the man away from the crowd and put his fingers into the man's ears. Then he spat and put his spittle on the man's tongue. He looked up to heaven and sharply drew in his breath. He said 'Open up' ('Ephphatha' in his own tongue). The man's ears were opened, his tongue was set loose and he began to speak plainly.

Mark 7:31–35

Reflection

A little sentence in this passage, that in English sounds so mild, calls for our attention. Before this deaf and half-mute man was cured Jesus looked up to heaven, and, according to traditional Bible translations, 'sighed'. But this was not a polite aside. It was more like the gasp that weightlifters let out as they strain every muscle in the body – they call it power lifting. Jesus needed to summon power, and power went out of him. This happened on other occasions, too, such as when 'virtue ebbed out of him' after a woman with a haemorrhage touched his cloak and was healed (Luke 8:46) and when he groaned before Lazarus was restored to life (John 11:37).

It takes effort, concentration to pray like that. We can't do it for everyone. The times when we can, and should do it may be few and far between, but don't depart this life without ever having done this.

Pause for thought

If you have never given your full concentration and strength to prayer for a person, look out for a right time to do this.

Prayer

God of outpouring mercy,
pour into us your love of the whole human family.
Move our hearts with compassion to cry mercy
for a world lost in illusion, greed and war.
Deliver us from praying our own agenda,
that we may seek your best for all.
Renew us in your Spirit with the passion to intercede.
Imbue us with your power
for a person straining to be set free.

Today's step

I step
away from ease
towards a bigger prayer challenge.

Spiritual breathing exercise

Your strength in.
Dis-ease out.
Healing.

SEPTEMBER 20

Persevering prayer

Bible reading

Jesus illustrated through the following story how they must keep praying and not lose heart: A magistrate who respected neither God nor his fellows had to face a widow who time after time pleaded with him to protect her from a man who was trying to ruin her. For a long time he refused. But in the end he concluded that she was such a nuisance that he would judge in her favour in order to get rid of her. Jesus commented: 'Notice how this ill-tempered magistrate behaved. Do you imagine that God, who is patient and kind, will not make sure justice is done for those who appeal to him day after day?'

Luke 18:1–8

Reflection

Scripture tells us two things that seem incompatible but in fact are not. We are told that the mere babbling of many words or the repetition of many religious services won't change God's mind; God wants our deeds, not our words. In this parable, it is true that a widow changes a judge's mind simply because she kept pestering him and for no other reason. In this passage justice is given to a sincere but powerless person who cries out for it. God heeds the prayers of people who pray after God's own heart, who cry out on behalf of the needy in body or soul. Luke, in introducing this parable, says it is about people's 'need to pray always and not to lose heart'. Jesus is making a point, with humour: never give up.

Many great movements of God have been preceded by sustained periods of prayer. John Wesley[39] recorded his prayer time at 3am on New Year's Day 1739. Half the nation was drunk on gin but he became drunk with the

Holy Spirit. In 1744 Jonathan Edwards[40] called Americans to a seven-year season of prayer which led to a spiritual awakening. The Pentecostal movement took off at Azuza Street, Los Angeles in 1903 following three years of sustained prayer. The Hebrides Revival fifty years ago was preceded by the sustained prayer of a group of women who met in one of their homes. George Otis's video series *Transformations* tells amazing stories of how cities and regions have been changed. Always this starts with the local church leaders finding unity and praying together.

Pause for thought

Never give up.

Prayer

Sovereign Lord, you made the heaven, the earth and the sea and everything in them. Enable your servants to speak your word with boldness. Stretch out your hand to heal and perform miracles, signs and wonders through the name of your holy servant Jesus.

Today's step

I step
away from throwing in the towel
towards the final goal.

Spiritual breathing exercise

Grit in.
Weak-knees out.
Please.

SEPTEMBER 21

Let prayer turn into mercy

Bible reading

Jesus said: 'The most important commandment is to love God with all your heart, soul, mind and strength; and the second most important is to love your neighbour as yourself.' 'You are right,' said the teacher, 'to do this is more important than all the rituals and ceremonies.'

Mark 12:30–33

Reflection

Prayer is not a technique that can be taught. It erupts in people who live life to the full.

The prayers of Silouan, the twentieth-century monk of Mount Athos and Paris, were at first a titanic struggle in order to slay the proud beast in himself and become a man, an authentic human being in the image of the perfect Man Christ – that is, to become meek and humble.

Gradually, however, sorrow for the world ignorant of God began to dominate his prayer. 'To pray for people is to shed blood,' said the staretz, who was taught of Christ-like love by the Holy Spirit. To love with Christ's love means to drink Christ's cup. The ascetic learns the great mysteries of the spirit through pure prayer. He finds his deep heart – reaches the core of his being; and looking into it sees the existence of humankind is not something extraneous to him but is bound up with his own being.

Through Christ's love all people become an inseparable part of our eternal existence. The staretz began to see in the command to love your neighbour as yourself a community of being. The Son of Man assimilates every person's existence into his own personal existence. He has accepted and suffered for 'the whole Adam' so that the whole human race may share his resurrection life (Romans 5:17). We, as the apostle Paul taught, ought to think and feel like Christ, 'having the same mind that was in Christ' (Philippians 2:5).[41]

Pause for thought

When you pray visualise all people as forming one body with yourself, and each separately as a member of the Body of Christ – look upon their infirmities, ignorances, sins, temptations and misfortunes as your own.

Prayer

O God,
deliver the oppressed, pity the unnoticed,
raise the fallen, show yourself to the needy,
heal the sick, bring back those who have strayed,
feed the hungry, lift up the weak,
remove the prisoners' chains.
May every people come to know that you are God,
that Jesus Christ is your Child,
that we are your people.[42]

Today's step

I step
away from mere words
towards mercy.

Spiritual breathing exercise

Heart prayers in.
Trite prayers out.
Mercy.

SEPTEMBER 22

Overcome denial

Bible Reading

The road that leads to destruction is wide and many travel on it. Only a few find the narrow road that leads to life. Watch out for false prophets. Outwardly they may look like sheep, but inwardly they are like ferocious wolves. You will recognise them by their fruit.

Matthew 7:13–15

Reflection

> We do not project on to the supernatural what belongs to the sphere of human responsibility.[43]

The Afrikaner novelist André P. Brink has an axiom: 'The truth is that which cannot be said.'

Father Silouan[44], who inspired his disciple Father Sophrony taught: 'Go to hell and find hope there.' He calls us to cross the darkness of our own inner hell in order to be reborn in the uncreated light which shines from the Word made flesh.

When Sundhar Singh was born in India in 1905 his aristocratic Sikh mother dedicated him to be Sundhar, a holy man. He became a wandering Christian mystic. As he sat on a rock in a forest he had a vision. A person who looked like a servant of God came, but his eyes glittered with deception. 'Holy servant of God,' he said, 'your unselfish life has made a deep impression on me, and you have sacrificed yourself for others, but have you been truly appreciated? As a Christian you have influenced only a few thousand other Christians, and even some of them mistrust you. Would it not be more worthwhile to become a Hindu or Muslim? Then you could be a really great leader, and millions of Hindus and Muslims would follow you.' Because Sundhar had daily practised resisting temptation, he immediately replied: 'Get out, Satan! You are the wolf in sheep's clothes. Your only desire is that I renounce the Cross and the path that leads to life, and travel the broad road that leads to death. My Master gave everything for me, so it is right that I give all to him.'

Our culture has swallowed the lie that celebrity is the highest thing we should aim for. It should be resisted. Re-enact the drama of the Tempter and the Saviour.

One of the many delightful, if quaint, prayers of the Hebridean islanders was a prayer for clearing the mote, from one's own eye, which the prayer below echoes.

Pause for thought

What is my blind spot?

Prayer

Thrice seeing King of Heaven,
dislodge the mote that is in my blind eye
and gently place it on my tongue
where I can spit it out.

Today's step

I step
away from false ambition
towards selfless giving.

Spiritual breathing exercise

Abandon in.
Ambition out.
Your will.

SEPTEMBER 23

Overcome dither

Bible reading

In the region around the river Jordan crowds came to Jesus . . . (Yet) Jesus led his twelve apostles all the way up to Jerusalem. They could not believe it, and those who followed on were frightened. Jesus took the twelve aside and explained what they would face on their arrival: he would be betrayed to the religious authorities, who would sentence him to death, and hand him over to be beaten by the foreign occupiers. These would belittle him, spit on him, beat him and kill him. However, three days after that he would rise.

Mark 10:1, 32–34

Reflection

Jesus had a choice. He could have continued as a successful celebrity in the south of the country. He chose to walk straight into the power centre of the capital city, where the authorities, feeling threatened by a rising popular force they did not understand and could not contain, plotted to be rid of him. Jesus' friends were mostly in denial about the situation. They would not look reality in the face. They wanted, perhaps unconsciously, to evade, or at least postpone the inevitable confrontation.

A poster in my gym says 'No gain without pain.' Spiritual initiative requires us to look reality in the face, to grasp the stinging nettle, to go through the pain barrier in order to overcome evil with good. For most of us, this starts with little things.

M. Scott Peck[45] describes how each day we may make a list of things we need to do. Our instinct is to do first the things we like, and leave to the last the things we find painful. Often we postpone these until tomorrow, and tomorrow always remains tomorrow. The answer, he suggests, is to consciously commit to do the most difficult thing first. This spiritual discipline he calls 'delayed gratification'. Although the gratification we feel about having done the nice thing is delayed, by dealing with the difficult thing first, we have created a space in which we can really savour and fully enjoy whatever it is.

Celtic Christians talk of letting your feet follow your heart through steep and dangerous places until you find your 'place of resurrection'. That is the reality Jesus brought to us. There is a reward for doing the right thing.

Pause for thought

What necessary but painful issue must I face?
Will I postpone this, and shrink,
or grasp it and grow?

Prayer

Lord,
in my hour of need, come to me.
In my weakness, give me strength.
In my actions, give me courage.
In my words, give me grace.

Today's step

I step
away from prevarication
towards the most difficult thing that needs to be done.

Spiritual breathing exercise

Now in.
Tomorrow out.
Your move.

SEPTEMBER 24

Overcome resentment

Bible reading

Jesus said to his disciples, 'You have been brought up with the idea of proportionate punishment, for example, if someone takes out your eye the judge will require them to lose one eye. I say to you, however, there is a better way to resist bad behaviour. If someone hits you in an insulting way, don't take it personally, give them a second chance and shrug it off. If someone goes to court to claim that some piffling item of yours belongs to them, disarm them by offering some more significant item! If someone abuses their authority by ordering you to travel one mile on some errand, go two miles. Give to anyone who asks you.

Matthew 5:38–42

Reflection

The law of tit for tat is as old as the code of the Babylonian Emperor Hammurabi, who ruled until BC 2242. The Jews adapted this. In practice, a judge would allow the guilty person to pay a fine as a substitute for losing an eye.

Gang warfare and indiscriminate revenge still rule in many troubled areas. The law of tit for tat does restrain these. If a member of one gang, (or tribe etc.) injures someone from another, the whole gang does not attack everyone in the other gang, instead the injured person gets a fair judge to give the attacker the same injury as he inflicted. This law is in fact the beginning of mercy. But, as Jesus points out, there is much more to mercy than this.

The non-violent response to a wrong which Jesus encourages is not an easy way out – it is in fact a harder, often a more effective, option. For with this approach one person, at least, remains a free spirit, and there is more chance than otherwise that both people become free of the vengeful spirit.

Pause for thought
Who is vengeful towards me?
How would Jesus respond to them if he was in my skin?

Prayer
Lord,
when we are insulted, help us to
refrain from hitting back
throw away resentment
and offer a challenge of tough love.
When our rights are overridden
or our privileges are taken for granted
help us to refrain from
enforcing them with malice
or selfishly clutching at them,
but to inspire, through acts of generosity,
the other person to change.
When a bureaucrat requires us
to carry out some uncongenial task,
help us to refrain from the sour face, catty remark
or grudging body language;
rather, help us to be cheerful, friendly,
and to soften up the bureaucrat by doing a little bit extra.

Today's step
I step away
from retaliation
towards the extra mile.

Spiritual breathing exercise
Forgiveness in.
Vengeance out.
Blessing.

SEPTEMBER 25

Overcome workaholism

Bible reading

Jesus explained to them that when the Final Appraisal before God comes many people will say, 'Lord, Lord, didn't we preach, cast out devils and do many things in your name?' But Jesus will say to them, 'Go away, you have worked on the side of evil.' Jesus then urged everyone who heard him to be like a person who builds a house on the rock of God's will rather than on the shifting sands.

Matthew 7:21–27

Reflection

A very active, energetic Christian worker confessed at a retreat that his temperament made it a joy for him to spend himself in service, but that the devil contrived, through his success, to deceive him over long years, and to stir him up to furious activity, filling him with dislike of the interior life, until now he had fallen over the edge.

It is easy for people like this to be carried away by the pleasure of living out of their natural energy, so that the supernatural, divine life gradually ebbs away. Activity has become a passion which is now fanned into a raging fever. This disguises the gnawing knowledge deep in the heart that all is not according to God. Their works, which in themselves are good, are turned against them like a two-edged sword which wounds the person who does not know how to wield it.

St Bernard warned the busy Pope Eugenius III against such a danger when he wrote: 'It would be very prudent for you to withdraw from such occupations, even if it be for only a little while, rather than let them get the better of you, and, little by little, lead you where you do not want to go . . . to indifference.' St Bernard concluded, 'Such is the end to which these accursed tasks will lead you . . . if you keep on as you have begun.'[46]

Pause for thought

To overcome work addiction I have to plunge heroically into the silence of being, suffering all the withdrawal symptoms, in order to overcome this evil with Good.

Prayer

Silent, surrendered, leaving all
open to you for yourself alone.
Into the seething mass within
pour your calm and still my being.

Today's step

I step
away from 'accursed tasks'
towards the Source of Being.

Spiritual breathing exercise

Being in.
Work addiction out.
Rock.

SEPTEMBER 26

Overcome hate

Bible reading

You have heard religious teachers tell you to love your neighbour and hate your enemy, but I tell you to love your enemies, bless those who curse you and pray for those who persecute you, that you may be heirs of your Divine Parent, who causes the blessings of sun and rain to fall on everyone, whether they are good or bad.

Matthew 5:43–45

Reflection

There are still teachers within the major religions who tell us to hate our enemies, whether these are people who dislike us, persecute us or simply who are unbelievers – infidels. Jesus, in contrast, tells us to love them. That is a hard call. It is one thing to practise non-violence, quite another thing to actively love such a person. How can we do this?

A form of intercession that we can all practise is to hold before us a photograph or a mental picture of a person we dislike, and place this side by side with a picture of Jesus. We then keep repeating the name of the person and the name of Jesus, visualising Jesus blessing that person. One person's hero can be another person's hate figure. The hermit Brother Ramon could not dislodge his dislike of Margaret Thatcher from his mind. So he placed a photo of her beside that of Jesus, and kept repeating the prayer, 'Margaret, Jesus'!

Sometimes a historical person becomes a symbol of our dislike of a nation or a culture. We do not have to like them, or approve things that are bad; we have to release them from our mental box, and desire their transformation. The USA author Catherine Marshall disliked Britain's King

Henry VIII because he symbolised oppression of women and people of conscience. One day she decided to release him, and therefore Britain, from her pigeonholing. She released them to the mercy and transforming powers of God.

We can be builders of a world free from prejudice, in which ever more people follow Jesus' example, and our example, of looking upon each and every person as a child of Love.

Pause for thought

Who is my hate figure – whether this represents the individual themselves or a wider group?

Prayer

Christ of the loving heart,
may we look upon everyone with a smile
that reflects a ray of the True and Universal Sun,
the smile of acceptance and understanding.
May we be builders of a world that is free from prejudice,
where everyone, however wayward, is seen as a child of Love.

Today's step

I step
away from hate, or coldness
towards the person I find difficult.

Spiritual breathing exercise

Jesus in.
Hate out.
Blessing.

SEPTEMBER 27

Overcome contempt

Bible reading

Do everything without complaining and arguing, so that you may behave like God's children, innocent, sincere and wholesome. Then, although you live in a warped, dysfunctional world, you will shine like lights in a dark place. For you hold in your hands the expression of God's life.

Philippians 2:14–16

Reflection

We live in a culture of contempt. The media denigrates everyone and everything until all are reduced to the lowest common denominator of worthlessness. They sacrifice us on the altars of their insatiable egos.

No individual psyche could withstand the destructive storm that has been unleashed by our media. Throughout an individual person's life, there is a constant need for self-criticism, self-analysis, and honesty. But the individual who plunges into the very depths of unmitigated ridicule and contempt as our nation states have done, would have entered into the realms of paranoia and melancholy; yes and into the realms of suicide itself . . . These days to believe is to be ridiculed, to hope is to be scorned, to trust is to be despised.

We are so ungrateful, we see nothing but angst.
We are so blind, we hear nothing but complaint.
We are so deaf, we feel nothing but pain.
We are so asleep, we experience nothing but nightmares.

Our culture decays because we no longer know how to be positive and kind. Or more to the point, because we invariably feel embarassed and unsophisticated when we harbour such thoughts. And so ingratitude becomes a cancer in our collective souls: eating us away until our nations are ugly.

Forgiveness and gratitude are the great grail castles upon our social and political quest, they are signposts to a new and undreamed of greatness: a healing and embracing greatness not as yet seen on our plant.[47]

Pause for thought

Replace a negativity with gratitude, a ridicule with affirmation, today.

Prayer

Mighty Anchor in our storms,
Brightest Light in our darkness,
lead us from
despair to hope
contempt to praise
falsehood to truth
hatred to love
violence to peace.

Today's step

I step
away from contempt
towards appreciation.

Spiritual breathing exercise

Gratitude in.
Complaining out.
Great!

SEPTEMBER 28

Overcome the rot

Bible reading

The Spirit of the Lord has sent me to bring good news to the people: to replace their ashes with a crown of beauty; to replace their grief with the oil of gladness; to replace their despair with the sounds of praise. Then they will be known as oak trees of goodness, planted by God to reflect the divine splendour. Then they will rebuild what is ruined and experience everlasting joy.

Isaiah 61:1-7

Reflection

A BBC newsreader, Martyn Lewis, once 'came out' and bemoaned the fact that in most areas of journalism there is peer pressure to give prominence to the world's ills rather than to its good things. In USA the CBS anchorman Dan Rather accused commercial television of 'putting more dead bodies, mayhem and lurid tales on the air to compete, not with other news programmes, but with entertainment programmes.'[48]

God calls us to reverse this trend. This is possible. Florence Nightingale denounced British hospitals at the time of the Crimean war as hospitals of hell. She told the Government and everyone who would listen that they could become hospitals of heaven. She not only held out this vision, she wrote a detailed plan of action that would help bring this about. In time, much of this was achieved.

When we see people carrying loads, cleaning, repairing, building, transporting, selling in cities, we thank God for them, for the good they do, for everything in them that reflects something of God's likeness – their work, their smile, their human presence. When we see people who seem to violate their bodies, others, the world, we pray

God's mercy upon them, even with tears. We do not glorify them, nor indulge in defeatism, instead we seek to build up and bless what is good.

Pause for thought
What good may I affirm today?

Prayer
Someone sent this prayer of a blessing to celebrate an organisation's tenth anniversary:

God bless you, my friends.
May your wisdom increase like a deep-rooted tree
and may peace always nest in its branches
to sing to you above the noise of storms.
May you always see yourselves
in God's plan for a blossoming earth.
And may the fragrance of your truth
be celebration for all.
God bless you, my friends.
Overcoming hells with heaven.[49]

Today's step
I step
away from what pulls us down
towards what lifts us up.

Spiritual breathing exercise
Blessing in.
Rot out.
Good!

SEPTEMBER 29

Missiles of peace

Bible reading

Haman, the enemy of the Jewish people, had cast lots (or purim as they are called) to determine the day for destroying the Jews; he had planned to wipe them out. But Queen Esther went to the king, and the king issued orders with the result that Haman himself suffered the fate he had planned for the Jews . . . The queen wrote a letter directing the Jews and their descendants to always observe the days of Purim.

Esther 9:24, 25, 31

Reflection

Have you ever had that awful feeling that somebody has got it in for you, and that there is nothing you can do about it? If so, take heart from the experience of Queen Esther, in the Bible, and of Samson of Dol.

A region of what is now France was cowed because an occupying king, urged on by his evil wife, had killed the head of estates, sentenced his son Judual to death, and oppressed the population. Samson stayed at the palace in order to negotiate Judual's release, to the fury of the queen, who tried one ploy after another to kill him. First, she pressed him to eat a meal, and instructed her servant to take him a poisoned drink. Samson made the sign of the cross over it and spilt it, saying calmly, 'This is not an appropriate cup for someone to drink.'

The king, softening after Samson had healed one of his staff, arranged for Samson to visit Judual: the queen arranged for an unbroken, angry horse to be brought for his use. Samson made the sign of the cross over the horse, and calmly sat astride it.

The queen was determined that Samson should never return, so when he was at the port she arranged for a hungry lion to be let loose. Samson invoked Christ and discharged after the beast 'his customary missiles as if from a catapult', saying: 'I charge you in the name of Jesus Christ who has given us power to tread under foot you and things like you, that your terrible power against the human race may from this day never rise again, but that you die quickly in the presence of all these people so that the people of this region may know that God has sent me here as a servant of Christ.' The lion died that hour, and everyone present, even the queen herself, pledged to support Judual's release and Samson's mission.

Pause for thought

What attack do I fear? What resources might I summon?

Prayer

Open my eyes to the poisons of our time,
that I may avoid them.
Alert me to the angry horses of our time,
that I may calm them.
Prepare me for the prowling lions of our time,
that I may bring them to nothing.

Today's step

I step
away from craven fear
towards the Cross of Christ.

Spiritual breathing exercise

Prayer in.
Panic out.
Praise.

SEPTEMBER 30

In the bottom of the pond

Bible reading

We who receive the gift of Christ are like cracked earth-ware which contain a treasure. It is like this to show that this glory comes from God, not us. We are hard-pressed on every side, but not crushed. We are perplexed but not in despair, attacked, but not abandoned, down but not out. We may carry signs of death in our bodies (it is Jesus who is being put to death again in us), but this is so that Jesus' resurrection life may also be seen in us.

2 Corinthians 4:7–11

Reflection

There is no pit so deep that Jesus cannot reach it.[50]

I fled him, down the labyrinthine ways
of my own mind; and in the mist of tears
I hid from him . . .
That Voice is round me like a bursting sea:
and is thy earth so marred,
shattered in shard on shard?
Lo, all things fly thee, for thou fliest me!
Strange, piteous, futile thing!
Wherefore should any set thee love apart?
Seeing none but I makes much of naught (he said),
whom wilt thou find to love ignoble thee,
save me, save only me?
All which I took from thee I did but take,
not for thy harms,
but just that thou might'st seek it in my arms.
All which thy child's mistake
fancies as lost, I have stored for thee at home:
rise, clasp my hand, and come!

Ah, fondest, blindest, weakest,
I am he whom thou seekest!
Thou dravest love from thee, who dravest me.[51]

Do not try to add one more thing to what you have to overcome. Stay where you are. Sink in to your weakness. In your vulnerability, simply repeat over and again 'Lord have mercy, Christ have mercy, Lord have mercy.' Picture Jesus climbing down the pit towards you, ready to throw you the rope. Hold it and repeat the words 'Lord have mercy, Christ have mercy, Lord have mercy.'

Pause for thought

St John of Kronstadt used to say: 'Go to hell and despair not.' It was said that St Kevin of Glendalough went to the place of his greatest weakness in order that there he might find God, whose strength is made complete in our weakness. Go to your place of weakness and seek God there.

Prayer

Lord have mercy, Christ have mercy, Lord have mercy.

Today's step

Stay where you are.
Let Mercy step in to you.

Spiritual breathing exercise

Mercy in.
Scream out.
Christ.

OCTOBER 1

One body

Bible reading

You all belong to one body, of which there is one Spirit. There is one Lord, one faith, one baptism, one God, one Father of us all . . . It is from the head that the whole body, as a harmonious organism, bound together by its joints grows, by the proper functioning of the individual parts, to its full maturity in love.

Ephesians 4:4–6, 16

Reflection

> As we study the history of the Celtic Church we rediscover the unity early Christian peoples had within the one universal Church.[1]

Jesus established one, universal Church with himself as its head. When the missionary apostle Paul wrote letters to local churches, he had no problem as to which address to use. They were addressed to those who had been ordained to lead 'the Church' in that town. Local churches were part of the one universal Church.

Of course, disagreements arose. These were resolved at ecumenical councils of the elders/bishops. Acts 17 gives an account of the first of these. Then there was the issue of which of the many inspirational writings should be treated as foundational by local churches, whatever their culture and country. Various lists were drawn up by the bishops. The Bible is the result. There still remains more than one list, but at least sixty-six books are regarded as part of the Bible by virtually all the world's churches. Then there were questions as to what teachings were fundamental to Christianity. The result was the Creeds. And there was ministry. For the first thousand years of Christianity the vast majority of Christians believed that Jesus not only left a message (enshrined in the Bible), he also left a means of transmitting Christian ministry (the apostles Jesus ordained laid hands on others, and handed down this practice).

These are bare facts. The wonder of it all is the presence of Christ flowing from himself, the head, through the rest of his universal Body. This is the essence of the Church. Whatever our viewpoint may be about the later fractures, today let us draw nourishment from the Head, and pray for every member of his Body in this world, that we may become fit for purpose.

Pause for thought

To get a right view of the Church, discard our jaundiced conditioning – go back to first principles.

Prayer

Bind us together, Lord,
bind us together, bind us together in love.
We are one family of God,
brothers and sisters in Christ,
called to give love to the world,
draw us nearer our Head.[2]

Today's step

I step
away from division
towards our Head.

Spiritual breathing exercise

Christ's Body in.
Dismembering out.
One.

OCTOBER 2

Repent of schisms

Bible reading

The eye cannot say to the hand, 'I don't need you!' The head cannot say to the feet, 'I don't need you!' Quite the reverse, those parts of the body that seem to be weaker are the most needed. God has done this so that all the members of the body should work together in a sympathetic relationship with one another – in order to avoid division. So, if one member suffers, all the others suffer too; if one member is honoured, all the others are honoured too.

1 Corinthians 12:21–27

Reflection

> We are constantly ashamed of our divisions, and we repent of the schisms that have occurred between the Eastern and Western Church and from the Reformation onwards.[3]

A Roman Catholic reader might say: 'I don't need to repent, it was you heretics who split the Church when you broke away from the Pope.' An Orthodox reader might say: 'I don't need to repent, it was you Papists and Protestants who imposed rulings in disregard of the bishops meeting in council.' An Anglican reader might say: 'I don't need to repent. We continued the same Church, but made it cleaner and more accessible.' An Independent Church reader might say: 'I don't need to repent. The true Church exists where two or three Christians meet with Bible and Sacrament – we need have no dealings with members of unbiblical Churches who are not true Christians.'

But Jesus, the Head of all these dismembered parts of his Body, is hurting and the world is betrayed. What we have today was never Christ's intention. The whole is greater than the parts.

We repent that Christ's beautiful Bride has been torn and tattered; that, if, on occasions, she has behaved like a whore, we have not wept for her as for ourselves. We repent that these splits were often made with vitriol rather than sorrow; that arrogance, or misuse of power too often marked the separating as well as the inherited Churches.

Pause for thought

Don't be like God's people in Moses' time who each 'did what was right in their own eyes'. Shed tears over our divisions.

Prayer

Thrice Holy God, eternal Three-in-One,
make your people holy, make your people one.
Stir up in us the tears for years of pride and power,
restore in us the trust that brings the servant heart to flower.
Thrice holy God, come as the morning dew;
inflame in us your love
which draws all lesser loves to you.

Today's step

I step
away from a schismatic mindset
towards other branches of the Church.

Spiritual breathing exercise

Penitence in.
Pride out.
Pilgrims together.

OCTOBER 3

The early Church in Celtic lands

Bible reading

Christ ascended to heaven, and showered gifts on his Church, in order that the whole universe, from highest to lowest, might experience his presence. These gifts were richly varied. He called some to be messengers, prophets, evangelists, teachers, spiritual guides. He gave these gifts so that Christians might be adequately equipped for their service, so that the whole body might be built up until the time comes when, in the unity of faith and knowledge of the Son of God we arrive at real maturity – that measure of development that is meant by 'the fullness of Christ'.

Ephesians 4:7–13

Reflection

> The Celtic Church honoured God-given strands of Christianity which later became separated.[4]

Members of early churches in Celtic lands were **biblical** Christians: St Patrick appealed solely to the Scriptures in support of what he taught. In a letter to a British chief he wrote, 'The words are not mine, but of God and the apostles and the prophets.'[5]

They were **catholic** Christians: None of us was a heretic . . . no one a schismatic; but the Catholic Faith, as it was first transmitted by you, successors of the holy apostles, is maintained unbroken' wrote the Irish monk Columbanus to Rome's Pope Boniface in 613.

They could be **protesting** Christians: 'Love for the peace of the gospel forces me to tell all in order to shame both of you who ought to have been one choir. Another reason is my great concern for your harmony and peace. For if one member suffers all the members suffer with it,' continued Columbanus in his letter, concerned that there were two power-hungry rivals for the 'Chair of Peter'.

They were **pentecostal** Christians: 'The man of God performed more and more signs and wonders' wrote Bede of Cuthbert, an English convert of the Irish Mission.

They stood for **justice** and supported the poor, they built **community**, loved **pilgrimage** and **contemplation**.

Of course, there were flaws and power struggles too. We should not read back into that period the 'isms' of today. Rather, we may recognise that it was possible for varied strands to flourish within one universal Church and we may honour and explore these strands today.

Pause for thought

We have highlighted ten strands. Reflect upon these today.

Prayer

Divine Weaver,
we bless you
for the many-coloured tapestry which is your Church.
We grieve with you
that so many strands have been torn apart.
Weave together in us
scriptural holiness and a catholic spirit,
pentecostal callings and contemplative calm,
radical justice and sacramental grace
that we may reflect your Body on earth
as it is in heaven.

Today's step

I step
away from wooden uniformity
towards life-giving variety.

Spiritual breathing exercise

Strand in.
Bland out.
Glory.

OCTOBER 4

Tearing apart

Bible reading
Some people asked Jesus why his disciples followed different practices to those of disciples of other religious leaders. Jesus replied: 'Nobody sews a patch of unshrunk cloth on to an old coat, otherwise the new patch tears away from the old cloth and the hole is worse than ever.'

Mark 2:18, 21

Reflection
Jesus was referring to his divine work in relation to self-centred forms of religion. What has happened in the two thousand years since is that Christ has continued to weave his everlasting threads into the warp and woof of the divine Weaver's world, but the self-centred weavers, including some in the Church, have tried to weave cloth that cannot last. So we have this tearing in Christianity, as well as the life-giving threads of God. That is why God now calls us to discern those threads that are God-given in every branch of the Church, and to weave these together.

Someone may object, 'But I don't like ecumenism. It is the lowest common denominator. It becomes like a tasteless soup. It loses distinctiveness. It blunts the cutting edge. It lacks passion.' This way of life has none of that. Instead, it inspires each of us to live to the full our own tradition. Thus, for example, it inspires Baptists to live their baptism fully – to be always immersed, not just sprinkled, in the presence of God. When what we believe becomes lived it becomes alive to others. We no longer need to define ourselves over or against others. Rather, rooted and overflowing in Christ, we reach out to others in love and connect with what is of God in them. In this way we indeed become weavers with God. This weaving requires the pain of being stretched on a loom and of being taken where the divine pattern dictates. Embrace the pain. God's weaving comes out of our vulnerability.

Several centuries after the Eastern Church and the Western Church split from each other in 1054, the Western Church divided along Protestant/Roman Catholic lines, and the Protestant side fragmented into thousands of subgroups.

Members of these differing churches regard themselves, in differing ways, as heirs to the original New Testament Church. Yet none can deny that their own Church has fallen short in certain ways, or that God has given graces, gifts and dynamic missionary fruit to Churches other than their own. Many new and would-be Christians are unwilling to be defined by these partial expressions of Christianity.

Pause for thought

What is self-centred about your approach to other branches of Christ's Church?

Prayer

Grant us humility to know that we did not create ourselves
and nor can we create your Church.
May we treasure one another as living stones,
each needed in the spiritual building
which makes up your Church on earth,
through Christ our Lord.

Today's step

I step
away from judging
towards supporting.

Spiritual breathing exercise

Weaving in.
Tearing out.
Holy cloth!

OCTOBER 5

Weave the strands together

Bible reading

Don't inflate your own importance and diminish others. Just as each of us has one body with many organs, and these organs do not all have the same function, so we, though many in number, make up one body in Christ and are fellow organs of the one body. If our gift is preaching, let us preach to the limit of our vision. If it is service, let us concentrate on our service; if it is teaching, let us give all we have to our teaching; and if our gift be stimulating the faith of others let us set ourselves to this. Let the person who gives, give freely. Let the one who has authority exercise it responsibly. Let the one with empathy act cheerfully.

Romans 12:3–8

Reflection

We seek to weave these God-given strands together again.[6]

A member of the State Church in Norway who has dedicated himself to this way of life writes this:

Celtic Christian spirituality is helping us to rediscover treasures in the Christian heritage, also in our own Christian history and heritage in Norway, and in our Lutheran tradition. It is helping us to hold together various strands in Christian tradition such as care for creation, seeking redemption, and opening up to charismatic gifts. We (with our mostly Lutheran background) are welcomed to become a little more Catholic, and Evangelical, and Pentecostal as well.

We are rediscovering the saints from the time before the reformation as role models. That is in accordance with the Lutheran confession (Confessio Augustana XXI) where saints act as role models. Their remembrance should still be honoured by praising God for them (but not by interceding to them).

And in that way we are also looking for role models in our later tradition, from the centuries after the reformation and up to today, and for role models in our personal faith-shaping history.

Pause for thought

Stories of those who have gone before us inspire and help us to make connections within ourselves. What connection do you make today?

Prayer

Triune God who mothers us all,
make whole the people through your Church.
Through her Scriptures, inform us.
Through her Sacraments, nourish us.
Through her ministry, enfold us.
Through her charisms, inspire us.
Through her prophets, challenge us.
Through her saints, sanctify us.

Today's step

I step
away from the part
towards the whole.

Spiritual breathing exercise

Finger-joining in.
Finger-wagging out.
One Body.

OCTOBER 6

The sacramental strand

Bible reading

Jesus said: 'I am the Bread of Life, whoever comes to me will never be hungry; whoever trusts me will never be thirsty. This living bread is my flesh.'
John 6:35, 51

Jesus took bread, gave it to them and said, 'This is my flesh given for you.'
Luke 22:19

Reflection

A Roman Catholic says, 'Christ is on the altar in the bread and wine.' A Protestant says, 'Christ is at the table in the hearts of believers as they imbibe the bread and wine.' These are two strands. Sometimes voices have been raised in dispute over this. When everyone realises that Roman Catholics and Orthodox, for example, when they repeat the words 'this is my body, this is my blood' are referring to the life of the *risen* Christ, barriers begin to go down.

Lindisfarne's seventh-century saint Cuthbert did not raise his voice when he presided at the celebration of the 'Saving Victim', as they described the Holy Communion service. Instead he so empathised with Christ pouring out suffering love on the Cross, that suffering love for the people poured out of him and he shed tears from his heart. Is that a way of weaving together these strands – to enter so deeply into the meaning of the symbols and actions that they become a living reality that substantially transfigures us?

Bishop John Chrysostom, fourth-century Patriarch of Alexandria, likened the water and blood which flowed out of Christ's side at his death to the nourishments of baptism (that is, saturation in God's presence) and Holy

Communion by which Christ feeds his people as a mother feeds her young with milk from her breast.

He wrote: 'The Church founded in Germany believes exactly the same and hands on exactly the same as do the Spanish and Celtic Churches, and the ones in the East, those in Egypt and Libya and Jerusalem, the centre of the world. As the sun, which is God's creature, is the same throughout the whole world, so the preaching of the truth shines in all places and enlightens all people who wish to come to the knowledge of the truth.'

Pause for thought

Feed and feast.

Prayer

Risen Christ,
you who can turn water into wine,
you who can transfigure damaged bodies,
you who through elements of bread and wine
can appear to us –
draw us by the mystery of your presence,
not into vain babblings, but to wholehearted worship.

Today's step

I step
away from head knowledge
towards heart knowledge.

Spiritual breathing exercise

Your life-blood in.
My theories out.
Jesus.

OCTOBER 7

Strands within the Eucharistic

Bible reading

The cup of blessing that we bless, is it not a sharing in the blood of Christ? The bread that we break, is it not a sharing in the Body of Christ? Because there is one bread, we who are many are one body, for we all eat of the one bread.

1 Corinthians 10:16, 17

Reflection

In the second millennium different Churches took one aspect of Holy Communion and made it their focus to the exclusion of others (the fellowship meal, the remembrance of the Lord's Supper, the sharing in Holy Communion, the re-living of the Lord's sacrifice and so on). We encourage today's Christians to see these as different facets of one diamond.

When we participate in the Eucharist we participate in the pouring out of the life of God in Christ. Holy Communion is a sharing together, at the deepest level possible, with the members of the Body of Christ in our locality, and with the Head of the universal Body of Christ. We are also connected to God's creation through the bread and the wine. What happens in the process of making bread and wine must also happen in us. Our grain must be milled and turned to dust (flour), then watered and leavened and turned to rise again.

The desert father Macarius wrote: 'As wine courses through the body, so that the wine is in the person and the person in the wine, so a person who drinks Christ's blood is filled with the Spirit of the Deity, who spreads through the whole soul, so that the soul is totally in him, and thus made holy . . . God has arranged for the soul to have meat, drink and garments, which truly give life to the soul, not from its own nature but from his own Divinity, from his own Spirit and Light. For the Divine Nature contains the Bread of life . . .'[7]

Pause for thought

If everyone seeks to experience the real presence of Christ in this sacrament, who or what can I justify shutting out?

Prayer

Father, I come to you as a cup emptied of self.
Fill me with your outpoured life – your light and love.
Overflow the chalice of my heart
into the empty cups of the world,
revealing your beauty among the ugliness of the world.

Today's step

I step
away from negative caricatures of this sacrament
towards the real presence of Christ.

Spiritual breathing exercise

Communion in.
Condemnation out.
At one.

OCTOBER 8

The leader-continuity strand

Bible reading

I passed on to you what I had already received from the other apostles. I am the least of the apostles. Since, before my conversion, I persecuted the Church I hardly deserve the name apostle. But by God's grace I am what I am, and that grace has not been fruitless. Far from it, for I – well, actually the grace of God given to me – have worked harder than any other apostle. But what matters above all is that I preach what they preach, and what we preached in common is what you all believed.

1 Corinthians 15:3, 9–11

Reflection

You come from an independent or Protestant church? Hear these words from a Roman Catholic: 'The Church is the universal Body of Christ, and no one part of it has a God-given right to act as if it is complete or may act in separation from that Body. Jesus bequeathed authority to the twelve apostles, who were led by the Spirit to ordain others, each of whom accepted the authority of the apostles and their successors. The individualism which later swept into Christendom was at root a prideful rebellion against God, even though there were indeed abuses that needed correction.'

You are a Roman Catholic? Hear these words from an Anglican-Orthodox representative: 'Jesus and the Holy Spirit led the early Church into a three-fold ministry of deacons, priests and bishops and every Christian should heed the discernments of all the bishops together in council. Jesus did not envisage a four-fold ministry, with a pope with political powers who can act outside the unanimous discernment of the bishops.'

OCTOBER 8

You are part of a historic Church denomination? Hear these words from a Christian who is not:

'I seek to follow Jesus and his teachings with all my heart. He called us to live the Beatitudes, but warned against following religious tradition such as that of the Pharisees. Wherever two or three Christians come together around the Word of God and the Lord's Supper, there is the Church.'

Now think about the apostle Paul. He was raised up independently of the first twelve apostles and had unique gifts. Yet he refused to be a law unto himself. He made sure everything he taught was in line with what they taught.

Pause for thought

What can you learn from the words of the above three friendly critics?

Prayer

Save me from being a law unto myself.
Save me from thinking that my church
is the centre of everything.
Grace me to listen to those who have oversight
in other parts of the Church.
Grace me with deep respect
for the Faith that has been handed down.

Today's step

I step
away from schismatic mindsets
towards the honouring of those in oversight.

Spiritual breathing exercise

Honouring others in.
Loose canons out.
One body.

OCTOBER 9

Honour those in oversight

Bible reading

Keep on loving each other as brothers and sisters . . . Obey your leaders and recognise their authority. They watch over you for your spiritual good, and they have great responsibility. Try to work with them, not against them, so that their work becomes a joy, not a burden, and this will help you, too.

Hebrews 13:1, 17

Reflection

We honour those in oversight in all denominations.[8]

A study of the word *peitho* in verse 17, which is usually translated 'obey', suggests that it would be better translated 'Be persuaded by your elders.' It argues for a conversation in which you are open, receptive but not coerced.

Mutual responsibility should not mean that everybody must do only what everyone has agreed. That way stultifies growth. Individuals can seek guidance for themselves, but they cannot decide what is right for the church. The community means all of us. Each has a duty to consult before changing what has been agreed. Each has a duty to connect with someone they disagree with, at least until a decision has been made by the whole community.

In order to reflect the love and glory of God we need to work in harmony, each member of the body working for the other. In the body each member has its own honoured place. The member who co-ordinates needs to be respected for that function. There is an honoured place for the overseer. Make sure you continue to honour the calling of the overseer, even if he or she shows weaknesses. 'When one member of the body suffers, all members suffer' (1 Corinthians 12:26).

Pause for thought

When we live oblivious of our past heritage and apostolic traditions, we could well be suffering from spiritual Alzheimer's. And when we behave in a disorderly manner, going whimsically our own way without any co-ordination with the head or other members of our community, it could be ecclesial Parkinson's.[9]

Prayer

Holy Spirit, fulfil through us the work begun by Jesus.
Invigorate our work, subdue our natural presumption,
raise us to humility and generous courage.
May no personal scheming
reduce our love to petty dimensions.
May all be accomplished according to the spirit
of your Son's last prayer for his Church
and through the Spirit of love which you send to us.[10]

Today's step

I step
away from self-serving
towards the ennoblement of others.

Spiritual breathing exercise

Embracing in.
Scheming out.
One people.

OCTOBER 10

Weave in the human strands

Bible reading

The wisdom that comes from God is authentic, peace-loving, gentle, approachable, full of tolerant thoughts and kind actions, with not a hint of favouritism or double standards. Wise people make peace and quietly go on sowing for a harvest of goodness – in others and in themselves.

James 3:17, 18

Reflection

We value all that is truly human in all people.[11]

There are many other strands we need to weave together, for example the mystical and the practical, work and prayer, this world and the next – but through it all we need also to weave the human strands.

I was commissioned by six Church streams, Catholic and Protestant, to 'establish one family of Christians' in a new neighbourhood. Unfortunately for me, representatives of three incompatible expressions of Christianity were among the first group. The first type thought born-again Christians should not waste time working with non-believers, Roman Catholics or Christians who used liturgy, which was of the devil. The second type thought 'the sea of faith' was so wide it should include people who did not believe in God. The third type was like Mother Teresa of Calcutta, who would not have wanted to spend her time in arcane discussions rather than in serving the poor. It seemed we had best give up on unity, until someone pointed out that we were each using the jargon and conditioned mindsets of the strand we had come from. If we declared our experiment a failure and each went back into their old boxes, it would be a defeat. If, however, we heeded the human part of us that was buried underneath the religious superstructure, we would become more real, more connected, and more like Christ. That is in fact what began to happen – we began to weave the golden and the dark threads of our common humanity.

> My life is but a weaving between my Lord and me,
> I cannot choose the colours he worketh steadily.
> Oft times he weaveth sorrow, and I in foolish pride
> forget he sees the upper but I the under side.
> Not till the loom is silent and the shuttles cease to fly,
> shall God unroll the canvas and explain the reason why.
> The dark threads are as needed
> in the Weaver's skilful hand,
> as threads of gold and silver
> in the pattern life has planned.[12]

Pause for thought

Watch out for jargon and partisan conditioning behind which I hide my real self.

Prayer

When I say, 'Don't' would you say it like that, Lord?
When I say, 'Them,' would you say it like that, Lord?
When I say, 'I,' would you, who called yourself 'I Am',
strain and push like that, Lord?
Break my brittle shell, Lord,
and make me as human as you.

Today's step

I step
away from being right
towards being human.

Spiritual breathing exercise

Sympathy in.
Scorn out.
Humanity.

OCTOBER 11

No longer strangers but pilgrims together

Bile reading

If your experience of Christ's love and encouragement means anything to you, if you have known fellowship of the Spirit, and the kindness and empathy that goes with this, then let my best hopes for you come true. Join together in harmony, relate to each other in love, as though you are of one mind, one heart. Never let rivalry or vanity spoil things. In humility think more of each other than you do of yourselves. Don't only think about your own concerns – learn to see things from the other's point of view.

Philippians 2:1–4

Reflection

> We look upon all fellow Christians not as 'strangers but pilgrims together'.[13]

'They are not Christians,' says a certain Evangelical of Roman Catholics. 'God looks on the heart. Do you know what God sees in the heart of every Roman Catholic?' his friend replies. 'You are separated brothers and sisters and therefore you cannot share at our altars,' say Roman Catholics to Protestants. 'Do you ask us to disobey our consciences in order to be allowed at the altars?' a Protestant replies. 'We are all pilgrims on this earth,' say others, 'so let us walk together, strangers no longer, and as one bring love to the world.'

Some people become voluntary pain-bearers,
absorbing the anger and hurt of others
and giving back acceptance and care.
These are the ones who refuse to blame and project . . .
We are a Community that knows deeply

that we belong to one another.
There is no place of escape from unlimited evil
in a bland suburban heart.
We pray and work for the well-being of all.
We search together for meaning and purpose.
We repent of what goes wrong between us.
We act to put things right and make amends.
We are alert to signs of God at work in the way we change
and the way things are being done,
the Lord striving through us
to transfigure the realm of this Community
into the realm of Christ.
We soberly remember that we are relatively well
at other people's expense.
We are a Community where we become more healed
by being prepared to bear more
for the sake of those who are less well.[14]

Pause for thought

How can you walk together with someone from a church which is officially not in communion with yours?

Prayer

O God, we thank you that you have called us to travel,
no longer as strangers but as pilgrims together
on the journey of your people on earth.
Lead us in the paths that are life-giving for the world.

Today's step

I step
away from rivalry
towards harmony.

Spiritual breathing exercise

Including in.
Excluding out.
Together.

OCTOBER 12

We resist things that damage unity

Bible reading

Warn your people before God not to fight wordy battles – this is a recipe for disaster. These help no one and can undermine the faith of those who hear these arguments. Avoid godless chatter. Those who indulge in this move ever further away from God and their teaching spreads like gangrene . . . God's servant avoids quarrels, is kind to all, teaches as a vocation, and never harbours resentment.

2 Timothy 2:14, 16, 24

Reflection

When there is a dispute in the wider Church how should we respond – by supporting one side and ostracising the other? Or by sitting on the fence?

Jesus was more concerned about people's purity of motive: 'You appear righteous on the outside but inside you are unclean' he told some religious protagonists (Matthew 23:28). When Jesus rebuked the city he wept over it. Is that our attitude to those we disagree with?

The apostle Paul advised a team member to keep away from troublemakers, but the motive was that they would come round. Always, in the New Testament Church, the motive of discipline is conversion of the offender, not control by the offended.

> Blessed are those who use the sword as a scalpel to be accurate and clear in their telling of truth, who protect and probe but do not destroy, whose wounds serve only to purify and prune.
>
> Blessed is the one who bears the community's pain, who loves and endures to the end,

who holds to the heart a wincing fellowship,
who surprises us with healing and hope.[15]

Pause for thought

Know the difference between discerning the spirit of the protagonist (a good thing) and defensiveness in oneself (not a good thing).

Prayer

From the spirit of force that overwhelms and subdues,
Good Lord deliver us.
From the power that exhausts the love
and giftedness of others,
Good Lord deliver us.
From bitter revenge, cruelty and indifference,
Good Lord deliver us.
From the risk of isolation and separation,
Good Lord, deliver us.
From unwillingness to see the nature and call of love,
Good Lord deliver us.[16]

Today's step

I step
away from idle or vindictive chatter
towards the speech that makes whole.

Spiritual breathing exercise

Kindness in.
Poison out.
Pure God.

OCTOBER 13

Do nothing apart that is best done together

Bible reading

If two of you come to a common mind on any matter it will be done for them by my Father in heaven. For wherever two or three people are drawn together intent to do my will, I am right there among them.

Matthew 18:19, 20

Reflection

We will not do separately what is best done together.[17]

Some people who talked with Father Bede Griffiths in his Christian Ashram in India concluded that his experience has to be restored to the heart of the Church if she is to face creatively the challenges before her: the challenge of finding unity in the spirit with all Christian communions, the challenge of embracing the non-Christian religions with the universal love of Christ present in the hearts of all people and which she has a special duty to release and identify. To meet these challenges each one of us must be personally rooted in the experience of God that Jesus brings.

The five churches in a small town met to explore how they could best serve their town's well-being. 'We are like the five fingers of a hand that seeks to serve this town,' said one representative. 'The trouble is,' complained another, 'that each finger is attached to its bureaucratic denomination and has no free space to serve the town. Should we cut off these attachments in order to serve the town better?' That is a dilemma faced by a million churches.

Be wise as a serpent. Do not cut off avenues that keep us in relationship to the universal Body of Christ. On the other hand, apologies sent in love, perhaps followed by a phone call, can help to free us from bureaucratic attachment and draw us into the loving priorities of God's kingdom.

Pause for thought

Imagine, for a moment, that you have total power, and then in a fit of craziness you decide to share it with nine other people. How much power do you have left? You have one tenth of what you began with. But suppose that you decide to share, not power or wealth, but love, or influence, or friendship or even knowledge, with nine others. How much would you have left? Would you have less than when you began? No, you would have more. For those things only exist by virtue of sharing them with others. The simple fact is that the more we give away the more we will receive – a 'win-win' situation that has huge consequences.[18]

Prayer

Help us, Lord, to respond to fresh initiatives of your Spirit
in a way that honours other Christians
and builds up the Body of Christ.

Today's step

I step
away from isolation
towards co-operation.

Spiritual breathing exercise

Your name in.
My name out.
You're here.

OCTOBER 14

Unity's primary and secondary colours

Bible reading

On one occasion Jesus said to his team: 'Don't think that I have come to bring peace on earth. The fact is that my coming brings division. Brothers will betray brothers, parents their children; everyone will hate you because of me . . . Anyone who loves their nearest and dearest more than me is not worthy of me.'

Matthew 10:34, 21, 22, 37

Reflection

The primary source of unity is oneness with the Source of all. The main cause of illness is separation, from others, from nature, from the Source. This primary alignment makes possible unity in diversity on an unimaginable scale. This, however, is costly. It dislodges parasites, leeches, and relationships based on possessiveness and false dependency. The secondary colours of unity can be separation. When a person puts God first, other people who wanted to be first in our lives can become hostile.

The qualities of Christian love:

Love never gives up,
love is self-emptying and merciful,
it cares more for others than itself.
Love does not steal what it does not have.
Love does not boast when it is afraid,
is not malicious – nor poisons life with revenge.
Love does not dominate or control in order to be safe.
Love does not explode violently when hurt.
Love does not use the sins of others against them.
Love does not gain pleasure
from the humiliation of its enemies.
Love rejoices in all truth – it does not take heart through evil.

Love contains all things:
the weakness of those who hurt and destroy,
the sins of its enemies,
the shadow of the whole world.

Love abandons itself to the way of God.
It protects – it trusts – it hopes –
it is committed to the end – it does not fail.
We are destined to be makers of love and peace,
passionately and tenderly.[19]

Pause for thought

What qualities of love will you pray for today?

Prayer

Dearest Christ, you have given love, given it exquisitely.
In your tiredness you washed your friends's tired feet,
in your generosity you gave bread to your betrayer.
In your all-seeing provision you bequeathed
a sacrament of nourishment for our souls
that makes you constantly present to us.
In your prayers you ever place your people in the divine heart.
Out of love for you, we, too,
will offer a many-splendoured love to the world.

Today's step

I step
away from secondary attachments
towards the Source.

Spiritual breathing exercise

God first.
Others second.
Unity.

OCTOBER 15

Reflect God's unity in diversity

Bible reading

If you have really seen me you have seen my Father. The words I speak are not my own, they are the Father's who lives in me. I will do whatever you ask that is in line with my character, so that the Son may give glory to the Father ... The Counsellor, the Holy Spirit, whom the Father will send in my name will teach you and remind you of what I have said to you.

John 14:9, 10, 13, 16

Reflection

Some forms of religion want to force the whole world to follow 'God's party line'. In fact many materialists, whether they admit it or not, want to eradicate local expressions of diversity because they 'hinder' maximisation of profit and efficiency in global commerce. No less a person than the former USA Attorney-General has called globalisation based on economic power, consumerism and materialism deadlier than armed conflict, because the spread of sameness – the same technology, the same kind of entertainment, the same junk food, the same desire for the same endless toys – will wipe out the distinction between one culture and another.

More fundamental than egocentric religious and economic ideologies is the Ground of Being. Christians have been given the hint, which they are to make known to the whole world, that the ultimate nature of life, of Being, is unity in diversity. That is what we mean when we say that God is Trinity.

Jesus said, 'I only do what I see the Father doing.' He also said that the Spirit only does what glorifies him.

Jesus' mother, Mary, is the exemplar of the human being who reflects the Trinity. She said, 'May whatever happens to me be according to your will.'

Pause for thought

Think of a way you can reflect the Trinity today.

Prayer

God who is One,
you create us in diversity.
God who is Three,
you draw us into unity.
We give you thanks for the little trinities
that reflect your nature to us in community.

We pray for places where community has been destroyed:
may the love of the Three give birth to new community.
May the life of the Three give birth to new creativity.
May the oneness of the Three give birth to a new unity.

Today's step

I step
away from proud isolation
towards humble up-building of another.

Spiritual breathing exercise

The Three in.
Me and them out.
Triune.

OCTOBER 16

A fellowship of love

Bible reading

My dearly loved ones, since God loved us so much, we ought also to love one another. No one has ever seen God; if we love one another, God lives in us, and his love is made complete in us . . . God is love, and those who abide in love abide in God, and God abides in them.

1 John 4:11, 12, 16

Reflection

Thomas R. Kelly affirms that when we are drowned in the overwhelming seas of God's love a new alignment of relationships takes place and a new kind of life-sharing arises. Those who, whether they have much or little talent, live continuously in the Centre, understand our leaping heart and are bound to us in the fellowship of love.[20]

The sharing of physical goods in the first Jerusalem church is just one particular fruit of a deeper sharing of a life, whose base is obscured to those whose work for God is still oriented around self rather than God, or is rooted only in social gregariousness. Every period of profound re-discovery of God results in an inter-knittedness of God-enthralled people. It emerges: we don't create it deliberately. It is the holy matrix of 'the communion of the saints'.

In this fellowship cultural and racial, religious and educational differences are levelled and transcended; each is at ease with the other: the scholar and the person who works with their hands and so on. Persons in this fellowship are related as are all mountains which go down into the same earth. This is an eternal fellowship which is shared in by every bird, stone and creature. This fellowship is deeper than democracy, for God co-ordinates the discernments of the members.

Frequency of personal contact within this fellowship is not imperative. The degree of self-disclosure we are given to make to others varies with time and place and person, and never is it complete. There are levels, seasons, overlappings of friendship. Sometimes we may carry in wordless prayer those whom we do not see for years. We do not strive to hold on, for all is flowing gift.

Pause for thought

Today, will we relate to every person – at a cash till, at the other end of the phone, at the workplace or school gate – through the divine compassion and will we greet each person with the eternal love?

Prayer

May the Christ who walks with wounded feet,
walk with us on the road.
May the Christ who serves with wounded hands
stretch out our hands to serve.
May the Christ who loves with wounded heart
open our hearts to love.
May we rest secure, secure in his love
and rise up to serve him with joy.[21]

Today's step

I step
away from surface scratchings
towards deep fellowship.

Spiritual breathing exercise

Love in.
Love out.
Love between.

OCTOBER 17

Build up others

Bible reading

Jesus was at a rather posh dinner party, and couldn't help noticing how the guests made for the best seats. So he offered this little word of advice: When you are invited to a wedding reception, it's not a good idea to sit in the best seat. For all you know someone even more distinguished than you has been invited. Your host might have to say, 'I'm awfully sorry, but would you mind giving up your seat for this person?' Then, because all the other good seats have by then been taken, you will have to take a back seat and suffer considerable embarrassment. This is the best tip I can give you: when you arrive at a reception, take the least conspicuous place. Then, when your host sees this, she'll say, 'Oh do come up here, we have a much better seat for you.'

Luke 14:7-10

Reflection

The seeds of disunity lie deep in the human heart – the lust to have one's own way, to look down upon others, to protect one's own comfort. I recognise this in myself. Often I have tried out Jesus' advice to take a servant position, the lowest seat, but I have not actually enjoyed this. How may we enjoy doing this? We may make an exciting game of it! I have found the following often works: Build up another person in your mind. Pray 'Lord, may your Spirit fill them and may they grow into their full stature.' Encouraging one another can be really satisfying.

We are called to build others up, not put them down. However, being a doormat does not create true unity. Sometimes we have to confront something that is wrong, even at the risk of a storm, in order to build a more fundamental unity. When a person humbly takes some new, but right action that upsets the status quo, others may stir up opposition for reasons of pride, prejudice or fear. The initiator reveals, but does not create, disunity for, although hidden, it already exists. The need to strive for unity does not mean that we do not stretch one another in pursuit of creative change.

If we care for unity, we will include others in the process, but we will not fail to take initiative. On the other hand a person who forces or opposes change out of a competitive, selfish urge *is* the cause of disunity.

Pause for thought

Who may I give up my place to, or encourage, today?

Prayer

Search out in me, O God, the seeds of disunity –
wilfulness, insecurity and ignorance.
Transform them into service, trust and awareness,
that unity in a common cause may be born.

Today's step

I step
away from hogging the limelight
towards encouraging another.

Spiritual breathing exercise

Other in.
Self out.
Union.

OCTOBER 18

Develop teamwork

Bible reading

We know God's love for us because Christ modelled it by laying down his life for us. We, in our turn, must model this love by laying down our lives for one another. Well-off Christians who shut their eyes and their hearts to their brothers and sisters – how can anyone believe that God's love is alive in them? Let us love with our actions, not just our words.

1 John 3:16–18

Reflection

Research has shown why geese fly in a V formation. As each bird flaps its wings it creates an uplift for the bird behind it. By flying in a V formation, the whole flock adds 71 per cent greater flying range than if each bird flew on its own. When people share a common direction and sense of community they journey better.

When a goose falls out of formation it feels the drag and resistance of trying to go it alone. So it gets back into formation to take advantage of the lifting power of the bird immediately in front. Who is the 'bird' in front of and behind you? Do not take them for granted.

When the lead goose gets tired, she rotates back in the 'V' and another goose takes her place. One might say that goose gets the point! Are you aware of when a colleague who has taken the brunt of things is bowed, bruised or burning out? That may be the time when, out of compassion, not out of a desire to control, you offer to take their place for a while. The geese honk from behind to encourage those up front to keep up their speed.

Learn, too, from horses. John C. Maxwell[22] describes how in the mid-west USA they used to have fairs where they had a horse pull. Various weights were put on a horse-drawn sled and pulled along the ground. The grand champion horse pulled a sled with 4500 pounds on it. The runner-up had a 4400 pound pull. Some folk wondered what the two horses could pull if they were hitched together. Separately they totalled nearly 9000 pounds. When hitched and working together as a team they pulled over 12,000 pounds.

Pause for thought

How can you encourage, without pressurising, those who are taking the strain?

Prayer

I pray for my sister, Lord, let me take the strain.
I pray for my brother, Lord, may he rest his brain.
I pray for the folk who've lost a bit of heart,
give them the oomph to make a new start.
I pray for the people at the bottom of the pile,
may you and I together take their loads for a while.

Today's step

I step
away from overload
towards assistance.

Spiritual breathing exercise

Do-it-together in.
Do-it-alone out.
Progress.

OCTOBER 19

A shared vision

Bible reading

I will survey the scene from a high place, to see what God will say to me. After I did this God said: 'Write down this vision, express it plainly so that even a jogger can get it at a glance. The vision relates to a particular season; it will ripen and come to flower. If this takes time, then wait for it, for you can be sure it will come to pass at exactly the right time.'

Habakkuk 2:1–3

Reflection

Peter Senge says that a shared vision is not an idea, it is a force in people's hearts. If it is compelling enough to get the support of more than one person it ceases to be an abstraction. When a shared vision which people genuinely want to achieve is lacking, forces in support of the status quo may become overwhelming. Minor disagreements, personal shortcomings and in-growing tendencies begin to dominate. The group becomes distracted and unfocused.[23]

In communities we need the vision that builds on common ground and connects up:

established and immigrant populations
businesses and the localities they serve
the marginalised and the various authorities.

One example of a grassroots initiative to build community in the UK's large cities is Citizen Organising Foundation (COF). This draws together schools, families, unions and religious congregations who seek to 're-weave the fabric of society'. They and their elected politicians engage in a listening-to-the-people process. They state: 'We do not believe that greed is good and we do not worship profit . . . We are not citizens that worship another false idol – that

of the government or even voluntary sector programme . . .
We value neighbourhood leaders to whom people naturally
turn – the lady in the corner shop or the tenants' leader
with a track record of care, attention, and a following . . .
We expect to be treated with the same respect and dignity
that the other traditional power players of business and
government are accorded . . . We are compelled by the
injunction of our holy and our history books to relate, to
reflect, to take action and to risk; to make the dry bones
of our broken neighbourhoods rise up, connect and live.'[24]

Pause for thought

In order for us to catch God's visions we may have to pull
back from activities and commitments that fill life to the
brim so that there is space to discern the nudges of the Spirit.

Prayer

We of this day are children of confusion:
restore the vision of God to us.

The noise of the city deafens us to the still, small voice:
restore the hearing of God to us.

The pace of modern living deadens us:
restore the altertness of God to us.

Reveal to us in our dreams
visions of your glorious truth.

Today's step

I step
away from small-mindedness
towards God's picture.

Spiritual breathing exercise

Looking in.
Not looking out.
Your vision.

OCTOBER 20

Churches without barriers

Bible reading

In the last week of his life Jesus went into the temple and drove out the traders who brought things there and pressed worshippers to buy them. He declared loudly, 'It is written in the Scriptures, "My house shall be a house of prayer for all peoples" but you have turned it into a kitchen for crooks.' There in the temple the blind and the lame came to him.

Mark 11:16, 18; Matthew 21:14

Reflection

> We seek to shed attitudes and practices that put up barriers between the Church and the people.[25]

Great leaders have the confidence to invite good people who disagree with them to be part of their team. The USA's President Lincoln famously stocked his cabinet with former adversaries who were nicknamed the 'team of rivals'. 'How can you do this?' he was asked. 'These are the strongest and most able men in the country,' he replied, 'the country's in peril. I need them by my side.' President Barack Obama has done something similar.

We instinctively push others out or resent their presence when they break into our circle. But if we see ourselves as a wheel with spokes from each of us into the hub, which is Christ, those who join us also look to the Christ and are no longer resented. They fit in fine.

Inclusive community does not mean that anything goes. It means that everyone is invited. Aidan lived alongside the people and refused to accept practices and customs that would distance him from the people and make him seem superior. He also challenged people, but they knew he did this because he loved them.

Pause for thought

Thoreau wrote in his book *Walden* about having three chairs in his cabin, one for solitude, one for friendship, and one for society. This was a metaphor. Each of these are to have an important place in our lives: none should crowd out the other.

Prayer

O God of the Great Heart,
may your churches be true to their birthright.
May they be places of prayer and eating,
living and learning,
work and celebration;
the warming, welcoming fire of Christ in their midst
drawing all peoples to you.

Today's step

I step
away from treating people as mere customers
towards treating them as God's children.

Spiritual breathing exercise

Inclusion in.
Exclusion out.
God's house.

OCTOBER 21

Indigenous churches

Bible reading

Many foreigners had become Christians in places such as Antioch. A delegation of strict Jewish Christians arrived who insisted that these converts should be circumcised in accordance with the customs taught by Moses. The missionary apostles Paul and Barnabus had intense discussions with them. It was agreed they should go to Jerusalem and decide such matters in an ecumenical council. After Paul and Barnabus described how the Holy Spirit had transformed these converts as completely as the Jewish converts, James declared, 'In my opinion we should not put obstacles in the way of these foreigners who have turned to God.'

Acts 15:1–19

Reflection

> The 'Celtic Church' was thoroughly indigenous to the people in a way that the Church has rarely been since.[26]

Wise people today, taking their cue from that first ecumenical council in Jerusalem, allow Christ's presence to emerge from within the culture. In our multi-cultural societies this calls for varied expressions of Church.

In nature, a fresh plant that grows up within its decaying parent plant, and from the same root system, is an endogenous plant. The best fresh expressions of Church are endogenous – they have roots. We will welcome expressions of Church in pub, internet or street culture, but we will ensure they have roots that go deeper.

There is yet a deeper point, which came home to me in Australia, where churches tend to be clones of a past colonial model or of a passé USA franchise model. Some

Australians sensed that an endogenous Australian Church emerges when the Christians embrace their own 'Shadow' and that of their land. In order to do this church planters might have to leave the cloned churches huddled around Australia's perimeter, journey into its vast desert heartland, and then let God work through the land and its Aboriginal people's ability to dream, to bring something authentically new to birth.

Pause for thought

What artificial traits should we allow to die in our churches, and what endogenous expressions need to grow?

Prayer

God of the memory held in genes and stones,
help us so to connect with the roots of our varied cultures
that fresh expressions of your Church may emerge
that are natural, true and attractive – and deeply Christian.

Today's step

I step
away from what is overlaid
towards what is authentic.

Spiritual breathing exercise

Natural in.
Unnatural out.
Real Church!

OCTOBER 22

The suffering Church

Bible reading

I suffer on behalf of all who have heard the Good News. I do not regret this because it gives me a chance to complete in my sufferings the immense pains which Christ suffers on behalf of his body, the Church.

Colossians 1:24

Reflection

Easy triumphalism and cheap grace have no place in the wardrobe of Christ's Bride, the Church. Suffering, however, is a necessary part of this Bride's beauty. Christ suffers on behalf of his bride, and the bride lovingly completes this necessary work.

Jesus promised that the Church would face persecutions. Sometimes, out of such persecutions, sanctity and many conversions have resulted: 'the blood of the martyrs is the seedbed of the Church'. For generations the Church in Cambodia was a tiny, dry stick. Then came the killing fields. Out of these came indigenous churches which flourish. Metropolitan Tryphon – Archbishop during the terrible persecution of Christianity in Soviet Russia – despite going blind and suffering the continual threat of exile and death, composed a remarkable hymn, 'Glory to God for all things!':

> In winter I have contemplated how in the silence of the moon, clothed in a white robe resplendent with diamonds of snow, the whole earth has quietly prayed to you. I have seen how the rising sun has rejoiced in you and choirs of birds have sung forth your glory. I have heard how mysteriously the forests resound of you, and the winds sing, the waters babble,

how choirs of heavenly bodies preach of you, harmoniously moving in endless space.

In countries besotted by material pleasures, the Church is tempted to become complacent or to become prey to the 'Prosperity Gospel'. Yet always God calls us to travail on behalf of souls, to weep with those who weep, to serve with sacrificial love, and to endure the hostility of those who repel challenge.

Pause for thought

For whom do you bleed? With whom do you weep?

Prayer

Life-giver, pain-bearer,
we offer you our tears for those broken by abuse
and our anguish for those who rebel against you.
We offer you the pain we endure from those who are hostile
and our burdens for the needy and poor.
May our sufferings contribute to the suffering
that your universal body needs to complete
in order to transform every last person and place on earth.

Today's step

I step
away from denial
towards the pain

Spiritual breathing exercise

Sacrifice in.
Insulation out.
Mercy.

OCTOBER 23

Churches that connect

Bible reading

Do not copy the spin doctors of religion – the Pharisees. They add to the baggage people are expected to carry, but they do not lift a finger to help ordinary people carry their load. They increase their religious paraphernalia in order to look important: everything they do covers up the actual grain of life. They take away the key to understanding: they don't actually enter themselves and they hinder seekers from entering.

Matthew 23:3–5

Reflection

> The Celtic Church honoured, trusted and went with the grain of the human communities it worked amongst.[27]

Let us be clear. Human populations are selfish. 'A church that marries the spirit of an age will become a widow in the next,' as Dean Inge observed. There is something even worse. That is a church married to the spirit of the bygone age which established its present framework, and which does not love the people of today enough to connect with them.

The phrase 'went with the grain of the human communities' should be understood in the sense that Christ is the light of every human being (John 1:4). Ultimately the whole human race is Christ's granary, therefore for us to go with the grain is to co-operate with all that is most fully human. Just as God's nature is reflected in the immense variety of creation, so is it reflected in the varied cultures and interests of humanity.

Today it is not so much religious people who subvert their profession as people in business, the media, politics:

they too often find out what people want and give it to them. Their motive is success or money.

Jesus connected not with people's 'wants' but with their deepest longings. He connected with people who already had a certain vision, for example, followers of John the Baptist. He connected with people in his area with whom he could talk while mending their fishing nets. He noticed a tax collector's curiosity and went to his home. Now, as then, Jesus enters the framework of people's lives in order to meet their eternal hungers.

The Celtic Church emerged from within the culture and grew around the natural patterns of the tribe. This was possible because the first missionaries accepted the hospitality of tribal leaders, made deep human connections, and established lasting friendships.

Pause for thought

Jesus walked where the people walked.
Where will I walk today?

Prayer

I pray for the people:
their patterns and their pastimes,
their work and their homes,
their love-making and their conflicts,
their dreams and their disillusionments,
their hopes and their eternal hungers.

Today's step

I step
away from unnatural airs
towards that which is human in another.

Spiritual breathing exercise

With-the-grain in.
Grating out.
God-centred.

OCTOBER 24

The ten community workers

Bible reading

Jesus prayed throughout the night up a mountain. In the morning he came down and chose twelve of his supporters whom he designated as apostles . . . Jesus campaigned in town and village. He took the twelve with him and some of the women who had been healed, who provided financial support.

Luke 6:12, 13; 8:1, 2

Reflection

Ten eager people started out as one,
one did not get his way and then there were nine.
Nine nervous people continued life together,
one was enticed away, and then there were eight.
Eight tetchy people continued life together,
one got bored with the chores and then there were seven.
Seven chastened people continued life together,
one crumbled when harsh words came
and then there were six.
Six battered people continued on together,
one saw the others' faults, and then there were five.
Five flawed people soldiered on together,
one ran out of stamina and then there were four.
Four weary people laboured on together,
one saw only problems and then there were three.
Three disheartened people struggled on together,
one said, 'I didn't come for this' and then there were two.
Two bleeding people gave everything to God,
then they stayed together, anchored in the call.

Someone else who'd done just that asked if they could join,
then there were three with nothing left but God.

Someone felt the realness, who longed to be real too,
she joined the others, and then there were four.
Someone sensed the listening, who longed to listen too,
he listened with the others, and then there were five.
Someone was touched by the way they served each other,
she asked to join them, and then there were six.
Someone saw the unity, who craved for union, too,
he asked to join the others, and then there were seven.
Someone grasped the clarity, who had clear vision too,
she asked to join the others, and then there were eight.
Someone enjoyed their creative ways, who was creative too,
he asked to join the others, and then there were nine.
Someone saw potential, who cared deeply for the world,
she asked to join the others, and then there were ten.

Pause for thought

The world has yet to see what God can do through twelve people wholly given to him.

Prayer

All that I am,
all that I do,
all that I'll ever be I offer now to you.

Today's step

I step
towards the call
away from distractions.

Spiritual breathing exercise

True path in.
Abdication out.
Calling.

OCTOBER 25

Slumdog community

Bible reading

Jesus told a story to highlight a feature of God's set-up:

A royal celebrity arranged a fabulous wedding banquet for his son. Invitations were sent to the powerful and famous. But one after another they made excuses and sent their apologies. As the preparations were almost complete, there were lots of empty places. So the host sent staff out into highways and byways, into slums and back alleys, and pressed invitations upon anyone they found there. In the end, the wedding festival was packed with all kinds of people, whether they were socially acceptable or not.

However, there was a twist in the tale. The royal host took a look at each guest to see if, in whatever small way, they had worn something that would show honour to the bride and groom. He came across one person who showed not honour, but disdain, and that person was bundled off by the security people to a hard place.

Matthew 22:1–14

Reflection

In the later 1970s the Venezuelan composer Jose Antonio Abreu started rehearsing with eleven slum kids in a garage. Thirty years later the youth orchestra *El Sistema* was the flagship of one of the most extraordinary social experiments ever. The young musicians were not just talented: many were brought up in the violent barrios of Caracas, where free lessons in classical music turned them from potential gang recruits into virtuosos. Abreu headed a nationwide programme involving 250,000 deprived children and more than two hundred local orchestras.

Sexual longing and aggression are the emotions that always and everywhere inform the music of the youth, both at its magical best and its mindless worst. What Jose Abreu realised is that this is not enough: that what easily enthrals, easily infantilises. It wasn't just the challenge of learning an instrument and the pride of belonging to a skilful group that redeemed the children of the slums. It was exposure to a range of emotions way beyond the limited horizons of adolescence. It was a chance to grow up.[28]

Pause for thought

Look for a slum, or a slump. What potential glory lies hidden under the negative appearances? Is your heart a place of royal hospitality? Do you despise or shut anyone out of your heart?

Prayer

May my heart be a place of royal hospitality
where cheerfulness and mercy abound.
May it unlock the song in every mind
and nourish every hungry soul.

Today's step

I step
away from snobbery
towards the street.

Spiritual breathing exercise

Connection in.
Aloofness out.
Music.

OCTOBER 26

Ubuntu

Bible reading

Be merciful in your actions, kindly in your heart, humble in your own estimation. Be gentle and patient. Bear with each other, always ready to forgive a grievance, as the Lord forgave you. Above all else, clothe yourself with love, for love binds all the virtues together in perfect unity. Let Christ's peace be like a referee in your hearts – always remembering that as members of one body you are called to live in harmony.

Colossians 3:12–15

Reflection

'I am drained by meetings but I am recharged by meeting' said a church leader. 'We need to discern,' said the Catholic before going to a gathering in Rome, 'the difference between avenues that help us relate to the wider Body of Christ, and unnecessary, bureaucratic growths which we *can* cut out.'

'Ubuntu' is a Zulu word which loosely translated means 'a person is only a person through other persons'. A popular definition of ubuntu is 'the belief in a universal bond of sharing that connects all humanity'. A person with ubuntu is open and available to others, affirming of others, does not feel threatened that others are able and good, for he or she has a proper self-assurance that comes from knowing that he or she belongs in a greater whole and is diminished when others are humiliated or when others are tortured or oppressed.

Nelson Mandela explained ubuntu as follows: A traveller through our country stops at a village, and he does not have to ask for food or for water. Once he stops, the people give him food, entertain him. That is one aspect of ubuntu but it has various aspects. Ubuntu does not mean that people should not enrich themselves. The question therefore is: are you going to do so in order to enable the community around you to improve? Desmond Tutu has said that the West's mantra is 'I think, therefore I am' whereas Africa's mantra is 'You are, therefore I am.'

Pause for thought

Become fully present to a person you encounter today.

Prayer

Weave in us this day;
silence of knowing,
clearness of seeing,
joy of serving.

Weave in us this day;
humility of listening,
depth of understanding,
grace of speaking.

Weave in us this day;
peace of being,
gift of loving,
power of meeting.

Today's step

I step
away from paper exercises
towards a person.

Spiritual breathing exercise

Ubuntu in.
Time-wasting out.
Meeting.

OCTOBER 27

Cultivate solidarity

Bible reading

In Christ I am a free person, I don't have to be anyone's slave. However, of my own free will I choose to be a slave, as it were, to everyone, in order that I might win as many as possible to Christ's Way. To the Jews I become like a Jew, to win the Jews. To those under the Jewish law, I become like one under the law, (though I am no longer, in fact, bound to it). To those who are not under that law I become like someone without law (even though, in fact, I cannot be lawless for I am bound to Christ's law). To the weak I become a weak person, that I might win the weak. I have been all things to all sorts of people so that by all possible means I might win some to God.

1 Corinthians 9:19–22

Reflection

> We seek to cultivate solidarity with all people in everything except sin.[29]

A preacher invited the congregation to imagine that human beings were ants and that a nature-lover felt sorry for them, for they were threatened by dangers they were unaware of. The nature-lover decided that the only way he could help them and communicate with them would be to become one of them. That is why a human became an ant. That story, said the preacher, is a parable of what God did for humans: God became one of us.

God calls us to follow Jesus' example by making acts of solidarity with groups and peoples who are not like us, as God lays this on our hearts.

The prophet Ezekiel left his position in the capital city to sit among the exiles by the river. The apostle Paul lived like a Jew when God called him to work with fellow Jews, and lived like a foreigner when God called him to work among them. He urges us to rejoice with those who celebrate and weep with those who suffer.

Some people adopt the dress or the patterns of a group they feel called to reach out to. We should all seek to be in solidarity with people in the way God is in solidarity with them – with their heart cries and their highest aspirations, with their God-given humanity, legitimate interests, and need to be understood, with their ache for God, for community and for a better world. 'God became one with us that we may become one with God.'

Pause for thought

Put yourself in the shoes of a group that is alien to you, and understand their way of thinking.

Prayer

Set us free, O God,
to put ourselves in others' shoes:
to be open to others in listening,
to be sensitive to others in praying,
that we may see Christ
in the face of each person we meet,
and cross barriers for you,
as you crossed barriers for us.

Today's step

I step
away from my comfort zone
towards another.

Spiritual breathing exercise

Their way in.
My way out.
Christ's way.

OCTOBER 28

Sobornost

Bible reading

Take a look at this – my servant, the one I uphold, my chosen one, the joy of my heart! I have put my Spirit upon him; he shall bring forth justice for the nations, neither by creating an outcry, nor by public broadcasting. No crushed reed will he break off; no dim-burning lantern wick will he snuff out. Faithfully he will bring forth religion, himself undimmed, unbroken, until he has established right ways on earth and even islands shall look to his teaching.

Isaiah 42:1–4

Reflection

This is one of four prophetic songs about a servant. Who is this servant? Scholars in the individualistic West come up with contrasting answers. In fact the servant is a corporate representative. At one time he is Israel, the entire nation. In the last song, Isaiah 53, he is just one person – which is why Christians apply it to Christ. In this passage the servant is a faithful minority who represent the nation. Always the servant's suffering is caused because he seeks to be in solidarity both with God and with the people while remaining true to self.

The West has become intoxicated with individualism. Even its Christians are blind to the corporate dimensions of the gospel. From Russia, however, comes the concept of sobornost which helps us to restore a biblical solidarity. Sobornost is rooted in the Holy Trinity. One cannot imagine the Father deciding something against the Son, or the Son against the Father, or the Holy Spirit, saying 'I'm not going along with this,' or 'I'll reserve my judgement'. Each eagerly bends towards the other, yields to the other, enhances the other, in the knowledge that they share the same origin, the same essence, the same ultimate fullness of achievement. Sobornost is total self-emptying and surrender to God, and through God, to that which is of God in other persons. Sobornost is the bending to one another, of our own free choice, preferring one another. This is the complete opposite of the 'self' that wants to manipulate others, that wants always to be right, that tries to impose its own will instead of praying that God's will be done.

Pause for thought

In your heart, yield to another now.

Prayer

Holy Trinity,
as you yield to one another
may we yield to you in each person we meet.
Help us to acquire, through pain,
a deep, God-given knowing
that builds the foundation of unity.

Today's step

I step
away from my affairs
towards the Ground of Unity.

Spiritual breathing exercise

Yielding in.
Imposing out.
Unity.

OCTOBER 29

Thinking alike

Bible reading

The nation that puts God first is truly blest. This nation is the people who enter into the heritage God has given them. God looks down on everyone on earth; the One who forms the hearts of all knows everything about them. No government is saved by the size of its military forces, for God oversees those who put their trust in the divine love to feed them and keep them safe.

We wait in hope for God, our sure help and defence, in whom we trust.

Psalm 33:12-22

Reflection

In the West people make an idol of democracy, they treat the will of the people as if it is God's will. But it is fatal to make a god of the people's will. The will of the people may be selfish, and this leads to disintegration. Muslims recognise this, and some therefore want to establish God's will by imposing Sharia Law. External laws however, cannot bring God's presence into every area of life.

Catherine Doherty suggests that sobornost[30] is born in the heart of a people who love God and follow him totally and completely, and who love their neighbour. When this is so, by the inspiration of the Holy Spirit, they experience the phenomenon of 'thinking alike', born of prayer. When God's people become truly 'bound' by the will of the Father, into a community, they take on the obedience of the Son. Sobornost is a unanimous decision by a group on a weighty – especially spiritual – subject where time is not of the essence. It is a deep unanimity that comes through prayer, and sometimes through fasting as well. It is something like a spring that wells up from the very heart of the Holy Trinity.

In a country or movement based on sobornost one might say that 'the voice of the people is the voice of God'. This, however, is not imposed, it is inculcated and commonly embraced.

Pause for thought

Become aware in prayer of the deepest God-chords that unite you to others.

Prayer

Increase our desire to enter into the world's life.
Make us secure enough to be with others.
Lead us into the deep divine-human chord.

Today's step

I step
away from my own agenda
down into the bonds of divine peace.

Spiritual breathing exercise

Deep fellowship in.
Fashion and fear out.
One.

OCTOBER 30

Ideologies that destroy community

Bible reading

Daniel interpreted the king of Babylon's dream for him: You saw an image, huge, gleaming and terrible to look at. The head was made of gold, its chest and arms of silver, its stomach and thighs of bronze, its legs of iron and its feet partly of iron and partly of clay. A huge stone struck this image and it broke into many pieces. Then the stone became a mountain that filled the earth. You are the head of gold. The silver represents the empire that shall follow you, the bronze a third kingdom which shall oppress the earth. The fourth kingdom, like iron, shall crush everything, but it shall be divided because of its feet of clay. Ultimately God will replace all these empires with a divine authority that shall never pass away.

Daniel 2:31–44

Reflection

Two ideologies compete for the world's allegiance. The first is the free market. This has individuals in control who use the mechanism of the market to achieve financially successful distribution of their products, often at the expense of communal well-being. The second is socialism, that forces people to accept equitable distribution at the expense of free choice and voluntary fellowship. A multitude of third ways are on offer, each centred on control, and each fails to reach the heart of our malaise. This is because they are all wedded to the mechanistic view of what makes us people. The way of community is to do those things that elicit the consent of the other, that brings out their best, that empowers them until each gives what they have for the benefit of the whole. Love does not flow in an environment that is dominated by control; it *can* flow in an environment that is dominated by co-operation.

The failure to live community has caused societies to heap ever more upon governments, which are too unwieldy to create well-being. If we are to heal our societies we need agendas that reach out to people and groups and which build relationships.

Pause for thought

The greatest challenge we face is that of reconciling the structural needs of modern economies with the intra-personal needs of the people.

Prayer

God of Community,
bring to birth a community of justice:
we pray for the powerful who impose their will on the weak,
may they come to know your defenceless love.
We pray for those who know only how to take
and not how to give:
may they become aware
that we each have something to offer.
Help us to recover a sense of belonging
by returning to the Ground from which we all come.

Today's step

I step
away from domination
towards your dominion.

Spiritual breathing exercise

Human family in.
Number one out.
Community.

OCTOBER 31

Healing of divided peoples

Bible reading

There is now no divide between Jews and people of other races, between slaves and employers, between male and female – all are one in Jesus Christ. You all belong to Christ. You are all children of Abraham. You are all heirs of God's promises.

Galatians 3:28, 29

Reflection

> We desire the healing of peoples divided by class, colour or creed and repent of our own part in these divisions.[31]

Individuals and the world are fragmented. Jews fight Muslims, and each thinks they are superior. Christians have fallen into the same trap. Protestants have fought and killed Catholics and vice versa. Zionists and Jihadists need to know that God's purpose in calling Israel into being is that it should help every nation to know that God loves and has a great destiny for it.

Those who are oppressed need healing of a victim mentality. After planes crashed into New York's Twin Towers on 9/11 a young Jordanian, Suleiman Bakhit, studying in Minneapolis, was beaten up. Instead of retreating into isolation or resorting to retaliation he started doing outreach work with USA schoolchildren to teach them that Arabs are human beings, too. He was flummoxed, however, when these kids asked him what comics and TV programmes Arab children liked. He realised that they had no great heroes. So he returned to Jordan and launched his own comics company, Aranim, which has since delighted Arab kids with tales of noble heroes.[32]

David Pott led the Lifeline Expedition, a Christian response to the legacy of the Atlantic slave trade. In recent years he has walked with a team along the meridian from Greenwich to the heart of Africa, in chains, to symbolise their recognition of the slavery their forebears promoted among Africans, and wearing T-shirts which say 'Sorry'. The Vice-President of Gambia was so moved to meet them that she personally took the chains from them and forgave them. Scenes like that, as those of England's two Anglican Archbishops (one white, one black) leading the team in a procession of penance and healing in a former slave port city, have hit the headlines. But David also told me of individuals of African descent who have experienced healing of false self-image during their travels together.

Pause for thought

What false self-image, caused by mistreatment in the past, can you identify and pray for to be healed?

Prayer

You whose order rules the atom,
you whose law propels the sea,
bring the nations, drowned in discord, closer to your harmony.
God of beauty, heal our sickness,
God of love, our fractures mend,
foster unity that binds us,
rich to poor and foe to friend.

Today's step

I step
away from national stereotyping
towards healing self-image.

Spiritual breathing exercise

Humanity in.
Hatred out.
Healing.

NOVEMBER 1

Big mission statement

Bible reading

Life from nothing began through Christ and so did life from the dead. That is why he, rightly, can be called Lord of all. The full nature of God chose to live in him. Through him God chose to reconcile the whole created cosmos, everything in the world of heaven and in the world of matter, to God's self, by virtue of the Cross.

Colossians 1:19, 20

Reflection

> Our aim is 'that the whole created order may be reconciled to God through Christ' (Colossians 1:20).[1]

If a person or an organisation stands for nothing, they are likely to go round in circles. Those that wish to stand for something often have a mission statement. A mission statement may be about multiplying a product or delivering a service. It may include a values statement, such as honesty in accounts or marketing. A church might have a mission statement that aims to double its members, or its income, or its number of charity projects.

What, however, would be the point if one Christian group aimed to double its converts by bolstering their prejudice towards one side in a conflict, while another group aimed to achieve peace between the two sides in this conflict? What is the point of one group drawing up a mission statement to halve the carbon footprint of its area, if the local Church centre uses ecologically unsound foods, energy and travel?

It is for such reasons that truly Christian mission statements need to be holistic. That is why the Community of Aidan and Hilda chose the above mission statement –

surely the biggest and most comprehensive mission statement in this, or in any world.

Of course this, too, has its dangers. A mission statement so big could be an excuse for doing nothing specific. Rome was not built in a day. The transformation of the world takes place in small, measurable steps. Each of these steps, however, should always be assessed in the light of the big picture, and should always lead to another step.

Pause for thought

Put into your own words the biggest mission statement that you can own as yours.

Prayer

Let there be
respect for the earth,
peace for its people,
love in our lives,
delight in the good,
forgiveness for past wrongs,
and from now on a new start.[2]

Today's step

I step
away from what is blinkered
towards the big picture.

Spiritual breathing exercise

Reconciled creation in.
Break-ups out.
Cosmic Christ.

NOVEMBER 2

Make disciples throughout the world

Bible reading

The risen Jesus met his eleven apostles up a Galilee hillside on his final day on earth. 'All authority in heaven and earth has been given to me,' he told them. 'Go to all ethnic groups in the world and make them my disciples, immersing them in the presence of the Father, the Son and the Holy Spirit. Teach them to observe all that I have commanded you, and remember this: I am with you always, even to the end of the world.'

Matthew 28:16–20

Reflection

'The Church is the only organisation that exists for those who are not its members,' said Archbishop William Temple. The nature of God is to reach out in love to every person. Since we are designed to reflect God's nature, our mission, whatever its unique elements, must also be to reach out.

Those eleven apostles who received Jesus' commission at first made disciples in Jerusalem. Following persecution and under the guiding of the Holy Spirit they spread further afield, as we can read in Acts of the Apostles. References in later records suggest that they went almost to the ends of the earth. Andrew may have died in Achaia; he left his mark most widely and became the patron saint of Greece, Russia and Scotland. Bartholomew died a martyr in Armenia, which became the first 'Christian nation'. James was the first of the eleven to be put to death: in AD44. Many now walk to Spain's Santiago de Compostella where some of his remains are buried. We know nothing of where James the son of Alphaeus went. John made many disciples in Asia, especially Ephesus. Judas Thaddaeus and his brother Simon of Cana are said to have reached

Persia (today's Iran). Judas healed the king of Edessa. Peter, of course, spread the faith in the world's largest capital city, Rome. Philip, who some believe to be also the deacon who interpreted the gospel to an Ethiopian finance minister, went to live in Hierapolis, Phrygia, and his Spirit-filled daughters spread the faith in all directions. Matthew spent his life preaching to Hebrew people, though a list of martyrs drawn up in Rome has him ending his life as a martyr in Ethiopia. Thomas took the gospel to India.

Pause for thought

Each apostle 'went far', even those who stayed near home. What does it mean for you to go far?

Prayer

Unfold to me the meaning of your commission –
may I not be blind to what you seek to accomplish.
Kindle in me the spirit of an apostle –
the willingness to pass on what you have imparted to me.
Reveal to me what it means to reach all the world –
whether near or far, may every bit of the world I touch
become immersed in you.

Today's step

I step
away from the bottleneck
towards the outflow.

Spiritual breathing exercise

Your words in.
Our words out.
Immerse.

NOVEMBER 3

Share what Jesus has done for you

Bible reading

The man who'd had all those demons cast out of him by Jesus, which then went into the herd of pigs, begged Jesus to let him travel with him. Jesus did not permit this. 'Go back to your friends,' he said, 'and tell them how much God has done for you.' The man went through all the Ten Towns telling what Jesus had done for him. Everyone who heard him was amazed.

Mark 5:18–20

Reflection

When a sixth-century missionary named Samson first landed on the beaches of Brittany he brought with him a team to begin a mission there. But God's first lesson for them was this: no amount of evangelistic organisation is a substitute for a prayed for, God-architected, God-timed healing encounter. Such an encounter can have a domino effect which influences a whole region before the organisation has even begun to get into gear.

As they were mooring their boat they saw a hut, and a man weeping and gazing out towards the sea. Samson went to the man and asked him what was the problem. 'I have now waited here three days and three nights,' the man told him, 'for someone to come from across the sea and help me.' He was a man of prayer who had a leprous wife and a deranged daughter. As he had prayed for them, God had told him that he was to wait at the harbour for such a man, who would heal them.

Samson went to the man's home and made extended prayers over the sick women, who were both restored to health. No doubt they all three told others. For this was the start of a wonderful ministry, and from there Samson established Christian communities throughout the region, one of which, at Dol, still flourishes today.

Pause for thought

Think of something Jesus has done for you and share it aloud – at first with an imaginary person, and as opportunity comes, with an actual person. Think of someone who, however faintly, signals for help. Your response could be God's opportunity.

Prayer

Thank you, Jesus, for your love for me;
for hurts you have healed, and faults you have changed;
for the thoughts you have inspired
and callings you have given.
May I share these joys
as naturally as we share the joys of a lovely day.

Today's step

I step
away from pressured programmes
towards shared treasures of life.

Spiritual breathing exercise

Shared blessings in.
Forced claims out.
Jesus.

NOVEMBER 4

Tell the good news

Bible reading

John the Baptiser sent two representatives to ask Jesus if he really was the leader they had been preparing for, or whether they needed to look for another kind of leader. While these representatives were with him Jesus healed many people of diseases, plagues, evil spirits and even blindness. So he replied: 'Go and tell John what you have seen and heard: the blind receive their sight, the lame walk, lepers are cured, the deaf hear, the dead are raised up and the poor have good news broadcast to them. The person who does not find my approach offensive is a blest person.'

Luke 7:18–23

Reflection

Now a confirmed atheist, I've become convinced of the enormous contribution that Christian evangelism makes in Africa: sharply distinct from the work of secular NGOs, government projects and international aid efforts. These alone will not do. Education and training alone will not do. In Africa Christianity changes people's hearts. It brings a spiritual transformation. The rebirth is real. The change is good . . . Christians, black and white, working in Africa, do heal the sick, do teach people to read and write, and only the severest kind of secularist could see a mission hospital or school and say the world would be a better place without it.

I observe that tribal belief is no more peaceable than ours; and it suppresses individuality. Anxiety – fear of evil spirits, of ancestors, of nature and the wild, of a tribal hierarchy, of quite everyday things – strikes deep into the whole structure of rural African thought . . . Christianity, with its teaching of a direct, personal, two-way link between the individual and God . . . liberates . . . Removing Christian evangelism from the African equation may leave the continent at the mercy of a malign fusion of Nike, the witch doctor, the mobile phone and the machete.[3]

Yes, we may admit with shame episodes when the Church has failed the people and not lived its faith, but don't be backward in putting forward the magnificent contributions Christ-led and Christ-like people have made and make now. For Christ is alive and at work in every continent and around the next corner.

Pause for thought

Rehearse in your mind some news of Christ at work today which is worth telling another.

Prayer

Thank you for the countless numbers
who have been made more whole through prayer.
Thank you for those who can now see, or write,
or believe in themselves for the first time.
Thank you for people of hate and violence
who now spread love and forgiveness.
Thank you for communities of hope
in an otherwise hopeless place.

Today's step

I step
away from denigration
towards affirmation.

Spiritual breathing exercise

Good news in.
Travesty out.
Hope.

NOVEMBER 5

Evangelism

Bible reading

Jesus came to live in Capernaum and preached in synagogues. He went to a deserted spot on the shore of the Sea of Galilee, but a crowd gathered. So Jesus asked Simon Peter to push his boat out a little from the shore, so he could speak to the crowd from the boat. After this meeting he urged Simon Peter to go into deep water and lower his nets. Peter had fished all night and caught nothing, but to please Jesus he did this. To his astonishment they had a huge, overwhelming catch. This had a deep impact on them and they felt quite inadequate. 'Don't worry,' Jesus said, 'from now on you'll be fishing for people.' They left their nets and followed Jesus.

Luke 4:31; 5:1–11

Reflection

The pastor said: 'You have to watch evangelists. They always talk but seldom listen. They make new converts, and leave old ones stranded. They take people out of the church on missions, but leave people in the church unsustained.' The evangelist said: 'If I did not do this nobody would.'

How did Jesus go about starting his mission in Galilee? He took lodgings in Capernaum. It seems quite likely he had room in the household of Peter. Archeological research suggests this had courtyards with a guest area. How did he first make such a contact? My guess is that when Jesus' family lived at Nazareth they took holidays in Capernaum. Maybe Jesus paid reconnaissance visits on his own. He went to the shore of the Sea of Galilee. People worked on their boats there. They had time to talk. And Jesus had time to observe, to intuit the spirituality of each person he talked with. He befriended Peter. When he was ensconced at the house of Peter, he did not rush into things. He made friends, arranged to meet a group. The group grew. He asked Peter to let him speak to them from the boat. The meeting ended. Jesus did not rush to create another meeting. He asked Peter to push out into deeper waters. They made a huge catch. This made an impact on these seasoned, unsentimental fishermen. Now, Jesus was not only a friend, he was a friend who HAD something. Whatever this something was, they wanted more of it. Jesus sensed the moment: then, and only then, he asked Peter to join him, not in something that made no connection at all with fishing, or which left him stranded, but in fishing for people. Connection. Connection. Connection. That is the best evangelism.

Pause for thought

How does the phrase 'less haste, more speed' relate to the way I reach out to people?

Prayer

Make us
patient in our observing,
sensitive in our listening,
generous in our befriending,
and compelling in our speaking,
that we may open new frontiers for you.

Today's step

I step
away from stale routine
towards your next command.

Spiritual breathing exercise

Responses in.
Refusals out.
Connection.

NOVEMBER 6

Tell your story

Bible reading

'King Agrippa,' Paul said, 'everyone knows how I lived from my youth among my own people in Jerusalem. They all know that I lived religiously as the strictest of Pharisees. At one time I thought it my duty to hound with all my strength the people who followed Jesus of Nazareth as their Lord. I was on my way to Damascus to do just this when, at midday, I saw a light far brighter than the sun which completely dazzled us. I fell to the ground and heard a voice say, "Saul, Saul, why are you persecuting me? It is not easy for you to go against your own conscience." "Who are you, Lord?" I said, and he replied, "I am Jesus, whom you are persecuting. I have shown myself to you for a reason; you are to be my witness."'

Acts 26:1–16

Reflection

After Paul had told his story King Agrippa said, 'If you go on like this you'll make me a Christian.' The best way to spread the faith is to tell our own story, to share our own experience of Jesus with all its ups and downs, warts and all. Preaching at people works in some cultures – witnesses to Jesus in one African country frequently come aboard buses and preach to the passengers with whom they already share a fellow feeling – but it rarely works in a European country where people feel they have a right for their personal space not to be invaded.

When we share our own experience it has authenticity and becomes interesting. It is important that we tell of our search, our journey, our encounters and our disappointments.

In order to tell our story we need a suitable context. For example, we may invite people to share a meal and tell something of their life journey. Others like to chat at the school gates or while in a queue. Research shows that more people are brought to faith through friendship than through any other means.

Pause for thought

Write or speak out what Jesus means to you.

Prayer

Author of life:
help me to tell my story –
the wonder of my birth,
the paths that led to glory
or what brought me down to earth.

Help me trace the times of light
when you were by my side;
through Scripture, prayer or insight
when I sang and when I cried.

Help me to share my story
dear Lord who for me died,
whose death became the victory
in which I now abide.

Today's step

I step
away from the hiding place
towards the telling place.

Spiritual breathing exercise

Recounting in.
Hold-back out.
Your story.

NOVEMBER 7

Give a reason

Bible reading

Always be prepared to give an answer to everyone who asks you to explain the hope that you have. Do this gently and with respect, keeping a clear conscience, so that those who speak maliciously against you may be ashamed of their slander.

1 Peter 3:15, 16

Reflection

The Scripture urges us to give a reason for our faith. This means that as well as sharing our experience of God we should, if we can, point out why our belief in God accords with reason.

Antony Flew, for fifty years one of the world's most influential atheists, changed his mind in 2004, and wrote a book entitled *There is a God*[4]. He faced up to the fact that modern science spotlights three dimensions of nature that point to God. The first is that nature obeys laws; how did these laws come to be? The second is that there are intelligently organised and purpose-driven beings; how could they originate from non-life? The third is the existence of nature; how did it come into existence? He came to the conclusion that it is more unrealistic to account for these by chance alone than by God.

He quotes Professor Stephen Hawking: 'You still have the question: why does the universe bother to exist? If you like, you can define God to be the answer to that question.' He quotes Einstein: 'We see the universe marvellously arranged and obeying certain laws but only dimly understand these laws . . . A little child entering a huge library knows someone must have written these books. It does not know how . . . That, it seems to me, is the attitude of even the most intelligent human being toward God.' He quotes Charles Darwin: 'I feel compelled to look for a First Cause having an intelligent mind in some degree analogous to that of man; and I deserve to be called a Theist.' He quotes Paul Davies: 'Atheists claim that the laws (of nature) exist reasonlessly and that the universe is ultimately absurd. As a scientist I find this hard to accept. There must be an unchanging rational ground in which the logical, orderly nature of the universe is rooted.'

Flew became convinced that the laws of nature seem to have been crafted so as to move the universe towards the emergence and sustenance of life. If the speed of light or the mass of an electron had been the slightest degree different, then no planet capable of permitting the evolution of life could have formed.

Pause for thought

Which is more odd, for something to come from nothing or from God?

Prayer

Eternal Mind, thank you for the minds
that make sense of the world.
Eternal Beauty, thank you for the beauty
that puts soul into the world.
Eternal Life, thank you for the lives
that point beyond themselves.

Today's step

I step
away from mindless assumptions
towards Omnipotence.

Spiritual breathing exercise

God in.
Denial out.
God is.

NOVEMBER 8

Turn enemies into friends

Bible reading

From now on we look upon everyone in a new light. It is true that at first we even thought of Christ in the way one human regards another, but this has changed. For we now know that anyone who is 'in' Christ is a new creation. The old has faded away, the new has come. All this comes from God, who through Christ changed us from being enemies into friends of God, and has given us the ministry of turning enemies into friends. Through Christ God was reconciling people to himself, and not holding their sins against them. That is why we are ambassadors for Christ, God appealing to the world through us.

2 Corinthians 5:16–20

Reflection

Friends are a little bit of heaven here on earth.[5]

The first step in reaching out is to build friendship. We make friends genuinely, from the heart. If there is purity in our friendships, we value people for themselves, and not only if they respond as we wish. God offers friendship regardless of sins.

Research into workplace satisfaction reveals that people with at least three close friends at work were 96 per cent more likely to be extremely satisfied with their life. Without a good friend at work only one in twelve engage with their job. But do we dedicate time to developing friendships?

A friendship may begin when we look for a common spark and take an interest in another. It strengthens when we affirm that person. Companionship grows when we identify common interests and pursue these. It can grow when we notice something that our friend could usefully develop and encourage them in doing so. It is watered by our prayer. It is secure when we can have fun together, be silent in each other's company, and cease to strive.

Pause for thought

Contact another in order to be with them, without any other pretext.

Prayer

Eternal Friend,
we thank you for the countless people who,
through the human gift of friendship,
have turned in to your friends.
Renew in us the gift of friendship,
and draw many folk in to the circle of your love.

Today's step

I step
away from self-interest
towards friendship.

Spiritual breathing exercise

You in.
Me out.
We.

NOVEMBER 9

Reach out

Bible reading

Jesus had trudged a long way and was tired out. He reached Jacob's Well, in Samaria, and sat down for a rest. A woman came to draw water. Jesus asked her for a drink. The surprised woman said, 'Jews don't talk to Samaritans, let alone to a woman, so why do you talk to me?' Jesus replied, 'If you had realised who I am, *you* would have asked *me* for something to drink, and I would have given you living water.' 'Sir,' she replied, 'you have no container with which to draw water. So how could you give me a drink? Where do you get your living water?'

John 4:4–11

Reflection

Our ego's brittle shell often refuses to admit that we have a simple human need, or that we can ask another to meet that need. Then, because we have refused to speak out of our vulnerability, it is not possible to share something that comes from our true self, from God in the core of our being, that might have been life-giving to the other.

How may I reach out to a sour-faced person I merely pass in the street? With a wave? A smile? A comment on the weather or on a football match result? Or maybe by sharing some information about my own needs or travels?

How may I break the ice with someone who seems frozen? By asking, 'How are you?' and waiting long enough to learn the answer.

How may I reach out to someone who strongly disagrees with me? By taking them seriously.

How may I reach out to someone whose moral stance I disapprove of? By embracing them in love, and letting trust grow.

How may I reach out to people who disdain or ignore me? Try and get your head round the way they think. Look for an occasion when you may relate to something on their agenda, or ask them if there is some way you can support them.

Pause for thought

If you have a need, share it with someone who can meet it. As you practise doing this, sooner or later it will be appropriate to share with one of them something life-giving that flows from God in your heart.

Prayer

Impart to us imagination
to find the places in people where we may connect.
Give us the grace of self-acceptance,
that we may accept a gift from another.
Grace us with love that empowers us to share of ourselves.

Today's step

I step
away from the closed heart
towards a shared human exchange.

Spiritual breathing exercise

Sharing in.
Superiority out.
Life.

NOVEMBER 10

Build bridges

Bible reading

The Jewish Christians heard that non-Jews had received the gospel through Simon Peter. When Peter came to Jerusalem some of these criticised him for eating with people who had not been circumcised. Peter explained how in a vision God had told him not to dismiss as unclean anything that God had made clean on the inside, even if it was externally or ritually unclean. He also explained how an angel had told an uncircumcised man to visit the house where Simon Peter was staying, and the Holy Spirit had come upon him there. When they heard this, they had no further objections and praised God, saying that God had given even non-Jews the privilege of a life-giving change of heart.

Acts 11:1–18

Reflection

The Maori people of New Zealand welcome people to their country with a *hongi*. First, they touch noses to exchange the *ha*, which is the breath of life. Then they touch foreheads, to exchange their dreams and aspirations with each other. Finally, they link arms and stand face to face. What a way to make a connection!

We can emulate the spirit of the hongi, even though we may choose other ways to connect with people. Jesus laid his life down in order to be a bridge between human beings and God. We can be bridge builders, too, as was Peter when he shared a meal with uncircumcised believers.

> When you're weary, feeling small,
> when tears are in your eyes, I will dry them all;
> I'm on your side. When times get rough
> and friends just can't be found,

like a bridge over troubled water
I will lay me down.
Like a bridge over troubled water
I will lay me down.[6]

Pause for thought

What word or action can connect me to a distant person?

Prayer

When a person sails by with eyes all glazed,
may my eyes give them rays of love.
When a person passes, cold or hard,
may my heart melt them with welcoming warmth.

Today's step

I step
towards a person in need
away from self concern.

Spiritual breathing exercise

Welcoming in.
Disdain out.
Hongi.

NOVEMBER 11

Culture-friendly mission

Bible reading

Some visiting Jewish Christians told believers in Antioch that they could not be saved unless they adopted the Jewish custom of circumcision. Paul and Barnabas sharply opposed this teaching. So the Antioch Christians sent them to the Church leaders in Jerusalem to sort this matter out in a council. They reported how many non-Jewish people had converted to Christ. The Jerusalem believers rejoiced at this news. Peter said, 'God, who understands peoples' hearts, has shown that he accepts these believers by giving them the Holy Spirit, just as he did with us. He makes no distinction between us and them. Then why should we provoke God by placing such an added burden upon these disciples?'

Acts 15:1–10

Reflection

How may we reflect Jesus' way of spreading the faith? As Jesus put himself inside a human skin so we put ourselves within the culture we seek to reach and let Jesus emerge from within it. Too few Western missions have adopted this principle. Many have set up a headquarters and urged the locals to leave their culture and come into theirs. Bruce Olsen[7] provides a shining exception. He went to live among the Motilone Indians of Columbia. Before he arrived he met members of another Indian tribe which had been evangelised by missionaries. 'Those Christians don't care about us,' they told Bruce, 'they do not sing our songs or wear our dress, and their churches are not like our buildings.' So when Bruce reached the Motilones, he lived as they did, contracted their diseases, learned their language and legends, and used their name for him,

Bruchko. Instead of dispensing his medicines himself, and thus demeaning their medicine man, he befriended him, sang his chants and taught him to combine the medicines with his practices.

Bruce prayed, 'Jesus, become a Motilone.' He developed a deep friendship with the son of a tribal leader named Bobby. One day Bobby told him that he had met Jesus, and that 'Jesus walks our trail.' Bruce held back his desire to preach to every Motilone he met. At the annual Festival the people sang their chants for hours. Bobby sang chant after chant about Jesus. Soon, many were singing them. A spiritual revolution swept through this tribe.

Pause for thought

If Jesus went to the lengths of putting himself into our skin, why can't we put ourselves in others' shoes ?

Prayer

Word of God, rays from you light people of many beliefs.
May these rays lead us
to the places where we may sit, and eat
and be one with those who are different from us,
until you emerge in their clothes,
revealing a new facet of your never-ending glory.

Today's step

I step
away from my framework
into another framework.

Spiritual breathing exercise

Incarnating in.
Imposing out.
Jesus.

NOVEMBER 12

Connect with other spiritualities

Bible reading

Make no mistake about this, everything that is good is a gift from above, from the Father of all light. God does not equivocate just because good comes in different frameworks.
James 1:16, 17

Reflection

It is being said that the divine Birther is bringing into being expressions of good within spiritualities that have no connection with churches and seeks to entrust the oversight of these to Christ-centred people who have discernment. To respond to this call they need to move out of a purely church box. They need to learn the language, and not expect these spiritual people to adopt all the church language.

A Christian blogger publicised ten commandments for bloggers. A witch saw them and recognised how good they were. She decided to adopt them for her own blog site.

In John's Gospel Jesus says, 'I do as I see my Father do' and 'I have other flocks'. Do these other flocks embrace Arab and Bengali, Chinese and Dinka, Hindu, Muslim and pagan? How does Jesus' Father, who even in the period when the Christian scriptures were recorded reveals himself under many names and in many ways, reveal himself to these?[8]

'What our encounter with India and the East is teaching us is something we should never have forgotten – that the essential Christian experience is beyond the capacity of any cultural or intellectual form to express. This is "the glorious liberty of the children of God" . . . This experience has to be restored to the heart of the Church if she is to face creatively the challenges before her; the challenge of the renewal of the contemplative religious life, the challenge of finding unity in the spirit with all Christian communions, the challenge of embracing the non-Christian religions with the universal love of Christ present in the hearts of all people and which she has a special duty to release and identify. To meet these challenges each of us must be personally rooted in the experience of God that Jesus personally knows and shares with us through his Spirit.'[9]

Pause for thought

Try to spot the good in a new spirituality.

Prayer

Good God,
from you flows all goodness, all light.
Help me to discern goodness wherever it surfaces
and to make common cause with it
for you are the Father of light.

Today's step

I step
towards the good in another spirituality
away from double standards in my judgements.

Spiritual breathing exercise

Good gifts in.
Misconstruing out.
Light.

NOVEMBER 13

Inter-faith dialogue

Bible reading

Jethro was a pagan priest of Midian whose daughter Moses married when he was a refugee there. God revealed himself to Moses as Yahweh – I AM – and called Moses to return to Egypt, whence he had fled, and lead his oppressed people out of Egypt to freedom.

Jethro and Moses' family came to meet him during the people's trek through the desert to their promised land. Jethro and Moses warmly greeted one another, went into the tent, and Moses recounted how God had guided his people. Jethro was delighted at all Yahweh's goodness to Moses' people and said, 'Now I know that Yahweh is greater than all other gods.'

Exodus 18:1–11

Reflection

People of other religions fear that Christians want to turn them into what they are not, and Christians fear this of other religions. The true passion of every Christian should be that each person becomes who they truly are. We ourselves, however, are still on a journey of becoming who we really are, since so much false and ego-centric conditioning still has a hold. Therefore we can neither boast nor preach down – all we can do is to share our journey.

Rapport, mutual respect and attentive listening grew between the pagan Jethro and the monotheist Moses. It was within that dynamic that Jethro, who was a good and open person, came to acknowledge Yahweh without necessarily ditching all his inherited beliefs.

No person can become the self that God has created unless they know and are known by God as God truly is. Christians do indeed believe that the greatest insight into the nature of God given to the human race is the defenceless, unconditional love made manifest in Christ – but over and over again we are blind to the meaning of this love, and other peoples and religions have beautiful insights into God that will greatly bless us.

So our approach should be human friendship.

The Columba Community in Bradford consists of believers of different religions who come together to pray, but they do not pray together; each prays in their own way but alongside one another. Then they share readings, dialogue and food together.

Pause for thought

With which non-Christian may I develop rapport, respect and attentive listening?

Prayer

Yahweh, people call you by a hundred names,
but YOU ARE. Help me to be.
Out of the silence of a listening heart
may compassion and rapport with others grow.
Out of the sharing of our treasures
may others come to bless you
and may you have all the glory.

Today's step

I step
away from being holier than thou
towards being a grateful companion.

Spiritual breathing exercise

Empathy in.
Arrogance out.
Yahweh.

NOVEMBER 14

Relate well to Jews

Bible reading

Jesus told this story-with-a-truth to some Jews: A farmer had two sons both of whom he dearly loved. In his will he left half his assets to each. The younger son claimed his half now, so he could travel the world. He got into trouble, and ended up destitute. Eventually he overcame his pride, returned home, and begged to be allowed to work as a waged servant. His father spotted him afar. He prepared a big banquet, and killed the best calf to provide meat. The elder son was furious. 'I have stayed at home and worked loyally and yet you don't provide me with a banquet,' he complained. 'My dear son,' said the father, 'that is because I always have you with me.'

Luke 15:11–32

Reflection

Pope John Paul II invited Christians to look upon Jews as their elder brother. It is important to understand an elder brother. This elder brother believes that Jesus cannot have been their messiah because he failed, as was prophesied of the messiah, to overthrow the oppressor and restore a God-led state. He believes that Christians are anti-semitic. Thus the Gospels, written after the failed Jewish uprising and the fall of Jerusalem in AD66, blamed the Jews so that the Roman authorities would not persecute Christians along with Jews. He knows that the eleventh- to thirteenth-century Christian Crusaders used the emblem of the Cross (on which Jesus was killed by Jews) as a reason for their mass killing of Jews.

In view of this suspicion we dare not be glib. We might say, 'We are brothers and sisters – may we become friends?' Later, when we have shared meals, and trust has grown, we may explain what we believe:

That Jesus challenged his fellow Jews to live, not to discard, their faith.
That early Christians, notably the apostle Paul, loved their fellow Jews and we love Jews too.
That we understand the Messiah, not as less than foreseen by prophets, but as cosmic and therefore greater in his influence.
That the Church, officially, does not put the blame for Jesus' crucifixion on to the whole Jewish race – it teaches that good and bad runs through every people and person.
That we are sorry for the Crusades, and some have made reconciliation walks along the Crusade routes.

Pause for thought

May the humbling of our pride replace the pointing of our finger.

Prayer

Crucified Jesus, you lived and died a Jew
with love in your heart towards all.
Risen Christ, you appeared under open skies
to those who did not recognise you:
embrace your Jewish family in your heart of love
and may we do the same.

Today's step

I step
away from blame
towards brotherhood.

Spiritual breathing exercise

Brotherhood in.
Anti-semitism out.
Celebrate.

NOVEMBER 15

Relate well to Muslims

Bible reading

Take heed that you never make an idol . . . Know this and reflect deeply upon it: that the Lord is God in heaven above and earth below and there is no other god. Therefore you shall keep his commandments which I give you today that it may go well with you and your children's children.
Deuteronomy 4:15, 39, 40

Reflection

Muslims, Christians and Jews believe in one God and abhor idolatry. However, the Prophet Muhammed met Christians who seemed to him to worship three gods, the Father, Jesus and Mary. He urged people to avoid the blasphemy of worshipping a mere mortal as God. The actual teaching of the Church agrees that it is blasphemy to worship mere mortals as God. We may reach out to Muslims by saying sorry that Christians in the time of the Prophet Muhammed believed such a travesty of true religion. Is it helpful if the only message on a church noticeboard is 'Jesus is Lord' when passers-by think this refers to the human Jesus, not to the triune God? The Christian belief in the triune God is a way of saying that love is not just something that comes from God to people, communing is within the very Being of God.

A Muslim said to a Christian: 'When this age ends Christ will return and all of us, Muslims and Christians, will follow him together; why wait until then?' So they followed him together. The Christian said: 'We both worship one God; let us listen to God together.' So they listened to God together. A Christian family invited a lone Muslim student to share their hospitality at Christmas. The Muslim said: 'We believe that Christ was born of the virgin Mary and is the only human being who is without sin; I will therefore celebrate this birth with you.' A follower of Jesus said: 'To be a Muslim means to submit to God, and to pray facing east, without shoes, five times a day. I will be a Muslim and join a mosque; there my fellow Muslims, who are meeting Jesus in their dreams, will come to love Jesus as much as I do.'

Muslims believe that God has one hundred names, and has power to manifest the meaning of these names. Christians believe that such a manifestation could even go to the length of incarnation.

Pause for thought

Jesus challenged Jews to be better or true Jews. If he met Muslims how would he communicate to them? Let him do this through you.

Prayer

O my Lord, make my coming in true and honest
and my going out true and honest.
And from your presence grant me your enabling power.
For you are the Creator of all.
You are the One and the only, the all-competent.

Today's step

I step
away from idolatry
towards those who honour one God.

Spiritual breathing exercise

God in.
gods out.
Almighty.

NOVEMBER 16

Relate well to Buddhists

Bible reading

Put to death your earthly desires: impure thoughts, lust, greed – these are all idols. Rid yourself of such things as anger, malice, slander and foul language. Do not lie, since you have replaced your former self-centred life with the new self . . . Therefore clothe yourself with compassion, kindness, humility, gentleness and patience.

Colossians 3; 5 ,9, 12

Reflection

One of Buddha's teachings that chimes with Christ's teachings is that of 'divine abiding'. The four states of loving-kindness (metta), compassion (karuna), sympathetic joy in others (mudita) and equanimity (upekkha), are known in the New Testament as 'fruits of the Spirit'. Both the Buddha and Jesus challenge the suggestion that these are unrealistic; rather, they say, without these we will never be able to see this world for what it really is. So there is common ground between some Buddhist and Christian practices, and both agree that the holy life, the divine abiding, is not some exclusive practice reserved for monks and nuns, but the necessary basis for all our lives.

There are differences between Eastern forms of Buddhism and Western forms of Christianity which are essentially cultural, but there are also some deeper theological differences. To Buddhists, belief in a God is one of the attachments that a person must let go of in order to be truly free of desire – for desire is an illusion. A Buddhist is unlikely to receive wisdom from a Christian who does not daily practise letting go of false attachments. A Christian believes, however, that although many of our human desires are false and need to be transcended, the Creator and Ground of Being has planted within us an eternal desire for union with the Divine: 'our hearts are restless until they find their rest in you'.[10]

That does not mean that there is no meeting point. It could be said that Jesus had to journey into 'nothingness' when he cried out on the Cross 'my God, my God, why have you forsaken me?' With hindsight we know that there is resurrection and intimate relationship with a personal God. Yet how many Christians give the impression that we can get a cheap ticket to heaven that avoids the journey into unknowing? To such Christians, Buddhists offer a challenge.

Let us journey together, casting away false attachments, embracing the 'four states' – which Jesus calls 'the kingdom of God' – and then perhaps our Buddhist friends will also journey with us through the dark night into the resurrection.

Pause for thought

What attachments do I need to throw away?

Prayer

May I be mindful in my speaking and in my eating.
May I be peaceful in my sleeping and in my rising.
May I be noble in my acting and in my dying.

Today's step

I step
away from acquiring
towards abiding.

Spiritual breathing exercise

Kindness in.
Cravings out.
Bliss.

NOVEMBER 17

Relate well to Atheists

Bible reading

God says: Stop your empty religious rituals. I cannot bear them. When you spread out your hands in prayer I will hide my face, even if you offer endless prayers. This is what I want you to do: stop doing wrong and start doing right. Seek justice and encourage the oppressed.

Isaiah 1:13–17

Reflection

My friend Howard was a militant atheist and president of the Student Union of what is now City University, London. He criticised politicians for being dishonest and corrupt. However, he himself had altered the voting figures of a motion he wanted to see passed. Some Christians invited him to join them in changing the world by listening to God, or, if he could not believe in God, to his conscience. He agreed to undertake this experiment. The first step in changing the direction of his life was to be honest at the next Union meeting about what he had done and reverse the decision. For him that act was linked with a commitment to be part of building a better world. It was nothing to do with believing in God, yet it caused inner liberation. It was about being true to what deep in his heart he felt to be right. He writes: 'Other religious people might say that, although I didn't recognise it, God was speaking to me. But the point for me, and for those challenging me, was not to get hung up on doctrinal concepts. The crucial issue was to be obedient to that compulsion within. We can believe different things about where that comes from. But to me it is that compulsion which we need to focus on as the basis of building trust across the world's divides, including the divides of belief. Having now become a

Christian I can identify with what Marcus Borg writes in *The Heart of Christianity* about Jesus as, "the decisive revelation of God and what a full life of God is like". But I still very much respect the beliefs of others, and try to honour what is precious for them.'

A friend of mine is a minister whose husband is an atheist for a good reason. He believes in integrity, and thought arguments his child mentors gave for believing in God lacked integrity. He supports the good works of the church. The church sent a Christmas card addressed to 'our atheist saint'!

Pause for thought

Be true to what deep in your heart you feel to be right.

Prayer

May I make common cause with those who do right.
May I not make a fuss about where good comes from.
May I let God look after himself.

Today's step

I step
away from disputation
towards doing right with others.

Spiritual breathing exercise

Honesty in.
Religiosity out.
That's better.

NOVEMBER 18

Relate well to other Christians

Bible reading

Jesus said, 'I am the way, the truth, and the life. No one comes to the Father except through me. If you really knew me, you would know my Father, too. From now on you will both know him and have seen him.'

John 14:6, 7

Reflection

Perhaps you, or some Christian you don't know how to relate to, thinks to a greater or lesser extent as follows: 'Every person who has not declared Jesus as Lord is of the devil. The founder of their religion, if they have one, was deceived by the devil. Do not make friends with them. There must be no dialogue. Preach to them, and let them convert to Christ and join our church. This is what the Bible says.'

As a Bible student who seeks to understand the mind of the divine author, you might respond along these lines: First, to preach to someone with whom we have refused to make friends is the opposite of Jesus' approach. Second, God specifically revealed to a narrow-minded Christian that God accepts people from every background who honour him (Acts 10:35) and can speak to them. Third, Jesus never stated that the founder of any religion was of the devil. Fourth, Jesus did point out that certain strict members of his own religion *applied* it in an inauthentic, dishonest way, and that to do *this* is of the devil who is 'the father of lies' (John 8:42–47). He said this to people who refused to dialogue and listen attentively.

Is this twenty-first century brother or sister in danger of falling into this same trap? In today's Bible passage Jesus teaches that *all* people who come to God as Father are doing this through him (John 14:6). Jesus could not have been referring to himself merely as the human being, Jesus of Nazareth, who lived but one generation on earth. The fact that no one comes to the Father but through him applies to all places and times: Jesus here makes a statement about his divine self, as part of the triune God, whose eternal role as Son is to do this. He did this for Abraham, even before Abraham understood. He does it for people today, yet he never forces himself on anyone. No wonder so many Muslims and pagans are meeting Jesus in their dreams.

Pause for thought
Repent if you have distanced yourself from, demonised or failed to listen to someone from another faith.

Prayer
Triune God, Forgiving One,
we pray for those who do not yet know you as Father.
As we take a fatherly or motherly interest
in one another's faith journey,
and share nurturing experiences,
reveal yourself to us all.

Today's step
I step
away from judgement
towards discernment of God in another.

Spiritual breathing exercise
Dialogue in.
Damning out.
Forgiving One.

NOVEMBER 19

Say it with actions

Bible reading

Jesus told this story-with-a-truth: A traveller was mugged, robbed and left half dead by the roadside. A priest saw him but passed by on the other side; so did someone in charge of religious worship. But a foreigner, of a race despised by these Jews, took pity on the victim. He tenderly washed his wounds and bandaged him. He put the man on his own donkey, brought him to an inn and cared for him. The next day he paid the innkeeper to look after this man, and promised to reimburse him on his next visit if more was needed.

'Which of these travellers was the neighbour to the man who was mugged?' Jesus asked his hearers. 'The one who treated him with mercy,' said one of them. 'Now you act like this yourselves,' said Jesus.

Luke 10:30–37

Reflection

Before Francis of Assisi founded a community or was known as a saint he passed by a leper. He felt sorry for him and threw him a bag of money. But his heart smote him for although, outwardly, he had given something like the good Samaritan in Jesus' parable, inwardly he had passed by and kept his distance. We do not know if Francis then approached the leper and kissed him, or whether the leper, thrilled with the money and sensing Francis' love, embraced and kissed him. But it seems that Francis saw the face of Christ in the face of the leper, and gave himself, and not just his money, to this needy person.

The term 'Good Samaritan' has passed into the English language as a synonym of someone who helps a stranger in need, and has given its name to a thousand good causes.

The Samaritans organisation offers a listening ear to people with suicidal thoughts in many lands. In Australia Samaritans is a leading welfare agency. And in red-light areas of city centres projects to support prostitutes are given this name.

The Bible story and the story of St Francis tell us much about how we should reach out to others. Christ's way is not to treat them as recipients of our preaching or purse, it is to embrace them as a brother or sister.

Pause for thought

Who do you choose to embrace?

Prayer

Lord, sometimes I feel beaten and battered
like that man in the story,
and I ask you to fill more of your people with compassion
so that one of them will come alongside me.

Lord, each day, if you open my eyes,
I see someone in need:
a child on a bus, bullied or excluded,
someone at work, hurting or mistreated,
the stranger in the street –
teach me to be generous, to give and not to count the cost.

Today's step

I step
away from my interests
towards the person in need.

Spiritual breathing exercise

Care in.
Self-concern out.
Good Samaritan.

NOVEMBER 20

Speak out for the poor

Bible reading

Jesus began his public mission by returning to Nazareth, where he had been brought up, and to the synagogue, as was his custom. He was handed the scroll of Isaiah. He unwound it until he found this passage:

'The Spirit of the Lord is upon me, for he has anointed me to announce good news to the poor . . .'

When he had returned the scroll Jesus told them, 'These words are becoming a reality right now.'

Luke 4:16–21

Reflection

> Our mission also includes speaking out for the poor, the powerless, and those unjustly treated in our society, and to minister to and with them as God directs.[11]

> The very poor tell us over and over again that a person's greatest misfortune is not to be hungry or unable to read, not even to be without work. The greatest misfortune of all is to know that you count for nothing.[12]

The compassionate life is the life of downward mobility! In a society in which upward mobility is the norm, downward mobility is not only discouraged but even considered unwise, unhealthy and downright stupid . . .

My whole life I have been surrounded by well-meaning encouragement to 'go higher up', and the most used argument was 'you can do so much good there, for so many people'.

These voices calling me to upward mobility are completely absent from the gospel. Jesus says, 'Anyone who loves his life loses it; anyone who hates his life in this world will keep it for the eternal life' (John 12:25). Finally he says . . . 'anyone who wants to become great among you must be your servant, and anyone who wants to be first among you must be your slave, just as the Son of Man came not to be served but to serve, and to give his life as a ransom for many' (Matthew 20:25–28).

This is the way of downward mobility, the descending way of Jesus. It is the way towards the poor, the suffering, the marginal, the prisoners, the refugees, the lonely, the hungry, the dying, the refugees, the tortured, the homeless – toward all who ask for compassion. What do they have to offer? Not success, popularity or power, but the joy and peace of the children of God.[13]

Pause for thought

Open your heart to the poor. Open your heart to fresh possibility.

Prayer

All-Merciful One,
who holds the poor closely to your heart,
forgive those of us who have enough
for closing our hearts to the poor.
Forgive those of us who have nothing
for closing our hearts to the rich.
Show us how each person and each place
can receive their worth
in the name of the One who had nowhere to lay his head.

Today's step

I step
away from a closed heart
towards the poor.

Spiritual breathing exercise

Action in.
Indifference out.
Good news.

NOVEMBER 21

Fight poverty

Bible reading

The world can seem like a living hell. Victims are crushed. The crooks and the abusers get away with it. But you take notice, O God, you listen. With you, the victim picks up; the hearts of the hopeless beat again. Orphans get parents, the homeless get homes. The reign of terror is over, gang rule is ended.

Psalm 10:14–18

Reflection

William Temple[14] worked with R. H. Tawney and William Beveridge to create the world's first Welfare State, a term which he coined. They sought to banish in Britain the five giants of poverty, unemployment, squalor, ignorance and disease. Surely we must now try to banish these five giants from the world?

Although there has been huge progress, especially in the world's increasing number of democracies, a backwards trend has also been at work. Electorates are selfish, and vote for politicians who pander to their selfishness. Wars are the outcome of the accumulated selfishness of nations. The free market, left to itself, means that the weak go under. Democracy, without a sufficient number of electors who seek God's will, or the common good, cannot fashion the world that we aspire to. William Temple wrote 'There is no hope of establishing a more Christian social order except through the labour and sacrifice of those in whom the Spirit of Christ is active,' and that 'the first necessity for progress is more and better Christians taking full responsibility as citizens for the political, social and economic system under which they and their fellows live.'[15]

This can't just happen by rich people pouring money into a bottomless pit, it involves effort, relationships and the modelling of a new way of living. Each person can do something. Some have started co-operatives. These can cause a chain reaction. Successful business people give the profits that remain beyond what they need to projects that change poverty-inducing patterns.

We consciously need to break with the consumer mentality – the lust to have. To practise detachment from material goods. To put God before career – to create 'an economy of communion'.

Pause for thought

For what aspect of social progress do you take responsibility?

Prayer

We plead for your justice to fill all the lands
as the waters cover the sands.

We cry until our voices are sore.
We weep for the hungry and poor;
the children mistreated;
those broken by force;
and the maimed who can't finish their course.

We pray against cruelty, hatred and pain;
against pride and greed for gain.
We pray for the homeless and victims of war;
the strangers to love at the door.

Today's step

I step
away from 'anything goes'
towards responsibility.

Spiritual breathing exercise

Care in.
Neglect out.
Welfare.

NOVEMBER 22

God's economy

Bible reading

The All-powerful Controller of planets and seas says this:

You trample on the poor, you take their produce but deprive them of representation in fair-trade agreements; your finance is a form of bribery.

You may have built yourselves lavish villas and estates, but you won't live in them for long. Stop being so complacent. Your turn will come to be oppressed.

Amos 5:3, 8, 12, 11; 6:1, 14

Reflection

We all get our living from a globally organised economy. It is not good enough for a Christian to say, 'All I want is Jesus,' while refusing to apply Jesus' values to that economy.

Injustice lies at the heart of the international monetary system. The power to create the forms of money used in international trade and payment transfers (known as liquidity) lies exclusively in the hands of the rich countries. Their weighted votes in the International Monetary Fund (IMF) give them 'special drawing rights'. In this way the rich get richer and the poor get poorer.

Capitalism makes a profit for some, and improves the material well-being of many, by providing products that people need and can buy. Capitalism without ethical values, however, leaves the poorest stuck in their poverty, mistreats the earth for short-term gain, and does nothing to create love of God and people. A counter view is promoted by people such as Bill Gates, founder of Microsoft, called 'creative capitalism'. Its aim is to do good (often with a nudge from socially aware activists) and to make a profit at the same time. Gates cites the example of Bono, who persuaded large multinational corporations to sign up to a scheme to help tackle global poverty, and to donate a portion of their profits to fight AIDS. Gates invites everyone to answer this question: how can we spread the benefits of capitalism and the huge improvements in quality of life it can offer to people who have been left out?

Creative capitalism is a step forward from the 'profit regardless of its consequences' doctrine, but it is not enough. Rich countries may break down because, lacking soul and meaning, their peoples become addicts, their families, communities and infrastructures fragment. In God-centred capitalism each company works to meet real needs, relates to its staff as whole people, and invests in the well-being of the environment.

Pause for thought

Review your spending and any investments you may have. Are they ethical?

Prayer

God of the Economy – the whole created universe:
teach us to use money as a servant of the common good.
Teach us to use the market as a guide, not as a god.
Teach us to invest in what brings long-term well-being
to the planet and its people.
And teach us to combat the cheats dressed in sheep's clothing.

Today's step

I step
away from selling others short
towards honest investment.

Spiritual breathing exercise

Good money in.
Bad money out.
Shalom.

NOVEMBER 23

Work with good leaders

Bible reading

Leaders will arise who rule uprightly and who make sure everyone is fairly treated. Each such leader is like a shelter from the wind, a refuge from the storm, like streams on parched ground, or the cooling shadow a great rock casts over a heat-weary land.

Under such leaders the people's creativity will flow: open eyes and ears will be welcomed; driven, pressurised people will be encouraged to think things over; shy and withdrawn people will flower; selfish fat cats and celebrities will be seen for what they are.

Isaiah 32:1–5

Reflection

Celtic evangelists worked hand in hand with those in authority to bring regions and kingdoms under the rule of God, and to open doors to the gospel. We seek to dialogue and work with people of good will in places of authority and influence so that our lands may be led by God, and become healed lands of the glorious Trinity.[16]

The highest type of leader is one of whose existence the people are barely aware.
Next comes one whom they love and praise.
Next comes one whom they fear.
Next comes one whom they despise and defy.

The Sage is self-effacing and scanty of words, when his task is accomplished and things have been completed, all the people say 'We ourselves have achieved it!'[17]

In the best schools, and in the best hospitals, and in the best families, those who work in them, or grow up in them, do so being able to act from their hearts . . .

Government, and especially he or she who leads the government, must be the 'still, small voice in the wilderness'. Most importantly, he or she must be a centre of integrity: there to foster, care for, look out for, and nurture all the righteous endeavours of the people . . . Any kingship, presidency, and premiership is a sacrifice.[18]

Pause for thought

Who are the good leaders in your sphere? How can you work with them?

Prayer

May each land find its well-being in your will.
Give us that dynamic which calls out
and combines the moral and spiritual responsibility
of individuals for their immediate sphere of action.
We pray for an uprising of people
who give leadership free from the bondage of fear,
sorry for the blindness of the past,
rising above ambition,
flexible to the direction of your Spirit,
reaching out with generous hearts to neighbouring peoples.

Today's step

I step
away from 'doing my own thing'
towards partnership with good people.

Spiritual breathing exercise

Partnership in.
Disconnection out.
Healing the land.

NOVEMBER 24

Peacemakers

Bible reading

The disciples were gathered behind locked doors for fear of their persecutors. Jesus came and stood among them. 'Peace be with you,' he said, and showed them his scarred hands and side. He said to them again, 'Peace be with you. As the Father sent me, so I am sending you.'

2 John 20:19–21

Reflection

The most universal greeting among Jews, Christians and Muslims is 'Peace'. The Jews say 'Shalom' and the Arabs say 'Salem'. Why don't we use all three words as appropriate?

The Christian vision, grounded in both earth and heaven, is that as long as bullies stalk the earth, states need to protect themselves under the law. This is what Christians mean by 'the just war'. This, however, is but a military shield, that allows other, more far-reaching work to proceed. The most important work is to cure the causes of war and create a peace which is far more than a mere truce in hostilities. Some Christians, such as those who enlisted as monks and nuns, were not expected to take up arms, for they gave their lives in a greater struggle – to turn enemies into friends – God's friends and theirs. To harness the energies of the population to great and noble causes.

> Working for justice and peace costs. Some of the reasons for that cost are to do with us. If we are to make peace, we have to let go of fantasy and obsession and the longing for control. We must be poor in spirit.
>
> If we are to make peace our attitude to the world around us must not be aggressive and acquisitive.

We must be vulnerable and receptive. We have to be meek. If we are to make peace we must know the need of it.

We must let ourselves be hurt by war and violence, oppression and injustice. And we have to learn to mourn.

If we are to make peace, we must feel our own loss and deprivation. In a world of injustice we must be hungry and thirsty for justice.

No wonder then that those who make peace are to be called God's children. They do God-like things. They are caught up into the making of wholeness on earth.[19]

Pause for thought

How can you contribute to the foundations of peace in the world?

Prayer

Make me a channel of your peace.
Where there is hatred, let me bring your love;
where there is injury, your pardon, Lord;
and where there's doubt, true faith in you.[20]

Today's step

I step
away from aggression
towards the aggrieved.

Spiritual breathing exercise

Vulnerability in.
Bombast out.
Peace.

NOVEMBER 25

International well-being

Bible reading

You go on your diets and your detox courses, but this is what I really want from you: stop blaming people, treating them with contempt, and taking them to court. End the unjust conditions that are put upon so many. Throw off burdens such as debt, abuse and violence. Set the people free. Share what you have with those who need it; don't turn away from those who belong to your own human family. When you do things like this your light will shine out, your wounds will heal, creativity will flow and your society will be like a watered garden. Almighty God will be behind you to guide you and satisfy your needs. You could then become known as 'the Restorer of streets that are worth living in'.

Isaiah 58:6–11

Reflection

In a speech to the Irish Government in 1913 the economist John Maynard Keynes talked about the hideous waste of an economic system that could not recognise art or beauty. US politician Robert Kennedy dismissed the use of Gross National Product (GNP) to set our priorities because it 'does not allow for the health of our children, the quality of their education, or the joy of their play. It does not include the beauty of our poetry or the strength of our marriages, the intelligence of our public debate or the integrity of our public officials. It measures neither our wit nor our courage, neither our wisdom nor our learning . . . it measures everything, in short, except that which makes life worthwhile.'

Pause for thought

What ugly part of our common life can you exchange for something beautiful?

Prayer

Beauty for brokenness, hope for despair,
Lord, in the suffering, this is our prayer.
Bread for the children, justice, joy, peace,
sunrise to sunset your kingdom increase.

Shelter for fragile lives, cure for their ills,
work for the craftsfolk, trade for their skills.
Land for the dispossessed, rights for the weak,
voices to plead the cause of those who can't speak.

Refuge from cruel wars, havens from fear,
cities for sanctuary, freedoms to share.
Peace to the killing fields, scorched earth to green,
Christ for the bitterness, his Cross for the pain.

Rest for the ravaged earth, oceans and streams,
plundered and poisoned, our future, our dreams.
Lord, end our madness, carelessness, greed;
make us content with the things that we need.[21]

Today's step

I step
away from unquiet ways
towards resolution.

Spiritual breathing exercise

Beauty in.
Madness out.
Well-being.

NOVEMBER 26

Be inclusive *and* accountable

Bible reading

Jesus told people that unless they got things more right than the official moral custodians they would miss out on God's reality. He gave them an example. Their famous law-giver, Moses, had taught that anyone who committed murder would be brought to legal account. Jesus went further, he said that anyone who hated another, thereby committing murder in their heart, would also suffer the inevitable fallout. Therefore, he urged, if you harbour a grievance against another, put it right before you come to the altar.

Matthew 5:20–24

Reflection

Western democracies require citizens to be universal and inclusive. No one can be discriminated against on account of their morals, practices or beliefs so long as they do not lead to public disorder or harm another person against that person's will. An unintended result of this is that for many younger people accountability has flown out as universalism has flown in. If everyone is free to do what they like, to whom or for what are we accountable – to the latest sales-driven vendetta trumped up by a newspaper?

Each human being has a moral choice. Each choice we make has its effects. We reap what we sow. Jesus is clear that we need to be accountable, not only for murder (which remains in law a punishable offence) but also for the 'root' of murder, which starts in the heart.

A civilisation collapses when its citizens no longer feel accountable; so does a person. Jesus describes this collapse as ending up in the scrapyard. Even though no external court imposes a penalty on us, we experience the penalty of the scrapheap. Jesus asks us to be aware of this, and to voluntarily make ourselves accountable to our conscience, our neighbour and our God. Community can only be sustained where there is accountability.

Pause for thought

Before you next take the bread and wine of Holy Communion, say or write that you are sorry to any person you have estranged without good cause.

Prayer

Lord, let our memory provide no shelter
for grievance against another.
Lord, let our heart provide no harbour for hatred of another.
Lord, let our tongue be no accomplice
in the judgement of a brother.[22]

Today's step

I step
away from an 'anything goes' attitude
towards moral choice.

Spiritual breathing exercise

Conscience in.
Indifference out.
Touching point.

NOVEMBER 27

The good society

Bible reading

Every plant that my Father in heaven has not planted will be pulled up by the roots. Don't take your cue from those who think they are the only custodians of the public good. In fact they are the blind leading the blind.

Matthew 15:14

Reflection

Liberal societies are shaped by the philosophy of John Stuart Mill that individuals should be free to do as they please provided they don't harm anyone else. In the name of protecting individual liberty religions are increasingly marginalised and some of their activities are made illegal, because by their nature they seek to evangelise or uphold moral standards. The blind lead the blind.

If citizens do not connect with the Source of Good evil will triumph and eventually ride roughshod over the many. It is precisely because Christianity has insight into the seeds of harm and of good that its flourishing is essential to the good society. Each generation must struggle to build on the good and dismantle the bad.

> Now understand me well – it is provided in the essence of things that from any fruition of success, no matter what, shall come forth something to make a greater struggle necessary.[23]

We must struggle for schools where children learn to love and love to learn; where they play outdoors and grow a bond with father and mother.

We must engage in the struggle of law over chaos, justice over revenge. We must struggle to outmatch the short war of hard arms with the long war of human arms – building institutions, infrastructures, police forces of character.

The West African poet Ben Okri hailed the third millennium as 'a wonderful excuse for beginning a clearing out of the garbage in our histories and our consciousness . . . (and) to transcend our grim ancient fears.' People who have been divided begin to hear one another. Terrorism is disempowered.

Pause for thought

Visualise society as a garden. What are the good and what are the bad plants?

Prayer

Good God,
may we never forget
that the blessings of prosperity and peace
come from eternal vigilance
in the struggle against greed, neglect and injustice.

May our nations be freed from the bondage of fear,
rise above selfish ambition,
and become flexible to your direction.

May the qualities that make democracy function flourish:
homespun qualities of faithfulness, honesty and care.

Today's step

I step
away from what rots the roots of society
towards what nourishes the good society.

Spiritual breathing exercise

Good seeds in.
Harmful seeds out.
Flourish.

NOVEMBER 28

The fall and rise of nations

Bible reading

Daniel fasted, prayed and mourned for the state of the world. A vision was given to him of an awesome figure who reflected the divine majesty. This person helped him understand what would happen to nations. Darius the Mede, the ruler of the Persian Empire had resisted him for a period, but Michael, the spiritual Protector of Israel, helped him turn things round. Four more rulers would assume power in Persia. Greece would fight against one of them. The fourth ruler would amass vast wealth and power and break the power of Greece but eventually his own empire would break into pieces. There would be the rise and fall of other powers. Then Israel and even its temple would be destroyed. There would be widespread distress. But Michael would also rise up, as would righteous people who had died.

Daniel 10–12

Reflection

We have seen that Walter Wink developed a spiritual critique of political powers and a biblical interpretation of the powers of a place. Power is the will to be. Power takes external expression in institutions, buildings, governments and processes. Each of the powers also has an inner dynamic, an ethos, a soul. God calls us to unmask those powers that are idols and to expose the means they use to cause degradation. The unseen spiritual rulers, authorities and cosmic powers that the apostle Paul refers to in his letter to the Ephesians 6:12 include these.

God also calls us to redeem each power by naming the original, God-given organising energy for which the idols are false substitutes. Speak truth to power. Transform power into love. Harness the nation or the power to its deepest sources of inspiration.

Acts of forgiveness that rise up when the time is ripe can release a restoring power that corrects the distortion which a process of evil established between two people groups.

Pause for thought

What is your nation's guiding principle? How is it turned into a god?

Prayer

Arbiter of the nations,
we confess that the twin evils of power and greed
have often usurped your values and torn us apart.
Humble our proud pretensions
that we can sustain a good society without you.
Replace our military walls with sacred, hospitable space.
Move us to build cities of friendship
between races and religions.
Raise up a new generation of God-inspired leaders.
Give us a soul that honours you.

Today's step

I step
away from my country's false substitutes
towards its true calling.

Spiritual breathing exercise

God's country in.
False gods out.
Glory.

NOVEMBER 29

Sustainable civilisation

Bible reading

Happy the people whose God is the Eternal Source.
May our sons be like plants that grow up strong.
May our daughters be like pillars that grace a palace.
May our stores be filled with worthy goods.
May creatures and crops grow into well-being.
May our streets be free from clamour and crime.
Happy the people whose God is the Eternal Source.

Psalm 144

Reflection

> Societies that create artistic and intellectual wealth in their cities also create the storehouses of knowledge, identity and self-confidence that allow them to survive and rejuvenate after periods of conflict or destruction. Their cultural assets are deep and indomitable, their reserves of civilisational protein substantial.[24]

> If the roots of your arts are firmly planted in your own soil and that soil has anything to give you, you may still gain the whole world and not lose your own souls.[25]

> Fine art is that in which the hand, the head, and the heart of man go together.[26]

> When we build, let us think that we build for ever.[27]

Writing of the USA during the 2008 election of Barack Obama as its first non-white President, the poet Ben Okri wrote: 'Nations become what they are because of certain crossroad choices they have made . . . There are those who have always believed that a new social vision could unite people of all colours, all the tribes of the human story. But to see it happen now, in America of all places, must count as one of the most significant moments in social consciousness since Mandela came out of prison (in South Africa) and unified a nation.'[28]

Pause for thought

What cultural or spiritual storehouses are you helping to create or sustain?

Prayer

From the point of Light within the Mind of God,
let light stream forth into human minds.
Let Light descend on Earth.
From the point of Love within the Heart of God,
let love stream forth into human hearts.
From the centre which we call the human race
let the Plan of Love and Light work out
and may it seal the door where evil dwells.[29]

Today's step

I step
away from bleeding civilisation dry
towards building it.

Spiritual breathing exercise

Creating in.
Grasping out.
Civilisation.

NOVEMBER 30

A prejudice-free world

Bible reading

To show favouritism is not compatible with belief in our glorious Lord Jesus Christ – it is inglorious. If a millionaire celebrity comes into your meeting dressed to kill, followed by a shabby tramp, and you give the celebrity special treatment, you have displayed discrimination, which is actually evil . . .

If you love each person as yourself you do well. If you show prejudice, you are a lawbreaker – you break God's law.

James 2:1–3, 8, 9

Reflection

A black woman, Rev Rose Hudson-Wilkin, has faced both racial and gender prejudice. Even if we do not believe women should at present be ordained, we can learn from her attitude. She says, 'There's a group that thinks it's OK to have women cleaning and decorating the church but they must not stand up and represent Christ. When you hear people denying your very being, as a child of God, you are entitled to a righteous rage. But God is fantastic. It didn't stop me loving them and presenting the gospel each week even though I didn't like their behaviour. We are the Body of Christ, we stand before God as one: Jew and Gentile, slave and free, male and female.'[30]

At a United Nations meeting to combat racism certain spokespeople said that Zionism is a form of racism and that Israel is Zionist. Some of these critics then revealed themselves to be racists, too, by calling for all Israelis to be treated as rubbish to be swept away. Diplomats and ordinary citizens alike are called to say and do what builds trust.

Bad deeds must be confronted, but they are confronted because they are an affront to the nobility of the human person and to the ideal of a prejudice-free world. Every person is a royal soul. We see Christ in foe and stranger.

Pause for thought

Who do I pigeonhole – for that is another form of prejudice? Adapt the following prayer to your own country.

Prayer

Mysterious, stranger God,
never confined by culture, colour, class or creed,
meeting us anew in the mystery of the stranger,
becoming in Jesus both refugee and migrant,
thank you for newcomers,
settling bravely in Australia's remoteness,
forsaking familiar, families and friends,
for strangers' insecurity in a strange land.
Stranger God of the stranger,
ever welcoming excluded outsiders,
celebrating life's richness in difference and diversity,
may your Spirit still stir this cultural mix, Australia,
that we may continue to embrace the gift of new migrants,
including their skills, valuing their difference.
And in them, meeting you.[31]

Today's step

I step
away from ostracising
towards building trust.

Spiritual breathing exercise

Acceptance in.
Prejudice out.
God's child.

DECEMBER 1

Trailblazers for our time

Bible reading

Rise up! Shine out! The Eternal, Uncreated Splendour will dawn upon you. Even though dark clouds threaten the world, God's light will break through, and the nations and their leaders will be drawn to the Light. Look around you. Already young people are flocking towards the Light. When you see them all, your heart will thrill . . . Walls will be rebuilt. Gates will remain open.

Just as I was the Hero of your spiritual figurehead of old, so I will become your Hero today.

Isaiah 60:1–5, 16

Reflection

The poet and novelist Ben Okri suggests that the economic crisis that hit the world in 2008 reflects a crisis of our civilisation: 'Individualism has been raised almost to a religion, appearance made more important than substance. Success justifies greed, and greed justifies indifference to fellow human beings . . . We are all implicated . . . We are now at a crossroad . . . To whom do we turn for guidance? Writers are entertainers . . . The Church speaks with a broken voice. Politicians are more guided by polls than by vision. We have disembowelled our oracles . . . What is most missing in the landscape of our times is the sustaining power of myths that we can live by . . . Find the values that were so crucial to our civilisation, but were lost in the intoxication of its triumphs . . .'[1]

Why are Aidan and Hilda so important? Real, gritty, historical characters from a nation-shaping period, they embody the sustaining power of a myth that our time can live by. They are signs of universal values.

Aidan is a sign that an ordinary person can be used by God to do extraordinary things. He speaks to our thirst to know how the greatness locked in ourselves may be released. Aidan lays down his life for a foreign people – he shows us we may build fellowship between different peoples. Hilda is a sign that someone with money and power need not misuse these, but can give their lives for the common good. Together, Aidan and Hilda are the answer to racism, sexism, and triumphalism. They live the values we have explored in this book – holistic learning, a pilgrim way of life, balance, simplicity, creation-awareness, growth into wholeness, standing for the poor, a vision for the world.

Pause for thought

What do you think is most missing in the landscape of our times?

Prayer

Help us bring to birth a civilisation inspired by love
and the values of respect and freedom,
the values of Aidan and Hilda.
Help us clear out the power and greed
that have usurped these values and torn us apart.
Raise up a new generation of God-inspired leaders.
Restore fellowship between races and religions.
Inspired by trailblazers of the past,
make us trailblazers today.

Today's step

I step
away from our false society
towards sources that can inspire civilisation.

Spiritual breathing exercise

Inspiration in.
Wasteland out.
Light.

DECEMBER 2

Pass on the flame

Bible readings

While I was meditating my heart was hot within me and the fire burned. Then I spoke out.
Psalm 39:3

Jesus said, 'I have come to bring fire on earth.'
Luke 12:49

What looked like tongues of flame separated and touched each person. They were all filled with the Holy Spirit.
Acts 2:3, 4

Reflection

The name Aidan means 'flame'. Aidan was born in Ireland shortly before the seventh century began. When Saint Columba, whose monastic family Aidan was to join, died on June 9, 597, the night sky lit up like fire and people far away saw this sign. I have sometimes wondered whether Aidan received his name because he was born that night.

As a boy Aidan would have heard stories of Patrick, who spread the faith to many parts of Ireland only two generations before. Perhaps he heard with baited breath how Patrick, in a stroke of inspired genius, celebrated his first Easter on the Hill of Slane. This was in full view of the Hill of Tara where Ireland's high king, with all his druids, lit a large fire to proclaim the rebirth of the sun after winter's death. Every other fire had to be extinguished until it was re-lit from this fire. So when Patrick lit a fire in the name of the risen Christ, the future of Ireland was at stake. 'If that fire is not quenched today it will burn forever, and it will overcome all the fires of our religion,' the druids told the high king. Many are the legends of how God used nature's wonders to extinguish the pagan fire and to keep the new flame burning.

At a meeting of the Community of Aidan and Hilda in London a young artist walked in who knew nothing of Aidan or of the Community. After a session he asked if he could say something. 'I had a vivid picture,' he said, 'of people carrying a torch of flame and carrying these through London to all parts of the world.' Only then did he learn that our logo is based on the Lindisfarne sculpture of Aidan carrying the torch of flame – ready to pass it on to us, like the relay athletes who pass on the Olympic flame.

Pause for thought

A flame burns out impurities, warms people, kindles fires and can become a beacon. Fire is used to describe one of the qualities of God's holy presence. What does God want to kindle in your heart?

Prayer

Fire of God,
may the flame of the fire warm our hearts,
may the sparks among the stubble dance in our hearts,
may the glow of the fire shine in our hearts,
may the crackle of the fire set us all ablaze
for the Three of Uncreated Love.[2]

Today's step

I step
away from dampening ways
towards ways that fire us up.

Spiritual breathing exercise

Fire in.
Damp out.
Blaze.

DECEMBER 3

Spiritual mothers

Bible reading

Many women were at Jesus' crucifixion, looking on at a distance. These women had followed Jesus throughout his Galilee mission and provided for his needs. Among them were Mary Magdalene, Joanna, Mary the mother of James and Joseph, and the mother of the sons of Zebedee.

Several of these women went to his tomb and adorned it with spices. As Sunday dawned they saw a bright light and were told: 'Jesus is not here – come in and see the empty tomb; he has risen from the dead. Go and tell the disciples to go to Galilee where Jesus will meet them. Do not be afraid.' Then they recalled all Jesus' words, ran with great fear and joy and passed on this message to everybody.

Matthew 27:55; 28:1–7; Luke 24:10

Reflection

The Ireland in which Aidan grew up valued the role of women. The parents of a boy like Aidan often entrusted him, at the age of seven, to the periodic care of a foster mother, who would be wise in both practical and spiritual matters.

Rumour had it that Aidan's father was Lugar, and was related to Saint Brigid of Kildare. Brigid has been described as the spiritual midwife who, following the labours of Saint Patrick, brought Christian Ireland to birth. It is feasible that Aidan's family visited Kildare. Who knows whether stories of Brigid that have come down to us were also told to Aidan? How she laid a spare place at the table in case Christ came in the guise of a stranger. How as a girl she was so keen to pray without ceasing that she lay down to sleep with her arms stretched out in the shape of a cross. How she developed a large faith community for men and women, and appointed Bishop Conleath to care for the men under her authority. How her network of faith communities replaced the military forts as the land's foremost guardian places.

Ireland was the first country outside the Roman Empire to become Christian and an idea was growing in the Irish imagination. Jesus not only had twelve male apostles, but also twelve spiritual foster mothers, like those who were the first witnesses of his resurrection. Each generation and each country needed the same. I think it likely that in his later mission Aidan came to realise that the brazen Anglo-Saxons would never be deeply converted unless they, too, had their spiritual foster mothers.

Pause for thought

What does this say to us?

Prayer

Great God who mothers us all,
develop among us those who will:
cradle the wee ones
and free the older ones to leave childish attachments
and face the world with love;
kindle the desire for holy living;
teach us to drink deeply from the wells of wisdom;
nurture a nation and shape it for God.

Today's step

I step
away from sexism
towards sensitivity.

Spiritual breathing exercise

Nurture in.
Bragging out.
Wisdom.

DECEMBER 4

Holistic learning

Bible reading

After the emperor of Babylon had conquered Jerusalem he ordered that the finest young men be brought to his palace to work for him there. These young men were physically strong and good-looking. They were also versed in every branch of wisdom, endowed with knowledge and insight, and competent to serve in practical matters. There they also learned the Babylonian language and literature.

One of these, Daniel, asked permission to keep to his disciplined diet and to refuse the foods and wines of the court that his religion forbade. He was allowed a ten-day trial. At the end of this he was in better condition than the others. Daniel also continued to pray three times each day, kneeling at his window to face Jerusalem in full view of others.

Daniel 1:1–16; 6:10

Reflection

It was said that Aidan's family lived near the river Shannon, the river which nurtures half of Ireland. Since he would later link up with the family of monasteries founded by Columba, whose clans came from the north, it seems likely that Aidan lived on the northern side of the Shannon, and would have joined one of several Columban monasteries that were within reach of his home. The largest of these, about which we know most, was at Durrow.

A monk's education at Durrow was what we call holistic. Columba, who like Daniel, was of fine stature and royal blood, forbade them to axe the sacred oak trees when they first built it. Its abbot Laisren at one time worked the monks too hard. On Columba's advice they learned to have periods of relaxation. The monks did building as well as intellectual and spiritual work. Once Columba, far away on Iona, saw a monk fall from the roof of a new house they were building, and commanded an angel to save him. In the kitchens they fed hundreds of hungry people. Durrow had a reputation for high-quality gospel manuscripts, using materials brought on ships from the Mediterranean. It was multicultural, and welcomed students from all sorts of countries, including one Northumbrian prince in exile.

The Burgundian Library in Brussels has a Rule of Life attributed to St Columba which, though probably of a later date, may reflect something of the spirit at the Columban monasteries. Two of its rules are:

> Three labours in the day – prayers, work, and reading.
>
> Forgiveness from the heart towards everyone.

This is about rhythm, roots and relationships. This is holistic learning.

Pause for thought

How can you sustain a good body-mind-spirit balance?

Prayer

Lord, when we cry out to you,
you bring us comfort and rest.
Be with us in all areas of our lives,
so we may labour with an easy heart.

Today's step

I step
away from one-sided living
towards the holistic.

Spiritual breathing exercise

Wholeness in.
Imbalance out.
Balance.

DECEMBER 5

Discretion

Bible reading

One person with wisdom has more influence than ten rulers.

I once came across this example of wisdom that greatly impressed me. A powerful ruler came against a village, and laid siege to it. A poor but wise man lived in that village, and saved it by his discretion. Nobody remembered that poor man, so I composed this saying: 'Wisdom is better than strength.'

Ecclesiastes 7:19; 9:13–16

Reflection

A Bishop Aidan was sent to oversee the hermits on the holy island in the mouth of the River Shannon which is known to the English as Scattery Island. O'Hanlon's *Lives of the Irish Saints* assumes this was our Aidan.

Senan established a village of God there about fifty years before Aidan arrived. It was said this fulfilled a prophecy of Saint Patrick that this feared and uninhabited isle would become the place of resurrection of a holy man. As a farming youth Senan's herd was stranded south of the Shannon after the tide had risen. The owner of a fort refused him shelter. God led him and his herd safely across the Shannon. Then and there he confronted a feared monster by marking the sign of the cross in its face, stuck his spear into the ground and dedicated this place to God.

Senan had courage, but he was stubborn and perhaps became possessive of his island, for we know that he refused to let any woman on to it. If the ethos fifty years later reflected those flaws, Aidan would have needed all the discretion which the historian Bede was later to extol in him.

In a time of prayer visualisation I imagined that when Aidan came to Senan's Isle he at first learned the brothers' story and imposed no new rules; that he slept in a disused cell, and himself repaired its neighbouring cell for use by guests. I imagined that gradually Aidan enabled the brothers to harmonise the work, listen to God, develop observation and discover the wider world as visitors came into the harbour.

Pause for thought

What situation most calls for your discretion? How might you use it?

Prayer

Divine Father, help us to affirm the good in others.
Divine Friend, help us to reach out warmly to others.
Divine Spirit, help us to connect well with others
across the shores that separate.

Today's step

I step
away from aloofness
towards accompaniment.

Spiritual breathing exercise

Discretion in.
Disregard out.
Flower.

DECEMBER 6

Iona – a lifetime's lessons

Bible reading

On the day that God delivered David from destruction at the hands of King Saul he composed and sang this song:

God is my rock and my fortress. Death stared me in the face, but I called upon the Lord. He sent angels. He sent arrows and scattered the enemy. He delivered me from those who were too powerful for me. You deliver a humble people. You are a shield for all who take refuge in you.

2 Samuel 22

Reflection

At some point Aidan was transferred to the monastery on the Isle of Iona. The Irish had colonised parts of northern Britain, including the area known today as Argyll and the Isles. Columba, who could perhaps have become high king if he had not become a monk, left his beloved Ireland, according to one story, as a penance for the three thousand lives lost in a battle between his and another clan, and in order to win the same number of people to Christ in a foreign land. His cousin was king of the Irish colony, and offered him Iona as his mother house. Columba agreed to settle there only if he could not see Ireland, for if he could, his heart would be torn between the two places. The Hill of Never Looking Back marks the highest point that confirmed that Columba could not see Ireland. No doubt Aidan, who arrived one generation after Columba's death in 597, climbed this, as do modern pilgrims, and assimilated this lesson: one cannot serve two bosses – one must be ready to lay down one's life unconditionally for another people.

Aidan would also have spent times on the little Hill of Angels where Columba communed with angels. On one occasion, as weary monks returned from work they experienced a fragrant scent as they passed that place. Their abbot said God was encouraging them by making them aware of the presence of their founder. Awareness of angels and of the prayers of holy forebears in their place of resurrection surely accompanied Aidan through the rest of his life.

Aidan would also have prayed in the hermits's cell where Columba engaged in spiritual warfare for a whole day, against what seemed like endless black darts at the end of which he announced to the brothers that plague would ravage the region, but that as a result of that day's warfare it would bypass Iona. Aidan understood spiritual warfare.

Pause for thought

Think about these three lifetime's lessons and apply them to your own situation.

Prayer

Break the ties that bind me to my past –
free me to go wherever you direct.
Bless the tiredness that blinds me to your presence –
grace me with the scents of the company of heaven.
Burden me with the evils that would ravage your children –
spur me to struggle until the tide is turned.

Today's step

I step
away from nostalgia
towards grace.

Spiritual breathing exercise

Faith in.
Fetters out.
Breakthrough.

DECEMBER 7

Forging strategic friendships

Bible reading

God endow the king with fairness in his actions, and his son with your righteousness. May he rule the people with justice and do right by the poor. May he rescue the children of the needy and send the oppressor packing. May he live on through the generations as the sun and the moon still shine. May he reign like gentle rain on mown grass, like showers that refresh the land. In his days may uprightness flourish, and his rule stretch from sea to sea.

Psalm 72:1–6

Reflection

Aidan and his brothers had close links with the rulers of their Irish colony of Dalriada and frequented the royal garrison at Dunadd by boat. On Dunadd's Rock Columba had installed the first king on British soil to be anointed in Christ's name and had chosen him as a result of divine guidance. That king, who became a monk, delegated much authority to his son Arthur, who won many battles between the two Roman walls. Hidden in the mists of this scantily recorded history lies a golden key – the faith, flair and friendships that drew into alliance groups from four previously warring peoples – the Picts, the Irish Scots, the native Britons and, in Aidan's time, the invading Anglo-Saxons, the English.

For after the king of Northumbria (the largest English kingdom) was slain, his family sought refuge in this Irish colony and embraced their faith. The four children who came were called etherlings, and were entitled for two generations to claim the Northumbrian throne. The King of Dalriada offered them fosterage – the king's son became their foster brother – and they were bound in covenant to defend one another. Their victories on behalf of the Irish helped them establish their reputation back in Northumbria.

Scholars assume that Aidan became a trusted friend, especially of Oswald. Oswald became a fine horseman, a consummate diplomat and a devout Christian. When the tyrant who had usurped their father's throne was killed, Oswald's older brother rushed back to seize the throne, but was himself killed. Oswald took an elite group of warriors from Dunadd. The night before the decisive battle he and his men knelt in prayer. He dreamed that Columba promised him victory, for it was a just cause. They won, against the odds. Oswald planted a cross in that field of battle and named it Heaven's Field. Back on Iona, Aidan and his brothers prayed and waited to hear the news.

Pause for thought

Did the inspired forging of fellowship between previously hostile peoples stir something deep in Aidan's soul? What does it say to you?

Prayer

High King of heaven and earth,
may the diverse authorities of our times,
acknowledge you as the Source of our common life,
emulate you as the Servant King,
and build trust and gratitude among their neighbours.

Today's step

I step
away from headstrong ways
towards the fellowship of service.

Spiritual breathing exercise

Perceptive friendship in.
Power games out.
Fellowship.

DECEMBER 8

Here am I, send me

Bible reading

In a vision I saw the Lord high on a throne, his trailing robes spread over the temple floor. Angels hovered around him, calling to one another, 'Holy, holy, holy is the Lord who commands infinite forces and whose splendour fills the entire earth.' The very foundations shook. I cried, 'I am unclean and live among an unclean people.' An angel then touched my lips with a burning fire and said, 'Now you are forgiven.' A voice said, 'Whom shall I send? Who will go for us?' I replied, 'I will go. Send me.'

Isaiah 6:1–8

Reflection

When Oswald came to the throne of Northumbria he asked the Irish leaders at Iona to send a mission team to introduce his pagan people to Christianity.

Under a previous king an Italian monk from the mission that Rome's Pope Gregory had sent to Kent had preached to and baptised those whom the king had summoned to royal centres, but when that king was killed they went back to their pagan gods. The first mission from Iona also failed. Its leader, Corman, a man of stern temperament, stayed for some time, but the people were unwilling to listen to him, and he returned to Iona.

At a post-mortem meeting of the Iona community Corman laid the blame on the Northumbrian people who, he said, were stubborn and uncivilised. The leaders discussed this matter for a long time, for this was the biggest missionary opportunity any Irish mission had been offered.

Aidan, who was present, said directly to Corman: 'It seems to me, brother, that you have been unduly severe with your ignorant hearers. You should have followed the guidance of the apostle Paul and offered them the milk of simpler teaching until, as they gradually grew strong in God's Word, they were able to take in a fuller statement of doctrine and carry out the higher commands.' As Aidan spoke, everyone turned and looked at him, and they carefully considered his words. The meeting finally resolved that Aidan should be sent to lead a second mission, because he had shown the gift of discretion, which is the mother of all virtues. So they consecrated him a bishop and Aidan said 'Yes' to the call.

Pause for thought

To what is God calling you?

Prayer

Here am I Lord,
I have heard you calling in the night.
I will go Lord,
where you lead me.
I will hold your people in my heart.[3]

Today's step

I step
away from armchair advice
towards the call.

Spiritual breathing exercise

Practising in.
Pontificating out.
The call.

DECEMBER 9

Aidan's manhood and mission

Bible reading

Here is my servant, my chosen one, in whom I delight. I have placed my spirit upon him. He will bring right judgement to the nations. He is not loud, he does not shout at people in the streets. He does not break a crushed reed or snuff out a faltering candlewick. He represents people faithfully. He is not a faint-heart. He will not cave in until he has established fair treatment on the earth. Coasts and isles are waiting for his guidance.

Isaiah 42:1–4

Reflection

There is a crisis in manhood today. As boys become men, hormones surge. Until recent times, these urges would impel men to hunt for food, battle against predator tribes, and take a woman who would provide children and a home. In today's spoon-fed, equal-rights society, what do men do with these undiminished urges? In circles where 'to be Christian' means 'to be nice' is a man's only option to neuter himself?

Aidan is a symbol of another option. Missionaries and monks in his day were often pioneers. Many came from the warrior class. As children their sports might have been running, wrestling and horse jousting; they would have learned to fish, skin animals and do hard physical labour. Those who became monks often continued to dig, fish, skin seals. They usually ceased to kill in battle, but they lived in such a way that they were thought of as soldiers of Christ. They remained warriors, but on a higher plane.

Aidan, who always lived near river and sea, was most likely a sailor, a horse-rider and a hiker. His childhood friends who chose to become warriors refused the challenge to face their inner demons. These they repressed, and in their blind rage brutally attacked their enemies. Those who, like Aidan, chose the course of fuller manhood, faced up to inner demons, learned to say no, to decide, to risk, and supremely to conquer fear and transform enmity.

Aidan was not only willing to embark on a hazardous journey by sea and foot into an unknown territory, he was willing to follow up a failed mission – to heroically attempt something against the odds – to change the barbaric English colonists.

Pause for thought

The Aidans of every age harness their manhood to heroic endeavour that requires every fibre of their body, mind and soul. Whether you are male or female, how does this challenge you?

Prayer

Heroic Love,
help me in my vulnerability
not to retreat, close up or pretend,
but to think clearly, act decisively,
confront lovingly, and go wherever you send.

Today's step

I step
away from prevarication
towards right decision.

Spiritual breathing exercise

'I'll go' in.
'No-go' out.
Sent.

DECEMBER 10

Colony of heaven

Bible reading

The believers were one in heart and mind. No one claimed that any of their possessions were their own; they shared all they had. The apostles witnessed to the resurrection of Christ with grace and authority. There were no needy persons among them. Sometimes wealthy people sold some land and gave the proceeds to the apostles to distribute to anyone who had need.

Acts 4:32–34

Reflection

Two ways to spread Christianity vie for supremacy. The first way is to make the Church the world's most powerful organisation – its buildings and its clergy the most grand. That approach had been tried in Northumbria by Paulinus, the bishop from the Italian mission whom a former king's bride had brought with her from Kent. It was the top-down approach. It seems Paulinus never went outside the royal centres. The people were commanded to come, were baptised, but when the king was slain they returned to their pagan gods. The second way, which Aidan introduced, was to live the message and model God's kingdom. It was the bottom-up approach.

Aidan taught his faith-sharing teams to memorise and meditate upon the Bible as they walked the tracks to a village. At least one of the team would carry a copy of the Gospels or the Psalms. He chose the tidal island of Lindisfarne, a few miles from the king's headquarters at Bamburgh, to build, very simply, a village of God. Monks lived in wooden huts clustered around the place of prayer. There they chanted the psalms and prayed five or more times each day. They established the first recorded school for English boys. They built a refectory and huts for guests, a scriptorium and library, cultivated crops, livestock and fishing. It was a colony of heaven.

The king, who rose early every day to pray, humbly followed Aidan's advice and at first acted as his translator. The initial team of twelve monks was soon joined by many more who flocked over from Dalriada and Ireland. Aidan taught these clergy many lessons about Christian lifestyle, but above all he modelled for them an example of simplicity and self-control. The best recommendation of his teaching was that way of life which he himself practised. He neither sought nor cared for worldly possessions, but delighted to hand over donations to any poor person he met.

Pause for thought

What corporate models of God's kingdom do you know of or strive to establish?

Prayer

May our faith communities be true to their birthright.
May they be places of prayer and hospitality,
living and learning, work and celebration;
the fire of Christ in their midst
drawing people to you.

Today's step

I step
away from imperious ways
towards Christ-like ways.

Spiritual breathing exercise

Your kingdom in.
Triumphalism out.
God's place.

DECEMBER 11

An authentic life

Bible reading

Since overseers are entrusted with God's work they should be blameless – not overbearing, hot-tempered or heavy drinkers; they should not pursue dishonest gain or be violent. Rather, they should be hospitable, lovers of good, self-controlled, holy and disciplined. They must live by the message they have been taught and which they can trust, so that they can encourage others by their sound teaching.

Titus 1:7–9

Reflection

In those days poor people would travel by foot, and the influential by horse. Aidan, however, insisted on travelling by foot in country as well as town, unless some urgent necessity forced him to do otherwise. So wherever he walked he was able to catch sight of people, rich or poor, and talk to them straightaway. If they were not Christians he would invite them to accept the mystery of the faith; if they already believed he would strengthen their faith and encourage them by his words and example in the practice of Christian giving and words of mercy.

It was the lovability of Aidan's missionaries which won the hearts of the people to Christ: when anyone met such a monk or priest on the road they ran to him and bowed, eager to be signed by his hand or receive a blessing from his lips. Whenever he spoke he was given an attentive hearing. When a priest visited a village, the people were quick to gather in some cottage to hear the word of life, for priests and clerics always came to a village solely to preach, baptise, visit the sick and, in short, to care for the souls of its people.

His teaching won the hearts of everyone because he and his followers lived out what he taught. He neither sought nor cared for the possessions of this world, and he loved to give away to the poor the gifts he received from the rich.

Bede, the monk historian from whom we know about Aidan in Northumbria writes: 'I have described . . . his love of peace and charity, temperance and humility; his soul which triumphed over anger and greed, and at the same time despised pride and vainglory . . . and his tenderness in comforting the weak, in relieving and protecting the poor.'

Pause for thought

What do you neither seek nor care for, and what do you love to give away?

Prayer

May your tender love burn inside me
and impel me on the road
to seek for Christ in the stranger's face
or, sensing his absence, introduce his presence.

Today's step

I step
away from my high horse
towards Christ in the person I meet.

Spiritual breathing exercise

Tender ways in.
Haughty ways out.
Christ.

DECEMBER 12

Speak truth to power

Bible reading

Jesus said to some leaders, 'It's a terrible lookout for you. You spend all your energy enforcing the letter of the law, but you neglect the important things such as acting honestly, dealing justly, and showing even a bit of tender loving care. You blind guardians of the public good: you make a fuss over a gnat and you swallow a camel. Inside you are full of greed and self-indulgence. First clean yourself up, from the inside.'

Matthew 23:23–26

Reflection

Neither fear nor favour made Aidan keep quiet about the sins of the rich and powerful; he would sternly correct them to their face if they did wrong, though, as far as we know, he maintained a relationship with them. He never gave money in order to buy influence.

> A Church that doesn't provoke any crisis,
> a gospel that doesn't unsettle,
> a word of God that doesn't get under anyone's skin,
> a word of God that doesn't touch the real sin
> of the society around it,
> what gospel is that?
> Very nice, pious considerations
> that don't bother anyone;
> that's the way many would like preaching to be.
> Yet does such a gospel light the world we live in?
> The gospel of Christ is courageous;
> it is the 'good news' of him who came to transform
> and take away the world's sins.[4]

> When Hitler attacked the Jews I was not a Jew, therefore, I was not concerned. And when Hitler attacked the Catholics, I was not a Catholic, and therefore, I was not concerned. And when Hitler attacked the unions and the industrialists, I was not a member of the unions and I was not concerned. Then, Hitler attacked me and the Protestant Church – and there was nobody left to be concerned.[5]

Pause for thought

When somebody you know habitually manipulates others in order to get their way, do you find the right way to confront them in love?

Prayer

We pray against the Pharisee tendency in our society.
We pray for:
the financial moguls who give a bit to charity
but milk the most vulnerable dry;
the media moguls who run down struggling public servants
and destroy rivals without a blink;
celebrities who smile nicely on camera
and abuse others the rest of the day and night.

Give us clarity about what is right
and courage to confront what is wrong.
May we do this in such a way that they know we care for them
and not just for those they abuse.

Today's step

I step
away from collusion
towards necessary confrontation.

Spiritual breathing exercise

Challenge in.
Cowardice out.
Resolve.

DECEMBER 13

Sharing our goods

Bible reading

Jesus said that God is like a king who summons all his subjects to appraise their actions. He placed the good on his right and the bad on his left. To those on his right he said: 'You are blest. Come in and inherit the kingdom my father has prepared for you, because when I was hungry you fed me, when I was thirsty you gave me drinks, when I had nowhere to stay you took me in, when I was sick you visited me, and when I was threadbare you bought me clothes.' They said, 'Sir, when did we see you like that?' The king replied, 'You did these things to me when you did them to my subjects, for actually they are my brothers and sisters.'

Matthew 25:31–40

Reflection

Bede records that under the young and saintly King Oswald, instructed by the wise Bishop Aidan, the kingdom of Northumbria expanded in all directions. It became by far the largest kingdom, and British, Pictish, Irish and English races were welded into one fellowship in Christ. Even Northumbria's previously warring sub-kingdoms of Deira and Bernicia were peacefully united.

Power did not corrupt Oswald. He was probably the first Saxon king to appoint an officer for the needs of the poor, as the following story illustrates.

One Easter he and Aidan sat at an Easter Day banquet at Bamburgh. A silver dish full of rich foods was placed before them. They were just about to bless the meal when the king's officer for the poor informed them that a crowd of needy people were begging outside.

Oswald at once ordered that the food set in front of them be taken to the poor. Then he ordered that the silver plate should be cut up into pieces and these also be distributed to them.

Aidan was so thrilled to see this Christ-like act that he grasped the king's right hand and said, 'May this hand never decay.'

This proved to be prophetic. For when Oswald was killed in battle his arm was cut off and brought back to the royal city where it was preserved in the local church. It is believed that Oswald's action was the origin of the custom, that still survives, whereby each year in an English cathedral the Sovereign gives a specially minted silver coin to ordinary people who have used their time to meet needs of local people.

Pause for thought

Why not ask God to give you a heart for the needy as they present themselves to you?

Prayer

I raise my hands and bless the hungry and the poor.
I lay these hands to tend the hurting and the sore.
I stretch out these hands to welcome the stranger at the door.

Today's step

I step
away from self-serving
towards the person in need.

Spiritual breathing exercise

Giving in.
Greed out.
Blessing.

DECEMBER 14

Freeing the slaves

Bible reading

If you are a landowner and someone sells you a slave to work for you, remember that after six years' service you must let that slave go free. More than that, provide for him generously from your livestock in order to give him a good start, for that is how God treats you. Always remember that you were once slaves in the land of Egypt and that your Eternal God rescued you.

Deuteronomy 15:12–15

Reflection

Aidan used money rich people gave him to visit the slave market and buy the freedom of those who had been unjustly sold as slaves. No doubt many of these became disciples. And perhaps some of them, after training and instruction, became monks or priests.

It is possible he had heard a famous saying of Gregory, Bishop of Rome. On seeing English boys (Angles) waiting to be sold in Rome's slave market he said: 'Not Angles, but angels,' and perhaps their plight ignited the compassion that led him to send a mission to the English.

Aidan modelled the message his mission brought. According to the historian Bede, Aidan's life was in great contrast to the lukewarm ways of the clergy of Bede's time. Everyone who joined his mission teams had to engage in some form of study, such as reading the scriptures or memorising the psalms. This was the daily task of Aidan and his teams, wherever they went. If, as sometimes happened, he was summoned to dine with the king at the royal headquarters, he ate sparingly and left quickly to study or pray with his team. Some Christians were so fired up by his example that they, following his example, fasted from foods during daylight on Wednesdays and Fridays throughout the year, except during the Easter to Pentecost celebrations.

It is said that William Wilberforce[6] invited influential people to his home in Clapham and gave them a good bowl of soup. As they finished savouring the ingredients brought, perhaps, by ship, each saw the words 'Abolish slavery' engraved on the bottom of the soup dish.

Pause for thought

Do you know who are slaves today? In your own area, who are the most unjustly treated? What can you do about this?

Prayer

We pray for an end to the injustices
which become breeding grounds of war.
We pray for the restoration of fellowship
and the building of integrity.
We pray for commitment
to the unending struggle against selfish ways
and violation of human dignity.
We pray for that peace
which is the full blossoming of our life together.

Today's step

I step
away from collusion
towards remedy.

Spiritual breathing exercise

Responsibility in.
Resignation out.
Freedom!

DECEMBER 15

Pour oil on troubled waters

Bible reading

When evening came Jesus urged his disciples to go to the other side of the lake. They took Jesus with them in the boat, just as he was, sitting there alongside other boats. A storm of hurricane proportions arose. Waves swept over the boat until it was almost filled with water. Jesus, however, was in the back of the boat, sound asleep! They woke him up and said, 'Master, don't you care that we are about to perish?' Jesus stood up, rebuked the wind, and spoke to the sea, 'Quieten down.' The wind came to a standstill; immediately there was a great calm. Jesus said to them, 'Why do you panic? Why is it you do not trust?' And they were filled with awe.

Mark 4:35–41

Reflection

Oswald was killed in battle and died with this prayer for his warriors: 'May God have mercy on their souls.' Following his death the two halves of Northumbria re-asserted their independence. Oswy ruled in northern Bernicia and his relative Oswin ruled in Deira. He invited Aidan to remain bishop of all Northumbrians, so his diocese was the means of a spiritual unity.

Oswy decided to marry a princess from Kent, and asked a senior cleric named Utta to escort her by boat. Utta feared possible shipwreck, so he asked Aidan for his prayers of protection for the escort. Aidan gave them a flask of blessed oil. 'You will meet storms,' he warned them, 'but if you remember to pour this oil on to the sea the winds will drop at once and you will come safely home.'

This is exactly what happened. The waves swept over all sides of the boat, which began to sink. However, at the last minute the priest recalled Aidan's words and poured oil into the sea. As Aidan had foretold, it immediately became calm.

A friend of Utta's personally recounted this story to Bede, who saw it as evidence of Aidan's prophetic spirit and believed that Aidan himself was there in spirit, calming the water. The phrase 'to pour oil on troubled waters' has passed into the English language ever since this event.

Pause for thought

I invited a primary-school assembly to suggest ways they could 'pour oil on troubled waters'. The headteacher allowed it to continue for well over an hour, and said he had no idea of the depths and inventiveness of the children's spirituality until that unique day. How may you pour oil on troubled waters?

Prayer

You who order the universe,
pour your oil on the troubled waters of our lives.
We bring to you the troubles in our places of work,
in our relationships, in our church and in the world . . .
Calm us, and help us rest in you.

Today's step

I step
away from unbelief
towards trust.

Spiritual breathing exercise

Calm in.
Panic out.
All's well.

DECEMBER 16

See, Lord

Bible reading

Peter and John were released from prison, where they had been placed for preaching that Jesus had risen from the dead. They went straight to the Christian community and told them what the authorities had said. On hearing this they all lifted their voices to God as one. 'Lord,' they said, 'it is you who made heaven and earth and sea, and everything in them. It is you who spoke through the Holy Spirit in the psalm written by your servant King David, our forebear: Why are nations so proud? Why do peoples make such futile plots? Kings setting out to war, people in positions of power making alliances against God and the One he has anointed. All this is coming true before our eyes. See, Lord, take note of their threats and help your servants to proclaim your message with boldness by stretching out your hand to heal and to work signs and wonders through the name of your holy servant Jesus.' As they prayed the house where they met was rocked.

Acts 4:23–30

Reflection

Aidan sometimes made retreat on Farne Island, which faced King Oswy's headquarters at Bamburgh.

Penda, Mercia's tyrant pagan king, made devastating incursions into Northumbria, and on one occasion, while Aidan was on Farne Island, he advanced upon Bamburgh itself. Since he could neither capture nor lay siege to it, his army built vast piles of thatch and wood, and waited for a favourable wind, in order to destroy the place by fire.

When Aidan saw the smoke and flames soaring up into the sky he wept. As Jesus had once before, Aidan raised his eyes and hands towards heaven and said, 'Oh

Lord, look at what evil Penda is doing.' As soon as he spoke those words, the wind changed direction and carried the flames into the faces of Penda's army. Some were hurt, and all panicked. The army retreated and they concluded that the city was under divine protection.

Pause for thought

What synchronicities can you find between the experience of the apostles Peter and John in today's Bible reading, and the experience of the apostle Aidan?

Prayer

Lord, the nations rage
and people around us
become vengeful.
You see it all.
The kingdoms of this world will become your kingdom.
So help me look upon what is happening
with the calm assurance and quiet confidence
of the Risen Christ
and leave the rest to you.

Today's step

I step
away from the panic of earth
towards the authority of heaven.

Spiritual breathing exercise

Faith in.
Fear out.
You see.

DECEMBER 17

Come off our high horse

Bible reading

If someone wants to sue you and claims something precious that you own in compensation, give them something even more precious! If a travelling VIP who gets lost presses you to accompany them for one mile, make it two miles. If a person in need of help asks you for something, give it to them. Don't even turn away a person who wants to borrow something . . . As you go about proclaiming God's kingdom heal the sick . . . and make no charge, for as you have received freely from God, so give yourselves freely to others.

Matthew 5:40–42; 10:8

Reflection

Oswin, King of Deira (roughly today's Yorkshire) was tall, handsome, courteous, pleasant of speech and generous to high and low alike. He was a true Christian, a great friend of Aidan and everyone loved him. One day he gave Aidan a highly bred horse with expensive royal trappings, so that, even though Aidan normally walked, he could cross rivers or fulfil urgent missions.

Shortly after this Aidan met a beggar who asked for a few coins with which to buy food. To his astonishment Aidan gave him the horse, complete with its expensive harness. When the king heard of this before he was to have dinner with Aidan, he was furious. 'Why did you give a beggar a horse that was fitted out for you? Haven't we plenty of less expensive things suitable to give to the poor?' Aidan swiftly replied: 'What are you saying, your Majesty? Surely this son of a mare is not dearer to you than that son of God?'

The king, who had just returned from hunting, warmed himself by the fire and thought about Aidan's words. Suddenly he gave his sword to a servant, threw himself at Aidan's feet and asked his forgiveness. 'Never again will I speak of this or presume to tell you how you should use what is given to you,' he told Aidan.

Aidan was not delighted, he was alarmed and tears formed. He told a friend, 'A king as humble as this cannot long survive.' Sure enough, the king was soon killed on the orders of his rival on the throne of Bernicia. And twelve days after that Aidan, too, was dead. Perhaps he had died of a broken heart.

Pause for thought

God does not mean us to give unwisely, but to give from our hearts without reservation. Try doing this today.

Prayer

Teach us, good Lord,
to serve you as you deserve,
to give and not to count the cost,
to struggle, and not to heed the wounds,
to labour and not to ask for any reward
other than knowing that we do your will.[7]

Today's step

I step
away from meanness
towards generosity.

Spiritual breathing exercise

Giving in.
Hoarding out.
Blessing.

DECEMBER 18

All gift, no threat

Bible reading

God loved the world so much that he gave his only Son, that whoever trusts him shall not perish, but have everlasting life. For God did not send his Son into the world to condemn the world, but that the world might be saved through him.

John 3:16, 17

Reflection

A radio tribute to someone who had died described their life as 'all gift, no threat'. Most of us are perceived as a threat in some way: because of our power, wealth, good looks, dismissive tone of voice, pushy manner, or the sense that we cannot be trusted because we are pushing a hidden agenda.

Aidan, more than most, deserves this accolade of 'all gift, no threat'. Corman, who preceded him, may have come under orders: Aidan volunteered. His gift of himself to an alien and ferocious society was for life. There was no guarantee that he would survive.

He and his missionary monks went out defenceless, to walk the lanes, to speak to people, to take whatever came to them.

Imagine Aidan explaining his strategy to his monks: 'We shall take a gently gently approach. We don't hit people over the head with the gospel. They would hardly notice: they are far too used to being hit over the head. First, we learn their language. Then, we talk to people, find out where they are, what they do. Don't rush in assuming they are pagans. Some of them may be Britons, and the Britons were Christians long before the Irish were. Remember that they are conquered, and angry. They'll connect us with the conquering king. Don't rise to taunts. On the other hand, you will meet English people who have never heard of the faith. Tell them about Jesus. Tell them there is a lot more to know, but ask them if they'd like to know more . . .'

The people, who would have initially seen these monks as a potential threat, soon saw them as a gift, and grew to love them. Of course, Aidan was a king's man, he could not be otherwise. But he soon showed that he was not there to be a drain on the people. His monks were welcomed to the villages because it was known they never sponged. Aidan may have seemed a threat to wealthy people who disliked his emphasis on justice. But he was not a threat to THEM, only to their false ways of life.

Aidan's total self-giving, to the people of the land, to his colleagues, to his rulers, surely flowed out of his self-giving to his God, who Aidan knew as the God of self-giving love, always being poured out without distinction.[8]

Pause for thought

How may you be less 'threat' and more 'gift'?

Prayer

Grace, grace, nothing but grace . . .

Today's step

I step
away from demand
towards Gift.

Spiritual breathing exercise

Giving in.
Pushing out.
Gift.

DECEMBER 19

Spiritual foster mothers of the English

Bible reading

When King Josiah was eighteen years old he sought God's will in the way the temple was rebuilt, and the workmen were so honest there was no need to check up on them. They discovered a copy of the laws Moses had given many centuries before, about which they were ignorant. When the king heard what was in this book he was devastated, and feared what dire consequences might afflict the nation for neglecting God's laws. He sent leading priests and civil servants to consult with Huldah. She was a prophet who lived in a housing estate on the outskirts of Jerusalem. Huldah confirmed that the nation would, indeed, reap what it had sown, but that because Josiah had listened to God the nation would be spared during his reign.

2 Kings 22

Reflection

When the English nation was being formed,
when the people's gods lost their shine
and the true God began to loom large;
when its Church was like a chrysalis emerging
from its Irish womb but did not yet know how to fly –
God placed a shining woman
on a throne not made by man
at the centre of two worlds no one else could span.
Her name was Hilda.

Aidan realised that the English could not be transformed without spiritual foster mothers.

Mother birds in the Bible describe God. The mother hen, (Luke 13:34); the mother eagle (Deuteronomy 32:11); the dove of the Spirit (Genesis 1:2) who broods over chaos to bring creation to birth. In Jewish wisdom tradition the bird building her nest (Ecclesiasticus 1:15) is a symbol of the 'shekinah' – God's feminine presence on earth. Stork in Hebrew is 'hasida', which translates 'tender mother' from its observed habit of staying with her young to the point of death. It is the same word as 'hesed' which means loving faithfulness, the word that describes God.

To begin with, Aidan encouraged solitary women to take vows. We know of Kenswith, who was St Cuthbert's spiritual mother. If legend is true, King Oswald arranged for the Irish princess Bega to find sanctuary in Northumbria, in which case Aidan must have received her vows. Then Heiu joined with a few other vowed women at a hermitage near the River Wear. The big breakthrough, however, had to await Hilda.

Pause for thought

What divine quality does God want you to recover or cherish?

Prayer

Triune God who mothers us all,
call into being those who nurture
tender shoots and thoughtful souls.
Soak your Church in new doses of tender loving care.
Raise up those who come alongside others,
foster their callings, and hold them in your heart.

Today's step

I step
away from competing
towards complementing.

Spiritual breathing exercise

Men and women in.
Chauvinsim out.
God.

DECEMBER 20

A baby of divine promise

Bible reading

In a dream an angel of God came to Joseph and said, 'Do not be afraid to take Mary home as your wife, because what is conceived in her is of the Holy Spirit.'

Matthew 1:20

An angel also appeared to Mary and announced, 'You have found favour with God. You will give birth to a son and are to give him the name Jesus.'

Luke 1:26, 30

Reflection

Hilda was born in 614. Her father was an Anglo-Saxon and a nephew of King Edwin. Both her parents were then pagans. Edwin was temporarily dethroned and sought refuge in the neighbouring Celtic kingdom of Elmet, as did Hilda's father, who was poisoned there before she was born.

While Hilda's mother, Breguswith, was pregnant she had a prophetic dream: her husband was snatched away and could not be found. But suddenly, in the midst of her painstaking search for him, she discovered a priceless necklace under the folds of her garment, and as she looked at it closely, it seemed to spread such a blaze of light that it filled all Britain with its splendour.

Through the years Hilda has been regarded as that jewel – a jewel of the Church, a spiritual mother, whose influence reached far beyond the boundaries of her own kingdom and who inspires ever more people in the twenty-first century.

In our losses come much grief and many tears. But never let us think that is all. For treasures are to be found in beds of nails. Even as we rise up and fold our clothes tightly round us in a vain attempt to hold in the pain, jewels are hidden in their folds.

Solveig Flugstad of Norway writes: 'My first encounter with Celtic Christianity was the story about the dream that Hilda's mother had when she was pregnant with her. If we believe that the Lord has created us, dreams are an obvious part of his creation and it is strange we do not pay more regard to what happens inside us during the night. People today who are open to this dimension in life live in an unbroken tradition from Old Testament times. Dreams are part of God's care and counselling for us, also!'

Pause for thought

Shake out your clothes. Listen to your dreams. Open up your life. See what treasures are there to be found.

Prayer

God, our vision,
in our mother's womb you formed us for your glory.
As your servant Hilda shone like a jewel in the Church,
so we now delight to claim the virtues and gifts
you delight to shower upon us.

Today's step

I step
away from despair
towards your gift.

Spiritual breathing exercise

Seeking in.
Panic out.
Treasure.

DECEMBER 21

Baptism and testing

Bible reading

Let us come into the still centre of God's presence, knowing that our hearts as well as our bodies have been washed. The One in whom we place our trust is faithful. Do not throw away that act of trust. Persevere so that when you have completed God's will God will richly reward you with what he has promised. We are not among those people who shrink back and fall to pieces; no, we belong to those who keep on trusting and whom God saves.

Hebrews 10:19–39

Reflection

When Hilda was aged two King Edwin regained the throne, this time of the whole of Northumbria. Hilda grew up in his extended household, which moved around the royal estates. When Hilda was eleven Edwin took a Christian wife from Kent, and agreed she could bring her chaplain, Paulinus, who was part of the mission team sent from Rome, to teach his people. On Easter Sunday, 12 April, 627 Edwin himself and thousands of his subjects were baptised in the river at York. Among them was the thirteen-year-old Hilda.

She probably married, since none of the accounts call her a virgin, and it was the done thing for royals to be married off at that age, often to one of the king's warriors. Six years later Edwin and his adult sons were killed, and, who knows, perhaps Hilda's husband was killed in that same battle? Hilda no doubt fled into exile, perhaps to the court of the Christian East Angles, where she had links, or perhaps beyond the northern boundary, south of today's Edinburgh.

Bede tells us that the people who had professed baptism

returned to their pagan gods, for their faith was skin-deep. Hilda, however, did not. It seems Christ himself, the King of kings had attracted her and drawn her allegiance for life. The waters of baptism had flooded her heart and her head, not just her body. Bede stresses her achievement in keeping the faith, perhaps while married to a pagan, certainly during years of pain and exile.

Hilda used this time to good effect. It could be that Hilda became a spiritual foster mother of the young Etheldreda, the daughter of the East Anglian King Anna, who would one day establish the great convent at Ely. There can be little doubt that she read widely and received an excellent education.

Pause for thought

Where do you wobble? Pray for the strength to grow ever more steadfast.

Prayer

Faithful God,
thank you for the glorious company of steadfast believers
and the friendship of spiritual mothers and fathers.
Establish our resolve.
Keep us steadfast, faithful and true
that we may climb every mountain
and overcome every obstacle.

Today's step

I step
away from fickleness
towards faithfulness.

Spiritual breathing exercise

Trust in.
Wavering out.
Reward.

DECEMBER 22

Your country needs you

Bible reading

Paul and the brothers on his mission team visited one town after another and the churches grew in faith. However, there was one occasion when the Spirit of Jesus would not allow them to go where they had planned. They were about to cross the border into Bithynia when a Macedonian appeared to them and kept on urging them to change their plan and come to Macedonia instead, to help them there. Once Paul had received this vision they lost no time in arranging a passage to Macedonia, convinced now that God had called them there.

Acts 16:7-10

Reflection

When King Oswald gained the throne it would have been in character for him to welcome back former exiles and especially to introduce to Bishop Aidan that rare, perhaps unique person, an exile who had retained the Christian faith. Hilda and Aidan became friends and Hilda was spiritually formed by the ways and teachings of the Irish mission. Here was an expression of the Christian faith which, unlike the mass conversions of the short-lived Roman mission, came alive in ordinary people's hearts, was lived out in common life, and which did not shut up the God of creation in a snooty church box.

Hilda's sister, Hereswith, married East Anglia's devout Christian King Egric. Perhaps after Oswald was killed in 642 she spent extended periods with her relatives there. When Egric was slain in battle Hereswith set out for Chelles, in today's France, where she became a nun at the monastery for men and women founded by Columbanus of Ireland. Hilda herself resolved to become a nun there –

no double or women's monasteries existed among the English.

When word of this reached Aidan he jumped. He said to her in effect, 'Your country needs you.' If there were no training monasteries for women in Northumbria, he and members of his team would disciple her through frequent visits and instruction. Aidan knew women's work must move forward among the English, and Hilda was the woman who could make this happen, for she was a natural leader.

Hilda was given a small area of land somewhere on the north side of the river Wear, in the area of today's Sunderland. There she developed a small band of Christian sisters who lived a rhythm of prayer and work. Aidan and his colleagues did indeed visit her often, instruct her mindfully, and love her heartily for her innate wisdom and devotion to God's service.

Pause for thought

Review your plans. Are you willing to change them if God should so direct?

Prayer

God of the Call,
make me willing to do anything and go anywhere for you.
All that I am, all that I do, all that I'll ever be
I offer now to you.

Today's step

I step
away from human proposals
towards God's leadings.

Spiritual breathing exercise

Your plan in.
My plan out.
Your call.

DECEMBER 23

Women transform the place

Bible reading

Everyone who felt moved by God made a contribution to the special meeting place with God. They came with brooches, rings, and all sorts of jewels. Anyone who possessed fine linen, scarlet yarn, rams' skins, leather, or wood useful for any good purpose brought that. Women with skills spun. The authorities provided essentials such as oil, and the people brought gifts of money as a free-will offering to God.

Exodus 35:21–29

Reflection

Hilda's women soon outgrew that first site. Heiu, the founder of a small monastery at Hart's Pool, on the headland, decided to become a solitary. Hilda was asked to take charge of the monastery, and she established a Rule of Life that embodied what she had learned from Aidan and of other wise teachers from Ireland such as Columbanus. Getting the Rule right was clearly fundamental, and she took great pains over this. Her greatest work began several years later. The king gave substantial land at what is now Whitby for the founding of a double monastery for men and women, and Hilda was asked to establish or reform it. She carried out her new task with great industry, and established the same Rule as at Hartlepool. Justice, devotion, purity, and above all peace and love were the goals she put before the members of the monastery. Following the example of the early Church in Jerusalem, no one was rich, no one was in need, because they had all things in common and none held on to private property.

They made small rectangular huts of wood and thatch. Daily tasks would be catching fish, rearing cattle and fowl, growing cereals, gathering fruits, spinning, making books and items for worship and the kitchens. They had to devote prime time to Bible-study, good works, and from Hilda's apprentices came a constant stream of candidates for ordained ministry. They must have displayed much energy, much creativity, much discipline and much love, for they grew fast. Hilda probably took twelve sisters and twelve brothers to Whitby. Soon it became the largest faith community for men and women among the English.

Pause for thought

What encourages growth and what stultifies growth in your sphere of life?

Prayer

Almighty God,
who gave to your servant Hilda gifts of vision and energy,
order and common sense, insight and devotion:
inspired by her example may we walk as one family
in the paths of love and obedience,
and attain the reward of the poor in spirit,
through Jesus Christ our Lord.

Today's step

I step
away from dither
towards duty.

Spiritual breathing exercise

Application in.
Inconstancy out.
Growth.

DECEMBER 24

Healing the land

Bible reading

When King Solomon had completed the building of God's temple and of his own palace, God appeared to him in a night vision and said: 'I have heard your prayer. I have chosen this place as my dwelling and will listen to the prayers my people offer here. If a time comes when there is prolonged drought, the land is ravaged or the people suffer an epidemic – if they humble themselves and seek my face and turn from their selfish ways, then I will listen, I will forgive their sin, I will heal their land and I will remain fully present to them.'

2 Chronicles 7:1–16

Reflection

King Oswy was superstitious. Perhaps to assuage a guilty conscience he promised his more devout wife that, if God gave him victory in battles, he would donate twelve estates where monasteries would be established. The first two of Hilda's monasteries were on such estates, and the third, at what is now Whitby, was perhaps a larger area linked to one of these. Some areas designated for monasteries were bleak, wild places where bad elemental influences accrued. Aidan had stressed the importance of cleansing such places by praying in them for forty days before beginning to build. Aidan's student Cedd did this at Lastingham. I have no doubt that Hilda, too, took prayer for the healing of the land most seriously.

She moved to Whitby in 657 to a engage in a task imposed upon her which she set about with great industry. She established the same Rule of Life which valued the virtues of justice, devotion, purity, peace and mutual love. Despite the fact that the community included royals, no one was rich, and no one was in need, for they had all things in common. Her students were required to spend so much time in study and so much time in practical service of others – this was holistic learning and it brought forth a fine crop of students fitted to be ordained priests.

Pause for thought

For centuries after the demise of Whitby the qualities that were cherished there seemed to have been vanquished from the Church. Make the following prayer, which was composed for a pilgrimage from Rome via Canterbury and Lindisfarne to Iona, your own.

Prayer

God of Hilda and the humble heart,
we confess with shame
the loss in the Church of integrity, humility and patience,
the crushing of spontaneity,
the caging of the wild Spirit,
the breaking-off of relationships,
the bruising of the crushed reeds,
the arrogance of the intellect,
the pride of empire-building.
Have mercy on us and forgive us.

Today's step

I step
away from possessive attitudes
towards the common life in Christ.

Spiritual breathing exercise

Shared life in.
Excluding postures out.
Community.

DECEMBER 25

Bring Jesus to birth

Bible reading

When the time had fully come God sent his Son, born of a human mother, to be our Saviour, so that we might no longer live like enslaved people but be freed up to truly live as members of God's family . . . My dear children, for whom I am again in the pains of childbirth until Christ is formed in you, how I wish I could be with you.

Galatians 4:4, 19

Reflection

On this, Jesus' birthday, let us remind ourselves that God is the Birther. Mary uniquely brought Christ to birth physically, and we, like Paul, Aidan and Hilda may bring Christ to birth spiritually.

In Jesus' language of Aramaic, according to Neil Douglas-Klotz, translator of the Aramaic version of the Gospels, the 'Abwon d'bwashmaya' (which in ancient English translated as 'Our Father who art in heaven') can mean 'O Birther, Father-Mother of the Cosmos'.

God brought to birth the cosmos. God brought himself to birth as a human in Jesus. God brings Jesus to birth through the Marys and Josephs of each generation.

In Aidan's Ireland Brigid was known as their people's Mary. They imagined her as the midwife present at Jesus' birth, and as the spiritual midwife who brought Christian Ireland to birth.

Aidan and Hilda in their turn brought Jesus to birth among the English-speaking people. And today, as often as possible, I hold in my heart the self-giving of God – giving himself to us always. I see it, feel it in Jesus. Then my heart begins to feel that mercy, that love, towards everyone in the world. Then our churches become places of giving, of generosity, of new birth.

Let the Son of God grow in you,
for he is formed in you.
Let him become immense in you
and may he become a great smile
and exultation and perfect joy.⁹

Pause for thought

Let us dedicate ourselves to Jesus' coming to birth in others through us.

Prayer

O Birther, Father-Mother of the Cosmos,
breathing through all creation,
breathing your life through a woman's womb
into a human form,
bring new birth to us who gather on this day of The Birth,
bring birth to our nation,
to this ailing, aging world
and bring to birth in us who are your people
the new creation which we stand on tip-toe to see.

God our Midwife,
contain in your hands the breaking of the waters,
the blood and din of your birth:
then, through our tears and joy, deliverer,
your wrinkled, infant kingdom may be born.¹⁰

Today's step

I step
away from what is barren
towards what brings Jesus to birth.

Spiritual breathing exercise

Birther in.
Terminator out.
Christmas!

DECEMBER 26

Songs in the fields

Bible reading

In some fields not far from the stable where Jesus was born some shepherds were keeping night watch.

An angel stood over them and the glory of God shone around them. They were frightened, but the angel said, 'Do not be afraid. I bring news of great joy for you and all the people. Today, in David's town, a Saviour has been born to you, and he is Christ the Lord.' Suddenly a great crowd of the heavenly host sang, 'Glory to God in highest heaven and on earth peace and good will towards all.' The shepherds hurried to see this event which God had made known to them.

Luke 2:8–16

Reflection

Although Aidan and Hilda's mission had spread the faith widely, the scriptures and the monastery church services were in the language that only educated people used, Latin. In Hilda's monastic village, however, an uneducated farm labourer named Caedmon kept watch over his cows by night. He seemed very ordinary, like the Bethlehem shepherds. He suffered from a low self-image. When his turn came to recite or sing at the social gathering in the big barn, he slid away to his cows, too shy to have a go. But that night an angel appeared to him, and asked him to sing something just for him. On what theme? Caedmon asked. On the creation of the world and of middle earth. In the morning Caedmon could remember both the lyrics and the tune. The foreman took him to Mother Hilda. She recognised that God had given him a gift, and took him in to the monastery as a lay brother. His role, she said, was not to do academic studies, but to compose songs of Bible stories. Caedmon became the first pop singer among the English, and his songs travelled far into the memories of people who never read a book.

'Let who will make the laws of a nation so long as I am permitted to make her songs,' said John Wesley.

The remaining fragment of Caedmon's first song contains the first recorded reference to middle earth, which J. R. R. Tolkien's *Lord of the Rings* has made world renowned.

Pause for thought

Hilda was very senior and very busy, yet she made time to take seriously the gift of someone with learning difficulties. Her example calls us to unlock the song in every human heart.

Prayer

God of shepherds and angels,
as Hilda drew out the songs
that were locked in shy Caedmon's heart,
may we draw out the music
that lies buried in a thousand lives:

The music of speech and seeing.
The music of laughter and loving.
The music of craft and creating.

Today's step

I step
away from flight
towards the flow.

Spiritual breathing exercise

Heart-song in.
'Can't do' out.
Hosannah!

DECEMBER 27

Two frameworks: one integrity

Bible reading

It is not for leaders to crave alcohol, to pour all their energies into sex or to deprive the oppressed of their rights. Rather, a leader should speak up for those who cannot speak for themselves and make sure that justice is upheld. By upholding justice a leader gives a country stability. When corrupt people rule the people groan. When good people rule the people thrive.

Proverbs 31:3–9; 29:4, 2

Reflection

In 664 King Oswy called a synod to decide whether Northumbria should follow the practices of Rome instead of Iona. It is a tribute to Hilda and the Whitby community that he asked her to host this: people from both sides respected her as a spiritual mother. We do not know whether she expressed views. We do know that following the decision to change to Roman practices Bishop Colman led all Lindisfarne's Irish monks and thirty of its English monks back to Ireland. This effectively marked the end of Aidan's framework and must have devastated many people, including Hilda.

Hilda remained the same person. She worked under the new framework with the same integrity and self-giving as before, yet she remained true to the spirituality she had learned from Aidan. She mentored the king's daughter, Elfleda. On Oswy's death she welcomed his widow Enfleda, who had always followed the Roman ways, and who would succeed Hilda as abbess. It can't have been easy. The Church was becoming the arena for turf wars. Enfleda supported the turbulent prelate Wilfred. Hilda's representative presented evidence at an enquiry in Rome under

Pope Agatho putting the case for a cleric whom she felt Wilfred was trampling on. Like Aidan, she was not afraid to stand up for people who were being misrepresented.

Yet people on all sides acknowledged her spiritual authority, and folk came from beyond the bounds of her own kingdom to consult with her. She had truly become a universal spiritual mother.

> Faithful host and reconciler,
> staying true through shifting ties,
> thankful in success and trial,
> always fair and always wise,
> meditator, motivator,
> wisdom's jewel and heaven's prize.

Pause for thought

How can you most wisely work through a framework you are required to operate under, and still retain your integrity?

Prayer

O God, who endowed Hilda with gifts of prudence and strength to govern as a wise mother over a large and fractious family, help us to sustain ordered lives where those of clashing views may find shelter and understanding, that our common life may be sustained and people may be excited by holiness.

Today's step

I step
away from partisanship
towards partnership.

Spiritual breathing exercise

Integrity in.
Prejudice out.
Holy God.

DECEMBER 28

Ceaseless struggle

Bible reading

Jacob, fearful of the coming meeting with his elder brother Esau, took his extended family and his possessions across the stream, and went back to spend the night alone in the desert. Someone wrestled with him until daybreak. Since the wrestler could not master Jacob, he struck him on the hip joint, which was dislocated and said, 'Let me go now.' Jacob said, 'I will not let you go unless you bless me.' The wrestler asked him his name and told him: 'You are no longer to be called Jacob. From now on you are to be called Israel, for this name means "you have struggled with God and have overcome".'

Genesis 32:23–30

Reflection

From the time Jacob wrestled with God, as if with a human partner, and eventually overcame, all Hebrews took their cue from and named themselves after this overcomer. Hilda's name, too, means 'one who struggles and overcomes'. The Jews' birthright, and ours, is to struggle and overcome.

Jesus' life-long struggle began amid King Herod's slaughter of Bethlehem's baby boys, to eliminate any future rivals, which the Church recalls on this day.

Hilda suffered many pains, some of which we may only guess at. She suffered the pain of losing her father before her birth, of losing her royal position and becoming a refugee when King Edwin was slain. If she married, she suffered the loss of her husband. She suffered the loss of the spiritual heritage of Aidan following the synod of Whitby, the pain of having to work with princes and prelates who played power games, and for the last six years of her life she suffered a fever and cough which racked her day and night. Yet, Bede tells us, 'during this time she never ceased to give thanks to her Maker and to instruct her flock both in public and in private. She taught them to serve the Lord wholeheartedly when in health, and always to return thanks when in trial or sickness.' No wonder that, after her death, a legend grew that Hilda's prayers could change dangerous serpents into stones.

Pause for thought

What adversity do you need to overcome rather than give in to?

Prayer

Help us, Lord, to trade with the gifts you have given us
and to bend our minds to holy learning,
that we may escape the fretting moth of littleness of mind
that would wear out our souls.
Brace our wills to actions
that they may not be the spoils of weak desires.
Train our hearts and lips to song
which gives courage to the soul.
Being buffeted by trials, may we learn to laugh.
Being reproved, may we give thanks.
Having failed, may we determine to succeed.[11]

Today's step

I step
away from capitulation
towards the struggle.

Spiritual breathing exercise

Grappling in.
Surrender out.
Birthright.

DECEMBER 29

Icon of wisdom

Bible reading

Wisdom calls to us wherever we turn: from the hill above us or the crossroads before us. She calls to all people: learn how to live. Come to your senses. Every word I speak is important: not one word is false or confusing to the person who practises honest reflection. I am worth much more than the most expensive jewellery. Nothing else is more worthy of your desire. I teach the Art of Thought, I work hand in hand with Discretion. Accept my discipline.

Proverbs 8:1–12

Reflection

In his book *Wonder: a Way to God* Eugene Stockton has a chapter headed 'Let's Play'. He writes: 'The Wisdom figure of the Old Testament is pictured as beside God, like a little child at creation, delighting in God – God's playmate.'

Thomas Merton[12] writes 'In *Sophia*, the highest wisdom-principle, all the greatness and majesty of the unknown that is in God and all that is rich and maternal in his creation are united inseparably, as paternal and maternal principles, the uncreated Father and created Mother-Wisdom.'

Hilda has become an icon of Wisdom and Wisdom – Sophia – has become an icon of the Eternal Divine Feminine.

When the Normans colonised England in 1066 they imposed a feudal, male-dominated society even in the Church, and belittled women. Not for a thousand years would a woman again be allowed to lead as had Hilda. In Durham Cathedral you can still see near the entrance the boundary line of tiles beyond which no woman was allowed to pass. Recently, however, the Dean welcomed women back, and has placed Edith Retien's icon of Hilda in its Galilee Chapel.

When the Community of Aidan and Hilda was launched in 1994 women were weeping both for the thousand years of belittlement and for the joy that the holy feminine was being honoured and released perhaps as never before.

Pause for thought

Wisdom:
begins in a mindful relationship with the Source,
forms when we observe,
survives when we exercise restraint,
strengthens when we learn from mistakes,
stabilises when we say 'no' to cheap blandishments,
matures when we look at both sides of an issue,
broadens when we ask questions,
widens when we extend our knowledge,
deepens when we resist headstrong ways,
heightens when we reflect.

Prayer

God our Wisdom,
who set Hilda as a mother in the Church,
may we now delight to claim her gifts of wisdom:
the wisdom of silence and the wisdom of speech,
the wisdom of observation and the wisdom of revealing,
the wisdom of memory and the wisdom of work,
the wisdom of deeds and the wisdom of being.

Today's step

I step
away from foolishness
towards mindfulness.

Spiritual breathing exercise

Wisdom in.
Pride out.
Sophia.

DECEMBER 30

Heaven's endowment

Bible reading

While the prophet Elijah was on a journey with his apprentice Elisha they met people from the school of prophets who said to Elisha, 'Did you know that God will take your spiritual father from you?' 'Yes, I know,' said Elisha, 'but keep the silence.' They passed over the river Jordan as if by a miracle. 'What may I do for you before I leave you?' asked Elijah. 'Let me inherit a double share of your spirit,' Elisha said. As they continued talking and walking they became separated by what seemed like chariots and horses of fire. Elisha kept crying out, 'Father, father.' He picked up Elijah's cloak that had fallen on him. He returned, struck the water, and the river Jordan parted for him. The community of the prophets who saw him in the distance said 'Elijah's spirit rests upon him.' *2 Kings 2:1–15*

Reflection

On Hilda's last day she received Holy Communion while it was still dark early in the morning, and called her sisters around her. Her final words to them were to preserve peace among themselves and with others. She died while she was exhorting them, and joyfully saw death approach.

At the same time, in a daughter monastery Hilda had established that year at Hackness, some thirteen miles away, a nun named Begu was dozing in her dormitory. Suddenly she heard the bell which called them together for prayer or when one of their number died. She opened her eyes and saw the roof rolled back. Light poured in and filled the whole place. She saw Hilda being borne to heaven in the middle of the light, attended by angels. The sisters were roused and gathered in the church, where they sang psalms of praise and prayed for Hilda until morning.

In the morning a brother arrived from Whitby with the news of Hilda's death. He was astonished to learn they already knew. Bede comments: 'By a beautiful harmony of events, it was divinely ordained that while some of them watched her departure from this life, others watched her entrance into the everlasting life of the spirit.'

Pause for thought

Elisha asked God for a double share of his Spirit that was in Elijah. What might we spiritual children of Aidan, Hilda and more recent role models ask God for?

Prayer

Great Spirit,
Encouraged by your cloud of witnesses,
give us an increased anointing.
Help us to take your word deep into our souls,
live it out, bravely, freely, creatively;
to be cheerful when we want to complain,
to be patient when we want to flare up,
to push on when we want to stand still,
to keep silent when we want to prattle
and to love when we want to harden our hearts.

Today's step

I step
away from resignation
towards divine supplies.

Spiritual breathing exercise

Glory in.
Withdrawal out.
You reign.

DECEMBER 31

The cloud of witnesses

Bible reading

You have come to something far more real than physical experiences and outward ceremonies . . . you have come into the community of the living God where millions of angels have gathered; you have been placed in the company of the spirits of the saints who have been made complete, and of Jesus.

Hebrews 12:18, 22-24

Reflection

The word 'saint' is used both for the figure in a stained-glass window and for the humble, self-effacing Christian down the street. In the apostle Paul's New Testament letters Christians were addressed as 'the holy ones'. In following centuries people who had attracted others to holiness were declared a holy person or saint by the local bishop at their funeral. It does not matter what we call them: it does matter that we be one.

The New Testament writer to Hebrew Christians sees our lives in the context of a sports arena. Past champions urge us on in our race. They have witnessed to Christ and they are now witnesses of our performance (Hebrews 11:1-12; 2:22-24). Believers who have passed from this life live consciously with Christ, though they await his Second Coming when they will be clothed with their glorified bodies at the resurrection of the dead. Athletes strive with double effort if they know that a stadium of famous Olympic athletes is watching them. How can a person avoid the struggle for greatness with an audience like that looking down upon them?'

B. F. Westcott[13] writes, 'They are more than spectators. They are spectators who interpret for us the meaning of our struggle, and who bear testimony to the certainty of our success if we strive lawfully.'

Pause for thought

We may visualise this great cloud of witnesses as round-the-world sailors, who cheer us on our voyage:

'Sail on, flowing freely, with the wind blowing your opened sails, God leading you. Sail on, your heart aflame, accompanied by the songs of creation. Sail on, your body and mind engaged in ceaseless struggle to overcome every obstacle, to be the person for others. Sail on, until the endless horizon comes into view.'

Prayer

Day by day, dear God:
teach me from your Word and your world,
lead me on my pilgrimage of life,
help me to live in your rhythms,
spur me to overcoming prayer,
strip from me all that clutters,
cherish through me your creation,
heal through me what is broken,
blow me to places beyond my comfort zones,
inspire me to foster unity,
reach out through me with your justice, truth and love,
that I may flame and struggle for you for ever.

Today's step

I step
away from my past
towards God's future.

Spiritual breathing exercise

The holy in.
The hellish out.
Heaven on earth.

Footnotes

January

1. Born 1918 in Spain. A Roman Catholic priest, he was Professor of Comparative Religion and Philosophy of Religion, University of Madrid.
2. St John of the Cross.
3. alt. Augustus Montague Toplady.
4. The Way of Life, Community of Aidan and Hilda.
5. From a reflection on one of the three Lent pillars, by Saint-Gregory of Nazianzus, Patriarch of Alexandria, d.389.
6. W. H. Vanstone (1977) *Love's Endeavour, Love's Expense*, Darton, Longman & Todd.
7. Echoes a prayer from Ghana.
8. T. R. Kelly (1941) *A Testament of Devotion*, Harper & Brothers.
9. The Way of Life, Community of Aidan and Hilda.
10. Alfred Lord Tennyson, *Idylls of the King*.
11. Life of Brigid.
12. The vision of Julian of Norwich, translated by Josef Pichler.
13. Guy Brandon in *Engage*, Issue 16 Spring 2007.
14. The Way of Life, Community of Aidan and Hilda.
15. Ibid.
16. T. R. Kelly (1941) *A Testament of Devotion*, Harper & Brothers.
17. The Way of Life, Community of Aidan and Hilda.
18. Saying of St Silouan the Athonite.
19. Saint John Climacus.

February

1. Henry Ford (1863–1947), Founder of the Ford Motor Company.
2. St Bede, Ecclesiastical History of the English People, Book 3 Chapter 5, Oxford University Press.

3. The Way of Life, Community of Aidan and Hilda.
4. Sun Chief of the Hopi people of Arizona, who studied in a USA institute, in *Touch the Earth: A self-portrait of Indian existence*, compiled by T. C. McLuhan (1992) Promontory Press.
5. Amplified Bible, Mark 11:11.
6. The presenting of the Holy Bible at the coronation of a British monarch.
7. The Way of Life, Community of Aidan and Hilda.
8. Quote by Martin Luther, initiator of Protestant Reformation.
9. The Way of Life, Community of Aidan and Hilda.
10. St Bonaventure.
11. Anamcaras song.
12. Echoes Moses' song at the Red Sea, from Exodus 15.
13. Echoes a prayer of King Soloman, see 2 Chronicles 6.
14. See Proverbs 6:6.
15. Bishop Basil of Caesarea.
16. Echoes sentences from Asser's *Life of King Alfred*.
17. Henri J. M. Nouwen (1994) *Here and Now*, Crossroad Publishing Co.
18. George Bernard Shaw.
19. Socrates.
20. The Way of Life, Community of Aidan and Hilda.
21. Andy Freeman, *Punk Monk: New monasticism and the ancient art of breathing*, p.139-140, 24-7 Titles.
22. Ben Okri in Commission on the Future of Multi-Ethnic Britain (2000).
23. From Alexander Solzhenitsyn's Nobel Laureate speech.
24. A Quaker saying.
25. Vincent McNab.
26. From Alexander Solzhenitsyn's Nobel Laureate speech.
27. An eighth-century Church catechism.
28. William Wordsworth.

29. From a prayer of the Ute people of North America.
30. Nicholas Heiney (2007) *The Silence at the Song's End*, Songsend Books.
31. The Way of Life, Community of Aidan and Hilda.
32. Ibid.
33. Ibid.
34. Ammon Hennacy 1893–1970, quoted in Shane Claiborne (2006) *The Irresistible Revolution: Living as an ordinary radical*, Zonderva Publishing House.

March

1. Ray Simpson.
2. Julia McGuiness, Reflections on life's road, from The Aidan Way, No. 12, 1997.
3. Ray Simpson.
4. Dag Hammarskjold, 1905–1961.
5. Taken from the hymn 'O God, our help in ages past', by Isaac Watts (1674–1748) alt. Based on Psalm 90.
6. From a sermon of Columbanus Hibernus.
7. Echoes the famous hymn by William Williams, 'Guide me O thou great Redeemer'.
8. The Way of Life, Community of Aidan and Hilda.
9. Heulwen Carrier.
10. Desert Elder in early Celtic Monasticism.
11. The Way of Life, Community of Aidan and Hilda.
12. The Times, January 5 2001.
13. Psalm 139:23, 24.
14. Catherine Doherty (2000) *Poustinia*, Madonna House Classics.
15. Echoes words of Catherine Doherty.
16. The Way of Life, Community of Aidan and Hilda.
17. After Ian Fosten, with permission.
18. Echoes a Muslim prayer made on arrival at a pilgrim centre.
19. Barbara Butler and Jo White (2002) *To be a Pilgrim*, Kevin Mayhew Publishers.

20. After John Bunyan.
21. Quoted in David Adam (2000) *A Desert in the Ocean*, p.20, SPCK.

April

1. From the musical *Sweet Charity*.
2. John O'Donohue.
3. The Way of Life, Community of Aidan and Hilda.
4. Irish authority on rhythm and blues music.
5. Taken from *David Copperfield*, by Charles Dickens.
6. Henri J. M. Nouwen (1994) *Here and Now*, Crossroad Publishing Co.
7. John S. Dunne (2008) *Deep Rhythm and the Riddle of Eternal Life*, University of Notre Dame Press.
8. Extract from 'Concurrence', from the collection *Candles in Babylon* by Denise Levertov (1982) New Directions.
9. Taken from Ruth Etchells (1994) *Just as I am: Personal prayers for every day*, Triangle Books SPCK.
10. Kristen Johnson Ingram, USA Wild Goose, Vol. 5, No. 4.
11. Rainer Maria Rilke, quoted in James Hollis (1996) *Swamplands of the Soul: New life in dismal places*, Inner City Books.
12. Brian Patten 'The Tree and the Pool', in *Stopping for Death: Poems of death and loss*, edited by Carol Ann Duffy (1986) Henry Holt and Co.
13. Jeremias, *The Prayers of Jesus*.
14. The Way of Life, Community of Aidan and Hilda.
15. Such as Ray Simpson's *The Celtic Prayer Book*, Kevin Mayhew Publishers.
16. From the Te Deum, fourth century, used in Anglican, Orthodox and Roman Catholic liturgies.
17. Quoted from Novatian in the encyclical, *The Splendor of Truth*, 108.
18. Alan P. Torey.
19. Christian theologian celebrated for his mystical writings.

20. From David's prayer, 1 Chronicles 16.
21. Ancient saying.
22. The General Thanksgiving, slightly adapted.
23. Artist and Recording Manager for Universal Classics and Jazz.
24. Taken from the article, 'The Cistercian monks being groomed for music stardom' by Emma Pomfret, Times Online, 17May 2008 http://entertainment.timesonline.co.uk/tol/arts_and_entertainment/music/article3931026.ece
25. Words of Joy Mead, St Giles' Cathedral, Edinburgh.
26. Lonnebo *et al* (2007) *Pearls of Life: For the personal spiritual Journey*, Wild Goose Publications.
27. Part of the Jesus Rosary prayer given to Jelena Vasilj at Medjugorje.
28. The Way of Life, Community of Aidan and Hilda.
29. Quote from John Ruskin (1867) *Time and Tide*.
30. Robert Baden-Powell, founder of the Boy Scout movement.
31. Noel Dermot O'Donoghue (1996) *The Mountain Behind the Mountain: Aspects of the Celtic tradition*, T&T Clark Publishers.
32. Echoes a prayer of Julia McGuinness.
33. The Way of Life, Community of Aidan and Hilda.
34. Richard A. Swenson (2004) *Margin: Restoring emotional, physical, financial and time reserves to overloaded lives*, NavPress Publishing Group.
35. Muirchu's 'Life of Patrick' in Liam de Paor (1993) *Saint Patrick's World*, Four Courts Press.

May

1. The Way of Life, Community of Aidan and Hilda.
2. Ibid.
3. Arsenius saying 38.
4. Dietrich Bonhoeffer, 1994.
5. The Way of Life, Community of Aidan and Hilda.
6. Ibid.

7. Ched Myers (2002) *The Biblical Vision of Sabbath Economics*, Church of the Saviour. Walter Brueggmann (1999) *The Liturgy of Abundance, The Myth of Scarcity*, Christian Century.

8. The Way of Life, Community of Aidan and Hilda.

9. St John of the Cross.

10. Anon.

11. Emeritus Professor Richard Whitfield, Initiatives of Change Newsletter, Jan–Feb 2003.

12. Echoes words of Kahlil Gibran.

13. Carl Jung (1965) *Memories, Dreams, Reflections*, Vintage Books USA.

14. Bieler *The Old Irish Penitential* 36, p.267.

15. The Way of Life, Community of Aidan and Hilda.

16. Richard Dell (2002) *Healing Nations: Eight steps to changing all our lives*, Albion Publishing Ltd.

17. Greg Anderson (1995) *The 22 (Non-Negotiable) Laws of Wellness*, Harper Collins.

18. John O'Donohue (2000) *Eternal Echoes: Exploring our hunger to belong*, Bantam Books.

19. Ignatius Loyola.

20. G. K. Chesterton, one of the most influential writers of the twentieth century.

21. The Revd James M. Gillis, author, editor and broadcaster (1876–1957).

22. Echoes a prayer from the Carmina Gadelica.

23. A Celtic rune of hospitality.

24. Prayer of St Brigid of Kildare.

25. George Monbiot, *The Guardian*, quoted in *The Week*, 31 August 2002.

26. Anon.

27. From the hymn *In the bleak mid-winter* by Christina Georgina Rossetti (1830–1894).

June

1. The Way of Life, Community of Aidan and Hilda.
2. J. Philip Newell (2008) *Christ of the Celts: The healing of creation*, Jossey Bass.
3. Irenaeus, *Against Heresies*, Vol. 5, 18:3. Irenaeus was a great teacher in the early Church.
4. http://www.bridgebuilding.com/narr/gmyc.html.
5. Excerpted with permission from Thomas Berry (2000) *The Great Work: Our way in the future*, Bell Tower, NY. Thomas Berry (1914–2009) was a cultural historian, author and teacher of religion.
6. Irenaeus, *Against Heresies*, Vol. 5, 36:1. Irenaeus was a great teacher in the early Church.
7. Hildegaard of Bingen, German abbess and author, she founded the monasteries Rupertsberg in 1150 and Eibingen in 1165.
8. Pierre Teilhard de Chardin, French biologist and priest.
9. Pierre Teilhard de Chardin, quoted in Ian Bradley (1990) *God is Green: Ecology for Christians*, Darton, Longman and Todd.
10. P. Evdokimov, quoted in Ian Bradley (1990) *God is Green: Ecology for Christians*, Darton, Longman and Todd.
11. St Maximus, 580–662.
12. Quoted in T. C. McLuhan (1992) *Touch the Earth: A self-portrait of Indian existence*, Promontory Press.
13. Werner Heisenberg, a German theoretic physicist (1901–1976).
14. Ian Skelly, 'Beauty Speaks', *Resurgence* magazine, issue 249, July/August 2008.
15. Taken from Dame Julian of Norwich, *Revelations of Divine Love*, paraphrased by Ray Simpson.
16. Gerrard Winstanley (1609–1676) English Protestant religious reformer.
17. Gerrard Winstanley, quoted in Ian Bradley (1990) *God is Green: Ecology for Christians*, Darton, Longman and Todd.

18. A Zulu prayer. The Zulus are a South African people traditionally living mainly in KwaZulu-Natal province.
19. Brother Lawrence (c.1614–1691) author of the classic Christian text *The Practice of the Presence of God*.
20. From Meister Eckhart's *Sermons*. Meister Eckhart (1260–1327) was a German Dominican; his writings form a vital part of Western mythical tradition.
21. *Touch the Earth: A self-portrait of Indian existence*, compiled by T. C. McLuhan (1992) Promontory Press.
22. From 'A Crystal Rim', by Hafiz, the celebrated Persian lyric poet.
23. Chief Luther Standing Bear of the Lakota people, born in 1868.
24. Quoted in *Touch the Earth: A self-portrait of Indian existence*, compiled by T. C. McLuhan (1992) Promontory Press.
25. Taken from Margaret Silf (2006) *The Way of Wisdom*, Lion Hudson plc.
26. Betty J. Eadie (1992) *Embraced by the Light*, The Aquarian Press.
27. The Way of Life, Community of Aidan and Hilda.
28. Alastair McIntosh (2004) *Soil and Soul: People versus corporate power*, Aurum Press.
29. Tim Clayton of the Eleuthero Community, Main Island, USA.
30. David Tacey (2004) *The Spirituality Revolution: The emergence of contemporary spirituality*, Routledge.
31. Hildegaard of Bingen, German abbess and author, she founded the monasteries Rupertsberg in 1150 and Eibingen in 1165.
32. Quote from *Hamlet*, William Shakespeare.
33. Paraphrased by Daniel Berrigan, poet, American peace activist and Roman Catholic priest.
34. Hildegaard of Bingen, German abbess and author, she founded the monasteries Rupertsberg in 1150 and Eibingen in 1165.
35. E. F. Schumacher, 1973.
36. Seventh-century saint of Glendalough, Ireland.
37. Abbot of the Monastery of St John on the Island of Patmos in the last century.

38. See Bishop Kallistos Ware lecture, *Through the Creation to the Creator*, 5.
39. Marie Connolly, a pilgrim to Glendalough.
40. William P. Young (2008) *The Shack*, Hodder & Stoughton.
41. Richard Dell (2002) *Healing Nations: Eight steps to changing all our lives*, Albion Publishing Ltd.
42. Echoes a prayer from Ashanti, Ghana.
43. From the lecture given by Al Gore when he received the Nobel Prize for Peace on 10 December 2007.
44. Arnold Mindell (1993) *The Shaman's Body*, Harper San Francisco.
45. Satish Kumar, *Resurgence* Magazine May/June 2008.
46. The Way of Life, Community of Aidan and Hilda.
47. Celtic Hymnbook No. 27.
48. Chief Luther Standing Bear, quoted in *Touch the Earth: A self-portrait of Indian existence*, compiled by T. C. McLuhan (1992) Promontory Press.
49. Arne Ness, Norwegian philosopher and mountaineer.
50. Lars Verket.
51. Albert Schweitzer (1875–1965).
52. Albert Einstein.
53. Author unknown.
54. From a benediction by Michael Klaper MD at the close of the memorial service for animals at Summerfest 2004.

July

1. From W. B. Yeats, 'The Second Coming'.
2. The Way of Life, Community of Aidan and Hilda.
3. John F. Kennedy.
4. Parts of this echo the prayer in Congressional Record-Senate, 78th Congress, first session, 89/5, July 5, 1943, 7160.
5. Wa'na'nee'che' (Dennis Renault) & Timothy Freke (1996) *Principles of Native American Spirituality*, Thorsons.
6. Catherine Doherty.

7. Dmitri Lvov, a respected economist at the Russian Academy of Sciences.
8. Alastair McIntosh (2004) *Soil and Soul: People versus corporate power*, Aurum.
9. A Scottish poet, Hugh MacDiarmid, writing of his homeland.
10. Author of *Healing Wounded History: Reconciling people and healing places* (2001) DLT.
11. The Way of Life, Community of Aidan and Hilda.
12. Caroline M. Myss and Norman C. Shealy (1998) *The Creation of Health*, Stillpoint.
13. Bill Jordan, General Secretary of the International Confederation of Free Trades Unions (ICFTU) representing 125 million trade union members in 137 countries.
14. John O'Donohue.
15. Extracts from *Instruction on prayers for healing*, issued by the Roman Catholic Congregation for the Doctrine of the Faith.
16. A Catholic online prayer for healing.
17. John O'Donohue.
18. From *For a Change* magazine, December/January 1998.
19. The Way of Life, Community of Aidan and Hilda.
20. A statement of the Infant Jesus Sisters, Dublin, printed for their Collegial Assembly 2007.
21. Words of Iago in act 3 of *Othello*, by William Shakespeare.
22. Also known as a whirly-whirly, or dust devil, a strong, well-formed, and relatively short-lived whirlwind.
23. Echoes Psalm 1, by Bruce Prewer, quoted in *Australian Prayer Rhythms*.
24. The Way of Life, Community of Aidan and Hilda.
25. North American Native Elder, Oriah Medicine Dreamer.
26. Matthew Lamont.
27. The Way of Life, Community of Aidan and Hilda.
28. Archimandrite Sophrony established the monastery at Tolleshunt Knights, Essex.

29. From chapter 4 of Archimandrite Sophrony (1999) *St Silouan the Athonite*, St Vladimir Seminary Press.
30. Howard Arnold Walter.
31. Marianne Williamson (1992) *A Return to Love: Reflections on the principles of a course in miracles*, Harper Collins.

August

1. The Way of Life, Community of Aidan and Hilda.
2. Echoes John Main (2002) *Essential Writings*, Orbis Books.
3. Isaac of Stella.
4. Alistair Maclean (1999) *Hebridean Altars*, Hodder & Stoughton.
5. Sayings of the Desert Fathers.
6. Russ Parker.
7. The Way of Life, Community of Aidan and Hilda.
8. Early Irish – sometimes attributed to voyagers such as St Brendan.
9. Joy Cowley (2008) *Come and See*, Pleroma.
10. From *The First Voyage of the Coracle*, Community of Aidan and Hilda.
11. Ibid.
12. Barack Obama (2007) *The Audacity of Hope*, Canongate Books.
13. Therese Luteke.
14. John Eldredge, author of the book *Wild at Heart*.
15. The Way of Life, Community of Aidan and Hilda.
16. Mother Teresa.
17. Inspirational Christian poem, author unknown.
18. Frederick William Faber (1814–1863) British hymn writer and theologian.
19. Robert Burns, 'To a Louse' 1786.
20. The Way of Life, Community of Aidan and Hilda.
21. Emily Mary Crawford d.1927.
22. 'The Acquisition of the Holy Spirit' in *The Little Russian Philokalia: St Seraphim of Russia* (2008) St Herman Press.

September

1. Traditional saying.
2. The Way of Life, Community of Aidan and Hilda.
3. C. S. Lewis' classic, *The Screwtape Letters*, in which a senior devil arms a junior devil with strategies to trip up a new Christian, highlights these truths.
4. Irenaeus was a great teacher in the early Church.
5. Verses from the *Altus prosator*, traditionally attributed to the sixth-century Irish mystic St Columba.
6. From 'Dream of the Rood', an old Northumbrian Anglo-Saxon poem.
7. From a hymn version of *St Patrick's Breastplate*.
8. St Abba Marcarius the Great (295-392) was among the most influential Desert Fathers of Egypt.
9. From the sayings of the Desert Fathers.
10. Godfrey of Ibelin.
11. Martin Buber, in a 1941 essay.
12. Echoes Daniel 9.
13. The Way of Life, Community of Aidan and Hilda.
14. From Bede's *Life of St Cuthbert*.
15. Genesis 18.
16. Deuteronomy 9:25–29.
17. 1 Samuel 1.
18. 2 Kings 19:14–20.
19. 2 Chronicles 6.
20. Esther 4:15–17.
21. Pslam 122:6.
22. Psalm 82:3.
23. Jeremiah 42:1-10.
24. Daniel 9.
25. Zechariah 8:20–23.
26. Matthew 9:38.
27. Matthew 5:44.

28. Luke 22:32.
29. John 17:21.
30. 1 Timothy 2:1, 2.
31. Ephesians 6:18.
32. James 5:14.
33. Ray Simpson (2005) *A Pilgrim Way*, Kevin Mayhew Publishers.
34. St Ninian is a Christian saint first mentioned in the eighth century as being an early missionary among the Pictish peoples of what is now Scotland.
35. Words of St Augustine.
36. Hugh MacDiarmid, significant Scottish poet of the twentieth century.
37. Selected sentences adapted from W. Jardine Grisbrooke (1967) *The Spiritual Counsels of Father John of Kronstadt*, St Vladimir's Seminary Press.
38. Adamnan of Iona, *Life of St Columba*, written in the seventh century.
39. John Wesley (1703-1791) Anglican cleric and Christian theologian.
40. Jonathan Edwards (1703-1758) was a colonial American Congregational preacher, theologian, and missionary to Native Americans.
41. From chapter 3 of Archimandrite Sophrony (1999) *St Silouan the Athonite*, St Vladimir's Seminary Press.
42. Clement of Rome c.200.
43. The Way of Life, Community of Aidan and Hilda.
44. Father Silouan, founder of the monastery of St John the Baptist, Essex.
45. M. Scott Peck, psychiatrist and author of *The Road Less Travelled* (1990) Arrow Books.
46. Echoes material in Jean Baptiste Chautard (2008) *The Soul of the Apostolate*, Tan Books.
47. Richard Dell (2002) *Healing Nations: Eight steps to changing all our lives*, Albion Publishing Ltd.
48. Martyn Lewis, *The London Times*, 17 November 1993.

49. Joy Cowley (2002) *Psalms for the Road*, Aotearoa New Zealand.
50. Corrie ten Boom (1892-1983) was a Dutch, Christian, Holocaust survivor who helped many Jews escape the Nazis during World War II.
51. From 'The Hound of Heaven' by Frances Thompson.

October

1. The Way of Life, Community of Aidan and Hilda.
2. Echoes the hymn by Bob Gillman, 1977, Kingsway's Thankyou Music.
3. The Way of Life, Community of Aidan and Hilda.
4. Ibid.
5. Letter to Coroticus, paragraph 20.
6. The Way of Life, Community of Aidan and Hilda.
7. Quoted from *Writings from the Philokalia on Prayer of the Heart*. Translated by E. Kadloubovsky and G. E. H. Palmer (1992) Faber and Faber.
8. The Way of Life, Community of Aidan and Hilda.
9. Said by The Vatican's Cardinal Ivan Dias to the Anglican Communion's 2008 Lambeth Conference.
10. Echoes a prayer of Pope John XXIII.
11. The Way of Life, Community of Aidan and Hilda.
12. Benjamin Malachi Franklin (1882-1965) U.S. Library of Congress, Washington DC.
13. The Way of Life, Community of Aidan and Hilda.
14. The Transfiguration Monastery, Victoria, Australia.
15. Drawn from the Grievance liturgy of the Holy Transfiguration Monastery, Victoria, Australia.
16. Ibid.
17. The Way of Life, Community of Aidan and Hilda.
18. Commonwealth Chief Rabbi Jonathan Sachs to the 2008 Lambeth Conference of Anglican Bishops.

19. The Transfiguration Monastery, Victoria, Australia.
20. 'Blessed Community' in T. R. Kelly (1941) *A Testament of Devotion*, Harper & Brothers.
21. Unknown author.
22. John C. Maxwell (2006) *Developing the Leaders Around You*, Nelson Thomas.
23. Peter M. Senge (2006) *The Fifth Discipline*, Random House Books. Senge is a professor of management.
24. See www.cof.org.uk.
25. The Way of Life, Community of Aidan and Hilda.
26. Ibid.
27. Ibid.
28. Extracted from Jeremy O'Grady, *The Week*, 1 September 2007.
29. The Way of Life, Community of Aidan and Hilda.
30. Catherine Doherty, *Sobornost*.
31. The Way of Life, Community of Aidan and Hilda.
32. *The Week*, 2 August 2008.

November

1. The Way of Life, Community of Aidan and Hilda.
2. A prayer of Churches Together in England.
3. Matthew Parris, The London Times, 27 December 2008.
4. Antony Flew (2007) *There is a God*, HarperOne.
5. Author unknown.
6. From 'Bridge over troubled water' by Simon and Garfunkel.
7. Bruce Olsen, a Norwegian born in the USA.
8. William P. Young (2008) *The Shack*, Hodder & Stoughton.
9. John Main, *Essential Writings*, selected by Laurence Freeman (2002) Orbis books.
10. Words of St Augustine.
11. The Way of Life, Community of Aidan and Hilda.
12. Joseph Wresinski (1917–1988) Founder of ATD Fourth World.

13. Henri J. M. Nouwen (1994) *Here and Now*, Crossroad Publishing Co.
14. William Temple was Archbishop of Canterbury during World War II.
15. Extract from William Temple's nation-changing book *Christianity and Social Order* (1942).
16. The Way of Life, Community of Aidan and Hilda.
17. Lao Tzu, *Tao Teh Ching* tr John C. H. Wu (1981) Shambala.
18. Richard Dell (2002) *Healing Nations: Eight steps to changing all our lives*, Albion Publishing Ltd.
19. Rowan Williams (2002) *The Kingdom is Theirs: Five reflections on the Beatitudes*. Christian Socialist Movement.
20. Author unknown, but attributed to St Francis.
21. By Graham Kendrick.
22. Northumbrian Office.
23. Walt Whitman 'Song of the Open Road'.
24. Rami Khouri, American University of Beirut, 2008.
25. Ralph Vaughan Williams quoted in Peter Ackroyd Chatto and Windus (2002) *The Origins of the English imagination*, Albion Publishing.
26. John Ruskin 'The Two Paths' 1859.
27. John Ruskin 1859 *The Seven Lamps of Architecture* (The Lamp of Memory Section 7).
28. *The London Times*, November 1 2008.
29. Part of 'The Great Invocation', the UN.
30. *The London Times*, August 2 2008.
31. Uniting Church in Australia.

December

1. The London Times, October 30 2008.
2. Echoes a prayer of Sister Dorothy Stella of OHP Whitby.
3. From the hymn by Dan Schutte, (1981) based on Isaiah 6, New Dawn Music.

4. Archbishop Oscar Romero in *The Violence of Love*, compiled and translated by James R. Brockman (2004) Orbis Books.
5. Pastor Martin Niemoller.
6. William Wilberforce, leader of the movement to abolish the slave trade.
7. Ignatius Loyola.
8. Drawn from a talk by Kate Tristram.
9. Isaac of Stella.
10. Gill Paterson, Christian Aid.
11. Echoes 'Homily of St Hilda', author unknown.
12. Thomas Merton, twentieth-century American Catholic writer. A Trappist monk of the Abbey of Gethsemani, Kentucky.
13. B. F. Wescott, Bishop of Durham from 1890 until his death in 1901.

Also by Ray Simpson

High Street Monasteries
Explores how the new monasticism is becoming the heart of our global village, focusing on community, peace and beauty.
1501179

A Guide for Soul Friends
Looks at the meaning of being a soul friend, how to get started and coaching techniques.
1501132

Celtic Prayers for Life Today
Over 700 prayers and blessings suitable for a wide range of needs and circumstances.
1500928

Celtic Daily Light
A Bible lectionary for each day, including a Psalm, Old Testament and New Testament readings and a piece of literature or material about Celtic saints such as Samson and Brigid.
1500600

A Pilgrim Way
A commentary on the Community of Aidan and Hilda's Way of Life.
1500745

www.ingramcontent.com/pod-product-compliance
Lightning Source LLC
Chambersburg PA
CBHW020347080526
44584CB00014B/926